THE WESTERN SAHARANS

The Western Saharans

BACKGROUND TO CONFLICT

Virginia Thompson and Richard Adloff

CROOM HELM LONDON

BARNES & NOBLE BOOKS
TOTOWA, NEW JERSEY

© 1980 Virginia Thompson and Richard Adloff
Croom Helm Ltd, 2-10 St John's Road, London SW11
ISBN 0-7099-0369-3

British Library Cataloguing in Publication Data

Thompson, Virginia, b. 1903
  The Western Saharans.
  1. Morocco - History
  2. Spanish Sahara - History
  3. Mauritania - History
  I. Title   II. Adloff, Richard
  964   DT314   80-41164
  ISBN 0-7099-0369-3

First published in the USA 1980 by
BARNES & NOBLE BOOKS
81 ADAMS DRIVE
TOTOWA, New Jersey, 07512

ISBN: 0-389-20148-0

Reproduced from copy supplied
printed and bound in Great Britain
by Billing & Sons Limited
Guildford, London, Oxford, Worcester

CONTENTS

ACRONYMS

AID	Agency for International Development
AJM	Association de la Jeunesse Mauritanienne
ALS	Armée de Libération du Sahara (Morocco)
BPN	Bureau Politique National
CADET	Centre d'Achat et de Développement du Tafilalet
CATC	Confédération Africaine des Travailleurs Croyants
CFDT	Compagnie Française de Développement des Fibres Textiles
CFTC	Confédération Française des Travailleurs Chrétiens
CHEAM	Centre des Hautes Etudes de l'Afrique et de l'Asie Moderne (Paris)
CMRN	Comité Militaire de Rénovation Nationale
CMSN	Comité Militaire de Salut National
Comaunam	Compagnie Mauritanienne de Navigation Maritime
Cominor	Complexe Minier du Nord (Mauritania)
Covima	Compagnie de Commerce des Viandes en Mauritanie
ENA	Ecole Nationale d'Administration
FAR	Forces Armées Royales (Morocco)
FDIC	Front pour la Défense des Institutions Constitution-elles (Morocco)
FLN	Front de Libération Nationale (Algeria)
FLU	Front de Libération et de l'Unité
GPRA	Gouvernement Provisoire de la République Algérienne
ICFTU	International Confederation of Free Trade Unions
IFAC	Institut de Fruits et Agrumes Coloniaux (France)
IFAN	Institut Fondamental de l'Afrique Noire (formerly Institut Français de l'Afrique Noire)
IMAPEC	Industries Mauritaniennes de Pêche
INEEP	Institut National d'Education et d'Etudes Politiques
MAS	Mission pour l'Aménagement du Sénégal
MDN	Mouvement Démocratique National (Mauritania)
Miferma	Mines de Fer de Mauritanie
Morehob	Mouvement de la Résistance des Hommes Bleus
MPAIAC	Movimiento Populár Autonomista para la Indepén-dencia del Archipiélago Canario
MRP	Mouvement Républicain Populaire (France)

Nahda	al Watanya al Mauritanya (Party of the Mauritanian Renaissance)
OAU	Organisation of African Unity
OCAM	Organisation Commune Africaine et Malgache
OCRS	Organisation Commune des Régions Sahariennes
OERS	Organisation des Etats Riverains du Sénégal
OMVS	Organisation pour la Mise en Valeur du Fleuve Sénégal
ONTP	Office National des Transports Publics (Mauritania)
ORSTOM	Office de Recherche Scientifique et Technique d'Outre-Mer (France)
PKM	Parti des Kadihines Mauritaniens
Polisario	Frente Populár para la Liberación de Saguia el Hamra y Rio de Oro
PPM	Parti du Peuple Mauritanien
PPS	Parti du Progrès et du Socialisme (Morocco)
PRM	Parti du Regroupement Mauritanien
PUNS	Parti d'Union National Saharienne (Sahraoui)
RASD	République Arabe Sahraouie Démocratique
RNI	Rassemblement National des Indépendants
SFIO	Section Française de l'Internationale Ouvrière
SIGP	Société Industrielle de la Grande Pêche (Mauritania)
SIP	Société Indigène de Prévoyance
SNIM	Société Nationale d'Industrialisation Minière (Mauritania)
UAM	Union Africaine et Malgache
UAR	United Arab Republic
UGTAN	Union Générale des Travailleurs d'Afrique Noire
UNFP	Union Nationale des Forces Populaires
UPM	Union Progressiste Mauritanienne
USMM	Union Socialiste Musulmane Mauritanienne
UTM	Union des Travailleurs Mauritaniens
UTM-R	Union des Travailleurs Mauritaniens — Renovée

GLOSSARY

abid   Black slave or servitor (often part of a name); descendant of a former slave of sudanese origin.

aman   Pardon or amnesty.

amel   Super-prefect or *chef de région*.

amghar nufilla   Supreme chief of the Ait Khabbache tribe.

azalai   Salt caravan.

Bafour   A people of unknown origin, believed to have occupied the Western Sahara prior to the second Almoravid conquest in the ninth century; possibly ancestors of the Imraguen.

baraka   A state of grace or habitual good fortune, indicating that its possessor enjoys divine favour.

bayoud (or *taka*)   A disease of the date palm for which as yet no cure has been found.

beidane   White tribes of Morocco, made up of *hassanes* and *zaouia* (q.v.).

bled- (or *blad-*) *es siba*   An area which has not accepted rule by the sultan (Morocco).

bordj   Fort or fortified settlement.

cadi   Judge of a Koranic law court (see *sharia*).

caïd Before independence, a tribal chief; subsequently a government-appointed official in rural areas, having limited judicial powers.

cercle   An administrative unit during the French colonial period.

chorfa (or *shorfa*)   Individuals believed to be descendants of the Prophet Mohammed.

daïra   A commune.

dahir   Royal decree (Morocco).

debiha   Act of submission indicating the status of vassal, by an individual or tribe, exacted by nomadic Berber warriors.

djemaa (or *yemaa*)   Communal council or assembly.

erg   Desert region of shifting sands.

fraction   Tribal group of 10 to 100 families.

friq   Group of tents, or a camp comprising 10 to 100 tents (5 to 25 persons per tent).

goumier   Indigenous militiaman under French command, in the colonial era.

graara   Small depression inundated by an *oued*; arable.

griot   Minstrel-clown.

guelb   Peak (plural, *eglab*); isolated conical mountains containing iron-ore (Mauritania).

guelta   Rainwater pool.

guetna   Fair held in Mauritania in June-July, usually for selling dates.

habous   Property held in trust to endow religious institutions, either directly (public *habous*) or after the death of the last family heir (private).

hammada   Vast calcareous or sandstone plateaux, whose highest parts have been denuded of all loose earth by the wind.

Hamallist   Left-wing splinter group of the Qadriya brotherhood (Mauritania).

harki   Auxiliary Arab or Berber troops of the French colonial army.

harratin   Black servitors, descendants of former slaves.

hassane   Member of a Moorish warrior tribe.

hassaniya   Arabic dialect spoken in the Western Sahara.

horma   Personal obligation owed by tributary families to their suzerains.

ijma   Assembly of tribal fractions in the Spanish Sahara.

indigénat   During the French colonial period, a native-status legal code imposable arbitrarily by French administrators.

jihad   War by Muslims against infidels.

katiba   Units of the Polisario armed forces.

khalifa   Representative of the *pasha* (Morocco).

khammes   Sharecroppers.

khum   Primary sector of the Ait Khabbache tribe.

ksar (pl., *ksour*)   Originally a fortified town built on an elevation; also refers to the elevated commercial centre of the oasis town.

leff   Ancient Berber system of tribal alliances (Morocco).

makhzen   The central government (Morocco).

marabout   A holy or saintly Muslim.

medersa   Islamic secondary school.

méhariste   Camel-mounted patrol.

mellamin   Blacksmiths.

moqqadan   Village headmen.

mouggar   Annual fairs in the Sahara.

obakh   Tribute paid to *hassane* tribes by freemen, or others cultivating the soil.

oued   Ancient watercourses; usually dry, they are sometimes subject to flash floods during heavy rains.

ouguiya   Monetary unit of Mauritania (abbrev. UM).

pasha Urban governor (southern Morocco).

Qadriya A major Muslim brotherhood.

reg Sandy and rocky desert plain.

rezzou Armed raids by nomads (sing., *razzia*).

rhettara (or *ghettara*) Subterranean canal.

sahel Semi-desert zone dividing the Sahara from the sudanese zone to the south.

sebkha Usually clayey land impregnated with salt; a salt lake.

seguia Surface canal.

sharia (or *cheriat*) Traditional code of Islamic law, both civil and criminal.

sudanese (zone) Zone between the *sahel* and the tropical forest to the south; grassy plains and scattered trees.

taka (see *bayoud*)

Tidjaniya A major Muslim brotherhood.

wilaya Province.

yemaa (see *djemaa*)

zaouia A Muslim brotherhood or fortified monastery.

zekkat Tax on animals (Mauritania).

TO GWENDOLEN CARTER

ACKNOWLEDGEMENTS

The basic material for this study has been gathered from libraries and archives and in the course of successive journeys to the Saharan countries beginning in 1936. Information concerning developments in the Western Sahara, in the form of documentation and of interviews with responsible officials as well as with knowledgeable individuals native to the area, was easier to obtain during the colonial period than in the post-independence years. Since the mid-century mark, the rise of nationalism has been responsible for creating both physical and psychological barriers between the governments of the Western Sahara and between those governments and foreigners — except for those journalists and officials whose support or influence are sought by the authorities concerned. Moreover, since war broke out in the western desert in 1975, it has become even more difficult for scholars to ascertain the facts needed to reach any valid or objective view of current developments there. Despite these handicaps, the writers have believed that the attempt to pull together and analyse such data as are available was worth doing.

In view of the many years covered by this study and the time required to gather and assess the relevant materials, it is obviously impossible to thank all of the numerous individuals who have helped us with our project, either by facilitating our acquisition or access to relevant documents, or by sharing with us their experience and views. Nevertheless, as regards documentation we would like to underscore the unique value of the unpublished papers prepared by former French administrators and officers which are in the archives of the Centre des Hautes Etudes de l'Afrique et l'Asie Moderne, which have been made available to us by its most obliging director, Colonel Georges Malecot. Outstanding, too, has been the contemporary material that was put at our disposal through the generosity of Mr Robert Cornevin, permanent secretary of the Académie des Sciences d'Outre-Mer and head of the Documentation Française services.

In the United States, we wish to express special gratitude to Dr Peter Duignan, curator of the African collection at the Hoover Institution, to Professor Carl Rosberg of the Institute of International Affairs at Berkeley, and to Dr Andrew Jameson of the University of California history department — all of whom have given us encouragement and constructive criticism of the manuscript.

December 1979

V.T.
R.A.

INTRODUCTION

For the vast and amorphous territory formerly known as the Spanish Sahara, the most recent maps of northwest Africa show a new name — the Western Sahara — and dotted lines divide its component parts, Saquiet El Hamra and Rio de Oro. Such lines suggest but — until 1979 — the maps prudently avoided confirming the occupation of those regions by Morocco and Mauritania respectively, as envisaged in the Madrid pact signed by those two countries with Spain on 14 November 1975. This cautious approach to the status of the area was adopted by many spokesmen for member governments of the UN, the OAU and the Arab League. By extension, the imprecise term 'Western Sahara' has come to be applied to all the desert regions included in the countries now disputing the land claimed by the Polisario (the Popular Front for the Liberation of Saquiet El Hamra and Rio de Oro), which was formed by some Sahraoui tribesmen of those areas.

The use of the term Western Sahara offers the advantage not only of avoiding a political commitment but also of concealing widespread ignorance about an area of which even generally well-informed persons have only scanty knowledge. The region's history has received attention not so much for itself as for certain peripheral or picturesque aspects, such as the upsurge of the Almoravids in the eleventh century and its influence on Spain's evolution, or the romantic appeal of Saharan nomadism to persons living in an industrialised society. Similarly, chroniclers of the picturesque have been attracted by Sultan Moulay Mansour's trans-Saharan expedition to conquer Timbuctu, and by the great caravan trade between the sudanese zone and the market towns of Morocco's deep south. In modern times, the survival of archaic peasant communities such as those of Oued Draa, as well as the post-Second World War rise of instant capital cities such as Nouakchott, have given rise to urbanisation studies. Surprisingly few anthropologists, however, have worked with the pastoral tribes of the Western Sahara, and most of the data available concerning the Reguibat, Ouled Delim, Ait Atta and Ma El Ainin were assembled by French and Spanish army officers who had the leisure and the inclination to record their observations about the peoples and areas they administered. As those tribes, especially the Reguibat, reportedly account for a large proportion of the Polisario troops now fighting in the Western Sahara, any analysis

15

of the present complex situation there, let alone any reasoned forecast for the entire Western Sahara, is handicapped by deficiencies in our basic information.

Nevertheless, since 1975 more journalists than ever before have visited and reported on that region. Indeed, the undeclared war there between the Moroccans and Mauritanians on the one hand and the Polisario and its Algerian sponsors on the other has brought the whole area into sharper focus and even given it a certain unity. In this light, new vistas have been opened up and the unique features of the region's development are now more evident. These features include the virtual disappearance of pastoral nomadism, the advent of Third World imperialism in the western desert and the birth of Sahraoui nationalism.

The decline of pastoral nomadism is a phenomenon common to all of the Sahara, and sedentarisation of the nomads has been a goal of that area's colonial and national governments alike, but in the western desert the concurrence of three phenomena has given it a distinctive aspect. Throughout the Sahara, the 1968-73 drought resulted in an even more pronounced void than before in the central desert, thus accelerating the southward migration of those nomads who had lost most of their animals. They were drawn to the towns and farming villages, where there were either wage-earning opportunities or government distributions of food and of jobs on public-works programmes. Such official benevolence had been a practice under the colonial regimes during periods of prolonged drought, but in the early 1970s, thanks to international aid, it was dispensed on a more generous scale than when the administering power had felt responsibility solely for its own subjects' welfare. Indeed, living off such handouts has become so much easier a way of life than the perpetual search for water and pasture that some Mauritanian nomads reportedly now prefer to remain indefinitely in the towns on public welfare and the depopulation of the central Sahara continues apace. This negative attitude testifies to the downgrading of the camel by the nomads. Formerly a nomad's most cherished possession and considered by him to be among Allah's noblest creations, the camel is now reared as a source of milk and occasionally of meat, and only rarely as a means of transport. This new trend has not only confounded those observers who had long assumed that the nomads were permanently committed to the pastoral life but has also alarmed the Mauritanian government lest a large percentage of the population become drones and a great proportion of the national territory that is suited only to pastoral nomadism may go unutilised.

The third and most recent stimulus to the decline of pastoral nomadism is guerrilla warfare in the western desert, which began in earnest late in 1975. The flight of hundreds of thousands of Sahraouis to camps in the Tindouf area of Algeria was, in effect, a mass migration on an almost unprecedented scale. It was analogous to (but different in composition and in some degree as to motivation from) the exodus of 1957-8, when the migrants were mainly Sahraoui town-dwellers of the Spanish Sahara who had fled to southern Morocco to escape bombardment by Franco-Spanish forces attacking the Moroccan Army of Liberation. Today, some of the refugees who sought shelter in Algeria during the early stages of the current war have been returning to their previous habitats, but this countermigratory movement affects only a small number of the nomads, most of whom continue to live on the bounty of international philanthropic organisations and of the Algerian government.

The birth of Sahraoui nationalism owed little to the contagion of nationalist movements in the Maghreb and black Africa but derived directly from the discovery of the Western Sahara's mineral resources. European geologists, in the early post-Second World War years, found extensive iron-ore deposits at Gara Djebilet in southwestern Algeria and vast phosphate deposits at Bu Craa in the Saquiet El Hamra region of the Spanish Sahara. These discoveries coincided with improvements in prospecting and mining techniques, the development of modern transport in the desert, a rapid growth in the world's population, and an ever-greater demand for raw materials on the part of the industrialised nations. The iron-ore of Gara Djebilet is situated so far from any shipping port that it has never been mined, but the proximity of Bu Craa's phosphate deposits to the Atlantic Ocean made it feasible and profitable for the Spaniards, who were concentrated in the coastal area, to mine and export its output. The Bu Craa mining enterprise (and to a lesser extent the Gara Djebilet deposits) gave monetary value for the first time to the Western Sahara itself, and prompted further prospecting in the hope of finding sources of water and energy, as well as of other minerals. Inevitably, it also aroused the covetousness of neighbouring countries, increased the Spaniards' determination to cling to their Saharan province, and alerted the Sahraouis to the possibility that underneath the sands over which they roamed lay fabulous wealth that could be claimed as their rightful heritage.

Gradually the attitude of the Sahraouis towards their Spanish masters became more aggressive, and their transition from docility to violence was encouraged by the national governments of Morocco, Algeria and Mauritania. From the medley of vested-interest groups proclaiming as their goal liberation from Spain or union with Morocco or Mauritania, there emerged the Polisario Front in 1973. The fighting spirit, capacity for organisation and uncompromising determination to be independent that were shown by its members won the respect of foreign observers and earned the Polisario its credentials as an authentic nationalist movement.

The third original aspect in the evolution of the Western Sahara has been its serving as a laboratory for four kinds of imperialism. Of these the two older European versions have now disappeared, but the two more recent African forms represent a novel experiment in Third World colonialism in west Africa. In both sectors of the former Spanish Sahara, the governments of Morocco and Mauritania in 1977 included the inhabitants of their newly acquired territories in their own electoral procedures, applying to them an assimilationist policy reminiscent of French attempts to make over Africans in their own cultural image fifty years earlier. To win the hearts and minds of its new Sahraoui constituents, Morocco is making heavy investments in the socio-economic development of the Saquiet El Hamra, whereas Mauritania, with far less funds at its disposal, was hard pressed to assure even the survival of its citizens, old as well as new, let alone undertake new projects. Rabat's determination to take over the Saquiet El Hamra, lock, stock and barrel, will be difficult for tribesmen as undisciplined and untrammelled as the Sahraouis to accept, even though the Moroccans insist that they are training the best Sahraoui talent for eventual administration of their territory and that the Sahraouis are now citizens of Morocco in every sense of that term. Yet unlike the Spaniards, who were in all respects aliens, lived aloof from the Sahraouis and were clearly transients in the country, the Moroccans consider themselves their cousins — if not brothers — and obviously intend to stay there indefinitely.

In reflecting on the occupation and rule of the former Spanish Sahara by Morocco and Mauritania, it should be noted that the governments of those countries have been the first in northwest Africa to breach the Organisation of African Unity's hitherto sacrosanct principle of the inviolability of inherited colonial frontiers. All the contestants are Muslim, were formerly colonies and now have Arab governments. Nevertheless, the war in the Sahara has had repercussions — in most instances disruptive — on the domestic policies of the countries most directly involved. Indeed, in Mauritania the war was the main cause of two recent governmental upheavals. Finally, in contrast to recent developments in Angola and the Horn of Africa, the fact that neither of the world's superpowers is appreciably involved in the struggle is a significant, if negative, claim to distinction in the contemporary African scene.

Certain aspects of the evolution of the western desert are less distinctive than those cited above, inasmuch as they are present in other Saharan areas as well. One of these is the universality of military governments there, for all of the powers that have ruled in the desert, whether European or African, have found army officers to be the most economical and effective agents for controlling a huge territory that is almost uninhabited, save for a few oasis-dwellers and some mobile and usually dissident tribes. Another development is one shared by Morocco with Algeria, Mauritania and Niger,[1] namely the discovery that beneath the desert sands lies a potential source of wealth that could make the territory where it is situated economically viable. Obviously this places a premium on the ownership of a region that, until minerals were discovered, was regarded either as a fearful barrier to communication between north and black Africa or, at best, as a transit zone for their trade. Realisation of the Sahara's mineral potential, in turn, has led to an upgrading of national economic interests at the expense of ideological goals, and Spain's impending surrender of its Saharan province in the early 1970s aroused the acquisitive instincts of its immediate neighbours. Consequently, early in 1976 all three of them, to varying degrees and at different times, reneged on their public commitment to the principle of the Sahraouis' right to self-determination — the principle which they had invoked in forcing the Spanish withdrawal.

Morocco and Mauritania justified this volte-face by proclaiming a higher priority for another principle that had been endorsed by the OAU — that of maintaining territorial integrity. Algeria, for its part, continued to uphold vehemently the right of the Sahraouis to vote in a referendum on their future status, but without waiting for such a plebiscite to be held it recognised the RASD (the Arab Democratic Sahraoui Republic) soon after it was proclaimed by the Polisario leadership. Algiers presumably took this action in the expectation that the new 'Sahraoui state' would accept its leadership out of gratitude for services rendered and, because of the RASD's landlocked position, for lack of more advantageous alternatives.

Differences in the motivation, the geographical milieu and, even more, the means at their disposal of all the powers that have governed in the desert account for most but not all of the variations in their policies. The stability and effectiveness of one colonial regime as compared with another have been determined less by the duration of its governance than by the site of its installation and the predisposition of the tribesmen nomadising in its territory to trade or to carry out armed raids. Thus Spain, the oldest of the imperial powers in the Western Sahara, was its weakest ruler because it had neither the means nor the incentive to develop a colony that apparently lacked any appreciable economic potential, and because the bellicose Reguibat were the dominant tribe in the area that Spain nominally ruled. It was largely to assure the defence of the Canary Islands and Spanish fishing grounds, and not the desire to acquire an empire on the adjacent mainland, that prompted Spain to occupy and to remain in the coastal region of the western desert. To varying degrees and at different times, the elements of nostalgia for the glory of their past empire, military defence, prestige and economic gain were factors in motivating and modifying Spain's policies in the Sahara.

Morocco's irredentism was motivated by most of those same elements, but to them was added the determination to expand its national boundaries and population. The Mauritanians, too, were moved by the remembrance of a vague Moorish 'cultural entity' in the history of the western desert, but the driving force behind their expansionism was the need to increase their mineral and fishing resources. As for France, the necessity to defend and bind together its black and white African dependencies was primordial, and the belated exploitation of Fort Gouraud's iron deposits played only a secondary role.

France's impact on the western desert was more effective, though of shorter duration, than that of Spain, which extended over some 400 years. It was not until the early twentieth century that France established its protectorate over Morocco, and Mauritania did not become a French colony until 1920. Moreover, those portions of the western desert that they theoretically encompassed were not wholly pacified until 14 years later. Then, too, both Morocco and Mauritania possessed large and economically productive areas, whereas the Spanish dependencies in northwest Africa, aside from the *presidios*, were long thought to be barren wastes. It is not surprising, therefore, that despite Spain's closer proximity to the western desert and its centuries-long presence there, Madrid made no effort to assert sovereignty over its desert hinterland until after the French had pacified the local tribes in their areas. Until the mid-1930s, Spain acted less as an imperial power in the Western Sahara than as the administrator of three small coastal colonies, inhabited almost exclusively by Spanish troops, civil servants and a few merchants. The main function of the local government was to provide training for the national army and to defend the area from any threat to the security and economic interests of the Canary Islanders. In

dealing with the local tribesmen, Spain found it easier and more economical to buy their goodwill with money and favours than to attempt
a military conquest. To be sure, the administrative framework in which
Spain ruled its dependencies was periodically revised, its original formula
of a dispersed military annex to the Canary Islands giving way to the
status of a Spanish province, but internal and external pressures had to
be felt before any basic changes in its rule and in its attitude toward
France were initiated.

Even before the Reguibat tribes finally surrendered to France in
1934, the Spaniards came to regard the French as dangerous competitors, and they would not co-operate in bringing dissident tribesmen
under control. Their attitude became more openly antagonistic during
the Second World War, and in 1953 Spain went so far as to refuse
recognition to the Sultan of Morocco, whom the French had installed
at Rabat. Farther south, they were reported even to have offered bases
in their territory to tribesmen hostile to France, from which to attack
French posts in Mauritania. It was not until 1957-8, a year after Morocco
became independent, that the Spaniards for the first and last time
joined with France in a military operation against the irregular Moroccan
forces that were threatening the rule of both powers in the Western
Sahara. After their brief and eminently successful joint military venture,
France and Spain resumed their separate ways in the desert until
eventually both powers were forced at different times — France in 1960
and Spain in 1976 — to withdraw from the desert after trying, largely in
vain, to preserve their economic and cultural interests there.

Just as their policies in the Sahara had diverged, so did the manner
of their departure from it differ, as did the destiny of their territorial
legacies in the desert. France, after briefly experimenting with autonomous regimes in its black African territories, made a mass grant of
independence to all of them, including Mauritania, in 1960. For Spain,
the turning-point came when the extent of Bu Craa's phosphate deposits
became widely known and aroused the covetousness of Morocco,
Algeria and Mauritania, not to mention that of the local tribesmen.
Representative institutions with limited power were introduced into
Spain's Saharan dependencies, but too slowly and too parsimoniously
to stem the rising tide of demands by all the indigenous forces for more
of the spoils. Despite the failure of its attempts to launch pro-Spanish
Sahraoui movements and the growing strength of Sahraoui opposition
to continued Spanish rule in the Sahara, Madrid clung to its largest
stronghold in Africa until it definitively withdrew in February 1976.

Spain's perseverance, or obstinacy, could not be attributed solely to its stake in the Bu Craa mines, for its Saharan territories were more costly than profitable to administer, and were less rich in resources than were the African dependencies to which France and Britain had granted independence 16 years earlier. Furthermore, Spain had no large settler colonies there comparable to those of the Portuguese in Angola and Mozambique, which Lisbon had abandoned in 1974. Probably the almost equally tardy and sudden collapse of the older Portuguese empire in Africa, the imminent death of Generalissimo Franco, the pressure exerted in unison by Morocco, Mauritania and Algeria in the UN, and, even more, the intensity of the Polisario's attacks on Spanish settlements and forts were the decisive influences in determining Madrid's decision to cut its losses in the Sahara by withdrawing, after making the best possible bargain with the leading candidates to its succession. By bequeathing the Saharan province jointly to Morocco and Mauritania in November 1975, the Spaniards hoped to salvage as much as possible of its economic and cultural assets, but at the last moment the Madrid government was beset by qualms concerning the effect its decision would have on its relations with Algeria and by uneasiness as to the fate of its legacy. By stating formally that it was transferring administrative authority but not sovereign powers over its former province, the Spanish government sowed the seeds of greater discord in an already troubled area.

One can only speculate as to what might have been the fate of the Western Sahara had knowledge of the extent of its mineral wealth remained limited to a few Spanish officials, or had France and Spain, instead of regarding each other as rivals there, early realised that their common interest lay in pooling their resources and in co-ordinating their defences against the forces opposing them. It is possible that the Sahara province might have continued to evolve gradually toward independence under Spain's tutelage, but more probably it would have been only a matter of time before the French and Spaniards were driven out of the desert by the growing strength of the local nationalist forces, to which their very presence (and that of the Sahara's vast economic resources) had given rise. Moreover, even though France and Spain left the Western Sahara peaceably, they are not wholly free of some responsibility for the bloodshed that ensued there. The Spanish government has been urged by its left-wing opposition — which in turn is being pressured by its Polisario friends — to repudiate the pact it made with Morocco and Mauritania. And France, to protect its nationals still living and working in Mauritania from being taken as hostages by the Polisario, and in response to pleas from Daddah, provided air support beginning in December 1977 to the Mauritanian forces — technically a breach of its neutral stand.

Another instance of self-defeating jealousy between two countries that might seem to have every interest in broad-based co-operation is that which has set Morocco and Algeria against each other over their Saharan inheritance. This case may be unique in the annals of imperialism in that initially the issue of nationalism was not involved, because the quarrel was one between rival officials of a common colonial power. In the early twentieth century, French bureaucrats and officials stationed, respectively, in Algeria and Morocco competed with each other for control of the undemarcated borderland area between those two dependencies of France. In this increasingly acrimonious dispute, the Paris government only occasionally intervened, and when it did so it usually took the side of the Algerian administration. The latter was favoured on the grounds that Algeria was bearing the cost, in terms of both manpower and money, of pacifying the Tafilalet-Guir-Zousfana-Touat region, but a more fundamental reason was to discourage the Sultan of Morocco from reviving his claim to that borderland area. Specifically, the officer in command of the attack on Tindouf in 1934 was instructed to occupy the town in the name of France and to use no Moroccan troops in carrying out that military operation.

During the Algerian revolt in the mid-1950s, the inclusion of Tindouf in Algeria was again confirmed by the French. This time, France reasserted its sovereignty there not only to obviate any Moroccan claim to that area but with a view to keeping Tindouf permanently under French control because in the 20-year interval between the capture of Tindouf and the outbreak of the Algerian revolt, Morocco was on the verge of becoming independent, and even more because French geologists had discovered at Gara Djebilet, near Tindouf, the largest iron mine in the Sahara. This find gave new significance to the ownership of that area, just as the discovery at about the same time of the Bu Craa phosphate deposits had immeasurably increased the economic importance of Saquiet El Hamra. The potential source of wealth represented by the Gara Djebilet deposits exacerbated the old dispute over ownership of the Algero-Moroccan borderlands, where France had never formally demarcated the frontier. In 1963, after France had left northwest Africa and both Algeria and Morocco had become independent, the same dispute flared into warfare.

Considering the intensity of the fighting between the rival claimants then and now, and the importance of the economic stakes at issue in the Western Sahara, the emphasis that has been and is still being placed on the legal aspects of the perennial Algero-Moroccan border conflict and of Spain's pact with Morocco and Mauritania seems academic and even contrived. Yet it is of major significance to all the belligerents involved, for the question of legitimacy weighs heavily on all revolutionaries, particularly those of the Third World, who seek to enlist foreign support for their cause. None of the contestants for control of the Western Sahara can afford to fight a war in the desert without the aid of those industrial nations that control the production and distribution of modern weapons. And in the less tangible domain of moral support, even Hassan II, the scion of a sultanate that has reigned in Morocco since the seventeenth century, could not long endure the opprobrium and the diplomatic isolation in the international community that was occasioned by his irredentist policies toward Mauritania and the Spanish Sahara.

It was to gain foreign approval of their projected seizure of Saquiet El Hamra and Rio de Oro that Morocco and Mauritania sent emissaries in 1975 to Third World capitals, and it was to justify their claims that they carried their case to the International Court at The Hague. Conversely, it has been to elicit the world's condemnation of those expansionist policies that Algeria has sought to have the Spanish Sahara question debated at every international conference where it could hope to have it included on the agenda. For similar reasons, the Polisario Front has been insistent that Spain repeat its statement of 26 February 1976 to the effect that it did not transfer sovereignty over its Sahara province to Morocco and Mauritania, but only administrative responsibility. The ambiguity of that statement has given the Algerian and Polisario leaders an opening to deny the legitimacy of Morocco's and Mauritania's occupation of Saquiet El Hamra and Rio de Oro although, initially, they had asserted that Spain had never had the right to rule in the Sahara.

The results of these efforts in the world arena have been inconclusive, partly because of differing interpretations and shifts in the priorities assigned to the two basic principles of the OAU that are subscribed to by all of its members. These principles are the right of peoples to self-determination and the right of nations to maintain their territorial integrity, and on occasion the same government in different situations has shifted its emphasis from one to the other of those principles according to its own advantage. Madrid, for example, has upheld the right of the inhabitants of the *presidios* to self-determination because the majority there are certain to vote in favour of remaining under Spanish rule, whereas it has denied that the same right should be exercised by the population of Gibraltar, which has voted to stay with the

British. Rabat had advocated self-determination for the Sahraouis until Spain proposed offering the option of independence to them as an alternative to perpetuation of Spanish rule or a union with Morocco. And Algeria has argued for the Sahraouis' right to determine their own political status but has not offered an analogous opportunity to the inhabitants of Tindouf or to its own Touareg nomads.

As events in the Spanish Sahara moved rapidly toward a climax, the international organisations most concerned in settling the dispute held meetings designed to head off the impending violence, and a number of Arab and African leaders tried to mediate between the opposing forces. But the incongruity between the ideals voiced by the contestants and their policies was too flagrant to be ignored, and the resolutions passed successively by the UN, the OAU, and the Arab League were themselves so contradictory as to be largely rhetorical and devoid of any effect. The International Court at The Hague, to which the case was referred in 1974 for an advisory opinion as to the respective historical rights of Spain, Morocco and Mauritania to sovereignty over the Western Sahara, handed down an opinion so ambiguous as to satisfy none of the litigants. In particular it failed to deflect King Hassan from his determination to take over the Spanish Sahara by one means or another. He utilised the breathing space provided by the debate before the Hague court to prepare meticulously a 'peaceable green march' by more than 300,000 of his subjects to the area under dispute. This recourse to direct action was planned to be a dramatic affirmation of the Moroccan people's support for their king's policy, but it also served as a smokescreen to divert attention from the negotiations for a legal transfer of the Spanish Sahara that the king was carrying on at the same time with Spain and Mauritania. They culminated in the Madrid pact of 14 November 1975, which insured Spain's withdrawal from the Sahara, allotted the Saquiet El Hamra to Morocco and Rio de Oro to Mauritania, and divided shares in the Bu Craa mining enterprise between all three parties.

A month later, the UN's members, faced with a *fait accompli*, approved two contradictory resolutions that neutralised each other, and the *impasse* to which this led was perhaps not unwelcome to the organisation's Third World members. The Arab League was equally stymied by failure to reach a consensus, and for the same reason the OAU has repeatedly postponed holding the special conference on the Sahara problem to which it was pledged. The Western Sahara was too isolated and remote, the minerals at stake there (iron and phosphates) were too moderate in value, and the issues were too confused and personal in the eyes of the major powers to warrant intervention. Their overriding concern was not the wishes or the future of the Sahraouis but to contain the conflict and, if possible, to restore peace to the region.

In the early 1960s the strongest support for Morocco's claims to Mauritania came from the Casablanca-bloc radicals — Guinea, Ghana, Mali, the Algerian provisional government and Egypt — whereas 15 years later it was provided by the conservative Arab states and the Western industrial nations, and Morocco's most implacable adversaries were Algeria, Libya and other 'revolutionary' regimes. Generally speaking, the further the country from the Saharan battle zone the more it was prone to judge the fighting there purely on ideological grounds, as did Madagascar and South Yemen, the first countries to recognise the RASD. Conversely, the nearer the country to the scene of conflict, the more it tended to be preoccupied with preserving its own economic interests and territory intact and to be swayed by its feelings of either fear or admiration for Algeria, as in the case of Mali and Senegal.

A middle ground between the two has been occupied by Egypt and Libya, owing to drastic changes in their leadership and consequent alterations in their foreign policies. In 1962 Nasser clearly showed his disapproval of Hassan, but in 1977 the king could be counted as Sadat's warmest Arab supporter, and this support was reciprocated in 1979 by the sending of Egyptian military aid to Rabat. Quite the opposite evolution has marked Libya's relations with Morocco, for the friendly ties that had existed between the two monarchs, Idriss and Hassan, did not survive the seizure of power by Colonel Khadafi in 1969. Nevertheless, Khadafi's attitude toward both Hassan and the Polisario remains somewhat ambivalent. He still strongly disapproves of Hassan as a conservative monarch, yet he applauded the king's sending of Moroccan troops to the Near East to fight against Israel, and has made agreements with Rabat to employ some thousands of Moroccans in Libya. Moreover, although he was the first Arab head of state to back the Polisario when it concentrated on forcing the Spaniards out of the Sahara, he has not recognised the RASD lest its existence as a separate state disrupt the 'Arab nation'. By and large, the key to the Arab attitude toward the Saharan question is first the preservation of Arab unity *vis-à-vis* Israel, and secondly the views of the various Arab governments in regard to Algeria's revolutionary socialism.

As to the superpowers, they have agreed only on their desire to prevent a 'destabilisation' of the Maghreb. Both the United States and the Soviet Union have believed that the collapse of the Moroccan monarchy — of whose expansion both nevertheless disapprove — would jeopardise the future of the region by unleashing disruptive forces as represented by the Polisario. Should Morocco, either through internal or external pressures, follow Mauritania's example by being defeated in the war, the anarchy thus generated could be held in check only by the (unlikely) combined efforts of the Polisario's present supporters — Algeria and Libya.

Ideologically, the USSR has been aligned with the Polisario which it supplies with weapons through Algeria and Libya, but it still refuses to recognise the RASD. In part, this is because Moscow wants to avoid offending Morocco, with which it signed in 1978 a long-term contract for supplies of phosphate, and also a less important agreement according Russians the right to fish off the Moroccan coast. Presumably, the USSR could make similar arrangements with whatever government in Morocco that succeeded in controlling those resources, but only after considerable delay and perhaps under less advantageous terms. The United States, for its part, has no such direct interest in Morocco's raw materials, but it is anxious to shore up a moderate government in the strategic area which Morocco occupies in northwest Africa, and to demonstrate to the Third World — sceptical since the fall of the Shah of Iran — that it will stand by a leader who has proved his friendship with the West by sending troops to Shaba in Zaïre and by supporting Sadat's overtures to Israel. At the same time, however, Washington wants to remain on good terms with Algiers, an important provisioner in hydrocarbons, and also to preserve its image as a supporter of peoples struggling for their independence. Nevertheless, the Polisario's Marxist stance and unproven capacity for nationhood might transform a fully independent RASD into a junior edition of revolutionary Libya, albeit without Tripoli's wealth. So the United States maintained a technically neutral position until late in 1979, when it tilted toward greater military support for Rabat's precariously poised regime. The primary concern of the United States and other Western powers has been to prevent the former Spanish Sahara from becoming another African magnet for Soviet and Cuban intervention, and also to preserve the balance of power in the Maghreb.

Concerning the support given to the combatants by Spain and France, the two European powers most directly concerned in the struggle for the Western Sahara, the involvement of the former has been both practical and psychological. All Spanish governments, of no matter what political stripe, have been committed to defend Spain's control of the *presidios* and the fishing privileges of Canary Islanders in the coastal waters of northwest Africa. For equally practical economic reasons, Madrid has wanted to remain on good terms with Algeria, not only as a source of

oil and gas but as an influential leader of the Arab world, which Spain
has been courting since the Second World War. The centrist government
of Adolfo Suarez has been trying to hold the balance between the
Spanish left-wing parties and the army, which, for different reasons,
favour the Polisario Front, and the Spanish business community, which
still hopes to get some return commensurate with Spain's investment
in the Bu Craa mines – a more likely outcome under the Alaouite
monarchy than under a Marxist-oriented RASD government.

Madrid's closer relations with Algiers further complicate Spain's
attitude toward the Polisario. Algeria has been prodding Spain to recognise the RASD by sponsoring the Canary Islands independence movement and the latter's making a common cause with the Polisario insofar
as creating a joint state and facilitating the Polisario's attacks on Spanish
fishermen. In so doing, however, Algeria has alienated even the Socialist
Workers Party, whose nationalist sentiments have once again prevailed
over ideology.[2] To offset its refusal to recognise the RASD as a sovereign
state, the Suarez government has tried to placate Algeria by permitting
the Polisario to open an office in Madrid, sending a party representative
to attend the fourth congress of the Polisario, and repeating in international forums its denial of having transferred Spain's sovereignty over
the Western Sahara to Morocco and Mauritania in 1975. Nevertheless, it
has stopped short of making the ultimate concession – that of recognising the RASD as a sovereign state.

France's far stronger emotional and politico-economic ties with all
the parties to the dispute have moved Paris to intervene more actively
in the Sahara than any other power than Algeria, and it has operated
there both as 'gendarme for the West' and in its own interests. Albeit
officially neutral, Paris has discreetly supplied Morocco and Mauritania
with arms, funds and technical aid; tried to mediate the dispute both
directly and through the good offices of the presidents of Senegal and
Ivory Coast; and refused to negotiate directly with the Polisario for the
release of its nationals held as hostages by that Front. In 1978-9,
however, Paris did move to warm up its increasingly chilly relations
with Algiers which were having adverse effects on the French economy.
It still refused, however, to cease aiding Morocco and also made it clear
that France would oppose by force, if necessary, any infringement of
Mauritania's sovereignty. As the foreign country with the most to lose
by continuation of the conflict in terms of influence and trade, France
has been the most active in seeking a negotiated settlement of the
desert war.

The absence of direct armed intervention by outside forces, excepting the support given Mauritania's army by the French air force between December 1977 and July 1978, seemed to confirm the futility of the combatants' various attempts to enlist the aid of foreign powers by appeals based on abstract principles. Mauritania's withdrawal from the war in August 1979 indicated clearly that the conflict would be settled according to the ability and determination of Morocco and of Algeria to assert what their respective governments believe to be their national interests. In this respect, a distinction should be drawn between the objectives of the leaders and their governments' refusal to submit the conflict between them to negotiation, on the one hand, and their insistence on continuing the undeclared war that has placed increasing strains on their manpower or financial resources, on the other, or both, and even more on their peoples' willingness to make the sacrifices that this policy demands.

As the war drags on, these sacrifices are becoming so heavy as to jeopardise the stability and solvency of the regimes participating directly or indirectly in the fighting. Of the three (now reduced to two) principals, Algeria has been the least threatened, for its resources are greater, it is not sending its own soldiers to fight in the desert and its land has not been invaded. To some degree, therefore, Algeria is engaged in a proxy war, wherein it simply provides funds and arms to the Polisario Front, which furnishes the actual combat forces. Although this policy demands of the Algerians no sacrifice of human life, it does drain off economic resources that could be more productively used in carrying out the official development plans that are designed to raise Algerian living standards.

The government's propaganda organs have been working overtime to awaken the Algerians' sympathy and support for their Sahraoui brethren, and by the end of March 1976 Algeria had subscribed some 20 million dinars (roughly £11 million) to send food and clothing to the refugees at Tindouf and for 'the defence of the homeland'. Nevertheless, the Algerians' general response to such pleas has ranged from lukewarm to clearly antagonistic on the part of a few politically conscious members of the elite. In the spring of 1976, a manifesto signed by four outstanding leaders of Algeria's war of independence (including Ferhat Abbas, former president of its provisional government) reminded President Boumediene of the support that Morocco had given to Algeria in its hour of need, and its authors urged him to end the fratricidal Sahara conflict and to co-operate with Morocco in building a united Maghreb.

It would be inadvisable to regard this manifesto as evidence of widespread discontent in Algeria with the official Saharan policy, although its authorship and the public's indifference, on the whole, to the Sahraoui question do suggest that there are limits to the Algerians' tolerance of a costly war with whose objectives they do not identify. To convinced Marxists this divergency in Algerian reactions to the Sahara conflict simply masks the underlying antagonism between the bureaucratic and entrenched capitalist wings of the Algerian bourgeoisie[3] and does not reflect the masses' response to the war.

Mauritania and Morocco, on the other hand, were at the outset direct participants in a war that was being conducted for what were to them very high stakes. In terms of manpower, economic resources and determination, Mauritania was the least able of the three major contestants to afford such losses as it suffered. The war brought Mauritania no material compensation commensurate with the sacrifices in manpower and money that it made and with the risk to its fragile national unity. Black Mauritanians were being called on in proportionately larger numbers compared to the Moors to fight a war that seemed irrelevant to their own needs and aspirations. As for the Arab and Berber Mauritanians, their small but influential radical elite not only resented the country's growing dependence on Morocco and France for their defence, but tended to sympathise with the Sahraouis' demand for self-determination. Although at first the Polisario's raids on the country's political and economic centres and the military posts within its 1960 frontiers aroused a patriotic reflex, soon there was a growing realisation that Mauritania was bearing the brunt of a war in which it had the most to lose and the least to gain. The increase in its losses in human life and the burden of taxation to meet the cost of defending the country and administering the new province of Tiris El Gharbia became intolerable even to the handful of professional officers in the Mauritanian army. So they overthrew the Daddah government and made their peace gradually with the Polisario and Algeria without hopelessly antagonising Morocco.

Of the countries involved directly in the Saharan war, Morocco alone has been actually strengthened morally by it and has a vital interest in its outcome. Doubtless because Morocco is the only country in northwest Africa that has an authentic national identity, the unity of its people has been strengthened and not shattered by a conflict that is costing them dear in human and economic terms. To the government, its control of the Bu Craa phosphate deposits seems essential in order to safeguard the country's remunerative export trade, and to the king, his unprecedented popularity comes from tapping the rich emotions that derive from Morocco's imperial past. Hassan's religious authority, as *imam*, has never been questioned, but now for the first time he has acquired a solid political base that embraces the whole gamut of local opinion.

The king, after surviving two attempts on his life and the waning of his influence as a leader in the Arab world, staged a brilliant comeback at home if not abroad. His army officers, far from trying to eliminate him, have been urging him to undertake a military offensive against Algeria. Moroccan radicals, for their part, have been threatening to out-flank him on the left and, paradoxically, his government risks being overturned not by pursuing the war but by making concessions to the Polisario and Algeria that could compromise Moroccan sovereignty over the Sahara. Thus far, both the mass of the population and the elite have been absorbed by the excitement and artificial prosperity generated by the war effort, and the serious attrition of the country's economy has been disguised by the influx of foreign aid and the opportunities for well-paid jobs in the new Sahara provinces and service in the army. Albeit increasingly isolated diplomatically, and hard pressed on the battlefield by Polisario raiders and on the home front by rapidly rising living costs, the king remains intransigent in the conviction that time is on his side.

Notes

1. Niger's uranium deposits are undoubtedly the main stimulus for Tripoli's inclusion of northern parts of that country in recent maps of Libya.
2. By a vote of 142 to 175 on 15 February 1978, the Cortes refused to re-nounce the Madrid pact of 1975 and the fishing agreement with Morocco.
3. E. Assidon, *Sahara Occidental: Un Enjeu pour le Nord-ouest Africain* (François Maspéro, Paris, 1978), pp. 43ff.

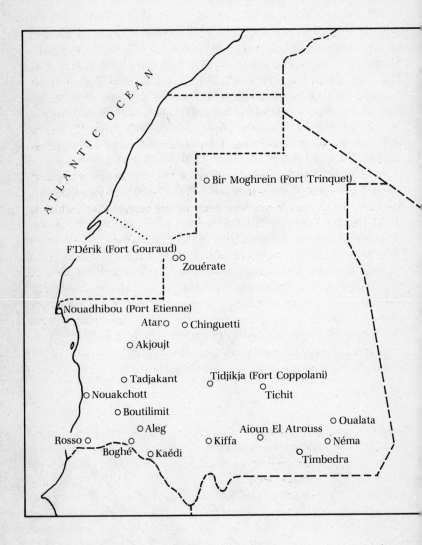

PART I: MAURITANIA

After Mauritania became a French colony early in the twentieth century, its area was twice substantially increased — in 1944 by acquiring the Hodh region of Soudan, and in 1976 by taking over the Spanish Rio de Oro — so that the country then extended from the Senegal River in the south to the new Moroccan border of Saquiet El Hamra in the north, and from the Atlantic Ocean in the west to the frontiers of Algeria and Mali in the east and southeast respectively. In 1979, after Mauritania made its peace with the Polisario Front, its boundaries became again those of 1960.

Most of Mauritania is a vast plain strewn with rocks (the *reg*), partly covered by moving or semi-stabilised dunes. The only arable regions are the alluvial belt on the northern bank of the Senegal River, which is 500 kilometres long by 5 to 20 kilometres wide, and the oases and depressions of Adrar and Tagant (*graara*). Until technology made possible improvements in the means of communication and the discovery of mineral deposits, Mauritania's most notable physical characteristics were its apparent lack of natural resources and the isolation of its small, dispersed and mobile population. Today it is still isolated from its neighbours to the north and east by immense stretches of the Sahara, and to the west by an inhospitable coastline, and, as in the past, Mauritania remains easily accessible only from the south.

History and Political Evolution

Local chronicles and Moorish tradition hold that before the Arabs invaded the Maghreb in the seventh century of the Christian era, negro tribes related to those south of the Senegal River lived on amicable terms with the Sanhadja Berbers, whose ancestors had come to Mauritania from Tafilalet and from the Draa and Saoura valleys. The main attraction for all these immigrants was the comparatively rich farming and pasture land, as well as the gum trees of the sahel region. This southward trend and the generally peaceable tribal relationships underwent a marked change in the eleventh century when a new Berber element entered the region. This was the Almoravid confederation, which used Mauritania as its base to conquer the empire of Ghana,

33

Morocco, southern Spain and western Algeria. Upon the conquered peoples the Almoravids imposed Islam, to which they themselves had been converted by the Arabs ten centuries earlier.

Immigrants continued to move into Mauritania at the time when European explorers and traders began to appear along its coast. By the fifteenth century, the dominant element among those arriving overland was the Arab tribe of the Beni Maql. Late in the seventeenth century disputes between the Maql Arabs (*hassane*) and the Sanhadja Berbers led to a 30-year war known as the Char Bouba, which culminated in the defeat of the Berbers in 1674. Consequently, the latter, who came to be called marabout or *zaouia* tribes, had to renounce warfare, assume exclusively religious and scholarly functions and pay tribute (*horma*) to and perform services for the *hassane* warriors. The ethnic division between the marabouts and the warriors was almost as clear cut as their occupations. The warriors were all Arabs except for the Berber Idaouich of Tagant, whereas virtually all the marabouts were Berbers of Sanhadja origin, some of whom claimed to be *chorfa* and hence of Arab stock. Nevertheless, the warriors and marabouts together formed a white aristocracy, each with its own *fractions* (kinship groups), vassals (*harratin*) and black servile castes, in which the marabouts were junior partners. The *hassane* Arabs monopolised the political power and leadership in war, which brought them booty in slaves and animals, and they also enjoyed extensive proprietary rights over cultivated land, fishing and the use of well water. As for the Berber marabouts, their energies were productively deflected to trading and to animal husbandry, and they also won renown throughout the Sahara for their Islamic learning and piety.

It took 30 years from the beginning of the twentieth century for the French moving north from Senegal to establish by diplomacy and conquest an effective control over the region which they named Mauritanie. After having been successively a protectorate in 1903 and a 'special civilian territory' in 1904, Mauritania became in 1921 a colony and a member of the French West African Federation. After the French established control over the Senegal River valley in the far south, negro and Peul tribesmen moved north into that area, which was organised administratively on the model of Senegal. To the north of it, however, a military government was retained in order to protect the cattle- and sheep-rearing tribes there, who had generally accepted French rule, from armed raids by the independent Reguibat tribesmen (see Annex) who roamed throughout the Western Sahara.

Until after the Second World War, the Paris government regarded

Mauritania not as of value in itself but in the light of French imperial concerns in west Africa, first as an indispensable frontier march to safeguard Senegal, and then as a link between the federation and Morocco. Such considerations, as well as Mauritania's lack of known economic resources, required that it be peaceful and stable and also that it should be administered as economically as possible. On both counts this meant the fewest possible changes in the established social order.

Subsidies from the metropolitan and federal governments were minimal, and never sufficed to develop Mauritania's few existing assets. Because the economy north of the Senegal River valleys was limited to date monoculture, animal husbandry and salt-mining, and because in the south a larger and more industrious sedentary population of different ethnic origin cultivated a more abundant and wider range of crops, Mauritania was in effect governed as two separate countries. The north was administered as a frontier march, while the south received more favoured treatment. Indeed, not only the south but all Mauritania became an appendage of Senegal, as was shown by the location of its capital at St Louis-du-Sénégal and by the handling of its foreign trade through the port of Dakar. This policy inadvertently proved to be costly, for the expenditures involved in maintaining a colonial administration with a top-heavy bureaucracy and a rudimentary economic and social infrastructure in the south were compounded by those of conducting military operations in the north. Moreover, the latter coincided with the world economic depression of the early 1930s, so that new taxes were imposed on the country's meagre resources. Since most of Mauritania's output was consumed by its producers and its amount was never precisely known, this fiscal policy was applied arbitrarily by generally inexperienced administrators and army officers who were frequently rotated in their posts. Although the tax rates were subsequently reduced, they continued to be collected by not disinterested local chiefs, who were already aggrieved by the government's suppression or reduction of their traditional revenues.

The widespread unrest caused by France's policy — imposing taxes, prohibiting armed raids and the slave trade, and restricting the trek areas so as to ensure closer control of the nomads — awakened the government to the need for dealing with Mauritania as an entity which had a personality of its own. In the mid-1930s the local authorities undertook their first serious study of the Moorish emirates, and required administrators and officers to undergo specialised instruction and on-the-job training before being assigned to responsible posts in the country.

The Second World War and especially the post-war reforms marked a turning-point in the evolution of Mauritania and its relations with France. Except for some incidents in the south which were due primarily to religious agitation emanating from Soudan,[1] there were no adverse political repercussions even after France's defeat in Europe in 1940. That the situation in Mauritania remained calm during the war attested to the wisdom of France's established policy of favouring the more peaceable, industrious and better-educated marabout tribes at the expense of the *hassane* warriors. Yet the whole population, especially those in the centre and north, suffered acutely from wartime privation.[2]

Never self-sufficient in foodstuffs, Mauritania experienced a decline in agricultural and pastoral production during the three exceptionally dry years of 1941-4, and it proved impossible to compensate for these deficiencies by imports. Rice could no longer be brought in from Indochina, and the millet normally obtained from Senegal and Soudan, which were equally drought-stricken, was unavailable. Trade with Morocco virtually ceased after the exportation of dates and animals from Adrar was forbidden, and Mauritania lapsed into a wretched subsistence economy. Herds were decimated for lack of pasture and many of the animals which escaped being requisitioned by the administration for meat or for transport were clandestinely sold in Senegal, Rio de Oro and Morocco. The contraband trade and a black market flourished, notably in sugar, tea and cloth. To offset shortages in those commodities and to combat the rapidly rising cost of living, the administration coaxed shipments from France and drew on its own stocks, which it tried to distribute equitably. It also established price controls on indispensable items in shortest supply, created public-works jobs, set up some soup kitchens in the largest settlements and gave food rations to the most indigent families. Late in 1942 the Allied disembarkation in north Africa slightly eased Mauritania's penury, but the war accentuated existing socio-economic trends, and on a smaller scale foreshadowed the more drastic situation that was to occur during the great drought of 1968-73.

Among the significant trends strengthened by wartime developments were the nomads' migrations southward to areas where pastures were more abundant, the rural exodus to towns where such supplies as existed were more available, and the flight to farming communities in Senegal and Soudan of the servitors whose masters were no longer able to feed them. The nomads' perennial search for pastures, always regulated by seasonal rainfall, now assumed a more permanent aspect in the south. Increasingly, the habit of selling their animals in Senegalese markets led the Moors to develop their talents as traders in a modern economy and to open small shops in the main Senegalese towns.

Among the innovations that carried over into the post-war period were the renewed strength of the chieftaincy, the birth of a mercantile middle class and the practice of working for wages. During the Second World War the chiefs throughout Mauritania had benefited by a general weakening of official controls following the departure of many French administrators and officers, whose replacements were slow to arrive. Of equal significance was the important role played by the chiefs in allocating and distributing food to their constituents, and in the larger rations which they themselves received along with other 'privileged' categories of the population — soldiers, government clerks and pupils attending state schools. Still another side-effect of the wartime rationing system was the rise of a new class of middlemen, who were the purveyors or smugglers (or both) of scarce merchandise. These were the livestock-rearing marabout tribes and Zenaga tributaries who possessed surplus animals as well as business acumen. By the end of the Second World War, therefore, Mauritanian society had acquired an embryonic bourgeoisie. It was composed of Western-educated government employees and traders whose power was based on money and not on traditional privilege, but they were too few to be considered at that time as a significant new force.

For the Moorish nobles the lure of the south was wholly materialistic, whereas such attraction as the north had for them was more religious and cultural. Although they and their animals found the southern climate unhealthy and humid, and looked upon the region's black inhabitants as inferiors, yet life there was easier and cattle husbandry more remunerative than camel-breeding. Furthermore, many of the noble immigrants owned arable land, especially in the southeast and in Soudan, which was farmed by their *harratin*. To get his share of the crop, the Moorish landowner formed the habit of leaving in place a member of his family to supervise cultivation. What began as a temporary expedient there became a permanent fixture: the caretaker married a black woman and their children were absorbed into the negro world.[3] In this process of adaptation, both nobles and *harratin* lost many of their Saharan characteristics of physical endurance, resignation to hardships and acceptance of the traditional social order.

Into this society marked by rapid transition, which had no shared group organisation beyond that of the tribe, the post-war reforms initiated in Paris fell precipitately and with an immediately disruptive effect. The grant of French citizenship and voting rights for representation in the three French parliamentary bodies and in a local assembly, the abolition of forced labour and the *indigénat* and the separation of executive from judicial authority in criminal cases were interpreted divergently by the various elements that made up Mauritanian society. As throughout French black Africa, the first reaction of the under-privileged classes was a refusal to work for their erstwhile masters and to pay taxes and tribute. Soon most of the servitors who were running short of food and other necessities returned to work for wages. Then the administration began to organise reimbursement of the *horma*, des-pite protests from the warrior tribes, for whom the *horma* had become their main means of subsistence.[4]

The new voting rights gave rise to other kinds of grievances. First of all, such rights were restricted to certain 'privileged' categories of the population — chiefs, government employees, *medersa* graduates, veterans and soldiers serving in the French army — who were most numerous among the black Mauritanians. Then, on the ground that Mauritania's population was small and dispersed, the country was associated with, and therefore subordinated to, more populous Senegal in electing a joint representative to the French constituent assembly. However, after the constitution of the Fourth Republic was accepted in October 1946, Mauritania had its own candidates for election to the National Assembly, Senate and French Union Assembly in Paris. This development awakened not the chiefs but the new mercantile class to the potential importance of the role of deputy to their interests. Their candidate was Horma Ould Babana, an obscure government interpreter, a member of the Idaouaich Tidjaniyist marabout tribe, and founder of the first local political organisation, the Entente Mauritanienne, which was supported by the French socialist party. His defeat of a well-known French administrator was hailed successively as a victory over the warrior chiefs and the triumph of Islam over the infidel. Soon, however, Babana's advocacy of socialism and the elimination of traditional insti-tutions, his excessive personal ambition and his political instability as a deputy caused concern to the chiefs as well as to the *hassane* and the *zaouia*, who joined forces. By 1946 the warriors and Qadriya marabouts had recognised the advantages of having their own deputy in Paris, and they threw their weight behind a conservative party, the Union Progres-siste Mauritanienne (UPM). With the backing of the French administra-tion, the UPM defeated Babana when he ran for re-election in 1951 and again in 1956. Embittered by his electoral defeat and expelled from the Entente Mauritanienne, Babana chose the path of exile. He eventually settled in Rabat, where he became Morocco's first effective advocate of its territorial claims upon Mauritania.

Under the aegis of the UPM, Mauritania remained for some years aloof from neighbouring countries, and internally it was but marginally affected by the political reforms of the early 1950s. However, the *loi-cadre* of 23 June 1956 gave considerable autonomy to French sub-Saharan Africa by enabling each country's territorial assembly to elect a government council that would share executive power with the French administration. Application of this law shattered the tranquil and super-ficial character of Mauritania's political life, and forced its population for the first time to make decisions on significant issues. Concurrently, external events became intrusive, in that Mauritania's foreign policy was shaped by the independence of Morocco (1956) and by the forma-tion of the Organisation Commune des Régions Sahariennes (OCRS). It was also in this period that international capital began to manifest an active interest in Mauritania's iron and copper deposits, with more enduring effects on the country's evolution.

At this critical juncture in its history, Mauritania was fortunate in finding a leader capable of constructively filling the void in its political leadership. He was Mokhtar Ould Daddah, a young French-trained law-yer who was elected in March 1957 to represent Adrar in the territorial assembly, and two months later was chosen by that body to head Mauritania's first government council. As a member of the distingui-shed Sheikh Sidya marabout tribe of Boutilimit and an austere Muslim Moor, he pleased the nomad chiefs, for whom he had briefly served as interpreter in the Fort Trinquet region. And as a Western-educated liberal married to a Frenchwoman, he was *persona grata* to the adminis-tration and the youthful elite, Moors and blacks alike.

Daddah often proclaimed Mauritania's vocation to be that of linking white with black Africa — a role that Niger also aspires to play — but in practice he veered from one side to the other as external circumstan-ces dictated. So long as Morocco's claims remained a threat to Mauritania's territorial integrity, Daddah sought and received support from France and other members of the Franco-African Community, which Mauritania joined after casting an affirmative vote in the consti-tutional referendum of 28 September 1958. But after Mauritania became independent and a member of the UN in 1960-1, Daddah pro-gressively dissociated himself from black Africa and cultivated closer ties with the Maghreb states and the Arab world. Inevitably, such inconstancy in foreign policy, accompanied as it was by tighter internal controls aimed at bringing about national unity under Daddah's aegis, had seriously divisive repercussions on a country so segmented in every way as is Mauritania.

The French Impact

Among the positive contributions by France to Mauritania's evolution was the concept of individual liberty, which was a by-product of the legal suppression of slavery. Among the unpremeditated contributions was the establishing of artificial frontiers for a region in which water and pasture were the vital needs of the nomadic population. Its obvious purpose was to bring the far-flung migrations of the nomads under closer control, but it unintentionally provided the geographical framework inside which a nation eventually could be created. Indirectly rather than directly, France modified intertribal relations, largely by eliminating the insecurity on which they were based. By ensuring peace and governmental stability, and by providing a rudimentary infrastructure and limited socio-economic services for the whole population, apart from the traditional order, France was responsible for a marked growth in Mauritania's human and animal population. More directly, by discovering and then to some extent developing Mauritania's mineral resources, France opened Mauritania to modern world economic circuits. And finally, by deliberately driving a wedge between the warrior and marabout tribes, mainly with a view to subduing the more turbulent *hassane*, France facilitated the rise of the more peaceable, industrious and educated *zaouia* tribes, among whom Mauritania has found most of its outstanding political and economic leaders.

The subsequent decline and underutilisation of the warriors, the administration of the south as an almost separate entity and, even more, the antagonism that developed between the Moors and the southern blacks, are often cited by critics of France's role in Mauritania as examples of applying there the classical imperial policy of divide and rule. Yet the southward drift of the Moors antedated the French occupation, and the northward movement of the Senegalese tribes across the river in the early twentieth century was not due to French coercion but to the attraction of peace in a more climatically favourable region from which its negro inhabitants had been driven out years before by the Berbers and Arabs.

Actually, it was to France's interest to maintain peace and not to sow more seeds of discord between the two major ethnic groups, and it was not until the eve of independence that major rifts between them became apparent. These rifts emerged because of the competitive appeals made to Mauritanians by their irredentist neighbours, Mali and Morocco, and they were intensified by the increasingly pro-Arab policy pursued by Daddah. Until some years after Mauritania became independent, it remained a bulwark of conservatism and peaceful coexistence. And if France did virtually nothing to promote national unity and very little to develop the country, its most permanent legacy was probably that its rule had acted indirectly as a solvent to Moorish society.

Moorish Society

The largest grouping of nomadic Moors is the tribe, whose organisation, way of life and mutual need evidenced its members' attachment to their social structure rather than to a geographical locality. Defined as the ensemble of tents (*friq*) or of joint families with common traditions, the tribe acknowledged the same chief and claimed as their ancestor the same legendary hero, and it was divided into *fractions* composed of ten to one hundred families. Over the tribes there was no single authority except in the emirates, and even there it was often challenged.

All Moorish tribes shared the same hierarchical structure, in which power and prestige were based on ethnic origin and functions. At the apex of the pyramid were the two white (*beidane*) tribes made up of Arab warriors (*hassane*) and Berber religious leaders (marabouts or *zaouia*). In their relationship, the *hassanes* provided protection to the *zaouia* in return for a payment called *horma*, but the latter were not vassals of the former as suzerains in the Western medieval sense of those terms. Their relationship was complementary rather than competitive in the modern period, and together they formed the aristocracy of the region. Around this 'nobility of the sword and the robe' gravitated tributary tribes, largely of Zenaga Berber descent. Beneath them were the *harratin* (liberated servitors) and at the bottom of the pyramid came the inferior negro or mixed-blood castes — the *griots* (minstrels), *mellamin* (blacksmiths) and *abid* (slaves). (Apart from the foregoing social structure, geographically and socially, lived the Imraguen fishermen and Nemadi hunters.) All, however, shared a way of life that was dictated by desert conditions, without visible disparities except in regard to the number of animals a tribe owned and the services its members commanded.

Warrior Tribes and the Chieftaincy

Never strong in nomadic societies, especially those of Berber origin, the chieftaincy was further weakened in Mauritania by the circumstances under which France conquered and then ruled the country. The French, who had established trading posts along the left bank of the Senegal

River, began in the nineteenth century to explore Trarza, Brakna, Tagant and later Adrar, where they made treaties with the principal chiefs – emirs or sheikhs – of those regions.

An emir's lot was not an easy one, for he risked assassination by rival candidates envious of his lucrative position, and his domain was periodically raided by the great cameleer Reguibat confederation from the north. Powerless to create unity or even to impose their will inside their own domains, the emirs soon showed themselves either incapable or unwilling to be bound by the treaties they made with the French. Tribesmen from the emirates, and especially those from Trarza, continued to pillage the river *escales* and to return to their home bases with impunity and their loot. In 1901 the governor of Senegal decided to 'pacify' the area, and he entrusted that mission to Xavier Coppolani, whose remarkable knowledge of the Maghreb Islamic world had been acquired while he served in the Algerian Arab Bureau and during a journey he made through the southern Sahara in 1898-9.[5]

In Mauritania, Coppolani conceived the policy of using the marabout tribes and religious brotherhoods against their warrior overlords, and of playing off rival *hassane* chiefs against each other. Within three months and without firing a shot, Coppolani won control over Trarza, thanks to his alliance with Sheikh Sidya of Boutilimit, and routed the Idaouaich of Tagant, but he soon realised that Adrar, whose massif offered shelter to the nomads, was the key to the conquest of Mauritania. To reach Adrar, Coppolani first had to establish French posts in the sahel zone, but while engaged in doing so he was killed at Tidjikja in 1905. After some delay, his successor, Colonel Henri Gouraud, transformed 'pacification' into military conquest, and in 1909 took possession of Atar and Ouadane. Five years later he won a spectacular victory over the Reguibat at Tichit, and in 1913 he launched a lightning attack on Smara, the mysterious stronghold of Ma El Ainin (see Annex), but his successes proved to be indecisive.

The emirates' instability was partly the result of internal weaknesses, but it was also due to the French administrators' misunderstanding of the nature of the emir's authority, for they assumed that he was a territorial rather than a tribal chief. According to Moorish tradition, an emir was elected by the assembly of warriors (*djemaa*) as a leader in war, but in time he came to be chosen always from the same noble family and was usually the dead chief's eldest son.[6] However, when the *djemaa* considered the heir to be incompetent or the heir's competitors became exceptionally aggressive, he could be eliminated or dismissed by the *djemaa* and replaced by another candidate of the same noble lineage. In principle, the chief presided over the *djemaa*, named judges (*cadi*), arbitrated disputes between fractions, granted pardons and negotiated with neighbouring tribes. In practice, however, his powers were restricted by the *djemaa*, where he was but the first among equals, and he was often victimised by his own jealous relatives.

France's decision in 1931 to impose taxes for the first time on the warriors serving as *goumiers* in the French army, who were then risking their lives in fighting the Reguibat, led to large-scale desertions. Compounding their discontent was the concurrent French policy of reducing the tribute owed to the warrior tribes by their Berber dependents. These measures were motivated in part by the government's desire to alleviate the latter's misery, which had been aggravated by the world economic depression of that period, and in part by France's determination to decrease the authority of the warrior chiefs.

The chiefs could justly complain that they were being given new responsibilities for keeping order and for guaranteeing their followers' loyalty to the French administration, while being deprived of some of the revenues they had formerly received from their tributaries and from armed raids. To be sure, they were left with their honorific titles, were relieved of the burden of defending their dependents, and were paid a regular salary as well as a share of the taxes they collected on behalf of the government. This additional income enabled them to extend the range of their patronage, and they were free to engage in trading and in animal husbandry, but so disoriented were they by the loss of their traditional occupation as warlords and of the prestige it had given them that they were unable to adapt themselves to the new order. Indeed, by the mid-1930s the emirs had already become so inept as chiefs that the French administration seriously considered abolishing the emirates when a particularly thorny problem arose over succession to the Trarza emirate.[7] After studying the chieftaincy as a whole, however, the government concluded that the emirate had become so institutionalised and modified that it should be retained. By then the emirs were playing a useful if limited role as symbols of indirect rule, as tax collectors and as intermediaries between the administration and the tribes.

The gradual suppression of the *horma*, completed in 1952, was the single most shattering blow to *hassane* society, especially in Trarza, which had always been Mauritania's most turbulent emirate. In 1958 the flight of the emir of Trarza to Morocco marked the ultimate disillusionment of an outstanding Arab warrior chief with the country's new political institutions that had voided his role of its traditional meaning. It was the more co-operative emir of Tagant, alone among the four emirates existing at the time of the French conquest, who was able to maintain his eminence and feudal way of life, as well as participate in the new political institutions as a territorial assemblyman. Under French rule, the chieftaincy declined steadily in terms of power but not in numbers. As of 1934, there existed four emirs, 50 heads of smaller tribes and 819 chiefs of fractions and subfractions.[8]

The Marabout Tribes

If the warriors were indubitably the losers under the colonial administration, the marabouts and the dependent tribes were clearly the winners. More numerous than the warriors, the marabout tribes had larger herds, controlled the sale of salt and gum arabic and dominated the caravan trade, and they also enjoyed religious pre-eminence. More democratic in nature, the organisation of the marabout tribes nevertheless resembled that of the warriors, although in their *djemaa* all elements except slaves were represented. The weakness of the marabouts' organisation lay in their *djemaa*'s propensity for interminable discussions and its members' inability to maintain a united front even in the face of a common danger. This failure explains the success of Coppolani's policy of enlisting the marabouts' support and the colonial administration's perpetuation of that policy.

After having been freed for two centuries from the need to defend themselves and then virtually exempted by the French from paying tribute to the warrior tribes, the marabouts could devote their energies to the new economic — and later political — opportunities opened up in Mauritania by France. Thus they added wealth to the prestige and social status they already enjoyed as repositories of Islamic learning and law. The marabouts' religious pre-eminence was paradoxical in that they were Berbers, defeated by the Arabs who had converted them to Islam. They were also unique in the annals of Saharan nomads in having smoothed the way for an alien infidel power to take control of their country. Better educated and more sophisticated than the Arabs, the marabouts were quicker to understand the bases of French rule and to adapt their own activities accordingly.

All Mauritanians profess Sunni Islam of the Malekite rite, and formerly almost all of them belonged to one of the two major rival brotherhoods of Qadriya and Tidjaniya, neither of which was indigenous to the country. The great majority of Mauritanians adhere to the Qadriya, which was propagated among them by the Kounta confederation (see Annex) and was generally supportive of the French regime. Its members were divided not by doctrinal differences but by allegiance to individual marabouts, notably those of Chinguetti and Atar. On the other hand, the Tidjaniya brotherhood, which was affiliated with the Fez *zaouia*, had a left-wing splinter group, the Hamallists, who originated in Soudan and were strongly anti-French. Many of the Tidjaniya Mauritanians belonged to the Idaouaich of Tagant, whereas the Hamallists were to be found in southeastern Mauritania. The Qadriya's opposition to Horma Ould Babana was due in part to his being a Tidjaniya adherent and in part to the socialist creed he professed. The Tidjaniya's close ties with the Fez *zaouia*, which in the early 1950s opposed the French protectorate in Morocco, go far to explain Babana's pro-Moroccan stance in 1958.

The Hamallist brotherhood, founded at Nioro in the late nineteenth century, constituted a social and religious protest movement which, by its egalitarianism and abridgement of the prayer ritual, antagonised the orthodox Qadriya marabouts. Bloody clashes between Hamallists and Qadriya followers in Soudan, beginning in 1924, recurred periodically during the next twenty years, spreading into Mauritania after Sheikh Hamallah had returned to Nioro from exile in 1934. During the Second World War, he apparently thought the time propitious for stirring up trouble for the French administration when it was recruiting Mauritanian blacks for military service.[9] The unrest this caused in Hodh and Assaba was severely repressed, the Hamallist *zaouias* there were destroyed, and Sheikh Hamallah himself was again exiled. Because most of the Hamallists were blacks and the bulk of the Tidjaniyists were Moors, their religious dissensions were compounded by ethnic antagonisms, and it was in part to end this 'settling of accounts' between them that Mauritania's southeastern frontier was extended in the mid-1940s to include all of the Hodh. Thereafter the Hamallist movement gradually disintegrated in Mauritania for various reasons: its leadership was decimated, the warring factions were placed under a single strong administration and the country's new political institutions diverted the disputants from doctrinal issues. An official demographic survey made in 1965 indicated that by then 82 per cent of the Mauritanian Muslims had no brotherhood affiliation, 10 per cent belonged to the Qadriya, and 8 per cent to the Tidjaniya. Even in eastern Hodh the Qadriya predominated, although that brotherhood remained weaker there than in Adrar, and stronger among the Moors than among the negro Muslims.[10]

Sharing the *hassaniya* dialect of Arabic and a common religion has been a unifying force in Mauritania, but Islam has not been a crucible there in which social inequalities and bitter memories of enslavement

have melted away. The progressive 'negrification' of Islam in the
Mauritanian far south is perhaps the local blacks' unconscious revenge
on their former white masters, whose orthodoxy becomes more intransigent as one draws nearer to the Sahara. The isolation enforced by the
desert has kept Islam in northern and central Mauritania remarkably
free of outside influences, and in the 1950s the UPM campaigned to
preserve that Islamic purity.[11] The austere piety of Mauritania's
marabouts, Qadriya and Tidjaniya alike, has been a source of strength
and renown in traditionalist Muslim milieus, but it also proved a weakness when confronted with Western culture. Few Moors have made the
Mecca pilgrimage, some have gone to study in Morocco, which is
Mauritania's closest link with the orthodox Muslim world, but no north
African missionaries have ever come to Mauritania, and there is little
evidence of Egyptian reformist proselytising there. On the contrary, it
has been the Mauritanians who have spread their influence and learning
north and south of their borders.

The *medersa* was a secondary-level school in which Islamic studies
were combined with elements of Western education — a compromise
designed by the French to check the erosion of the marabouts' institutions of higher learning in Adrar, Tagant and Assaba, which formerly
had been renowned for their theological and juridical teaching and
which now received fewer students. Throughout the 1930s the retro-
gression of Islamic learning affected study of the law (*sharia*), in which
the marabouts' scholarship and strict observance had been one of their
proudest distinctions. Justice of the type dispensed by the French
throughout sub-Saharan Africa was applied in Mauritania only to the
southern blacks. Yet encroachments by the French administration on
traditional justice[12] everywhere in Mauritania modified the *sharia* as
to both its application and its principles. The suppression of slavery,
the institution of loans through creation of provident societies (*sociétés
indigènes de prévoyance*) and the changes made in legal procedure and
penalties all served to alter customary justice to such a degree that the
Moors had recourse to it less and less frequently.

For many years, nevertheless, the marabouts certainly fared better
than the warriors in terms of status at home and abroad, as well as in
wealth. They continued to collect alms from their faithful constituents,
still kept the indispensable genealogical records for the tribes, and their
Koranic tent schools were as well attended as before. It was the loss of
their monopoly of education, beginning at the higher levels, that was
the main cause of their decline. So long as the Moorish aristocracy
refused to send their children to French schools, notably to that for the

sons of chiefs at St Louis-du-Sénégal, the marabouts continued to dominate the pedagogic field. During the interwar period, however, the Moors' hostile attitude toward the state schools began to diminish, and with it the marabouts' pre-eminence. Apparently the *medersa* represented the limit of their adaptability, and at the primary level they resisted any attempt by France in the post-war period to tamper with what remained of their control over Moorish youth. Psychologically, the French authorities had to overcome the resistance of nomad parents to being separated from their children, losing the latters' services, and combining Koranic with secular instruction — an innovation that the Moors regarded as useless and possibly harmful.

In time, however, the very functioning of even the limited French school system and, above all, the earning power of its graduates revealed to the Moors the anachronistic character of the traditional Koranic schools and the material advantages of government employment, to which the state system alone gave access. Of the three occupations open to the Moors – trade, animal husbandry and the bureaucracy – the last-mentioned seemed the surest means of satisfying the nomads' newly acquired needs in tea, sugar and cloth. An equally cogent argument used to overcome the Moors' antipathy to French lay education was their fear lest the civil service be monopolised by the blacks, who had provided the first and largest contingent of pupils in the state schools. Consequently, throughout the 1930s attendance in those schools by Moorish children steadily increased.

The post-Second World War reforms led to changes in the French school system, some initiated by the colonial administration and some as a response to Moorish demands. In Trarza an experiment began in 1947 to integrate the French primary-school curriculum into tribal life through the agency of teachers who would travel with the tribe. Three years later, seven nomad schools had been set up in encampments which had no strong marabout teacher and where parents were willing for their children to be taught the three Rs at the same time as they studied the Koran and did their daily chores.[13]

After some years of fitful experimentation, the nomad school gave way to a new type of permanent school, whose curriculum embodied a compromise between the pre-existing French system and the changes requested by Mauritania's territorial assembly.[14] Mauritania's newly elected representatives asked that religious instruction be introduced into French primary schools, that Arabic be taught in state secondary schools, and that *medersas* be replaced by Franco-Arabic institutions at a higher level. Such innovations, however, raised delicate questions politically, for they would breach the lay character of French public instruction and expose Mauritania to the currents of Pan-Arabism. Nevertheless, in 1953 the colonial regime did transform the Boutilimit *medersa* into an Islamic institute, which grew rapidly. Seven years later, when Mauritania became independent, the institute had a 30-member faculty and 400 students, who came from both francophone and anglophone west Africa, and it added Toucouleur to the *hassaniya* Arabic and French which from the outset had been its linguistic vehicles.

To some extent, the institute safeguarded the marabouts' position, and their co-operation with the Institut Français de l'Afrique Noire (IFAN) — which in 1959 established a Mauritanian branch separated from its Dakar headquarters — assured them support and facilities for their research and libraries. Increasingly, however, the youthful elite preferred to attend French universities and technical schools abroad. With the passage of time, the marabouts risked more and more being outflanked on the left by foreign-educated Mauritanian youths determined to lead their country along a more radical, nationalistic and materialistic path. As applied to education, this reorientation meant placing greater stress on Arabic and practical studies than on Islamic learning, and the original Muslim culture that the Mauritanian marabouts had created and propagated was in jeopardy.

Tributary Tribes

Compared with their fellow-Berbers, the marabout tribesmen, the Zenaga represented a minor but growing force in Moorish society, forming the largest element in both *hassane* and *zaouia* encampments. Defeated successively by the Almoravid and Arab *hassane*, the Zenaga owed tribute to individual tribes among both warriors and marabouts. The Zenagas' status resembled that of vassals in medieval Europe, but their dependent and inferior position was attenuated by the egalitarian Berber traditions and by their strong family organisation.

Unable to rise in the Moorish hierarchy through religious learning or military skill, the industrious Zenaga tributaries devoted themselves to trade and livestock-rearing. Thanks first to *pax gallica* and then to profits they made during the Second World War, the Zenaga increased their herds to the point where, by 1947, they owned the largest number of sheep in Adrar and of camels in the Mauritanian sahel.[15] Yet during the colonial period the Zenaga never succeeded in wholly freeing themselves from their traditional obligations,[16] nor did the administration provide freed tributaries with the means of earning a livelihood other than by the occupations that had been traditionally their lot.

Black Harratin and Abid. Altogether the blacks, including Moors with a strong admixture of negro blood, formed about a fourth of the Moorish society into which they were integrated. Under French rule, the categories of *harratin* and *abid* into which the black Moors were divided became so fluid that their status was increasingly difficult to determine. Often the term *harratin* was used as a synonym for freeman, yet many *harratin* remained in the service of their former masters, out of habit, or timidity, or the lack of alternative occupations. Like the other tribes that made up Moorish society, the *harratin* and *abid* were organised into *fractions*, and they usually lived near their masters, whose language, religion, and way of life they shared. *Harratin* and *abid* did the same kinds of work: caring for the herds, cultivating the soil, collecting dates and gum, and performing domestic tasks. The basic difference, however, was that the *harratin* were paid for their services, could buy off their obligations with their earnings and were free to seek employment elsewhere.

French law did not admit the existence of slavery in Mauritania, yet in fact it survived throughout the colonial period.[17] In the eyes of the administration, the *abid* were freemen, and they were protected by the authorities if they brought complaints against their masters, which was rare; slave traders were severely punished if they were caught, which was seldom; and a few *abid* managed to escape to Senegal or to a French military post. But even when they were freed voluntarily by their masters, as happened during the Second World War when the latter could no longer feed their slaves, the majority of *abid* stayed on as *harratin*. Many *harratin*, including former slaves, sought work in Senegal or Soudan as farmers, herdsmen or labourers, on either a permanent or seasonal basis.

Generally speaking, the black Moors seemed to accept their inferior status so long as they were protected and reasonably well treated. However, by the time Mauritania became independent, the more militant among them had formulated specific demands. These were freedom to marry, recognition of the legality of their marriages, a separate listing in the national census and above all suppression or a drastic modification of their traditional obligations.[18]

The Bafour. The vague term 'Bafour' has often been applied to any low-caste Mauritanian who is not Arab, Berber or negro.[19] Victims of the Arab-Berber wars, they were forced either to submit or be dispersed over a huge area. The opprobrium with which the Bafour are regarded may be due to their being pagans, but probably it is because many

Bafour belong to the despised and feared caste of blacksmiths (*mella-min*). There is a Moorish saying to the effect that the Bafour are not a tribe and have no fatherland.

The Nemadi. Probably of mixed Arab and Berber origin, the Nemadi have been studied by French scholars as an anthropological curiosity and as physical specimens of extraordinary endurance.[20] The Nemadi are not a tribe but comprise a few hundred individuals drawn and kept together by their chief occupation, that of hunting big game in the Djouf desert. Initially, the vastness of their area of nomadism, covering some 1,000 square kilometres extending from Chinguetti to Hodh, isolated them from other Mauritanians, with whom they have little in common except the *hassaniya* language and — at least superficially — the Muslim religion. Changes in their way of life came about through the restrictions placed by the French on their trek area and the development of the means of communication and the introduction of firearms, which led to the destruction or dispersal of the great antelope herds. Thus, both directly and indirectly, French rule in Mauritania forced many Nemadi to abandon hunting and to seek employment as *goumiers*, guides and nightwatchmen in the larger towns.

The Imraguen. The 5,000 or so Imraguen, of mixed Berber and negro origin, are nomadic fishermen who live for most of the year along the Atlantic coast. They are based on land, live almost exclusively by fishing and their habitat is determined by the fish migrations. During the summer months when fish desert the Mauritanian coast, the Imraguen move inland to sell part of their salted or dried catch, or work as dockers, labourers or porters in the main Mauritanian towns, Rio de Oro and the Canary Islands.

The Imraguen are loosely organised into groups of a dozen or more families headed by a chief selected by them for his technical skill. Members of each group of two or three families are either tributaries or *harratin* to a specific warrior fraction, to whom they pay tribute in dried fish at the time of the February fish fair (*guetna*).[21] Along the southern coast, the lord of the littoral is the emir of Trarza, who periodically rewards his most deserving followers by ceding to them a portion of his rights over an Imraguen *fraction*. In the north, where the Imraguen are fewer in number, even more miserable and almost totally unorganised, the proprietary rights of their warrior overlords are more confused. However, the latter are so jealous of even such poorly defined rights as to refuse all other Mauritanians the right to fish in their section of the coast.[22] Despised by the hinterland tribes for their lowly origin and occupation, and forced to pay tribute to their overlords as well as taxes to the administration, the Imraguen at the end of the colonial period seemed destined for extinction, yet they have survived.

The Islamic Republic of Mauritania

During the 1960s President Daddah encountered almost insuperable difficulties, both external and internal, in his striving to make Mauritania an independent, viable and united nation in the face of foreign aggression and internal conflicts. First Morocco's offensive and the Mali Federation's subversive activities compelled him to seek support inside and outside Mauritania. Then the referendum on the constitution of the Fourth French Republic in September 1958 required him to make a decision concerning Mauritania's future relations with France and the Franco-African Community that largely determined the nature and degree of such support.

Foreign Relations

Mauritania's foreign policy has been a major disruptive factor in its history as a sovereign state. In the years immediately preceding and following independence, both black and white Mauritanians were encouraged by their covetous neighbours — who played on the fears that each ethnic group had of being dominated by the other — to secede from Mauritania and join Mali and Morocco respectively. At this stage in the Mauritanians' evolution toward nationhood, ideology counted for little compared with ethnic and cultural affinities, and they viewed Mauritania's treaties of co-operation with France as the surest bulwark against foreign aggression. Black Mauritanians were attracted to the Mali Federation less by its socialist principles than by the prospect of being united with their fellow-tribesmen and of escaping from a government dominated by the Moors. The young Moors, for their part, formed such groups as the Association de la Jeunesse Mauritanienne (AJM) and the Nahda, both of which reacted to current developments but with divergent objectives. The AJM at its constituent congress in July 1956 urged the Entente Mauritanienne and the UPM to merge into a single party so as to move the country towards autonomy.[23] The Nahda, on the other hand, advocated close ties with Morocco, whose history and religious affinities its members, particularly those in Adrar, felt they shared. To them, the cherifian monarchy offered an appealing alternative to an administration that was then largely in the hands of France and of French-educated blacks, whom they regarded as inferiors. A common religion (Islam) and language (the *hassaniya* dialect of Arabic) were in themselves insufficient bonds at that time to hold in check the Mauritanians' centrifugal tendencies.

Daddah's foreign policy between 1957 and 1974 could be described as moderate and pragmatic, in contrast to his domestic policy which was generally more conservative and authoritarian. These dissimilar policies conformed with the views held by Daddah's main constituents, the chieftaincy and noble Moors at home, and by moderate francophone leaders of sub-Saharan Africa and of Tunisia, whose president, Habib Bourguiba, was Daddah's sole Arab champion abroad for some years. To offset the picture of Daddah as a French puppet, as portrayed by Moroccan propaganda to the Third World, and also to prove that Mauritania was an authentic Arab nation, Daddah felt impelled to withdraw more and more from the French orbit — a choice between conflicting loyalties and needs facilitated by the end of the Algerian war in 1962 and the diminishing danger of Moroccan aggression. He began cautiously by leaving the Franco-African Community in 1961 and supporting Tunisia in the Bizerte crisis in 1962. As his dependence on France's military, technical and financial support declined to the point where he could renounce French subsidies for Mauritania's operating budget in 1963, Daddah became openly critical of French nuclear tests in the Sahara, left the OCAM and sought allies among the 'progressive' Arab and African states.

Not only was Daddah extraordinarily successful in so doing, but in the process he isolated Morocco from its erstwhile Third World allies and also won over the conservative Arab leadership. Thus virtually all the oil-rich and pious Muslim leaders, ranging from Boumediene and Khadafi on the one hand to King Faisal and the Persian Gulf emirs on the other, vied with each other in financing Mauritania's development projects, as in the ideological sphere the Chinese and Eastern European bloc leaders competed with each other and, to a minor degree, with the Western powers.

Even more remarkable was Daddah's ability to enlarge the range of his followers and adapt his ideology without immediately or wholly alienating his former supporters. Daddah's first change of course, beginning in 1964 — to align Mauritania with the Arab world — produced adverse reactions among the black Mauritanians, but it was accepted with remarkable equanimity by the leadership of the Union Africaine et Malgache (UAM) and by France. In 1969 Daddah's patient nine-year courtship of Morocco was rewarded by King Hassan's formal acknowledgement of Mauritania's sovereignty, and four years later Mauritania was accepted into the Arab League. Such a prestigious confirmation of Mauritania's Arab credentials, as well as the Arab governments' lavish funding of his development projects, may have made Daddah less prudent in dealing with his black-minority population and with France, as well as more susceptible to pressures from his internal Moorish opposition.

Successive radical measures in the early 1970s — Daddah's creation of a national currency, his takeover of the Miferma company and his insistence on a revision of the co-operation agreements with France — went far to placate the student and labour critics of his foreign policy, and they also helped to reconcile opponents of the growing centralisation of his government and continued reliance on the — albeit diminished — chieftaincy and Western capital. By a combination of strong-arm methods and occasional concessions to the black Mauritanians, Daddah early quelled their active opposition, and by cultivating good relations with neighbouring countries to which they had been attracted he apparently eliminated the danger of their secession. Coincidentally, the severe drought of 1968-73 awakened the sympathy of Western nations and elicited generous aid from them, especially from France, with which relations had cooled since Daddah's nationalistic moves. Extenuating circumstances, Daddah's diplomatic skill and the diversity of his sources of support once again saved Mauritania from what might have been the disastrous consequences of Daddah's changing alliances. In brief, Mauritania might have successfully pursued its zigzag policy to attain total sovereignty had it not been for the intrusion of the Spanish Sahara problem. Daddah's momentous decision in 1974 to take over the Rio de Oro, just a decade after he had launched his first major policy change, so altered his relations with black Africa, the Maghreb and the Arab world as to place his country's future in jeopardy.

Sub-Saharan Africa. Leaders of the moderate francophone African states who formed the Brazzaville Bloc in 1960, which became successively the UAM and the Organisation Commune Africaine et Malgache (OCAM), strongly supported Mauritania's independence. Mauritania's only adversary at that time in sub-Saharan Africa was its eastern neighbour, Soudan, which in 1960 became the Mali Republic. Soudan's opposition to a sovereign status for Mauritania was motivated by its desire to recuperate the Hodh area which it had lost to Mauritania in 1944, and also to include the black Mauritanians of the Senegal River valley in the Mali Federation which Soudan was in the process of forming with Senegal.

The political ferment of the late 1950s gave birth to regional associations in southern as well as central and northern Mauritania. Among the former were the Bloc Démocratique du Gorgol, the Union Nationale Mauritanienne, and the Union des Originaires de la Vallée du Fleuve, all of which favoured joining the Mali Federation. In backing such secessionist movements, the Soudanese were more aggressive than their Senegalese partners, whose interest in Mauritania was largely concern for their fellow-tribesmen there and for the trade in livestock. The break-up of the Mali Federation in 1960 for reasons unrelated to Mauritania thwarted Soudan's imperialistic designs on Mauritania. Although Soudan, after becoming the Mali Republic, continued to oppose Mauritania's independence, this attitude was motivated mainly by its membership in the Casablanca Bloc organised by Morocco in 1961, and it melted away with that bloc's dissolution following the creation of the Organisation of African Unity (OAU) in 1963.

In the euphoria generated by the formation of the OAU, Presidents Daddah and Modibo Keita negotiated a treaty at Kayes that same year which affirmed the inviolability of the Saharan frontiers inherited from French colonisation and provided for the peaceable settlement of future border incidents along their common frontier. Incidents, some of them violent, recurred there periodically, but they were dealt with by negotiation, and the two leaders of Mauritania and Mali met occasionally to discuss common problems. The friction seemingly inseparable from close geographical proximity was offset by the big stake which they shared with President Senghor of Senegal in promoting the Organisation for Improvement of the Senegal River Valley (the OERS, later OMVS).

As to Senegal, the Moors' only apparent concern was to disassociate themselves as rapidly and thoroughly as possible from Dakar. For some years they had wanted their country's capital to be transferred from St Louis to Mauritanian soil, and their trade to be handled through a Mauritanian port instead of Dakar. The cost of such changes, however, seemed at the time prohibitive, and the choice of sites bred disagreement. Atar, as the Moors' historical and cultural centre, would have been their choice for the capital, but it was difficult of access, far from the sea and climatically untenable the year round. Nouakchott therefore was chosen because it was only four kilometres from the coast, had a comparatively good climate and an adequate if remote water supply and above all marked the dividing line between the nomadic and sedentary areas. Although this involved building a capital from the sand up, France agreed to finance construction of Mauritania's Brasilia, and work was begun in March 1958. To replace Dakar as Mauritania's foreign-trade port, Daddah persuaded China to pledge aid in building a deep-water port at Nouakchott.

On the whole, the leaders of black Africa accepted with fair grace their being downgraded in the scale of Daddah's priorities except when he sought their support in Mauritania's hours of need. Nor did they apparently resent his withdrawal from such organisations as the OCAM and the West African Monetary Union when such groups no longer served what Daddah considered to be Mauritania's national interests. On the personal level, Daddah cultivated good relations with the heads of both revolutionary and moderate black African states. As president of the OAU in 1972 he actively promoted African unity, and he always joined in the perennial chorus of denunciations of white rule in southern Africa, the Biafra secession, neocolonialism and the like. In the early 1970s Daddah established himself as spokesman for the Maghreb in persuading the black African states to cut their ties with Israel and to back the Palestinian movement as well as all other liberation groups in Africa itself. So long as Daddah's activities in the Western Sahara were directed toward freeing it from Spanish rule, his efforts were enthusiastically applauded by African leaders of all political stripes. But his popularity plummeted when he allied himself with Morocco and reneged on the UN resolution calling for a referendum in the Spanish Sahara, although he was not subjected to as much opprobrium as that heaped on King Hassan by some of black Africa's revolutionary leaders.

The Maghreb and Other Arab States. Beginning in 1960, successive military and diplomatic efforts by Rabat failed to prevent the granting of independence to Mauritania by France and its being admitted to the UN as a sovereign nation. In 1969, however, Daddah and King Hassan reached an understanding that led to economic co-operation, diplomatic co-ordination, and finally a defensive alliance in 1976. The causes of this extraordinary volte-face by Rabat were multiple and largely external to Morocco, although domestic pressure exerted by the king's Moroccan opponents played a minor part. Hassan met with his first setback in being unable to find valid allies among the Mauritanians aside from a few disgruntled individuals (notably Horma Ould Babana, Emir Ali Ould Omeir of Trarza and two ministers in Daddah's government council, Dey Ould Sidi Baba and Mohammed Mokhtar Ould Ba), a small political party (the Nahda al Watanya al Mauritanya) and a minority of the Afro-Asian group in the UN. But Hassan's goal of creating a Greater Morocco reaching south to the Senegal River and east to include Tindouf and the Touat oases encountered a major stumbling block, Algeria, after that country became independent in 1962.

Frustrated by the continued presence in the Western Sahara of French troops until 1964 and of Spanish garrisons until 1976, and by the long delay that followed the inconclusive Algero-Moroccan border war in 1963, Hassan came to realise that he must trim his Saharan sails and confine his irredentist aspirations — at least temporarily — to the Spanish zone. There the king found some ready-to-hand advantages that were lacking when he began his offensive against Mauritania in 1957. These were that the Spanish Sahara was a European colony and therefore vulnerable to Third World attack, and that it contained rich phosphate deposits, the control of which would enhance Morocco's already strong position as the world's major exporter of that commodity. To eliminate Spain from that region required the co-operation of Mauritania and, if possible, that of Algeria as well, so as to present a united front against European imperialism. But Mauritania, too, had been laying claim to some of the Spanish Sahara since 1957, and its co-operation would necessitate some *quid pro quo* in that area as well as meeting Daddah's perennial insistence that Morocco should recognise Mauritania's independence. Furthermore, Daddah did not want to jeopardise the substantial aid he was receiving from Spain to help develop Mauritania's fishing industry. Presumably, letting Mauritania take over the Rio de Oro would ensure Daddah's willingness to participate in Morocco's Saharan venture, but Hassan had no comparable inducement to offer Algeria except the satisfaction of helping to force Spain to surrender its last important foothold in Africa, and perhaps a share in developing the Bu Craa phosphate deposits.

King Hassan's strategy comprised several stages, which began with meeting Daddah, as arranged by President Boumediene at the Islamic conference held at Rabat in 1969. Soon after Hassan eliminated the post of Minister of Saharan Affairs in his cabinet, Morocco and Mauritania exchanged ambassadors, and the king, Daddah and Boumediene met in 1970 and 1973 to co-ordinate their moves to exert pressure on Spain directly as well as indirectly through the UN. In order to break the stalemate in 1975, Morocco, with Mauritania's concurrence, carried their case to the International Court at The Hague, but their cause was not advanced by that court's ambiguous conclusions a year later. Secret agreements allegedly reached in December 1974 between Morocco and Mauritania, the Madrid government's preoccupation with the succession to Generalissimo Franco and the much publicised Green March into the Sahara, contributed in varying degrees to Spain's formal withdrawal from the Sahara in February 1976, so that Mauritania and Morocco were able to divide the Spanish territory between them leaving Algeria no share in the spoils.

There has been speculation as to why and when Daddah chose to align himself with Morocco, his erstwhile enemy, rather than Algeria, whose president had rendered Mauritania invaluable services and had voiced the same principles that Daddah himself often professed in regard to self-determination of the Saharan population. Apparently Daddah believed that what his country stood to gain — Rio de Oro, a vast territory of considerable if unknown economic potential, rich resources in fish, and a share in the phosphate production of Bu Craa — outweighed the risk of losing Algeria's material and moral support. Daddah probably did not foresee that Mauritania might be mired down in costly and prolonged guerrilla warfare, his country be occupied by Moroccan troops indefinitely and the national unity he had so carefully nurtured be rent asunder by the reinforcement of internal dissensions.

Although Daddah, after he came to power, had supported Algeria in its revolt against France, he had no official contacts with the GPRA. This may well have contributed to the FLN's consistent hostility to his regime, and caused its representatives at the UN to avoid meeting the Mauritanian delegates until after Algeria became independent.[24] By 1963, however, because the two countries had a common adversary in Morocco, the tide of Algerian opinion had turned in Mauritania's favour, for after Daddah had praised Ben Bella for winning the support of his people, the latter stated soon thereafter in a press interview that 'Mauritania is a reality'.[25] Of greater significance in the Arab world was the cordial welcome given the Mauritanian delegation by Nasser at the founding congress of the OAU at Addis Ababa in May of that year. This implicit recognition of Mauritania's sovereignty by north Africa's most influential leader, followed by Bourguiba's vain efforts to reconcile King Hassan with Daddah, paved the way for other Arab governments to reconsider their support of the Moroccan thesis. In 1966 Algeria backed Mauritania's claims to the Spanish Sahara and Daddah made a state visit to Algiers. It was not, however, until after Hassan and Daddah were formally reconciled, in part thanks to Boumediene's good offices, that Algero-Mauritanian co-operation went into high gear. Algerian aid took the form of a loan of 5 billion CFA francs in 1973, facilities for Mauritanian students in Algeria and support for Daddah's

nationalisation of the Mauritanian economy. However, relations between them rapidly chilled after Mauritania and Morocco negotiated
the Madrid pact with Spain.

Throughout 1975 Daddah engaged in shuttle diplomacy to avoid a
rupture in the tripartite agreements reached at the Agadir and Nouakchott conferences of 1970 and 1973, but to no avail. Daddah asserted
that at their last stormy meeting at Béchar in September 1975, Boumediene used pressure and threats to induce Mauritania to renounce its
claims to the Spanish Sahara,[26] but when Daddah stood firm the die
was cast. By the end of 1975 their joint ventures in shipping and fishing
were halted, Mauritanian students in Algeria were sent home and the
Mauritanian soldiers in training there were transferred to military
schools in France.[27] Then Boumediene's recognition of the RASD in
February 1976 impelled Mauritania and Morocco to break off diplomatic relations with Algeria on 7 March.[28] Algeria's alleged participation
in the Polisario Front's armed raid on Nouakchott three months later
caused Daddah to denounce forcefully Algeria's 'acts of war' at the
OAU ministerial meeting on 29 June, yet this was not Daddah's last
word. As recently as 13 August 1976 he told a correspondent of *Al
Ahram* that he was ready to normalise relations with Algeria if that
country would cease training recruits for the Polisario and supplying
it with arms and funds.

Daddah's relationship with President Mouamar Khadafi of Libya
followed much the same pattern as that with Boumediene, but it never
reached the same degree of intensity. Under King Idriss, Libya did
not acknowledge Mauritania's independence, but recognition quickly
followed the military *coup d'état* at Tripoli in 1969 – the same year
that Mauritania not only reached an agreement with Morocco but also
drew closer to such varied Arab countries as Iraq, Syria, Kuwait and
Saudi Arabia. In May 1970 Daddah made his first state visit to Tripoli,
and Khadafi reciprocated in February 1972. During the tour of Mauritania's Islamic shrines at Chinguetti, Ouadane and Oualata on which
Daddah conducted Khadafi, Daddah attempted to tone down the harsh
comments made by the ebullient colonel about Spain, with which
Mauritania wanted to remain on good terms. But Daddah publicly endorsed Khadafi's stress on Arab solidarity and puritanical Muslim ethics,
and even warmly welcomed Khadafi's pledge of funds for restoring
Mauritanian mosques, promoting use of the Arabic language in Mauritanian schools and upgrading the Muslim institute at Boutilimit. In 1973
Khadafi's largesse was extended to more secular projects, such as a loan
to support the new national currency (*ouguiya*) and the building of a

road from Atar to Chinguetti and a power plant and water-distribution system for Nouakchott. When the Mauritanian-Moroccan secret pact of 1974 became public knowledge, however, Khadafi began to look with favour on the Polisario Front despite a lightning visit by Daddah to Tripoli in December 1975 to dissuade him. Khadafi's attitude was due less to his disapproval of Daddah's policy than to his long-standing hostility toward King Hassan and his more recent friendship with Boumediene.

Tunisia, like Libya, judged Mauritania's policy in the Sahara not solely on its merits or demerits but also in the context of inter-Arab relationships and of national interests and ideologies. Since 1960, Bourguiba has consistently supported Mauritania, not only because Daddah's pragmatism and moderation were akin to his own but also because of his generally uneasy relations with Algeria. Differences deriving from Tunisia's role during the Algerian revolt and then from its claims to part of their common frontier region caused Bourguiba to view Daddah and King Hassan as potential allies in holding Algerian expansionism in check. Although he was careful to maintain correct relations with his neighbour to the west, Bourguiba publicly endorsed the division of the Spanish Sahara between Mauritania and Morocco. Daddah, for his part, appreciated Tunisia's moral support but was well aware of Bourguiba's anomalous position in the Arab world and of Tunisia's inability to provide appreciable material aid. Therefore, when Bourguiba proposed that Mauritania join the short-lived Tunisian-Libyan union in 1974, Daddah remained noncommittal. It was on the Arab countries with enormous resources that Daddah trained his sights, and until 1974 he did so with spectacular success.

As the majority of Arab nations began withdrawing their support for Morocco's thesis that Mauritania was a French satellite, their leaders came to regard Daddah as 'Monsieur Bons Offices', a genuinely independent Arab leader who could bridge the gap between the Maghreb and black Africa. As such he was welcomed in September 1973 into the existing organisations for Maghreb co-operation, and two months later Mauritania became a fully fledged member of the Arab League. This was the reward for Daddah's espousal of Arab causes, especially his role in persuading black African governments to sever their ties with Israel, and for his assiduous cultivation of all the Arab leaders, conservatives and radicals alike.

Beginning in 1974, Daddah redoubled his efforts, personally visiting or dispatching missions to all and sundry black and Arab countries to explain his new Saharan policy. By then, however, his image had changed, for no longer could he claim to be the disinterested foe of Spanish imperialism and an independent Arab spokesman for the Maghreb in its dealings with black Africa. By 1975 Daddah found himself not only openly opposed by the presidents of Algeria and Libya but aligned with the conservative Arab monarchies and emirates, which had loaned Mauritania 4 billion *ouguiyas*. Furthermore, he had also sought and received support from those Western powers which only recently he had alienated by his nationalistic policies. Black African reactions, to which Daddah was more sensitive than King Hassan for historical and geographical reasons, were mixed and on the whole moderate. Some leaders, Arab as well as black, were genuinely shocked by Daddah's seizure of Rio de Oro, whereas others approved of it, if only on the grounds that it was a better solution than the creation of still another unviable, small and so-called independent country.

Because of Mauritania's military weakness in 1976-7, its foreign policy — which had won it respect and aid from a wide spectrum of nations as well as the support of its own radical nationals — had to be reversed to the point where at Daddah's request Moroccan troops were occupying strategic points in the north and French planes from Dakar were flying military missions against the Polisario guerrillas. Ironically enough, it was from the grip of those very two countries that Daddah had striven hardest to extricate his nation.

Internal Developments

Mauritania's political and labour organisations were initially affiliated with metropolitan parties and trade unions just as were those of French West Africa. No branches of the French Communist Party or Confédération des Travailleurs Chrétiens, however, could flourish in Mauritania because of that country's industrial and urban underdevelopment, inadequate means of communication, the Muslim Mauritanians' opposition to Christian schooling and the hierarchised structure of conservative Moorish society. The association of the Entente Mauritanienne and the Union Progressiste Mauritanienne with the French Socialist and Catholic parties, respectively, was both brief and tenuous, for their goals bore no relation to the ethnic conflict that caused the basic division between Mauritanians. For similar reasons, the Mauritanian branches of the metropolitan or black African labour federations did not long survive the advent of national independence.

As for the indigenous political groups that in December 1961 joined together — the PRM, the UPM and the Mauritanian Muslim Socialist Union (USMM) — to form the Parti du Peuple Mauritanien (PPM), none at that time represented more than an ethnic or Muslim affiliation, and virtually all their leaders came from the warrior or marabout families that were already prominent in the nineteenth century. The labour unions, for their part, were then composed primarily of bureaucrats and miners, and both those groups lacked homogeneity and stability. Those in the public sector were Europeans, Moors and blacks, whose earnings varied markedly with the category of their employment. Manual labourers, most of whom were employed by the Miferma company, were almost exclusively black Africans of various nationalities, whose number fluctuated with the type of work and the degree of skill required by mining operations at a given time. In both the public and private sectors of wage-earners, the Moors long remained a minority.

On 29 March 1959 Mauritania's territorial assembly accepted a constitution of the parliamentary democratic type but with a few distinctive features. These were the designation of Arabic as Mauritania's national but not official language, which remained French, and of Islam as the state religion. That constitution, however, did not long survive Mauritania's accession to independence on 28 November 1960, and it was succeeded by a presidential regime on 29 May 1961. Three months later Daddah was elected head of state as well as head of the government, and within the following seven months general secretary of the newly formed PPM, which in 1965 became the country's only legal political party.

Armed with these new powers, Daddah felt strong enough to change course politically, in domestic as well as in external affairs, when the danger of foreign aggression had clearly receded. As the focus of political activity shifted increasingly to the local scene beginning in 1964, Daddah tried to promote national unity by expanding the administration to remote areas in the north and west, and by beating back any challenges to the authority of the PPM — and by extension, to himself — from the government, the civil service, the national assembly and organised labour. Between 1957 and 1969 the cabinet was reshuffled thirteen times, the politburo (BPN) was revised three times and the legislature was twice renewed. Changes in ministerial posts as in the party's leadership largely reflected Daddah's estimate of shifts in personal or regional strength among the very limited number of individuals in whose hands the power was concentrated. And he effectively stifled any dissent from the assemblymen by deluging them with bills that occupied their debates for an entire session.[29]

The main challenges to the pre-eminence of Daddah and the PPM came from the civil service and organised labour, but trials of strength also developed at different levels — between French- and Arabic-speaking bureaucrats, between the former and the government, between the local elected bodies and party leaders, and between them and the central administration. In the later stages of these power struggles, the element of ideology further confused the picture, creating for the first time bonds above and beyond those of the ethnic and regional loyalties through radical creeds that threatened the established political and social order on which the PPM's support rested.

In the course of time, Daddah's experiment with administrative decentralisation and local elections was discreetly phased out, to the enhancement of the central government's authority, but to some extent the bureaucracy still escaped its control. The tension between black and white Mauritanian civil servants was somewhat eased by their common opposition to competition from alien Africans as well as from the growing number of local school and university graduates. By the early 1970s, however, the revolutionary doctrines preached by some of the young intellectual elite had bridged the gap between organised labour, the bureaucracy and a loose coalition of clandestine opposition groups, and together they succeeded at the PPM congress of 1975 in forcing the party to adopt policies in conformity with their views. National unity and independence remained Daddah's basic objectives, but the party through which he worked to attain them acquired a drastically altered power base and leadership. Its unity, which rested on its new leaders' interpretations of Islam, socialism and centralism, was disputed by traditionalist forces, and its ideological cohesion — albeit soon submerged by the upsurge of newborn nationalist emotions — was jeopardised by the political and economic repercussions resulting from the war for control of the former Spanish Sahara.

Civil Servants and Local Government. Within twelve years of Mauritania's becoming a sovereign state, the number of civil servants had more than doubled, to some 8,000.[30] As of 1960, only about two dozen Mauritanians had been sent abroad for training in government service. Although fifteen years later their number had grown to 529, in addition to the 181 students receiving higher education locally, neither in quantity nor in quality did the bureaucracy yet meet its country's needs. Mauritania's finances did not permit granting a pay rise to such a swollen bureaucracy until February 1974.

During this quantitative increase and qualitative decline, the country's basic ethnic problem surfaced. The seriousness of this problem was shown by the series of strikes led by black civil servants, notably the

1,200-member teachers' union, protesting against the law of 30 January 1965 which made obligatory the teaching of Arabic in all secondary schools. Among the 19 signatories of their manifesto were a magistrate, several engineers and some secondary-school teachers, who feared lest the new linguistic regulation jeopardise the virtual monopoly that black Mauritanians, thanks to their schooling in French, then enjoyed of the middle and lower echelons of the civil service. The government reacted by dismissing the civil servants and expelling the students who were involved, but in January 1968 a new strike wave, motivated by the same fears, was set off by a law requiring all civil servants to swear fealty to the PPM. It was not ended until that party's politburo, in a conciliatory mood, agreed to reinstate all the functionaries who had participated in the strikes, on condition that they take the loyalty oath.

Beginning in 1960, the number of administrative units was increased, particularly in the nomad areas, which had long been underadminis-tered, and in the north, which had been placed under a military regime. The *cercles* and subdivisions were renamed regions and departments, with comparatively few changes in their boundaries. Progressively, how-ever, the largest of them were broken up into smaller units, and by 1970 seven regions had been formed.[31] The former *commandant de cercle*, now termed governor, was given wider powers and two assist-ants, one for economic affairs and the other for party business. As of 1976, Mauritania had eleven regions, whose governors were responsible to the head of state, and which were divided into 55 departments, hea-ded by prefects under the authority of the Minister of the Interior, and there was one urban district, Nouakchott.

The foregoing reorganisations were undertaken in the name of regional decentralisation, as was the concurrent creation of local elec-ted councils for the regions and communes, both urban and rural. Fur-ther down on the local-government scale came the elected communal councils, to which limited financial and legislative powers were to be delegated. A deficit of 200 million CFA francs in the operation of the rural communes led to new regulations in 1965 that defined the condi-tions under which they could be dissolved and be replaced by special delegations. They were finally eliminated in 1970, when councils in the newly created regions took over their revenues and their responsibilities, and by 1970 even the budgets of the regional councils had to be appro-ved by the central government.[32]

Thus Daddah's goal of regionalising the administration proved in-compatible with that of centralising the political apparatus, which he deemed more essential to achieve national unity. The enhancement of the PPM's authority, however, did not end regionalism or bureaucratic dissidence, particularly in the southeastern frontier area adjoining Mali. In 1971 another experiment — this one in regard to electing local party officials — was terminated within two years because it had allegedly encouraged tribalism and regionalism, as well as party-bureaucracy rivalry.[33]

Labour and Student Dissidents. In contrast to the civil-servant disorders of the mid-1960s, the strikes in that period involving labourers were generally non-violent and concerned differences in pay and working conditions for Mauritanian and Senegalese workers in the mining industry. A serious conflict, however, occurred at Zouérate in May 1968 when, for the first time, workers of Mauritanian, Senegalese, Dahomeyan and Guinean origin presented a united front against the Miferma company.[34] To quell the ensuing disorders, the government sent in troops, which opened fire, killing eight workers and wounding 25, according to the official count. In 1969 and throughout the 1970s strikes were endemic and violence increased in frequency and scope.

The strikes against Miferma generally concerned working and housing conditions and pay, as well as the Mauritanisation of its personnel. But increasingly the government was accused by the workers and their student allies of being the tool of international capitalism in its support of a 'foreign company that is in reality a military base'.[35] The regime was also accused of 'illegally imprisoning patriots' and of failing to relieve the misery of a population suffering acutely from the drought. The growing violence and the injection of an ideological element into what had begun as labour disputes derived from two revolutionary forces — the clandestine radically oriented political groups and the Union des Travailleurs Mauritaniens — Renovée (UTMR), composed of about twelve left-wing unions that had broken away from the mainstream of the labour movement in 1969.

The UTM had been founded at Nouakchott in June 1961 by the six existing labour unions, which had been formed in the early 1950s by Senegalese and French organisers. Having been created six months before the PPM, the UTM managed to retain considerable autonomy, and in 1964 it won a notable victory when it pressured the government into nationalising road transport in Mauritania.[36] At the party congress held at Kaédi that same year, the PPM acquiesced in the UTM's refusal to become integrated into the party, but it insisted on close collaboration by the UTM in return for recognising the latter as the only organisation representing Mauritanian workers. The PPM, however, did not agree to the UTM's demands for wage increases commensurate with the rising cost of living, effective price controls and the creation of an import-export company under state control.[37]

As of 1964, one-third of the 9,300 or so workers in the modern sector of the economy were foreigners. Some 60 per cent of all Mauritania's wage-earners and 98 per cent of those in private employment were concentrated in the north and along the Atlantic coast — that is, the most productive sector was heavily concentrated in the least populous area. Furthermore, nomadic habits, difficult working conditions and the lack of motivation for sustained effort all militated against forming and retaining a stable indigenous labour force, once a worker's pressing needs for money had been met. In 1966 the labour turnover in the private sector averaged 40 per cent, ranging from 30 per cent at Zouérate to nearly 100 per cent in the building industry.

As drought conditions worsened in the Mauritanian sahel, employers had an ever-larger reservoir of manpower on which to draw, but this advantage was offset by the nomads' distaste for regular manual labour — especially when it involved working for a foreign company — and above all by their lack of skills.[38] At Nouakchott, the Collège d'Enseignement Technique was opened in 1966, and vocational courses were introduced into the curriculum of Mauritania's four *lycées*, as well as specialised schools for training teachers, nurses, midwives and agricultural monitors. By 1974, students attending technical and vocational schools totalled 1,591, far below the population's potential and the economic demand, but their orientation was directly related to the current needs of the labour market.

The scarcity and lack of skills of local labour, as well as its instability, accounted for the large number, status and salaries of the foreigners employed in Mauritania. The alien Africans, who were sometimes used as strikebreakers by Miferma, were paid slightly higher wages than were the Mauritanians, but the wage scale for both was appreciably higher than the official minimum wage, even after the minimum was raised by 15 per cent both in 1961 and in 1969. The Europeans, who held most of the managerial and technical positions, received half the total wage payments and repatriated a large percentage of their earnings. Mauritanian wage-earners, who filled two-thirds of the jobs in the modern private sector, received only one-third of the total wages paid out. Nevertheless, they averaged an income that was five times that of workers in the traditional economy, who accounted for 85 to 90 per cent of the active population.[39] Together with the Mauritanian civil servants and traders they were on their way to becoming an embryonic middle class. Since 1969 their number has remained fairly stable, and by 1975 they totalled some 17,000 but constituted only 3.5 per cent of the country's active population, then estimated at about 500,000.

It was not until the spring of 1973 that the UTM, following a revision and census of its membership, accepted integration into the PPM, which thereby acquired control over 73.4 per cent of Mauritania's nearly 15,000 unionised workers.[40] Nevertheless, the most contentious members of the UTMR − the teachers' and students' unions − were not placated by the contracts negotiated with foreign employers in Mauritania at the end of 1973 by the government on behalf of Mauritanian wage-earners, which met many of the unions' demands for improved pay and working and living conditions, and for the Mauritanisation of those companies' personnel.

The Government, the Party and the Opposition. Like other African single parties, the PPM was given a pyramidal structure of committees topped by a national politburo, whose members directly or indirectly named cabinet ministers, appointed high-ranking administrators and selected candidates for election to the legislature. The thirteen-member politburo was chosen by the national council, which in turn was elected by the party congress, in accordance with the president's wishes. According to Francis de Chassey,[41] a former sociology professor at the Nouakchott *lycée*, the leadership group was so small between 1957 and 1968 that the 175 top posts were filled by only 112 persons, 38 of whom occupied all but 74 of them. At first this concentration of power in the hands of so few people could be attributed to the shortage of qualified personnel, but in time it became clear that unswerving loyalty to the president and his party was the prerequisite for eligibility to high office. Ministerial appointees had to be party members, but this was not required of candidates for the civil service. Some of the friction between party officials and bureaucrats, especially in the rural areas, could be traced to the difference in their qualifications and training, as well as to the obvious power struggle. The hundred-odd students each year at the Ecole Nationale d'Administration (ENA) in Nouakchott received a professional education very different from the ideological indoctrination given to party cadres at the Institut National d'Education et d'Etudes Politiques (INEEP). At no time could the PPM claim to be a mass party: until it was reorganised in January 1968 throughout the country, its membership was haphazard and its structure deficient.[42]

Of the four national congresses held by the PPM prior to the war in the Sahara, two were turning-points in the country's history: the second congress at Kaédi in 1964, which reoriented Mauritania's domestic and foreign policies,[43] and the fourth at Nouakchott in 1975, which marked the final stage in radicalising the government and the party. At the third congress, held in 1966 at Aioun-el-Atrouss, the existing party hierarchy was confirmed, and the economic zones of Mauritania were made identical with its administrative regions. That congress also reinforced the centralisation of the administration and the authority of the PPM, and it sought to 'repersonalise' Mauritania by raising the official status of Arabic.

The fourth congress revised the structure of the state and the party, as well as their relationship, accepted a party charter that spelled out the country's overall orientation, adopted the third economic-development plan (1975-9) and chose candidates for the next presidential and legislative elections. To end the rivalry between party and state, PPM regional leaders were no longer to be locally elected but were to be appointed by the central authorities, and all party memberships were to be 'renewed'. Control over the government was to be assured by a more tightly knit politburo, while at the same time the national council — enlarged to include more elected members — was to exercise supervision over the politburo itself. To curtail the 'excessive autonomy' of cabinet members, the fourth PPM congress reorganised the government by creating seven super-ministries (whose incumbents were all politburo members), and gave them supervision over 21 junior ministers (of whom eleven were newcomers to the political arena). And finally, to liberalise elections to the legislature, voters were allowed to choose two-thirds of the deputies from their own areas, but to obviate regionalism and tribalism each region was required to vote for all 70 deputies.

The Nouakchott congress's crowning achievement was the PPM charter, slated to become the country's fundamental law and the basis for revising the 1961 constitution. Mauritanian socialism, as defined by the charter, called for state control over the key sectors of national life, setting up joint ventures, especially in mineral prospecting and processing, keeping a niche for private enterprise that would be content with moderate profits, and, most significantly, eliminating all feudal rights to the unremunerated services of fellow-Mauritanians. This charter, which seemed to herald a fundamental restructuring of Moorish society, expressed the goals of the government's erstwhile left-wing opponents, whose spokesmen in the government were the five young university-trained technocrats who became ministers on 18 August 1971. Thus the principles of the PPM charter were not innovative, but the unanimity they evoked at Nouakchott was new.

How well Daddah had succeeded in inculcating Mauritanians with the twin sentiments of nationalism and Arabism was shown during President Pompidou's state visit in 1971, when he was greeted by slogans denouncing him as a 'Zionist banker who owns 19 per cent of the Miferma trust'.[44] This demonstration, however, as well as the 1968 strikes at Zouérate, also revealed the new element of Marxist ideology, which was hostile not only to France's economic investments in Mauritania but also to Daddah's government because it had permitted international capital to play the dominant role in the country's economy. Hostility to the regime was intensified by the government's increasingly harsh treatment of its radical adversaries in 1973-4, when between 200 and 300 labour leaders and students were arrested for subversive activities.

Radical ideology supplied the framework for the new supratribal and supranational groupings that brought together a motley array of individual malcontents. Some of them believed that their personal position would be improved under any government other than that led by Daddah, whether foreign or indigenous, but the newer stratum was composed mainly of youthful urban intellectuals who for ideological reasons objected to Daddah's toleration of – if not support for – the traditional institutions, notably the chieftaincy, and wanted a drastic revision of Mauritania's social and political structure. Numerically and organisationally weak, but highly articulate, some of the Leninist-Marxist, Maoist, Nasserite and other Mauritanians came together in 1973 to form a loose federation called the Mouvement Démocratique National (MDN), whose extreme left wing was the proletarian Parti des Kadihines (PKM). In its organ, *The Cry of the Oppressed*, the PKM advocated Leninist-Marxist doctrines, the formation of a youth front and the overthrow of Daddah's 'feudal-imperialist' regime. At the other end of the spectrum, right-wing dissidents formed the Justice Party. It proposed a federation of Mauritania, Senegal and Morocco, whose co-operation would help Mauritanians to develop their economy and solve the Sahara question. Significantly, however, both groups denounced the government for its denial of democratic freedoms and, while castigating those 'tyrannical' religious leaders who allegedly had been the allies of colonialism, urged respect for the traditional values of Islam.

By 1973 the government was finally forced to admit the existence of clandestine opposition groups because their increasing violence made maintaining silence no longer tenable, harsh repressive measures had become counter-productive, and the officially created national-reconciliation commission had proved ineffective. Convinced by some PPM leaders, including Madame Daddah, that dialogue would prove more constructive than force, and operating under the old principle that he must join opponents he could not defeat, Daddah took successive steps to persuade them of his sincerity in promoting Mauritania's independence culturally, economically and politically. After setting up a Ministry of Youth, Daddah finally adopted the radicals' basic programme, although he still tried to maintain a balance between them and the forces represented by the traditionalists and the country's regional interests. The stress placed by the charter on a nationalistic version of orthodox Islam was a concession to the traditionalists, whose opposition concerned social and economic rather than political questions.[45]

The social changes that have gradually taken place in Mauritania since independence have been due largely to forces already at work during the late colonial period, although some were the result of governmental action and of the great drought of 1968-73. The rise of new social classes, first discernible during the Second World War, was accelerated by the expansion of education and capital investments, the increased size of the bureaucracy and the wage-earning component, and the overall growth in the population, especially in the urban centres, to which all categories of drought victims flocked. To eliminate tribalism and regionalism, the government encouraged the development of nationwide organisations, such as the UTM, the women's association and above all the PPM. The influx into Mauritania of alien Africans was due partly to the new economic opportunities opened up there and partly to the government's need for their services, but it had the unexpected effect of uniting black and white native Mauritanians against them.

The evolution of the chieftaincy in independent Mauritania has differed markedly from that in sub-Saharan francophone Africa. Yet in both areas the chiefs have been tribal and religious leaders rather than autocrats or wealthy landowners, their posts are not necessarily hereditary, and they receive salaries from the state. Even before independence, however, black African chiefs were first controlled by the colonial regime and then forced into an adversary position by the rising politicians,[46] whereas in Mauritania there has been no major confrontation between the chiefs and the youthful elite, largely because Mauritania's geographical isolation and the physical separation of its two major ethnic components long immunised it against radical influ-

ences emanating from the south. Indifferent to the representative institutions created in the late 1940s, the chiefs finally formed a political
party which they easily dominated and which served to maintain the
status quo.

After the Mauritanian territorial assembly in 1958 made three
inconclusive efforts to define − that is, limit − the chiefs' powers, the
government, following the French example, decided simply to utilise
the existing structure, given the shortage of qualified government personnel and the influence that the chief still retained, especially in rural
areas. Furthermore, in nomad society the *djemaa* played a role in
limiting a chief's authority that had no counterpart south of the
Sahara, and it was with members of the *djemaa* that the government of
independent Mauritania preferred to deal. In 1963, therefore, it was
decided that when a chief died, his post would either be left vacant or
be filled by an amenable candidate.[47] Although the emirs varied as
regards wealth, tribal strength and personality, they continued to
receive preferential treatment. They retained their ceremonial functions, all four were elected to the national assembly and two of them
also to the PPM politburo. Only the venerable emir of Tagant remained
a feudal lord in respect to his honorific titles, perquisites and retainers,
but he took his orders from the PPM-appointed governor. The emir of
Trarza might have played an influential role locally had he not chosen
to cast in his lot with Morocco, as a result of which he was succeeded
by his more docile brother-in-law. Indeed, his defection and subsequent
eclipse may have served to keep the remaining important Moorish chiefs
in line.

As to the evolution of the noble Moors as a whole, the warriors continued to predominate in the army and gendarmerie, and the marabouts
worked even more zealously than before to safeguard the values of the
traditional social order, which they realised were being eroded.[48] Yet
both warriors and marabouts had become increasingly aware of the
advantages to be derived from a Western education, even though it was
clearly the most potent levelling influence in Mauritanian society. The
rate of school attendance, albeit still only 16 per cent of the school-age
population in 1975, was more than twice that of the last pre-independ-
ence days. Of the 175 Mauritanians who occupied key posts in the
power apparatus in 1973, all but 13 had attended school or been at one
time government agents; 156 of them currently were chiefs, sons of
chiefs or Notables; and 162 were members of the noble Moorish tribes
or of black chiefly families.[49] These data suggest that because opposition to the government came largely from urban-based students and

labour leaders, the regime was cultivating its old ties with the rural aristocracy.

After both the PPM and the Justice Party had dissolved themselves at the fourth PPM congress, Daddah felt justified in claiming at its closing session that such a degree of political unity had been achieved that 'if there still are opponents [to the regime] they can be counted on the fingers of one hand'.[50] In the by-elections of 8 August 1976 nearly 85 per cent of the registered electorate, which numbered 861,416 persons, voted for PPM candidates to the legislature. Moreover, Daddah, as the master of compromise and arbiter between the old and new forces in Mauritania, received almost unanimous endorsement when he sought his fourth mandate as president of the republic. Yet the precarious unity that he had only recently achieved was both challenged and reinforced by the disruption caused by the war that broke out late in 1975 for control of the former Spanish Sahara. Once again, forces external to Mauritania reopened old wounds, reversed the established foreign policy and served to disrupt further an already divided people.

The Armed Forces

In the Mauritanian Sahara, periods of intense military activity have occurred more frequently than in the equivalent areas of Mali or Niger. Some observers attribute such frequent recurrences to the greater prowess of the Reguibat as warriors and as armed raiders compared with other Saharan nomads, but the key to the endemic strife in the Western Sahara has been the Reguibat's proximity to foreign sanctuaries and sources of supply, first in Rio de Oro and then, after Spain withdrew from Africa in 1976, in the Tindouf area of southwestern Algeria.

During the inter-war years, the line of Mauritania's northern defences ran from Port Etienne through Akjoujt, Atar and Chinguetti to Fort Gouraud, all of which were military posts manned jointly by black *tirailleurs* and Moorish *méharistes*. Many Mauritanian warriors were induced to join the camel corps by the regularity of pay, freedom of action and confirmation of their noble status that was conferred automatically on those possessing firearms. They lived apart from the regular colonial army, whose black *tirailleurs* they regarded as mercenaries. France never gave them military training until they served under the same conditions as French soldiers during the campaign against the Moroccan Army of Liberation of the Sahara (ALS) in 1957-8.[51]

Although at the time of Mauritania's independence its armed forces were organised on the French model, that country was unique among the francophone African states in having no officers who had been commissioned in the French army, and no armed forces in the professional sense of the term. The ALS's invasion of northern Mauritania in 1957-8 had been repulsed by France's army, and its units stationed in Mauritania continued to assume responsibility for defending the country so long as Morocco threatened to take it over by force.

By January 1966 the last French troops had left Mauritania, with the exception of an air squadron based at Atar and some French instructors who were training Mauritania's armed forces. In the early 1970s, however, rising nationalist pressure forced a renegotiation of Mauritania's agreements with France that eliminated military cooperation. All French military personnel — by then totaling only 58 officers and NCOs — who had been technical advisers to the Mauritanian army and had worn Mauritanian uniforms — simply left the country on 1 April 1973.

In December 1961 the congress that gave birth to the PPM opted for a people's army, but Mohamed Ould Cheikh, Minister of Defence until 1966, persuaded the new politburo that military personnel should remain aloof from politics.[52] On 27 March 1962, therefore, members of the army and security forces, except for police officers, were forbidden to join the PPM. Three months later military service was made obligatory for all Mauritanian youths 18 years of age and older, but enforcement of that measure was lax because the government preferred to spend its limited funds on economic development, and was, moreover, reluctant to train and equip an army that perforce would comprise more blacks than Moors as conscripts.

The question of politicising the armed forces was reopened by the army's reaction to the ethnic violence that erupted at Nouakchott in February 1966 over the issue of making Arabic along with French the language of instruction in Mauritania's secondary schools. At the PPM's third congress in January 1968, Daddah's project to model Mauritania's armed forces after Guinea's people's army was accepted, and a programme was drawn up to lighten the army's military tasks so that soldiers and officers alike could receive ideological indoctrination and participate actively in the manual work required to increase Mauritania's economic production. In the summer of 1969 a mission was charged with preparing the armed forces psychologically for their eventual integration into the party.

This neglect of military training and the transformation of soldiers into party militants and manual workers, along with the PPM leaders' conviction that Rio de Oro would fall into Mauritania's lap without the army's needing to fire a shot, explains the country's almost total unpreparedness for the war that broke out in the Western Sahara in 1975.

The Mauritanian Economy

The Peoples

As elsewhere in the Western Sahara, the flow of migration has been from north to south and, less extensively and for shorter periods, from west to east. In the dry season, the nomads have trekked south to the better-watered sahel and soudanese zones. There they have had conflicts with the black farmers whose fields their animals often damage and have also risked contracting tropical diseases affecting man and beast, but they could sell or rent their animals out for transport service there at higher prices than they fetch farther north. Two different currents have formed the west-east migrations: one by herders seeking temporary pastures and the other by servitors escaping from their overlords to the 'free villages' of Soudan (and also to Senegal). Equally long-established and transient has been a contrary northwestward migration. From the time of the Almoravids to that of the Polisario Front, the prospect of pillage and, to a lesser extent, that of conquest has lured the Moors northward and westward, just as the hope of economic gain has impelled the southern blacks and a few Moors to seek jobs in the mining and fishing industries of those areas.

Independence, with its stress on political and economic sovereignty, has encouraged the northwestward movement while discouraging that to Senegal and Mali. Nouakchott as the new capital rose out of the sand as an administrative centre, and Nouakchott and F'Derik-Zouérate grew with the country's industrial development. Even before independence, garrisons in the Spanish Sahara, at Tindouf and in northern Mauritania were reinforced, and they grew markedly with the current military operations in those frontier areas. Offsetting this northward movement have been the migrations resulting from the drought of 1968-73, which drove the nomads and their decimated herds to the southern and western settlements, where food and medical care were more available. How permanent this trend will be depends on natural phenomena, the outcome of the war in the Western Sahara, and the degree to which the nomads accept the government's policy aimed at stabilising them.

Before independence, only 5 per cent of the population was urban, including the oasis-dwellers, but by 1976 this element accounted for 24 per cent of the total population. As of 1974, the number of northern refugee families that had moved to the towns was estimated at 10,000, but the return of normal rains that year caused 3,000 or so families to return home.[53] Nevertheless, the official census carried out during the winter of 1976-7 showed a net increase in the number of town-dwellers. Between 1962 and 1976 the population of Nouakchott had grown from 77,000 to 134,986, that of Nouadhibou from 6,500 to 23,000, of Zouérate from 5,000 to 17,471 and of Atar from 9,500 to 15,326. The annual population growth rate of Mauritanians is about 2.1 per cent, but it varies from one region to another, ranging from 0.01 per cent in Tiris-Zemmour to 7 per cent in Guidimaka.

According to the 1964 survey made by two specialised French agencies,[54] black Mauritanians were increasing more rapidly than the Moors, who are generally monogamous and marry later than do the blacks. The reported growth in the sedentary component also indicated that even before the recent drought there had been an increase in semi-nomadism, for what had formerly been wholly nomadic tribes were now spending more time in the oases to gather dates and harvest crops, and were restricting the seasonal movements of their herds. Furthermore, in the far north and in Hodh, the great camel-breeding tribes — for whom statistics are the least reliable — were numerically even fewer than had been supposed, and their number was further reduced by the drought of 1968-73. Journalists visiting Mauritania since 1974 have reported that many of the newcomers to the shanty towns of the south and west prefer remaining there on government bounty to resuming their precarious pastoral life. Two of the fastest growing towns have been Nouadhibou and Zouérate, whose numerical fluctuations were caused by variations in the number of transient labourers, and another has been Atar, whose sedentary population tends to be more stable, albeit increasing.

As is true in other south Saharan states, Mauritania is most densely populated in its permanent river valley, its black element is increasing faster than its Arab and Berber inhabitants, and the latter are becoming more stabilised as a result of the expansion in their human and animal population, recent and generally adverse climatic conditions and government pressure. Mauritania has been distinguished from its eastern neighbours — sometimes more in degree than in kind — by its recurrent northward pushes, the predominance of nomadism, the compartmental-isation of its two major ethnic communities (in which the white ele-ment still predominates in every respect), the sudden upsurge of urban-isation in a country where the pace of such a phenomenon has always heretofore been slow and the instability of its towns, both ancient and modern.

In Mali, Niger and Tchad, as well as in southern Morocco, formerly flourishing markets and relay points for caravans have virtually disappeared under the sand, following shifts in trade routes and the advent of new means of communication. In Mauritania those settlements that were, and to a slight degree still are, religious and cultural centres, such as Chinguetti, have survived a little better than, for example, Oualata and Timédra. Atar is almost the only northern town that has consistently increased in importance and in population, thanks to its strategic position, religious prestige, thermal springs, rock paintings and, above all, its large and productive palm grove, for which a packaging plant was opened there in 1967.

The first reports on the official census carried out during the winter of 1976-7 gave a total population for Mauritania of 1,481,000, of whom 942,000 were sedentaries and 539,000 were nomads. Although there is no doubt but that the proportion of nomads to the total population has permanently declined, Mauritania's demographic situation has been in such a state of flux since the drought of 1968-73 and the warfare in northern Mauritania as to render all forecasts invalid. It is clear, however, that the growing disaffection of the Moors for a pastoral life has led to such a large-scale and rapid sedentarisation as to create problems of medical care, unemployment and housing that are beyond the government's expectation and its capacity to cope. Politically more significant is the growth of the black component in numbers and discontent, and should the Polisario Front achieve a merger with Mauritania and thus swell the Arabo-Berber element, the Senegal River tribes might either revolt against reinforced white domination or simply secede and join their fellow tribesmen to the south and east. Thus the two salient characteristics of the current evolution of Mauritania's population are its rapid stabilisation and urbanisation and its imminent reversal of the dominant ethnic balance of power.

Planning

Taking stock of the situation in 1967, Daddah apparently had every reason to be pleased with the effectiveness of his first four-year plan (1963-7). Mauritania's budget was balanced, its public debt had been negotiated on a long-term basis, its trade balance was favourable, and investments amounting to some 30 billion CFA francs had exceeded expectations.[55] By the late 1960s economic growth, which was running at the annual rate of some 10 per cent, had become synonymous with the fortunes of the Miferma and Imapec companies, and their output was increasing. Moreover, Mauritania had succeeded in obtaining foreign aid from China and Spain as well as from the EEC countries, which still provided the major share. Yet the plan was abandoned at the end of 1966, and a few months later Mauritania asked the World Bank to send a mission that would propose new guidelines for drafting its next development plan.[56] Subsequently, most of the mission's recommendations were adopted by the PPM at its third congress in January 1968. They concerned primarily the means for reviving the now stagnant rural economy, by reducing Mauritania's dependence on foreign funds and personnel, and for participation by the state in all the companies operating in Mauritania.

The most urgent task facing those drafting Mauritania's second four-year plan (1971-5) was to redress the growing imbalance between the modern and the traditional sectors of the economy. By 1969 the former accounted for 40 per cent of the GNP compared with 6 per cent a decade earlier, but it directly affected only about 5 per cent of the local population.[57] Miferma and Imapec, the outstanding producers in the modern sector, were foreign enclaves as regards their capital, technology and upper-echelon personnel, and their fortunes fluctuated with world market prices. In general, their importance to Mauritania was confined to the royalties they paid the government and the wages they paid to their Mauritanian workmen, to some of whom they also gave limited training. Situated in northwestern Mauritania, whose few and scattered nomad inhabitants considered fishing and mining demeaning occupations, the foreign companies had very little contact with the local population and did not even provide a market for the latter's output of meat and vegetables. Propinquity did not break down the barriers between members of the two sectors that were inherent in the Moors' social structure and value system.

In allocating investments designed to strengthen the national economy and assure a more equitable distribution of income, Mauritania's planners have misjudged the viability of such costly ventures as the fish-processing plant at Nouadhibou, the national airline and the refrigerated abattoir. Even under the most propitious circumstances, Mauritania's vast size, small and scattered population and limited resources made it unlikely that such industries would generate profits. Nevertheless, national pride and generous foreign sponsors involved Mauritania increasingly in ventures of dubious economic validity albeit of social utility, such as an oil and a sugar refinery, experimental rice-farming, road building, a desalination plant and the like. Beginning in 1972, the nationalistic motivation in the government's economic policy was given free rein when Daddah moved swiftly to Mauritanise the private sector, creating state companies or joint ventures to which monopolies were granted in the key areas of mining (to SNIM), the importation of prime necessities (to Sonimex), the export of meat (to Covima) and land-freight and sea transport (to Comaunam). Daddah's determination to establish state control over the entire economy gathered momentum with Mauritania's withdrawal from the franc zone and its creation of a national currency, the *ouguiya* (UM, worth 0.10 French franc), in June 1973, the nationalisation of Miferma in November 1974 and the absorption of Somima in April 1975.

These successive radical steps plunged Mauritania into multiple and complex operations designed to safeguard the *ouguiya* (notably by severely restricting the movement of capital out of the country), to negotiate compensation to the shareholders of the nationalised companies and to cope with the ensuing disruption of the established trade circuits and the rapid rise in the cost of living. The primary goals of Mauritania's third plan (1976-80) are to promote industrialisation, mineral prospecting and employment, and also to stimulate food production, notably that of fish and rice — all worthy activities but of little direct interest to Mauritania's Saharan peoples. To be sure, some of the plan's projected 32 billion UM of investments have been allocated in the north to the reconstitution of herds and to hydraulic improvements, and also for providing more health and educational facilities in the northern settlements. However, no mention has been made of any grants to the Kankossa date-palm station, which is of vital importance to the oasis-dwellers of Adrar and Tagant.

The sahel drought accentuated the dual character of Mauritania's economy, accelerated the decline in its pastoral life and widened the gap between the mining operations and the rural population, whose survival was assured largely by international aid. And the disruption occasioned by the war for control of Tiris El Gharbia, intensified by the subsequent political upheaval and its aftermath, has not only delayed execution of Mauritania's third development plan but has jeopardised the country's very existence as a sovereign state.

Transportation and Trade

Mauritania's inhospitable coast, difficult terrain, vast distances and sparse population account for the country's lack of ports and paved roads, as well as for the important role — potential rather than actual — of aviation in Mauritania's transportation and trade.

Except for the salt-caravan route from Idjil, the old caravan trails have fallen into disuse. The first tracks (*pistes*) built by France to provision its military posts reflected the general view held in Paris at that time that Mauritania's main function was to serve as a land link between Morocco and Senegal. As the needs of Mauritania grew with its population, and as the process of supplying the military posts along Transsaharan Track no.1[58] was depleting Mauritania's camel herds and causing resentment in their owners, whose services were also requisitioned, new routes were developed during the 1920s that permitted swifter and surer transport of merchandise by truck. Much of the importance of the old military posts and their supply routes was eliminated by pacification of the Western Sahara in 1934 and the shift in trade and trade routes after the Second World War.

Over the years, exports from north and central Mauritania have changed more than have those regions' imports, largely through the addition of mineral ores to the traditional shipments of animals and animal products, salt and gums, whereas imports — still geared to the nomads' austere needs — have continued to consist predominantly of supplementary foodstuffs and textiles. With the increase of the local population, more of the north's production of dates and fish has been locally consumed, but the concurrent growth in animal herds has outpaced local consumption and enlarged their sales abroad, notably in Goulimine (Morocco) and Louga (Senegal). The Moors' ability and experience as stock-breeders have made them successively masters of the caravan trade, of truck transportation and of the animal retail markets even in towns beyond their own borders.

In recent years political developments, along with economic ones, have altered the trading pattern in northern Mauritania. One qualified observer[59] pointed out that the Second World War upset the economic balance in that area by reorienting Mauritania's economy away from the Sahara and towards Senegal as its major market and provisioner. Even during the inter-war period, trade routes had been moving closer to the coast, thereby spelling the decline of Atar, which had been the successor to Oualata as the Western Sahara's major marketplace, and marking the rise of Port Etienne, despite the latter's lack of a supporting hinterland and of a nearby supply of fresh water. Then in 1957-8, during the Army of Liberation's offensive, the closing of Mauritania's frontier with Morocco cut Atar off from its main animal market in Goulimine. At the same time, Atar's trading ties with Tindouf were also severed because of intensification of the revolt in Algeria. The foregoing developments accelerated the southward drift of the Adrar tribes, which had long been attracted to the Senegal River valley as a source of cheap millet and as an animal market. Inevitably, Adrar's date-palm oases were progressively abandoned, especially as their water table was falling and the possibility of wage-earning in the mines of Fort Gouraud and Akjoujt was further weaning the oasis-dwellers away from agriculture. Iron and copper ores added enormously to the volume but did not change the character of northern and central Mauritania's exports. Like the area's traditional exports of gum arabic and salt to a lesser degree, they were not simply the surplus output of locally consumed products but commodities extracted almost exclusively for sale abroad.

Following the independence of Morocco in 1956 and that of Senegal and Soudan in 1960, customs posts were erected along the new national frontiers. These impediments to the Western Sahara's traditional trade naturally gave an impetus to smuggling between Mauritania and its neighbours, including Rio de Oro. They further enhanced the attractions of Port Etienne, which some time earlier had been made a free-trade zone so as to offset similar facilities existing in Spanish territory. Completion in 1963 by Miferma of the 675-kilometre railway from Fort Gouraud to the coast, and the enlargement of Port Etienne to include a fishing port as well as ore-loading and commercial port facilities, confirmed Port Etienne's primacy as Mauritania's economic capital.

Building the railway and mineral port were obviously Miferma's enterprises, but by the time they were completed the government was already working on a transport system that would serve wider national interests. In 1962 it had created Air Mauritanie to provide regular service between Nouakchott and Néma and irregular flights to the Canary Islands. By 1971, when it was responsible for operating 22 airfields and five planes, Air Mauritanie served not only the river *escales* and the main towns of central Mauritania, but also the northern settlements of Atar, Akjoujt, Zouérate and Bir Moghrein (Fort Trinquet).

Of wider significance than Air Mauritanie's limited and expensive service is the wharf completed at Nouakchott in 1966 to handle some of Mauritania's foreign trade that had formerly passed through the port of Dakar, and also to give central and southern Mauritania direct access to the sea. By 1971 the wharf had increased its capacity to 150,000 tons and Nouakchott had become the shipping port for copper-ore exports from Akjoujt. For more than a decade studies have been made and funds sought to build a deep-water port at Nouakchott, but its viability is believed to depend on its handling some of Mali's foreign trade, and this in turn is related to execution of the Senegal River development (OMVS) programme. As a vital part of its plan to link Mauritania's natural regions by national highways, the government in 1965 obtained a loan from AID to start building a highway that ultimately will connect the capital with Néma, the most westerly *ksar* of Hodh, and be linked by branch roads to the centre and to the north. Indeed, road-building has occupied an important place in all of Mauritania's plans because the government considers roads a main means of bringing isolated regions together, developing national consciousness and helping free Mauritania from its chronic dependence on Senegal's transport network.

Mauritania's present road system is still primitive and inadequate, for it consists of only two paved highways, one from Nouakchott to Akjoujt and the other from the capital to Rosso. Like most of the country's development projects, road-building cannot be justified in purely economic terms and must to some degree be considered from a political angle. The Nouakchott-Néma highway will not only provide means of communication to isolated and comparatively populous Hodh but also help to integrate an area which has long been highly vulnerable to centrifugal influences from Mali. Political considerations have also determined the choice of Nouakchott and Nouadhibou as the transport hubs for the country: the capital's only real link with its back country is to the copper mine at Akjoujt, and Nouadhibou is situated 500 kilometres from the oasis of Atar and 650 kilometres from F'Derik-Zouérate.

Similarly — but in this case to Mauritania's economic advantage — political and not economic considerations have impelled the Arab countries to finance Mauritania's transportation projects. To some extent, however, those foreign donors that have been most lavish in aiding Mauritania have encouraged expenditures gratifying to Mauritanian national pride but economically burdensome, or at best dubious. A case in point is the prop-jet plane given by the USSR, which was so costly to operate that Air Mauritanie found it more economical to ground the plane than to fly it.[60] Above all it was Algeria, beginning in the early 1970s, that provided funds and technical aid to launch a host of activities, such as an ocean-shipping service, but most notably the creation of a national currency. Boumediene even invited Daddah to attend the meeting of Saharan borderland states at El Goléa in April 1975 to discuss the itinerary for a trans-Saharan road, although there was no question of its passing through or even near Mauritania. Two years later, it was again for political reasons that the conservative Arab countries relayed Algeria in helping Mauritania to solve its transport problems, after Boumediene abruptly cut off all aid to Mauritania.[61] The initial motivation behind that Arab aid was to keep Mauritania in a war that would hinder the spread of Algeria's revolutionary influence. Then, after Nouakchott made its peace with the Polisario Front, and by extension with Algeria, the conservative Arab states for the same reason bolstered Mauritania's economy so as to preserve that country's existence as a buffer state.

Mining

Rock salt is easily extracted from the *sebkhas* that are found throughout Mauritania's coastal plain, of which the most productive are those of Idjil and of N'Tenert in Trarza (sometimes called the *salines de Dahar*). Mauritanian salt is reputed for its quality, reserves appear to be almost inexhaustible, and it is still distributed mainly by caravan to markets in the south. To promote rock-salt mining and also to encourage fishing on an industrial scale, the government in 1971 considered forming companies to increase the output of Idjil and N'Tenert, and also to develop that of the marshlands around Nouadhibou.[62] This was to be done in anticipation of an expanding market, especially that for Nouadhibou's growing fishing industry. Thus salt, like copper and iron, is slated eventually to be mined primarily to supply local industries rather than for export as a raw material.

Geological studies during the late 1940s led to the formation of the Mines de Fer de Mauritanie (Miferma) in 1952 and the Syndicat d'Inchiri in 1953. Their capital came from international sources and their main problems at the time concerned adequate water supplies and transportation. After those problems were solved, however, the evolution of iron and copper mining in Mauritania diverged, only to be subjected eventually to an identical fate — that of nationalisation.

From the outset French capital was dominant in the Miferma consortium, whereas Anglo-American funds and technology came to predominate in the copper company (named successively Micuma, Socuma and Somima). Miferma began exporting iron within a decade of its formation, and it grew steadily stronger to become by far the greatest force in Mauritania's economy. On the other hand, the successive companies formed to mine Akjoujt's copper encountered such financial and technical problems as to necessitate multiple reorganisations and to delay production until 1970. Periodically, Miferma was plagued by strikes, some of which had racist overtones and were directed against the highly paid French personnel which held all the top and middle-echelon posts in the company. Miferma's role was that of a state within a state, and its aloofness from the mainstream of Mauritanian life, as well as its overwhelming ascendancy in Mauritania's economy, aroused the resentment of the country's youthful radicals, who considered Miferma symbolic of renascent French imperialism. Except for the

3-per-cent share of its capital acquired by the government in 1963, all of Miferma's capital was foreign, as were its management and shareholders, who, furthermore, were entitled to buy its output at reduced rates. Only in a juridical sense could Miferma have been considered to be a Mauritanian company.

The government's attitude toward Miferma combined respect for its achievements and apprehension about its power with some disappointment that it had not done more to modernise Mauritania's economy and finance its development plans. By the time Miferma was nationalised, its business turnover (*chiffre d'affaires*) was appreciably larger than Mauritania's operating budget, its investments totalled some 3 billion CFA francs, and it paid taxes and royalties that in 1975 provided the state with one-third of its revenues. It employed 4,182 persons (of whom 3,725 were Mauritanians) or one-fourth of all the country's wage-earners, and it had built villages to house them at Consado and F'Derik-Zouérate.[63] Furthermore, because of prospection and development of new deposits of lower-grade ore, production had exceeded expectations, rising to 10.5 million tons in 1973. Nevertheless, the big profits that both Miferma's management and the government had anticipated failed to materialise, largely because of higher production costs, declining world prices for iron-ore and new competition from Brazil and Australia. To this disappointment was added annoyance over Miferma's delaying tactics in implementing its pledge to Mauritanise a larger percentage of its cadres and, above all, concern about mounting political opposition, of which Miferma at that time was the target as the epitome of neocolonialism.

All these factors explain Daddah's decision in 1972 to prepare the way carefully for nationalising Miferma. His first step was to create in July the Société Nationale d'Industrialisation Minière (SNIM) to take over Mauritania's entire mining industry eventually, but whose task initially was to extract and export gypsum on a small scale, and then to manufacture some 3,000 to 4,000 tons of explosives a year at a new plant in Nouakchott. Other measures culminating in Miferma's nationalisation on 28 November 1974 were the creation of a national currency, revision of Mauritania's co-operation agreements with France and the enactment of regulations requiring Miferma to invest all its profits locally. Five months later, SNIM unexpectedly absorbed Somima, but for reasons very different from those that had led to Miferma's nationalisation.

Mauritania's known deposits of copper at Akjoujt are estimated at 27.8 million tons, of which 7.7 million consist of oxide-ores with 2.52

per cent of copper content, and nearly 20 million tons of sulphide-ores with 1.76 per cent copper. Financial disagreements and delays in perfecting the procedure for reducing oxides by the Torco method were not wholly resolved when Somima was created in 1968. However, the new company, in which the Charter Group of London held 54 per cent of the shares, was able with government help to pave a 250-kilometre road between Akjoujt and Nouakchott for carrying its concentrates to the coast and to build housing for its employees at Akjoujt. Production rose unsteadily from 14,900 tons of concentrates in 1972 to 32,000 tons by October 1974, when it abruptly ceased because Somima was then losing money at the rate of $1 million a month and would require $60 million to repair its facilities and to continue mining during the ensuing three years. A loan hurriedly granted by Morocco enabled Somima to stave off its foreign creditors temporarily.

Despite its disappointing performance and financially shaky position, Somima never incurred the opprobrium directed at the efficiently managed and soundly financed Miferma, because it met most of the nationalists' criteria. At the time of its takeover, 22 per cent of Somima's shares were held by the state, a larger proportion of its 700 Mauritanian employees were cadres, 10.4 per cent of its total investments of 17 million CFA francs came from international agencies, and the road it built between Akjoujt and Nouakchott also served the general public. Consequently, Somima's misfortunes were blamed on the decline in world demand and price for copper rather than on its negligent management, excessively high salaries and prerequisites for its local personnel, and poor maintenance of its equipment.[64]

SNIM's acquisition in rapid succession of Miferma — now renamed Complexe Minier du Nord, or Cominor — and of Somima enormously complicated and amplified its field of operations and competence. Undaunted, SNIM planned also to build an industrial complex at Nouadhibou, comprising a steel mill, a copper foundry and an oil refinery. Yet by 1978 the desert war, combined with a steady decline in the world price for iron, had made SNIM's operations unprofitable, and it was also becoming clear that the Kedia d'Idjil deposits would be exhausted within a decade. The only hope for the iron industry's survival in Mauritania was to extract and enrich the huge deposits (estimated at some two billion tons) of the *guelbs* region east of Zouérate. They were expected to 'prolong iron mining in Mauritania for more than a hundred years' but would require the largest single investment ever made in that country.[65] Negotiations to raise $900 million needed from the project's 14 international financiers, notably Kuwait and Saudi Arabia, were not

completed until the summer of 1979, and the psychological cost to
Mauritania was high: SNIM was required to slough off its economically
unviable subsidiaries, dismiss several hundred employees, including the
able director (Ismael Ould Amar), and reduce the state's share in its
capital to 51 per cent.[66] Inasmuch as this restructuring of SNIM coincided with the conclusion of peace between Mauritania and the Polisario,
its future now seems assured.

Like other Third World countries dependent for their revenues on
wasting assets, Mauritania is determined to modernise as well as control
its economy by means of rapid industrialisation. Its leaders realise that
its iron and copper will eventually be exhausted and it was surely the
economic potential of Tiris El Gharbia, not to mention a share in Bu
Craa's burgeoning phosphate production and Dakhla's fish resources,
that induced Daddah in 1975 to undertake his disastrous Saharan venture.

Fisheries

Along with mining, fisheries are the most productive sector of the
modern Mauritanian economy and also that in which foreigners have
played the dominant role. Independent Mauritania's goal has been the
development of a national fleet that would eliminate foreign control
and bring into the state's coffers the profits from fishing that have
always gone to companies from abroad. In the process of trying to get
more returns from its fish resources, and to reduce foreign control of
fishing in its waters, Mauritania has distributed fishing concessions more
widely among alien companies, but the state has incurred heavy debts,
and it still plays a minimal part in fishing as an industry. A major obstacle to enforcing its regulation is the government's inability to control
the 500 or more 'factory' ships that elude supervision and process their
catch on board, thereby failing to use more than 30 per cent of Nouakchott's port facilities and 20 per cent of its processing installation. As of
1978, foreign fishermen were reported to have done business in Mauritanian waters estimated at $1 billion, of which only $30 million were of
direct benefit to the country.[67]

In 1970, when the annual catch of cod, sole, tuna, mullet and lob-
sters was roughly estimated at 270,000 tons, the head of the World
Bank mission to Mauritania warned that overfishing was depleting the
country's fish resources.[68] Although these resources were appreciably
increased in 1976 by the acquisition of Tiris El Gharbia, those rich
fishing grounds — as well as the need to protect them — were eliminated
three years later by Mauritania's sudden withdrawal from that region.

In practical terms, the major obstacles to Mauritania's formulation of a rational fishing policy have been its government's inability to enforce its regulations, need for larger revenues from fishing, and lack of any complete inventory of the area's fish species. The last-mentioned deficiency should eventually be remedied, however, for in August 1977 the cornerstone of an oceanographic and fish-research centre was laid at Cansado.

The only Moors who could be called professional fishermen have been the Imraguen tribesmen.[69] Using primitive equipment, they have long fished for turbot and mullet, which swim near the coast during the summer months. Under the colonial regime, most Imraguen fished on behalf of their overlords, the Oulad Bou Sba,[70] or for French companies, although the few who were self-employed sold their surplus catch in the Port Etienne market. Their total catch probably never exceeded 1,000 tons a year, as compared with the 15,000 to 30,000 tons caught annually by black fishermen in the Senegal River, and in both cases most of the catch was consumed by those who fished it.[71]

Since independence, the Mauritanian government has tried to assert more control, both by treaty and by force, over its fishing grounds, which increasingly attract fishermen from many regions and nations. In its 1963-6 plan, the government earmarked some $10 million for the development of Port Etienne (later renamed Nouadhibou) as a fishing and fish-processing port, and at the same time President Daddah moved to build up a national fishing fleet. The fisheries code of 1962 extended Mauritania's territorial waters from three to six nautical miles, beyond which trawling was forbidden for another six miles; the fishing season was limited to six months; and fishing by foreigners inside the twelve-mile limit required official permission.

Enactment of this code necessitated a revision of the Franco-Spanish agreement of 1901, whereby Canary Islanders were granted the right to fish under more stringent conditions, and also committed Spain to help finance an industrial plant at Nouadhibou. By late 1968, Spain had invested 2 billion CFA francs in the Société des Industries Mauritaniennes de Pêche (Imapec), inaugurated four years later with the capacity to can, dry, salt and freeze some 9,000 tons of fish annually, including 2,000 tons of the Canary Islanders' catch.[72] That Europe had become the principal and growing market for Mauritania's fish exports has been indicated by the rising share of frozen and canned fish in the Nouadhibou plant's total output and the concurrent decline of production of salted and dried fish.

An early agreement was reached with France whereby a few French companies that had long been fishing off Mauritania were allowed to continue their operations and to sell their catch under favourable conditions in French markets. In return for these concessions, France agreed to train Mauritanian fishermen and to finance generously Nouadhibou's industrial complex, especially its refrigerating operations and fish-meal production. Not all the foreign companies frequenting Mauritanian waters proved so amenable. In particular, the Japanese, whose catch in 1967 amounted to 87,000 tons, did not recognise Mauritania's extension of its territorial waters. Negotiations between the two governments were at an impasse until the seizure by Mauritania of two intruding Japanese vessels resulted in an agreement between it and a consortium of Japanese companies.

In the foregoing cases, Mauritania succeeded in realising greater monetary returns from the fishing rights it granted over an expanded area of territorial waters, but not the full implementation of the concessionaries' pledge to train or to employ more Mauritanian fishermen or technicians. Nor has the government itself been able to persuade the Moors in any appreciable number to become professional fishermen or even to consume fish.[73] Fishing and the industries associated with it would have to be made much more remunerative for the Moors to overcome their distaste for such a lowly occupation, and yet the government will have to find many more native candidates if it is to man the national fishing fleet of 50 to 100 units that it has been trying to build up.

Inexperience and precipitate action were the main cause for Mauritania's inability to create a viable national fishing company. In February 1963 a French firm launched the first fishing boat wholly built in Mauritania, but so eager was the government to build up a national fishing fleet quickly that it bought or rented foreign vessels with their crews at huge expense, only to find that the great majority of them were unsuited to Mauritania's coastal waters. By 1970 some 7 billion CFA francs had been invested in Nouadhibou's industrial plant, but its capacity to process fish had already outrun its supplies. Of the 70,000 tons of fish landed at Nouadhibou in 1974, Canary Islanders brought in 14,000 tons, Japanese 12,000, Norwegians 7,800, Russians 6,500 and Mauritanians only 3,500.[74] Inasmuch as the Nouakchott government is now less able than before to correct this imbalance, the trend is more and more to undertake joint ventures with foreign governments or with private fishing companies.

Animal Husbandry

Animal husbandry and iron-mining are reputed to be Mauritania's largest revenue-earners, but livestock is a far more vital asset to the nation than iron because it concerns at least 70 per cent of the population. Although sedentary farmers have acquired more livestock in recent years, animals are the main source of food and sole source of wealth for most of the Moorish and Peul nomads. As of 1968, animals and animal products accounted for a fourth of Mauritania's GNP, although their owners received far less than the maximum monetary returns from their herds. Before the 1968-73 drought, the nomads used whatever cash they had at their disposal to buy more breeding stock. This practice may not recur with the return to normal climatic conditions, as the nomads are reportedly reluctant to resume their pastoral life.

Naturally, climatic conditions have determined the habitat of Mauritania's various animal species. Although there is some geographical and ethnic overlapping, cattle, sheep and goats generally form the bulk of the herds owned by the marabout tribes and the Peuls in the south, whereas the warrior tribes and their tributaries in the north usually own mainly camels and goats. The 1968-73 drought and the war in the Sahara have altered the normal geographical distribution at least temporarily, for some areas such as eastern Hodh are said to be now totally devoid of animals.

The size of Mauritania's herds has never been accurately gauged because of their mobility and because of the nomads' reluctance to divulge the number of animals they own. A local superstition holds that counting animals is injurious to their health. More cogent, however, is the obvious relationship between their number and the amount of the animal tax (*zekkat*), which impels their owner to dissimulate the size of his herd. Because official animal censuses are made by guess and by Allah, it is not surprising that the statistics vary markedly from one census to another in the same region and even more for the same breed of animals.[75] Despite such fluctuations, however, animals of all categories, especially cattle and sheep, have increased notably since the early days of the French occupation. Losses resulting from the 1968-73 drought have reduced the number of cattle by 45 per cent, of sheep and goats by 30 per cent and of camels by 5 per cent, but all four breeds are still more numerous than they were in the early post-Second World War years.

Whereas the growth in Mauritania's cattle and sheep herds reflects in part the sedentaries' recent acquisition of such animals, variations in the camel population and their habitat bear a more direct relationship to the history of French colonisation in Mauritania. Even before France conquered that country, the rising power of the Reguibat tribesmen had disturbed the existing equilibrium between human and animal resources in the Western Sahara. As that marabout Berber tribe began moving east and south from Saquiet El Hamra and Zemmour in the late nineteenth century, they became great camel-breeding warrior nomads. They enlarged their herds by armed raids (*rezzou*) and at the same time pushed the *hassane* Moors into smaller and poorer pastures farther south, with a consequent diminution in the latter's herds.[76]

With time and security, however, the number of camels grew. *Pax gallica*, established in the north by 1934, put an end to camel raiding, hence the nomads in that region tended to disperse into smaller units, especially as it was easier to find pasture for a few animals than for a big herd. The far-ranging nomads divided their camels into two groups, taking with them only those that would provide milk and leaving the rest to be guarded by their tributaries. Also responsible for the upsurge in camel husbandry was the work of the colonial veterinary service and the growing trade with Senegal and Soudan, especially that of the camel caravans carrying salt south from Idjil and returning with millet. Furthermore, rich southern merchants began to invest in camels, not only because camels were less vulnerable to drought than were cattle and sheep, but also because of a 'deep-rooted Muslim conviction that the camel is the supreme good created by Allah'.[77]

Included in Mauritania's first four-year plan were about a dozen projects related to the development of animal husbandry. They comprised inoculation centres in addition to the 80 already operating, a well-digging and well-maintenance programme for Hodh, a bacteriological laboratory at Nouakchott and, above all, refrigerated abattoirs at Kaédi, Nouakchott, Kiffa and Aioun-el-Atrouss. Kaédi being the country's most important animal market, the first abattoir was built there, and it was intended to supply hides to a nearby tannery and to be provisioned from an adjacent ranch where animals were to be collected and fattened. At the same time as the Kaédi abattoir was inaugurated in January 1968, a Compagnie des Viandes de Mauritanie (Covima) was formed, with state and private funds supplying 30 per cent and 15 per cent, respectively, of the capital, to manage the abattoirs, supply them with animals and sell their output. From the beginning, Covima had difficulty in getting sufficient supplies of good-quality animals, the model ranch that was to have been built nearby never materialised, and the tannery, completed a year earlier than the Kaédi abattoir, had to import its raw materials from Mali. The abattoir's production declined from 1,200 tons in 1973 to 200 in 1975, largely because of the drought and its consequences.

Traditionally, herdsmen bring their animals to Kaédi, Kiffa and Néma, where middlemen take them in charge and drive them — often clandestinely — across the frontier to Senegal and Mali. In the process the animals lose weight and also much of their sales value, and the state is deprived of revenue through smuggling. The scale of this contraband trade can be seen by comparing the livestock-export figure for the last pre-drought year, 18,000 head, with the unofficial estimate of 52,000 head. The drought that began in 1968 swelled the clandestine exports and also diminished the returns to their owners. Unable to feed their surviving animals and needing money to feed themselves and their families, the nomads accepted whatever price they could get, with the result that exports soared in 1974 to an estimated 100,000 head of cattle, one million sheep and goats, and 30,000 camels.[78] Because such huge exports also created a meat shortage in Mauritanian towns, the government transferred the monopoly for the sale and exportation of meat and livestock from Covima to a new organisation, the Société Nationale pour l'Industrialisation et le Commerce du Bétail (Sonicob).

Under normal conditions, it should be noted, livestock exports represent less than 1 per cent of Mauritania's total herds.[79] Because the nomads eat more meat than do any other Mauritanians except town-dwellers, and consume virtually all the milk their animals produce, as their basic diet, they have a vital interest in enlarging their herds as an ambulatory food reserve. The element of prestige is also involved, for the Moors and even more the Peuls view the increase in their herds as an addition to their capital rather than as a productive investment. Although to some extent they appreciate the veterinary service's inoculation campaigns and the improvement in water supplies, they have become increasingly negligent since independence about subjecting their animals to disease-control regulations.[80] Furthermore, the increase in all Mauritanian herds has led to widespread overgrazing, especially near wells and waterholes.

The 1968-73 drought, by destroying or displacing so many animals and their owners and by deflecting government funds to meet emergency conditions, has caused some of the projects under the development plans to be abandoned. So dire was the plight of the herdsmen that four months before the government drafted its emergency plan in November 1972 it had suspended the collection of the animal tax for a five-year period, during which time it aimed to devise a more equitable fiscal system. Foreign aid has more than offset this loss of tax revenue. In 1971 the World Bank granted Mauritania a loan of $4.15 million, and in 1972 the Common Market Development Fund allotted 600 million CFA francs to be used, in part, to form a model herd of 5,000 cows, improve animal fodder, increase water supplies and develop intensive pilot animal-husbandry centres in Kaédi and Rosso. Reconstituting Mauritania's herds is a major problem facing the government, but even more difficult is that of deciding how far it can or should go in stabilising the nomad populations, even supposing it can win the latter's co-operation. In carrying out its policy to control and modernise the nomads through sedentarisation, the Nouakchott government rests uneasily on the horns of a dilemma: either it must continue to subsidise them in the main settlements around which they now cluster in idleness, or let them resume their traditional way of life in areas that can support only pastoral peoples.

Agriculture

Mauritania's agricultural potential is sharply limited by its arid climate, its mostly mediocre soil, the predominantly nomadic character of its small population and their predilection for animal husbandry and distaste for farming. Generally speaking, farming is practised only by black tribesmen in the sudanese zone and in the more northerly oases, where they cultivate date palms and the market-garden crops that grow in their shade. Thus the clear-cut geographical distribution of agriculture is matched by the ethnic division between black farmers and semi-nomadic or nomadic Arab-Berber herdsmen of the central zone and northern desert.

Millet and dates are Mauritania's major food crops; wheat, barley, corn, rice, peanuts, henna, indigo and tobacco are cultivated on a small scale almost wholly for domestic consumption; and gum arabic is virtually the only agricultural export. Even in years of normal rainfall, Mauritania has never been self-sufficient in food production, and the droughts in 1904, 1918, 1941-5 and above all 1968-73 necessitated ever-larger food imports to feed Mauritania's growing population. Government policy, at first fitfully during the colonial regime and more consistently since independence, has aimed, with the aid of foreign funds and technology, to increase the volume of food crops and to improve their distribution. As yet, however, Mauritania's production is not on a scale sufficient to meet its people's nutritional needs and, more significant, the government has not thus far found the means of coping with the socio-economic revolution that has been greatly accelerated by the repercussions of the drought and the undeclared war in the Western Sahara. In fact, the area under cultivation has declined with increasing rapidity over the past 19 years, as a result of the rural exodus, which has been caused by adverse climatic conditions, locust damage and attacks by the Polisario guerrillas. A recurrence of the drought, beginning in 1977, has required the authorities to reactivate their emergency plan and to solicit donations of food from international sources. Already by mid-1979, such gifts in kind had amounted to 57,000 tons for that half-year.

In northwestern Mauritania there existed a primitive irrigation system utilising seasonal flood waters. Elsewhere the Mauritanians depended on natural cisterns (*gueltas*), primitive water holes dug in the beds of dry rivers (the *oueds*) or earthen dams built to retain flash-flood water. Today in the north, wells are still few and far between, their water is heavily impregnated with magnesium, and they tend to run dry as the summer approaches. These disadvantages and the recurrence of droughts induced the colonial administration to undertake a survey of Mauritania's hydrology. Later, the French built the first two concrete dams, in Brakna and Assaba, and planned to construct similar dams in other regions. But interest in dam construction lapsed until 1951, when it was revived, along with the rehabilitation of many old wells, by the newly created Rural Engineering Service. This programme and other innovations ran into difficulties because of complex questions of traditional landownership and water rights, which dated from 1672 when the *hassane* Arabs in the war of Char Bouba defeated the Sanhadja Berbers. Since then, the warrior and marabout tribes together have controlled the flow of well water and the ownership of land, including date palms, which were cultivated by the Arabo-Berbers' black servitors. Because of this quasi-monopoly of the arable land and water in central and northern Mauritania by largely absentee owners, in conjunction with the far greater agricultural and human potential of the Senegal River valley, the French concentrated their irrigation programme and water-prospecting in southern Mauritania.

The colonial administration chose the Sociétés Indigènes de Prévoyance (SIP, or Native Provident Societies) as its main agency for increasing the country's food production in general and its water supply in particular. Although the SIP repaired old wells and built new cement ones, rehabilitated aging date palms, distributed seed as well as hand mills to grind millet flour, stocked food crops and on rare occasions lent small sums to needy members, they failed to take root in Mauritania, so that by the Second World War they totalled only ten. Under the austerity conditions created by that war, their number grew rapidly, as did their unpopularity. The principle of co-operation was too alien to Mauritanians, and this, together with the obligatory aspect of their membership and especially their domination by local administrators of varying abilities and degrees of good will, were largely responsible for their failure. Furthermore, among Mauritania's solidly Muslim population, especially among the Moors, the SIP ran counter to the Koran's prohibition of usury. Despite modifications in the organisation of the SIP, time has shown that Mauritania's socio-economic structure does not lend itself to the development of such institutions, regardless of their sponsorship. Since 1967, the independent Mauritanian government has tried to organise and increase co-operative associations of various types, but by February 1976 their membership totalled only 1,400, and the great majority of these were rice and market-garden farmers to whom considerable material aid had been given.[81]

Agronomic research in Mauritania, aside from date culture, was also largely concentrated in the south and operated jointly with Senegalese or metropolitan institutions.[82] Only the Ajouir station for date culture, in Adrar, was operated independently by the local agricultural service. All these stations did some teaching in connection with their research and experimentation. On a less specialised level, about eight Centres d'Expansion Rurale popularised modern agricultural techniques. A more general agricultural education was offered Mauritanians at the Katibougou school in Soudan and at the apprenticeship centre at Louga in Senegal, but no Moors ever filled the three places reserved for them at Katibougou, and only black Mauritanians attended the Louga centre.

The protection of crops against locusts and predatory birds (the *queléa-queléa* or *mange-mil*) was under a French bureau for all French West Africa, and it was allotted one-third of the local agricultural service's budget. Much of the work of the date-palm stations was devoted to eradicating a malady locally called *taka*,[83] which was largely responsible for frustrating the post-Second World War Monnet Plan's scheme to double the number of Mauritanian date palms within a decade. By and large, the French planners operated on the principle that water control was the key to food-crop increase, but the dams and irrigation canals built during the colonial regime did not protect Mauritania's agriculture against recurrent climatic hazards. Nor was much done effectively to promote the transport and marketing of crops from surplus to deficient regions, and this placed Mauritania in the anomalous position of being both a grain-importing and grain-exporting country.

Post-independence Mauritania. In Mauritania's first post-independence development plan, 1962-3, agriculture was given as low a priority as it had had before then, and for the same reasons. These were Mauritania's meagre agricultural potential, the complexity of its traditional land-ownership and water-ownership rights, and the indifference of the great majority of Moors to farming, as well as the larger monetary returns expected from investments in mining and fishing. To be sure, the existing programme and research institutions continued to operate under their French sponsoring organisations. Co-operation between the scientific bodies working on both banks of the Senegal River was continued, including the frequently modified and ever-more-ambitious programme of the Mission pour l'Aménagement du Fleuve Sénégal (MAS). After its creation in 1935, the MAS was successively oriented to developing cotton and then rice culture, and finally to controlling all the Senegal River that formed the boundary between Senegal and Mauritania after flowing from its source in Guinea through much of Soudan. In 1967 the MAS was expanded to include Mali and Guinea, and was renamed first the OERS and then, after Guinea withdrew, the OMVS.[84]

The Mauritanians who drafted the second development plan (1963-6) showed more awareness of the need for increasing food-crop culture than did their predecessors. Even if the goal of a 2-per-cent annual increase in food crops had been achieved, it would not have met the needs of a population growing at the rate of 2.2 per cent a year. Moreover, racial tensions between the Arabo-Berbers and the blacks and the strong attraction felt by the latter element for their fellow-tribesmen in Senegal and Mali added a political motivation to economic necessity in developing the south as a means of preserving national unity. The planners, however, were handicapped by the lack of basic data on the country's geology and hydrology, the inadequacy of its infrastructure, the scarcity of qualified personnel and the insufficiency of investment funds.

Food self-sufficiency being the declared goal of both the colonial and independent Mauritanian governments, it might seem logical that millet and sorghum, the crops that were grown in the largest quantities and were the basic foods of the largest number of Mauritanians, should receive favoured treatment, but this has not been the case. On the eve of independence, Mauritania's annual millet and sorghum production was estimated at 50,000 to 60,000 tons, and by the mid-1960s it had risen to between 80,000 and 100,000 tons. Increased irrigation facilities and experiments with animal traction had augmented output but not yields, and very little had been done to improve the storage of those cereals or assure their transport and sale to regions outside the producing areas. In part this was due to Mauritania's inadequate communications network, but in Hodh it also resulted from the Malian franc's devaluation in 1962, which was responsible for flooding Hodh with millet from Mali. In view of the difficulties impeding the sale and distribution of the country's grain surplus, Mauritania's planners found it advisable to concentrate use of the country's costly irrigation facilities for the new Chinese-directed experiment in rice culture at the M'Pourié farm station on 4,000 hectares in the Gorgol plain.

The Gorgol project — the most important innovation in Mauritania's rural economy since independence — is a water-control and irrigation scheme involving about 30,000 hectares of farmland in the Senegal River valley and vast stretches of pastureland as far north as Tagant. Launched in 1967, the project revived a scheme drawn up by the French administration 20 years earlier and now expanded to comprise millet, sorghum, rice and sugarcane. The project involves controlling the flood-waters of the Senegal River at Kaédi. When completed it should create an artificial lake containing one billion cubic metres of water and provide a bridge for vehicular traffic, all of which eventually would be integrated into the OMVS project.

Even in its early stages, some doubts existed as to the efficacy of the irrigation plan in appreciably increasing agricultural production. Richard Westebbe, head of the World Bank mission to Mauritania in 1967, believed that the output from the inundated land would be insufficient to justify the cost of building dams and that the dam sites, by their seasonal attraction for masses of animals, would cause overgrazing. Jacques Cherel, former technical adviser to the Mauritanian Ministry of Development, also was convinced that large-scale dam-building had two objectives that were incompatible because of a time conflict between the respective needs of farmers and of herdsmen.[85] The former wanted the maximum water for irrigation in the sowing season at the same time that the latter also needed the dam water for their animals and to revive their pasturelands. Only in the extreme south whenever the rainfall is normal can the farmers' needs for water be met. North of a line running between Boghé and Bassikourou, herders decrease the flow of water into the dams by digging their own wells and constructing earthen dykes. These objections have not deterred the UN Development Fund from granting more than $2 million to Mauritania for well-digging, water-prospecting and the training of Mauritanians for such work. Everywhere well-digging has increased, and some new water resources have been found in Trarza and Dahar, but little has been done in this respect for the northern region except to install water-distribution systems for the towns of Atar and Chinguetti.

Official efforts to improve the traditional agriculture have concentrated on date-palm culture in the north, where dates as a high-calorie, easily transportable food play a role analogous to that of millet for the south. Mauritania probably has some 800,000 palms growing on 3,000 or so hectares, of which about half are in Adrar and a fourth in Tagant, the balance being divided between Assaba, Affolé and Hodh. Yet despite these efforts to increase production, as of 1967 they were producing about 10,000 tons of fruit, or approximately the same amount as in 1959.[86] The oldest palms are those of Chinguetti and Ouadane, and it is only in Adrar and Tagant that numerous groves containing 5,000 or more comparatively young trees are to be found. Before independence the SIP and the agricultural service rehabilitated many groves and created new plantations. Pierre Munier, an expert who studied Mauritania's date palms between 1951 and 1955, believed that the area planted to dates there could be increased by 2,650 hectares and the number of palms by 530,000.[87] In 1946 the Monnet Plan called for a doubling of the number of date palms during the following decade, but for reasons independent of the drought of 1968-73, date production declined from about 15,000 tons in 1960 to 12,500 in 1974.[88]

The causes for this decrease are both physiological and economic. Among the former are the progresssive depopulation of such oases as Chinguetti, Ouadane and Tichit, and a reduction in ground-water levels in Adrar due to overpumping. A more serious physiological cause has been the destruction wrought for many years by the parasitic cochineal, and it has been to combat that pest that the IFAC station at Kankossa and even more its laboratory at Atar have devoted much of their work. IFAC experts have succeeded in introducing a biological predator, the coccinella, which by 1968 had rid the Adrar groves of their infestations. In 1971 they began a similar experiment in Tagant, and planned to extend it to all the other date-growing regions. To preclude the possibility that the coccinellas after eliminating all the cochineals might starve to death, a reserve stock of coccinella has been built up at the Kankossa station for possible future use.[89]

This success may account for the surprising maintenance of date production levels during the severest drought years just when millet in the south was declining disastrously. However, the authorities have not yet been able to cope with the two major economic handicaps to further increasing date production. One is the difficulty of marketing dates, which is linked to the twin problems of transport and lack of demand.

These handicaps have also adversely affected the vegetables and fruit harvested in the palm groves. Despite the research done on those crops at the Ajouir station, they amount to only some 400 tons a year. Almost all of Mauritania's dates are consumed locally and only about 500 tons are exported, mainly to Senegal and Mali. These exports might be appreciably increased if the trucks returning north from the Senegal River valley could find sufficient freight. Even before 1960, the Kankossa station began experimenting with the preparation and packaging of fresh and dried dates in the hope of enlarging their market south of the border.

It is upon the unlikely event that Mauritanian dates will sell at a price remunerative to their growers that the success of the official programme of increasing output depends. To the drawbacks of a poor marketing organisation, a plethora of middlemen and the high cost of transport must be added the traditional landownership system. Most of the palms have absentee owners whose chief occupation is rearing livestock. They seem content with the income received from leasing their groves seasonally, and their tenants, for their part, give little care to the palms, from which they receive one-tenth to one-half of the crop, simply consuming the dates they need and selling the surplus. The date palm takes five years to bear fruit, and neither the owner nor the lessee has the patience, interest or capital required to modernise and enlarge their operations, even though this would produce more abundant and better-quality dates, bringing them larger returns. Under the existing system, the Mauritanian tributary tribesmen or freemen pay the 'masters of the land' that they farm a fee called *obakh*, whose counterpart was the *horma* paid by the marabout tribes to the *hassane* warriors for protection.[90] But so many and so diverse are the customs regulating rights and obligations, as well as the size of plots in different regions of Mauritania, that they defy codification.[91]

In 1968 began the longest and most severe drought in all the Saharan sahel, but Mauritania showed more foresight than its neighbours in regard to its implications. For the first time in Mauritania's history, the PPM congress gave priority to agriculture in general and to water development in particular. Although the execution of the 1970-3 plan was delayed by the time required to appraise the efficacy of existing projects, the plan's adaptation to emergency conditions, and its integration into the larger OMVS programme, a considerable part of the 30 to 40 billion CFA francs needed for its implementation was forthcoming from foreign sources. The emergency plan included a greater effort at agricultural development in the north, although the government's energies and resources were largely absorbed in distributing foodstuffs and coping with the problems arising from the flight of the nomads to the south. A Centre National de Recherches Agronomiques Tropicales was created in 1974 to take over management of existing research facilities, including the encouragement of market-crop gardening and pineapple culture at the Ajouir station.

Foreign aid on a generous scale came early to Mauritania, and it was matched by the government's own efforts to cope with the crisis. In the spring of 1969 a food programme was devised by the government with the aid of foreign countries and international agencies, and that year some 10,000 tons of foodstuffs were distributed throughout the country at less than cost.[92] As the drought persisted, almost all the grain consumed in Mauritania had to be imported, and much of it was used to induce farmers and the unemployed to increase crop output, build dams, dig wells and undergo relevant training, for which equipment, fertilizers and insecticides were also provided. The Food and Agriculture Organisation of the UN (FAO) was the main international agency involved, and the major donors were the United States, Western Europe and Canada, with Morocco, Algeria and Sudan in that order contributing smaller food tonnages. By buying 20,000 tons of food in the world market, the Mauritanian government itself made a major effort. As of mid-1973 it had spent 33 million UM to hold down the prices of goods of prime necessity, devoted 5 per cent of the national revenue to relief operations, and created an Office des Céréales for food distribution. By imposing taxes on wage-earners and business firms it amassed 600 million UM with which it bought trucks to carry food to remote areas.[93] A report issued in July-September 1973 by an international team that surveyed Mauritania's nutritional needs and incidence of disease not only helped the government to increase the effectiveness of its food-distribution programme but also underscored the plight of the nomads, which it claimed were feeling the primary impact of the drought more than were the sedentaries.[94] Consequently, the government sent supplementary food to the nomad children suffering acutely from malnutrition and related diseases. If the drought had made Mauritanians realise how dependent they were on their government in time of stress, it had also awakened the government to a better realisation of the vulnerability of its nomadic population.

In analysing the causes of the great sahelian drought, members of a colloquium meeting at Nouakchott in December 1973 divided the responsibility between nature and man. Although there was evidence of a trend toward increasingly arid climate over the past 5,000 years, the inhabitants of the sahel themselves had aggravated its effects by abusive hunting, deforestation and overgrazing around waterholes. Politically radical analysis of the 1968-73 crisis attributed major responsibility to the colonial regime, which had broken up the existing Moorish social structure, destroyed the traditional trade patterns and imposed taxes, requisitions and forced labour on the population in order to introduce capitalism into Mauritania.[95] A more moderate view was that taken by the eminent scientist, Théodore Monod, who believed that the equilibrium between man's destructive powers and the regenerative forces of nature in the sahel had been thrown out of balance primarily by overgrazing — the indirect consequence of *pax gallica* in the area and the direct result of the work done by French veterinaries in Mauritania.[96]

Inasmuch as climatic changes are irreversible and colonialism's responsibility is today a moot question, the Mauritanian leaders are now more concerned with devising long-term programmes that, insofar as possible, will obviate a recurrence of the conditions that led to the recent drought disaster. By 1975, foreign aid, the government's own efforts and several years of normal rainfall seemed to have provided a breathing spell in which to seek solutions to the problems arising from the socio-economic revolution that the drought did not bring about but which it aggravated and accelerated. That this hope was illusory was proved by the recurrence of drought conditions in 1977 and of political instability in 1978.

Notes

1. See p. 45.
2. Roger Lafeuille, 'La Crise Economique chez les Nomades de Mauritanie de 1940 à 1944' (CHEAM, Mémoire No. 756, 5 Sept. 1945).
3. M.R. Lemoyne, 'La Transformation Moderne de l'Economie des Nomades du Sahara Occidental' (CHEAM, Mémoire No. 1009, May 1946).
4. See De Luze, 'La Société Maure de 1942 à 1946' (CHEAM, Mémoire No. 2246, 9 Oct. 1953).
5. See G.M. Désiré-Vuillemin, 'Coppolani en Mauritanie', *Revue des Colonies*, trimestres 3-4 (1955).
6. H.P. Eydoux, *L'Homme et le Sahara* (Gallimard, Paris, 1943), p. 90.
7. O. du Puigaudeau, *Le Sel du Desert* (Plon, Paris, 1940), p. 67.
8. R. Delavignette, *Les Vrais Chefs de l'Empire* (Gallimard, Paris, 1934), p. 124.
9. De Luze, 'La Subdivision de Tamchakett en 1945' (CHEAM, Mémoire No. 2169, 1953).
10. *Enquête Démographique* (Ministère de Finance, du Plan et de la Fonction Publique (Mauritania), Paris, 1972); C.C. and E.K. Stewart, *Islam and Social Order in Mauritania* (Clarendon Press, Oxford, 1973).

11. A recent tribute to the purity of Moorish Muslim practices was paid by Professor Vincent Monteil, who chose Mauritania as the site of his formal conversion to Islam in September 1977 because 'the faith there has remained almost intact . . . and has shown great tolerance in its human relationships'; *Le Monde*, 9 September 1977.

12. Among the Moors, the *cadi* replaced the chief as judicial head of the tribe, and the court consisted of the local administrator assisted by the *cadi* and a Notable, if the case involved more than one tribe.

13. M. Lenoble, 'L'Enseignement Français en Pays Maure' (CHEAM, Mémoire No. 2454, 1954).

14. See Mauritania Territorial Assembly minutes, 27 Nov. 1947.

15. A. Trancart, 'Base et Structure de la Société Maure' (CHEAM, Mémoire No. 1024, 1947).

16. J. Beyries, 'La Mauritanie' in *L'Economie Pastorale Saharienne* (La Documentation Française, No. 1730, 21 April 1953); 'Evolution Sociale et Culturelle des Collectivités Nomades en Mauritanie' (Comité d'Etudes Historiques et Scientifiques d'AOF, *Bulletin*, tome XX, 1937), pp. 465-81.

17. According to reports made by the Institut National de la Statistique et de la Recherche Economique and the Société d'Etudes pour le Développement Economique et Social in 1964-5, 200,000 freed slaves were still living with their former masters. See also F. de Chassey, 'Tension Politique en Mauritanie', *Le Monde Diplomatique* (June 1973).

18. 'Les Populations de Race Noire d'Aioun El Atrous' (CHEAM, Mémoire No. 3503, 1961).

19. According to Professor Capot-Rey, their origin is mysterious, but they certainly occupied Mauritania before the Almoravid conquest and may have created the first palm groves in Adrar. See R. Capot-Rey, *Le Sahara Français* (Presses Universitaires de France, Paris, 1953), p. 153.

20. The outstanding authority on the Nemadi is Philippe Fanacci.

21. R. Anthoniez, 'Les Imraguen Pêcheurs Nomades de Mauritanie', *Bulletin de l'IFAN*, série B, part I (July-Oct. 1967).

22. A. Kone, 'Perspectives d'Avenir d'une Communauté Mauritanienne' (CHEAM, Mémoire No. 3932, 1964).

23. See B. Fessard de Foucault, 'Le Parti du Peuple Mauritanien', *Revue Française d'Etudes Politiques Africaines* (Oct. 1973).

24. J. Limagne, 'La Politique Etrangère de la République Islamique de Mauritanie', *Revue Française d'Etudes Politiques Africaines* (March 1972).

25. Agence France Presse dispatch from New York, 25 Oct. 1963.

26. *West Africa*, 23 Feb. 1976.

27. R. Taton, 'Mauritanie: Les Combats du Sahara ont Cimenté l'Unité de la Nation', *Europe-Outremer*, no. 552 (Jan. 1976).

28. *Chaab*, 9 March 1976.

29. A.G. Gerteiny, *Mauritania* (Praeger, New York, 1967), p. 142.

30. R. Taton, 'Le Pouvoir, l'Administration, et l'Opposition', *Europe-Outremer*, no. 519 (April 1973).

31. In the areas that were mainly desert, eastern and western Hodh became Regions 1 and 2; Tagant and Brakna, Region 5; Trarza, Akjoujt and Inchiri, Region 6; Adtat, Tiris-Zemmour, Baie du Levrier and Port Etienne — the largest of all — Region 7; and Nouakchott was made a district.

32. *Marchés Tropicaux*, 12 March 1976.

33. Ibid., 1 Aug. 1975; B. Fessard de Foucault, 'Le Quatrième Congrès du Parti du Peuple Mauritanien', *Revue Française d'Etudes Politiques Africaines* (May 1976).

34. J.L. Ormières, 'Les Conséquences Politiques de la Famine' in *Sécheresses*

et Famines du Sahel (Maspéro, Paris, 1975), vol. I, pp. 131-45.

35. *Marchés Tropicaux*, 13 April 1973.

36. C.H. Moore, 'One-partyism in Mauritania', *Journal of Modern African Studies* (Oct. 1965).

37. Radio Nouakchott, 1 May 1964.

38. A. Baro, 'L'Enseignement Technique et la Formation des Cadres', *Europe-France-Outremer*, no. 490 (Nov. 1970).

39. R. Westebbe, *The Economy of Mauritania* (Pall Mall, London, 1972), p. 44.

40. Taton, 'Le Pouvoir'.

41. De Chassey, 'Tension Politique'.

42. M. Wolfers, 'Letter from Mauritania', *West Africa*, 13 Jan. 1975.

43. See pp. 52, 61-5.

44. *Le Monde*, 8 Feb. 1971.

45. *Afrique Nouvelle*, 2 Sept. 1975.

46. De Chassey, 'Tension Politique'.

47. Moore, 'One-partyism'.

48. Stewart and Stewart, *Islam and Social Order*, p. 389.

49. De Chassey, 'Tension Politique'.

50. *West Africa*, 1 Sept. 1975.

51. De Luze, 'La Société Maure'; H. de Boisboissel, 'De l'Adaptation des Maures au Cadre d'une Armée Moderne' (CHEAM, Mémoire No. 3500, April 1961).

52. Fessard de Foucault, 'Le Partie du Peuple'.

53. *Afrique Nouvelle*, 12 Nov. 1974.

54. *Enquête Démographique*.

55. *Marchés Tropicaux*, 26 Aug. 1967.

56. See R. Westebbe, *Mauritania: Guidelines for a Four-year Development Program* (World Bank, Washington, DC, 1968).

57. *West Africa*, 26 March 1971.

58. Dakar to Casablanca via St Louis, Atar, Fort Gouraud, Tindouf, Tiznit and Agadir.

59. Lemoyne, 'l'Economie des Nomades'.

60. Westebbe, *The Economy of Mauritania*, p. 75.

61. See p. 58.

62. *Marchés Tropicaux*, 19 Dec. 1975.

63. *Afrique Nouvelle*, 21 Jan. 1975.

64. P. Chambard, 'La Politique Minière', *Europe-Outremer*, no. 549 (Oct. 1975).

65. P. Chambard, 'Le Nouveau Drame de la Sécheresse', *Europe-Outremer*, no. 574 (Nov. 1977).

66. *Jeune Afrique*, 14 Feb. 1979; *Chaab*, 12 Oct. 1979.

67. *Marchés Tropicaux*, 20 and 27 Oct. 1978.

68. Westebbe, *The Economy of Mauritania*, p. 62.

69. See pp. 50-1.

70. See Annex.

71. Capot-Rey, *Le Sahara Français*, p. 447.

72. *Afrique Nouvelle*, 30 Nov. 1966.

73. Gerteiny, *Mauritania*, p. 67.

74. Chambard, 'La Politique Minière', *Europe-Outremer*, no. 549 (Oct. 1975), p. 43. In 1976 the catch came to 60,000 tons.

75. See *Afrique Française* (Aug. 1933); *L'Economie Pastorale Saharienne* (La Documentation Française, No. 1730, 21 Apr. 1953); Westebbe, *The Economy of Mauritania*, p. 66; Chambard, 'La Politique Minière', *Europe-Outremer*, no. 549 (Oct. 1975), pp. 41-2.

76. See C. Le Borgne, 'Les Nomades Chameliers de Mauritanie. Evolution du Nomadisme et de la Richesse Chamelière' (CHEAM, Mémoire No. 2241, 8 Oct. 1953).

77. Ibid.

78. Chambard, 'La Politique Minière', *Europe-Outremer*, no. 549 (Oct. 1975), pp. 41-2.

79. *Marchés Tropicaux*, 20 Jan. 1968; Gerteiny, *Mauritania*, p. 171.

80. *West Africa*, 7 July 1972.

81. *Marchés Tropicaux*, 6 Feb. 1976.

82. Among the local stations were those managed by the Institut des Fruits et Agrumes Coloniaux (IFAC) at Kaédi for Senegal River crops and those for dates, first at Kiffa and then at Kankossa; the Boghé cotton plantation under the direction of the Compagnie Française de Développement des Fibres Textiles (CFDT); and the Office de Recherches Scientifiques et Techniques Outre-Mer (ORSTOM), which undertook soil studies.

83. *Taka* was probably identical with the plant disease called *bayoud* in other parts of the Sahara.

84. See pp. 54, 282, 307.

85. J. Cherel, 'Secteur Traditionnel et Développement Rural en Mauritanie', *Tiers Monde*, vol. VIII, no. 31 (July-Sept. 1967).

86. *La République Islamique de Mauritanie* (La Documentation Française, *Notes et Etudes Documentaires*, No. 2687, 29 July 1960); Gerteiny, *Mauritania*, p. 167.

87. P. Munier, *Le Palmier-Dattier* (Maisonneuve et Larose, Paris, 1973).

88. *Marchés Tropicaux*, 10 Dec. 1975.

89. Ibid., 10 Oct. 1973.

90. See D. Bombote, 'Nationalisation de la Miferma: Révolution Economique?', *Afrique Nouvelle*, 21 Jan. 1975.

91. Gerteiny, *Mauritania*, p. 167.

92. *Marchés Tropicaux*, 22 March 1969.

93. J.R. Pitte, 'La Sécheresse en Mauritanie', *Annales de Géographie*, vol. 466 (Nov.-Dec. 1975).

94. M.H. Greene, 'Impact of the Sahelian Drought in Mauritania', *African Environment* (April 1975).

95. P. Bonte, 'Pasteurs et Nomades — L'Exemple de la Mauritanie' in *Sécheresses et Famines du Sahel*, vol. II, pp. 62-80.

96. Interview with Théodore Monod, *Jeune Afrique*, 24 Sept. 1976.

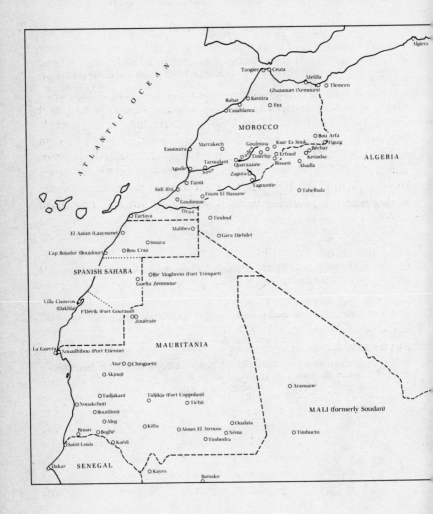

PART II: THE SPANISH SAHARA

Spain, unlike the other colonial powers in west Africa, did not seek to extend its domain or its trade on the mainland but remained entrenched along the coast, oriented politically, economically and culturally overseas to the north and to the west. In the twentieth century the government in Madrid, whether a monarchy, a military dictatorship or a republic, continued to be nostalgically attached to this vestige of Spain's great era of discovery, but could see little of current interest in its sterile foothold in the Sahara, especially as compared with its Mediterranean *presidios* of Ceuta and Melilla.[1] Indeed, it was only when other powers, European or African, began casting covetous eyes on Spain's desert colony that the Spaniards dug in and reinforced the military defence of their scattered coastal settlements. And it was not until France had pacified most of the western desert in 1934 that the Spaniards began venturing deeper into the Sahara to claim their internationally recognised rights there. During the Second World War, because of the Nazis' designs on northwest Africa, Spain began taking an inventory of its Saharan holdings and initiated successive reorganisations of their administration.

Far from challenging the nomads' right to carry out raids and to wander freely throughout Spanish territory, the local authorities sought to placate the outstanding tribal chiefs by a combination of benevolence and concessions calculated to ensure that Spain's possessions along the littoral would be left in peace. This *modus vivendi* lasted until Morocco attained independence in 1956, after which it was broken not so much by the nomads' own initiative as by irredentist Moroccan irregular troops who attacked Spanish rule in one of the regions that Moroccan nationalists termed *le Grand Maroc*. As this Moroccan offensive was also directed against France's sovereignty in Mauritania and Algeria, the two European powers co-operated militarily for the first time in that area, and through their joint efforts the status quo there was restored.

The discovery at that time of the Western Sahara's mineral wealth was another new element that exacerbated resurgent nationalism throughout the area. The great iron deposits of Mauritania and Algeria and the vast phosphate resources of the Saquiet El Hamra not only stimulated Morocco's cupidity, but gave Spain its first economic incentive to hold

103

on to and develop its Saharan territory. In practical terms, the prospect of acquiring riches from mining also 'created' a spurious Sahraoui[2] nationalism among tribesmen who had been for centuries traditional enemies and to all of whom the desert had been of interest only insofar as it provided enough pasture and water for their herds.

In its physical make-up, its tribal structure and to a lesser degree its history, the territory commonly called the Spanish Sahara[3] closely resembles Mauritania and southwest Algeria. In this region lacking natural frontiers, one finds throughout the Western Sahara the same sterile rocky plateau (*hammada*), dried alluvial plain covered with stones (*reg*), zones of dunes (*erg*) and clayey depressions some of which contain arable soil (*graara*) and others salt deposits (*sebkha*). As in Mauritania, the ocean's proximity somewhat mitigates the high temperatures along the inhospitable coast and for a short distance inland, but also creates fog that makes navigation hazardous. Only very rarely and in the northern region known as Saquiet El Hamra (Red River Valley) is there any flowing surface water. Rio de Oro, lying to the south, has only dry river beds (*oueds*) and few watering points. For many years Rio de Oro's reputation as one of the least-watered Saharan areas accounted for its failure to attract European explorers. As of 1958, in all of Rio de Oro's 184,000 square kilometres there were only 25 known wells, as compared with 35 in Saquiet El Hamra's 82,000 square kilometres, and in both cases the great majority of those watering points lay along the main caravan trails.[4] The discovery in 1964 of one of the world's most extensive subterranean lakes of fresh water drastically changed the economic prospects of Villa Cisneros and its environs.

History

In early modern times Spaniards from the Canary Islands showed a fitful interest in the nearby African mainland, especially in Tekna country, as a source of slaves and of cowries, and even more in the coastal fish resources. Although for centuries Spain failed to penetrate the hinterland, its occasional presence in the area served to forestall other possible European claimants, notably British traders striving to gain a foothold on the coast. Such was largely the motivation behind the formation of the Sociedad de Africanistas y Colonistas, which took possession of nearly 500 kilometres of the littoral following two explorations that it sponsored in 1883-4 and treaties made in that society's name with chiefs of the Oued Noun region. Although fishing, shipping and trading were the bases for such interest as the Spaniards had in the west African coast, in the late nineteenth century there was also a nationalistic and even imperialistic concern to assert Spain's historic rights in that area.

November 1884 saw the founding of Villa Cisneros, Angra da Cintra and La Guera, and one month later, in conformity with the Act of Berlin, Spain announced its protectorate over Rio de Oro and the adjacent regions locally called Oued Eddahab. Although commercial and shipping companies in Spain and the Canary Islands were granted permission to operate concessions there, their financial difficulties progressively involved the government in paying their debts, though it did not share in such profits as they made from their monopolies.[5] Inasmuch as cultural, commercial and political interests converged in the Rio de Oro, the Spanish government installed a small garrison at the territorial 'capital' of Villa Cisneros.[6] On 6 April 1887, a royal decree placed the area between Cape Bojador and Cape Blanc, as well as 150 kilometres into the interior, under the authority of the governor general of the Canary Islands. In reality, Spanish influence was confined to the coast; to the east of the Spanish settlements of Villa Cisneros and Santa Cruz de Mar Pequeña (allegedly the site of Sidi Ifni), nomad tribes wandered freely in search of pastures for their herds.

The first years of the twentieth century heralded significant changes in the area. In 1900 Ma El Ainin,[7] the erudite and fanatical leader of the nomads' holy war against European invaders in the Western Sahara, founded Smara as his fortress and religious centre in the Saquiet El Hamra. Ma El Ainin's crusade and the emergence of France and Spain as the dominant powers in northwest Africa in the years preceding the First World War impelled Sultan Moulay Hassan of Morocco to send a military expedition to southern Morocco and to support Ma El Ainin's *jihad* against the French. In 1912 France established a protectorate in Morocco and was then well on its way to controlling northern Mauritania, and Spain was installed firmly in the *presidios* and at Villa Cisneros. Those two powers had delimited their respective zones of influence in the Western Sahara in the agreements of 27 June 1900, 3 October 1904 and 27 November 1912. Specifically, France recognised Spanish rights over a vast part of the desert, including Rio de Oro and Saquiet El Hamra, as well as the land lying between 27°40' north latitude and the course of Oued Draa, which both were agreed belonged to Morocco. That area was administered by Spain as a protectorate under the name of Spanish South Morocco until 1958, when it was retroceded to Morocco and thereafter called by its former name of Tarfaya.

Tarfaya was briefly named Villa Bens in honour of Captain Francisco

Bens, who from 1903 to 1925 governed in Villa Cisneros under the Canary Islands military command. Bens strengthened Spain's hold on the west African coast by occupying Cape Juby in 1916 and La Guera in 1920, but he failed in his four attempts to take Ifni. The policy associated with Bens's long incumbency was popularly known as the 'sugar-lump policy',[8] but officially called 'restricted occupation'. In the hinterland it could be summed up as indirect rule by tribal chiefs, whose goodwill was assured by regular gifts of tea, sugar and cloth, and by a consistent refusal to co-operate with France's efforts to conquer the Western Sahara. The assumption lying behind this largely negative policy was that the Saharan settlements' principal value to Spain was that their possession prevented any possible attack on the Canary Islanders fishing off the west African coast. That coast's lack of ports, of sources of fresh water and of marketable local produce would have made the cost of a military conquest of the hinterland prohibitive. In the late 1920s, however, the stationing of small garrisons in the coastal settlements, the creation of the first *méhariste* unit (camel-mounted corps) and the establishment of penitentiaries at El Aaiun, Villa Cisneros and Cape Juby for political prisoners, bespoke a more positive policy on the part of Spain's recently installed military dictatorship.[9]

With the advent of the Spanish Republic in 1931, the pendulum swung back briefly to an attitude of *laissez-faire* toward the west African possessions. In 1932, however, the desertion of 30 Ouled Delim members of a *méhariste* unit with their arms, reportedly because of irregularity in their pay, served to change the new republic's attitude toward the Sahara to one of greater albeit still limited co-operation with France, after the latter's campaign to pacify the western desert proved effective. Following the French defeat of the Reguibat at Tindouf in 1934, the Spaniards began to recruit more nomad troops and to venture beyond their coastal forts. They captured Ifni on their seventh attempt, patrolled the desert and its watering points from the Draa to Tantan, built tracks and airfields near their desert military posts, which were now garrisoned by the Spanish Foreign Legion (Tercio Africanos), and finally occupied Smara.

The three coastal settlements were adminstered from Villa Cisneros by a governor general whose delegates were stationed at Cape Juby and in the Ifni enclave, but no attempt was made to relate this military regime to any tribal organisation, and the policy formulated by Bens of 'paternalism, friendliness and appeasement' was not altered. That formula envisaged that the Sahraoui should evolve in their traditional milieu without interference by the local Spanish authorities, who were instructed to win the nomads' confidence and to avoid wounding their sensibilities. Spain, in contrast to France, made no attempt to collect taxes from the nomads, or to restrict their possession of firearms; hence Spanish territory inevitably became a refuge for dissident tribesmen escaping from French control. Moreover, the Spanish settlements became a pole of attraction for all the West Saharan nomads after the coastal towns were made duty-free markets provisioned from Europe by sea.

The Second World War actually served to enhance in Spanish eyes the value of Spain's west African dependencies and thereby contributed to their development. Beginning in 1940, Spanish experts undertook the first scientific exploration of the Saharan hinterland, to such effect in the first post-war decades that the *Estudios Saharianos* published in Spain by the Higher Council for Scientific Research came to rank among the most scholarly work on the Sahara yet undertaken.[10] In terms of concrete achievements, the state increased its contributions to the Sahara budget and vastly improved the colony's economic and social infrastructure.

The foregoing developments could not but further sour Franco-Spanish relations. With a view to strengthening Spain's bargaining position in Africa and undermining France's status there after the war, the local Spanish authorities caused prayers to be said in the mosques of their territory in the name of the sultan of Morocco and no longer in that of the Blue Sultan, Ma El Ainin. They also encouraged nomads throughout the Western Sahara to buy in the well-stocked markets of their settlements, which contrasted sharply with the meagre ones in wartime Mauritania. Although the defeat of the Axis blunted Spain's openly anti-French propaganda, its Saharan territories, according to a British authority, played 'an important supporting role for Franco's aggressive post-war policy, which hinged on Spain's Moroccan protectorate and served to legitimize Spain's voice in the councils of Europe.'[11]

In March 1956 Spain lost no time in recognising Morocco's independence and promised to retrocede to it the protectorate of southern Morocco. Its failure to do so promptly, however, was due to the growing agitation in the Spanish Sahara by Tekna and Reguibat tribesmen and, more serious, to attacks by elements of the Moroccan Army of Liberation for the Sahara (ALS) allegedly with King Mohammed V's authorisation. Within a month of Morocco's declaration of independence, anti-Spanish demonstrations occurred in Ifni. These were followed by the murder of Spaniards and their supporters, destruction of the Cape Bojador lighthouse, and attacks on Spanish posts and convoys throughout the Spanish Sahara, culminating in the siege of Sidi Ifni and an assault on El Aaiun in late 1957 and early 1958.

A rapidly organised joint Franco-Spanish campaign (*Opération Oura-gan*) mobilised some 14,000 troops and 60 to 70 planes in February 1958. Within a month the Moroccan ALS's attempt to overrun northern Mauritania had been checked, Spanish control over its desert colony was restored, and the first large-scale refugee problem in the Western Sahara had been created by the concentration in the environs of Agadir of some 10,000 tribesmen who had fled there from as far afield as Atar and Tindouf.[12] The speed and decisiveness of this Franco-Spanish victory was attributed to heavy air support and the sizeable number of troops deployed, as well as to their concentrating on control of that crucial area in the Saquiet El Hamra where the frontiers of Morocco, Algeria and Mauritania converge.[13]

The violence that marred the end of nearly a century of Spain's generally peaceful presence in the Sahara, the discovery of the region's mineral wealth and the contagion of Morocco's aggressive nationalism inevitably induced Madrid to reappraise its role in west Africa. Not surprisingly, in view of Morocco's irredentist offensive and the desert's enhanced economic value, Spain strengthened its military establishment there to 9,000 men, encouraged Spanish settler immigration and reorganised the administration so as to bind it closer to the central government. The tardy retrocession of Tarfaya to Morocco in April 1958 only temporarily placated Rabat, for it heralded a reinforcement of Spain's grip on its remaining dependencies in the Western Sahara and also an intensification of its efforts to deepen the nomads' attachment to the Franco regime. Far from reducing its expenditure on behalf of the nomads, Spain increased its largesse for them, raised the minimum wage for labourers, allotted larger funds to improve the socio-economic infrastructure, and promoted the dissemination of Spanish culture. After 1961, Madrid's expenditures on the Saharan populations were appreciably increased and were reinforced by the pledge that all locally generated revenues would be used solely for the benefit of the Sahraouis.

Evolution of the Administration

Spain made no perceptible effort to give its desert territories a government suited to their particular needs until after the Second World War. In July 1946 Spanish West Africa, including the Ifni enclave, was detached from Spain's Moroccan protectorate and reconstituted as a colony under the Dirección de Plazas y Provincias Africanas. The attacks on the Spanish dependencies in 1956-7 by the Moroccan ALS caused Spanish West Africa to be divided in 1958 into the two provinces of Ifni and the Sahara. As a result of this change, the latter was composed of only Rio de Oro and the Saquiet El Hamra following the retrocession to Rabat of the southern Moroccan protectorate — now called Tarfaya — in April of that year. Each province was assigned a governor general — a high-ranking army officer — who as before was indirectly responsible to the Spanish premier. The Canary Islands' military authorities remained in command of the armed forces of the two provinces, which then numbered some 9,000 men and included units of the Spanish Foreign Legion.

By a law of 19 April 1961 El Aaiun became the capital of the Sahara province, largely because of its strategic situation and its proximity to the Bu Craa phosphate deposits. That same law organised the Sahara's judicial system, combining tribal customary law with Spanish legislation, and also gave the Sahara an administration modelled in part on that of the Canary Islands. Just as the eclipse of Sidi Ifni and of Villa Cisneros to the benefit of El Aaiun reflected a shift in the focus of political and economic power from Rio de Oro to Saquiet El Hamra, so the elevation of the Spanish colony to the status of a province of Spain with representation in the Cortes reflected the Sahara's enhanced value in the eyes of Madrid.

Although the Ifni enclave, which was without representation in the Cortes, had only a municipal council and was divided into districts and circumscriptions, the Sahara province was provided with a more complex structure. The two governors general at Ifni and El Aaiun, their secretaries general, civil servants and delegates in some minor settlements continued to be the highest local authority and responsible to the Madrid government for maintaining order. For the first time, however, the law of 19 April 1961, supplemented by that of 29 November 1962, gave the government of the Sahara a pyramidal base having three tiers. These consisted of the elected municipal councils (*ayuntamientos*) at El Aaiun and at Villa Cisneros, chaired by a mayor (*alcalde*); assemblies for some of the smaller settlements (at Smara and La Guera), each with an appointed mayor and elected members; and the nomad *fractions,* now legally recognised as more representative of the population than were the larger and more dispersed tribes. Between this base and the top Spanish hierarchy was placed a provincial council (*cabildo*), which met at El Aaiun and whose powers, procedures, and functions were regulated by law.[14]

The municipal elections were held first in 1963 and at two-year intervals thereafter. The council members were chosen, as were their Spanish counterparts at that time, both by direct vote and indirectly by economic, cultural and professional bodies. Generally speaking, the franchise was granted only to the head of a Sahraoui household or of a business. Specifically, the qualifications for membership in the two town councils were such that the candidates could only be Spaniards or sedentarised Sahraouis. Six members of the El Aaiun town council were selected by mercantile, industrial and trade associations, and the remaining six by the nomad *fractions*.[15] As to the provincial *cabildo*, half its members, as well as its president, Khatri Ould Jamani, were Sahraouis, as was also the mayor of Villa Cisneros, Suilen Uld Abdelahaye.

Rudimentary as was this local framework of local representative government, it filled a void in the Spanish Sahara's political structure. Yet because of the failure to provide for a general Sahraoui assembly, the Spanish Sahara still lagged far behind neighbouring countries. Furthermore, such progress as was made by this reform was due to external factors: these were the contagion of the nearby black Africans' rapid progress toward self-government, the international pressures generated by the rapid decolonisation of Africa in the early 1960s, and Spain's fear of losing to others the mineral wealth of its Saharan province. Certainly the Spanish policy could not be attributed to any expressed demand on the part of the Sahraouis at that time for a greater share in the government. The Sahraoui deputies in the Cortes warmly endorsed the policy of Spain in the Sahara, and in December 1966 six Sahraoui chiefs submitted to the UN in person memoranda signed by hundreds of local Notables — allegedly representing 91 per cent of the nomad population — couched in similar terms.[16]

It was largely to forestall possible Sahraoui demands for more power, to counter international criticism of Spanish rule in the desert and to stabilise the nomadic population, that in 1962 Spain began to finance liberally a plan for the economic and social development of its Sahara province. More indicative of Madrid's greater responsiveness to current trends in Africa was its creation on 11 May 1967 of a *yemaa*, or general assembly, for the Sahara. A few days later, the Spanish Minister of Defence told the tribal chiefs assembled at El Aaiun that Spain was determined to defend the Sahara against all comers. Of the *yemaa*'s 82 members, including the president of the *cabildo* and the province's two mayors, half were to be tribal or *fraction* chiefs, 36 would be elected every four years by all the adult male nomads and the balance — as well as the *yemaa*'s secretary general — were to be appointed by the governor general.[17]

Participation by the Sahraouis in the *yemaa* would be wider than that in the *cabildo* because of a reduction in the minimum age required of candidates and voters alike, and its competence, albeit still exclusively advisory, was to include initiating measures conducive to improving existing legislation and the government's proposals. As regards tribal representation, the constitution of the 1967 *yemaa* confirmed the pre-eminence of the Reguibat, who controlled 49 of the *yemaa*'s seats, and the Ouled Delim ran a poor second. In 1971 the Sahara's second *yemaa* was voted into office by a larger percentage of the Sahraoui than before. Candidates now included men of the fishing tribes and all male Sahraouis 21 years of age and over, and altogether 280 competed for office. Otherwise it differed little from its predecessor except that a Delim tribesman replaced a Reguibat as president of that body.

Nevertheless, there were indications at about this time of a change in attitude on the part of the Madrid authorities. In 1969 the transfer of Ifni to Morocco prompted Madrid to alter the name of the governmental department handling Saharan affairs to the less offensive one of Dirección General de Promoción de Africa. Then on 30 April 1973 the *yemaa* was enlarged to either 102 or 190 members, depending on whether or not one accepts as legitimate the election on the following 11 June of 88 sheikhs to the new assembly. In any case, new regulations that same year sought to restructure the chieftaincy and consequently the chiefly component in the *yemaa*. To some degree this legislation reflected Spain's desire to exert some control over, and to establish a hierarchy among, the desert's multiple and disparate chiefs, but the change was due even more to the influence of external forces that were trying to force Spain to grant self-government to its Saharan territories. Thenceforth the requirement that chiefs were to be elected only by the young adult males of their family, *fraction* or tribal assembly who held an identity card denoting their Spanish nationality was designed ostensibly to insure the representativeness of the leaders they chose. The chief so elected, however, had to pledge his 'fealty to Spain in the accomplishment of his duties and respect for the law that regulated the life of his community'.[18] The implications of this requirement, as well as the administration's strategy in devising boundaries for the electoral circumscriptions, contributed to the confusion that arose as to the membership of the *yemaa* elected in 1973, and partly accounted for the contradictory claims later made by Morocco and the Polisario Front as to its legitimacy.

Spanish Paternalism and Culture

Foreign observers of the Saharan scene during the 1960s and early 1970s concurred in pronouncing Madrid's policy of lavish paternalism to be highly successful in winning the acquiescence if not the enthusiastic endorsement of the Sahraoui chiefs to the prolongation of Spanish rule in one form or another. The monthly stipends, access to imported goods virtually at cost price, truck transport of camels and their herders to new pastures, free schools and clothing for nomad children, and airplane trips to Mecca were enumerated by a qualified observer as attractions far superior to those offered in any of the surrounding countries.[19] John Mercer noted that in 1963 the seating arrangements in the first official photographs of the provincial *cabildo* placed its Sahraoui members in the centre of the picture and the Spaniards on each side, and that in 1967 the Spaniards began to address Sahraouis as 'don' rather than 'sidi'.[20]

In terms of material advantages and honours, neither Mauritania nor Algeria nor even Morocco, the most serious contender, could compete with the Spaniards. Had not the Third World in the UN been stirred up by anti-colonialist resolutions passed at the instigation of those three countries, had not the prospect of great wealth to be derived from the desert's mineral resources whetted the Sahraouis' appetites, and finally had not Spain in consequence felt compelled to form a representative assembly and a supportive pseudo-political party, the tribal chiefs of the Spanish Sahara might have been content to settle for an autonomous government under Spain's aegis. Until 1970, it seemed as if the *yemaa*'s pleas to stay with Spain and Franco's antiphonal reassurances that he would never abandon the Sahraouis might continue to be exchanged indefinitely.

Similarly, in the cultural sphere, Spain moved during the 1960s from the negative attitude of simply not interfering with indigenous traditions and practices to the positive policy of promoting religion and education locally. Islam and its substratum of animism play much the same role in the life of the Sahraouis as among the Arabs and Berbers of Mauritania. Because the learning if not the piety of the Moorish marabouts has long been recognised by the Sahraouis as superior to that of their own religious leaders and brotherhoods, Sahraoui children are often sent to Koranic schools taught by Moors. In keeping with their long-standing policy of respecting the Muslim religion, the Spanish authorities built mosques in their three main settlements and paid the salaries of some teachers of that religion.[21]

Western-style education was very limited, and for many years in the colony it was virtually restricted to young Spanish children. Although school attendance by the Sahraouis increased greatly after the Second World War, the number of Spanish students in primary schools (2,688) in 1972 still slightly exceeded that of the Sahraouis (2,516), and in the province's two secondary schools the disparity was even greater (883 and 141 respectively).[22] For obvious reasons, no valid statistics on nomad literacy are available.

Once Spain had decided to offer modern education to Sahraoui children, its generosity in this respect was typically exemplary — at the primary level. Children attending urban primary schools were given not only free education, food and clothing but also a monthly allowance; and in El Aaiun and Villa Cisneros 'national institutes' were opened in 1963 to prepare those who would go on to secondary schools. All-Sahraoui rural schools were created in the minor settlements throughout the province. 1967, an eventful year politically, also witnessed the start of vocational schools in the two main towns and of a training centre for local administrators and judges, as well as the use of radio broadcasts to provide elementary instruction for illiterate adults. John Mercer has estimated that between 1968 and 1972, there was on average one Sahraoui receiving secondary education to four Spaniards,[23] a remarkably high percentage considering the recency of its introduction into the Sahara.

Some critics of Spain's cultural policy claimed that modern higher education was deliberately restricted to the youthful members of the most docile Sahraoui tribes, or that those who received scholarships for study abroad discredited such schooling in the eyes of their family chiefs by their behaviour on returning home. A case in point occurred in 1972 when 20 youths selected from different Saharan regions were sent to secondary schools in Las Palmas where, reportedly, they soon abandoned their studies and used their scholarship funds to buy alcoholic beverages and drugs, thereby scandalising their families.[24] As of 1973, there were only six Sahraouis studying in Spanish universities and another handful in Moroccan institutions of higher learning, and it was they who became the fiercest critics of Spain's policy of limited acculturation and who were the promoters of the various Sahraoui nationalist movements.

The Peoples

During the colonial period, official census-takers recorded, and qualified observers hazarded, such wide-ranging estimates of the Spanish Sahara's nomadic tribes and sedentary population as to inspire little confidence even in their approximate accuracy. First the political upheavals in 1957-8 and then, in 1975, guerrilla warfare in the Western Sahara brought about the withdrawal of Spain, the advent of Moroccan and Mauritanian officials and officers, and such large-scale migrations of the Sahraouis as to render previous data concerning their number and location even more obsolete and invalid. Mobile peoples, *per se*, are hard to enumerate, and this handicap is aggravated in the Western Sahara by the nomads' antipathy to being counted lest this lead to official controls limiting their independence and increasing their taxation.

The statistics gathered by the Spanish administration at ten-year intervals, beginning in 1950, as well as the estimates made during those intervals, disclose the small size of the total population and especially of its urban component. Generally speaking, such figures may be considered comparatively accurate only for the sedentary element, but even in that case confusion is often caused by confounding the population figure of a region with that of the settlement to which it has given its name. Even though both Spanish and Sahraoui town-dwellers were clearly increasing in number throughout the 1960s, the Spaniards were essentially transients, being in great majority civil servants or military men whose tour of duty in the Sahara was normally based on two-year contracts. As to the Sahraoui accretion, this could be attributed in part to the years of drought that, as always, have driven the nomads to seek food and medical care in the towns. The last official census, taken in 1974, cited the largest concentrations of nomads around urban centres as being those in the regions of El Aaiun (2,315), Cape Bojador (2,235) and Smara (1,898).

The official figures for the post-Second World War period suggest that the total population virtually doubled between 1950 and 1960, and that it tripled between 1960 and 1970. The increase of the Spanish element was proportionately greater than that of the Sahraouis, for it grew from 1,340 in 1950 to 5,304 in 1960, and to 16,648 ten years later, whereas the corresponding official figures for the Sahraouis' increase were 12,287, 18,489 and 59,777. In particular, the urban population grew by 40 per cent between 1963 and 1967[25] and by 1974 it totalled some 40,000. This marked growth in the number of both urban Spaniards and sedentary Sahraouis seemed to reflect the former's determination to remain entrenched in the territory and to make life there more attractive to the nomads, as well as the allurement that the amenities and material advantages of town life increasingly exerted upon the latter.

In the autumn of 1974 a special count of the Sahraoui tribes was undertaken by the administration with a view to holding the long-promised — and as frequently postponed — referendum on the province's future. Published in June 1975 in a volume of 158 pages, *Censo/74*[26] recorded the total Sahraoui population as 73,497, of whom 38,336 were men and 35,161 were women, and of these 40,988 were under 18 years of age and 2,025 were over 70. Of the eight major tribes, divided into 45 *fractions,* living in the Western Sahara at the time this census was taken, the Reguibat Lgouacem predominated in the coastal area of Saquiet El Hamra, in southwestern Algeria and in northern Mauritania, whereas the trek area of their fellow-tribesmen, the Reguibat Sahel, lay farther south, astride the Mauritanian frontier. The Izarguin Tekna frequented the El Aaiun area and also the Moroccan littoral between Rio de Oro and northwestern Mauritania. The region of the Ouled Delim and the Bou Sba was the area later known as Tiris El Gharbia. Along the coast farther to the north were found successively the Tidrarin, the Arosen (or Assoussyines), the Filala and the Ait Lahsen.

As to occupations, *Censo/74* divided the active Sahraoui population into 8,078 herders, 5,465 labourers, 1,341 soldiers and policemen, 981 merchants, 707 drivers of motor-vehicles, 358 skilled workers, 345 industrial workers, 226 sheikhs, 190 government employees, 149 fishermen, 141 teachers of primary and secondary schools, 119 nurses and paramedical personnel, 38 judges of Islamic law and 17 teachers of Muslim theology. Abdelaziz Dahmani, in commenting on this remarkable division of gainful activities, noted the extraordinary number of sheikhs, and an even more noteworthy phenomenon, the parity between the number of tailors and that of farmers (17).[27]

The foregoing enumeration cannot but arouse bemused scepticism, even though the Spanish administration claimed to have used more efficient methods than before to arrive at an accurate count of its Sahraoui population and to distinguish between residents of a town and those of its surrounding region. Admittedly, the ebb and flow of those nomadic peoples across political frontiers according to the changing state of the desert pastureland and the current relationships between the tribes would make any tally of their comparative numerical importance unrealistic. Furthermore, the political climate in 1974 was so tense as to render the results of *Censo/74* unacceptable to any of the parties most directly concerned.[28] Moroccans and Mauritanians held that the figure purporting to be the total number of Sahraouis was excessive, whereas advocates of Sahraoui independence considered it an under-estimation. Aside from any other flaws in this accounting, its basic one was the

failure to define acceptably first who was a Sahraoui. There is little disagreement, however, as to the outstanding importance of the Reguibat
confederations and of the Ouled Delim tribe.

The traditional tribal structure of the Sahraouis has been, not surprisingly, similar to that of the Moors, as was the intricate network of
rights and obligations that holds nomadic society together. The tribe
was divided into *fractions,* themselves made up of several families each
of which possessed its own tent and animals.[29] *Fraction* chiefs were
chosen by the oldest men of the member families, and together those
chiefs formed the assembly or *ijma*, although the marabouts could and
did settle minor disputes. Warriors occupied the highest rank, socially
as well as politically, followed in descending order by the marabouts,
tributaries, *harratin* and black servitors, with blacksmiths and fishermen
forming groups marginal to the basic tribal structure. The markedly
superior position of the warrior tribes contrasted with their generally
lower status in contemporary Mauritania. In the Spanish Sahara, the
absence of strong governmental control encouraged the maintenance of
the warriors' bellicose traditions, and they have remained so prestigious
that some Berber tribes have tried to claim Arabic or even *chorfa* origin.
Moreover, as compared with Mauritania, the harsher climatic conditions
in the Spanish Sahara and the fewer opportunities to acquire learning,
wealth and prestige there accounted for the inferior position of the marabout tribes. And finally, the number of blacks, and especially of half-
castes, was far smaller than among the Mauritanian tribes. Moreover,
the status of the former was more menial even though the Spaniards
claimed to have emancipated 2,000 slaves in their territory,[30] and the
opportunities open to freed blacks are more restricted.

Villa Cisneros, the *doyen* of Spanish towns in the Western Sahara, was
named after a distinguished Africanist of Spain but was called Dakhla
by its native inhabitants — a name later revived by the Mauritanians.
After the Second World War, Villa Cisneros was superseded as the provincial capital by El Aaiun. As a fishing port it was rapidly overshadowed
by Port Etienne in nearby Mauritania, and it also suffered from competition by the more recently founded settlement of La Guera. Even
after the Spanish army had taken over control of the town from the
Transatlantica company and Villa Cisneros became the site of a peniten-
tiary for Spain's political prisoners, it retained a certain urban elegance
among the reinforced Spanish military posts. Thanks to its peninsular
situation and unique natural harbour, Villa Cisneros held its own as a
fish-processing centre, developed a sea-salt industry and acquired a
modern airport. Moreover, during the 1960s it was provided with a

hospital, a mosque, a church, vocational and secondary schools and a municipal council headed by an elected mayor. The discovery of a vast local water supply bolstered its economic autonomy by increasing its agricultural potential. Yet in every significant respect, including the scope of its anti-Spanish activities in 1972, Villa Cisneros with its population of only 5,370 ran a poor second to El Aaiun. Between late 1975 and 1979, the town was successively administered by the Polisario Front, Mauritania and Morocco.

The Ifni enclave, 60 kilometres long by 25 wide, was ceded to Spain by the sultan of Morocco after his defeat in the 1859-60 Hispano-Moroccan war. Yet it was not until 1934 that the enclave's sole settlement, Sidi Ifni, was occupied,[31] having been chosen by the military for its location near land that could be transformed into a sizeable airfield and for its long beach front. Sidi Ifni became a garrison town *par excellence*, created by and for the military, and they and their families accounted for most of its 5,000 or so residents prior to the Second World War. The enclave's other 30,000 to 40,000 inhabitants were semi-nomads of the Ait Ba Amran confederation. Their meagre resources consisted of the wheat and barley grown on a total of about 300 square kilometres, some 20,000 cattle and 80,000 goats, and a portion of the fish catch, most of which was taken by Canary Islanders.[32]

After the Second World War, Sidi Ifni enjoyed brief prominence and an expansion as capital of the newly created Spanish West Africa, and work was begun on building an artificial port there in 1953. Four years later, however, the development of Sidi Ifni was halted by a revolt of the Ba Amran tribesmen, instigated by the ALS.[33] Thereafter its role as an administrative centre was taken over by El Aaiun, although it remained a strong if somewhat obsolete military bastion. By an informal agreement with Rabat in April 1958, the Spaniards effectively occupied thereafter only Sidi Ifni, its beach and airfield, and a radius of 7 to 8 kilometres around the town.[34] Barricaded inside Sidi Ifni, its 8,700 residents, mostly military, were, like the Ba Amran tribesmen, permanently underemployed. The former, and to a lesser extent the latter, however, enjoyed there the amenities (and endured the boredom) of a small Spanish town, including bars, churches and shops provisioned from Spain and the Canary Islands, and heavily subsidised by the Madrid government. The retrocession of Ifni to Morocco in 1969 brought to an end this windfall for the Spanish military overseas, but it also brought relief to the Spanish taxpayer, as well as compensation and repatriation to Sidi Ifni's small Spanish civilian contingent.

The military operations in and around Ifni in 1957 did not result in

the immediate acquisition of that enclave by Rabat, but they did indirectly attain two other important and seemingly unrelated Moroccan
objectives. These were the cession to Rabat of Villa Bens and the Cape
Juby area, renamed Tarfaya province, and a better control over the
ALS by the Royal Armed Forces (FAR). To protect Goulimine and
adjacent Moroccan territory against a possible Spanish invasion from
Ifni, units of the FAR at Agadir were moved south so as to encircle that
enclave.[35] There the FAR later served to make that enclave a refuge for
rebels and gave protection to refugees fleeing from the Franco-Spanish
bombardment of the area, as well as to either disarm ALS irregulars
resistant to the Rabat military command or to push them across Oued
Draa, where they could and did continue to harass Spanish troops. The
cession of Tarfaya to Rabat in April 1958 was in fact a consequence
of the near defeat of the Spanish at Ifni. And the lessons learned by
Morocco from the delays and embarrassing mistakes of Prince Moulay
Hassan and Major Oufkir in taking over the ceded area[36] prompted
moves to organise the FAR more efficiently and to employ it in the
economic development of Tarfaya province.

When on 17 April 1958 the Moroccan troops finally passed through
the sand-eroded walls of Villa Bens, what they saw confirmed Saint-
Exupéry's description of that settlement as 'the outpost of desolation'.
The almost desperate situation of its few hundred remaining inhabitants
was treated as a challenge by the FAR, which governed Tarfaya as a
military province for the next two years. Hassi Tantan and Tarfaya were
developed as military bases, wells were dug and airstrips and roads were
built in the area. By 1960, despite some Reguibat raids on the new province, Tarfaya's population numbered some 6,000, three times that of
Villa Cisneros at the time, and about the same as that of El Aaiun.[37]
Then, beginning in 1974, first as a staging centre for the Green March[38]
and then as a military base for the FAR fighting the Polisario Front,
Tarfaya became a new target for the latter's attacks.

When Franco decided to establish the capital of the Spanish Sahara
at El Aaiun after the Second World War, that garrison town had few
visible assets. It was situated some 24 kilometres inland and had a small
population of somewhat more than 5,200, of whom about 3,000 were
Europeans. Yet El Aaiun possessed a relatively abundant water supply
and, more important, it was only 100 kilometres or so south of Tarfaya
and about the same distance from the Bu Craa phosphate mines. The
last-mentioned advantage was not then known except to a very limited
Spanish milieu, so that the large sums poured by Spain into creating El
Aaiun from scratch puzzled foreign observers, who noted that 'every-

thing in this curious town from telegraph poles to doorknobs has had to be carried ashore in amphibious vessels'.[39]

The pay scale in El Aaiun, more than twice that in Spain, lured settlers and labourers there in sufficient numbers to make it the province's largest city, and building was that town's most flourishing industry. In 1974, thirty years after its founding, El Aaiun boasted a population of some 28,000 and had a mosque, a hospital, a cathedral, a library, a secondary boarding school, a stadium, shops galore, a modern airport and 30 saloons, not to mention ample housing for both Spaniards and a few Sahraouis. To all appearances, the town's architects had deliberately fostered nostalgia for Spain by building El Aaiun in the image of a Spanish city, yet such an ambiance was also in keeping with the overall Spanish attitude towards west Africa. Particularly in El Aaiun, the Spanish imprint was so pervasive — numerically, militarily and politically — that the Spaniards' departure in 1976, as well as the flight of an unknown number of Sahraoui residents, faced the incoming Moroccans with a void that challenged their ability to fill.

Smara, the only authentically Sahraoui settlement in the Spanish Sahara, was chosen in 1895 by Ma El Ainin, because of its water supply and its position at the crossroads of caravan routes, to become a fortress-monastery for his followers. Before its construction could be completed, however, Smara was destroyed by the French in 1913, but for the nomads of the area it retained its sacrosanct and military character.[40] Four years later, Spanish troops occupied Smara without bloodshed. Yet in 1957 they were forced to abandon it by the ALS, whose forces, entrenched in the half-finished fort, the Spanish managed to oust in the next year.

Under Spanish rule during the following 18 years, Smara resumed its role as a market and a garrison town. In the 1960s it experienced the same building boom as El Aaiun, with which it was connected by a paved road. The housing built by the administration for Sahraouis attracted many settlers, and by 1974, according to the census of that year, it had a population of 7,200 — larger than that of Villa Cisneros. Despite or because of its chequered history, Smara also revived as 'the religious heart of the western Sahara, a rallying point for the nomads, with whom it still enjoys prestige'.[41] Morocco was to learn to what degree Smara had become a religio-political symbol for the desert tribes not only when it occupied that town in 1975 and tried to win over what remained of its population but when Smara became the target of successive Polisario attacks in late 1979.

The only remaining Spanish Saharan settlement of any importance was La Guera.[42] Acquired by Governor Bens for Spain in 1920, La Guera served as a minor fishing centre whose inadequate water supply and poor anchorage were major handicaps to any increase in its population beyond about 1,000. Yet, along with Smara, it was provided in the 1960s with an embryonic municipal council of four elected members and an appointed mayor, and in the last years of Spanish rule it enjoyed a boom as a shopping centre for Moorish smugglers, who bought there radios, cigarettes, tinned goods, perfume and the like for sale in Mauritania.[43] When its Spanish residents suddenly abandoned La Guera early in 1976, the Mauritanian authorities who took over were obliged to bring in provisions of food and water by plane for its Sahraoui population. Three years later the Mauritanians in turn left La Guera hastily when Morocco took over Tiris El Gharbia.

The Economy

Finances

Until 1958 the budget for Spanish West Africa, aside from military expenditure, came to 87 million pesetas.[44] Four-fifths of the territory's revenues were provided by Spanish public funds, and the balance by taxes on animals, motor-vehicles and fishing enterprises.[45] With the start of oil-prospecting and the launching of the area's first socio-economic development plan in 1960, investments — notably in the infrastructure — and ordinary expenditures rose vertiginously until 1963, when the hope of striking oil was dashed.

In the plan's first budget, 44 per cent was earmarked for education, health and postal services; 16 per cent for public works; 13 per cent for urban construction; 11 per cent for telecommunications; and only 1 per cent for mining.[46] The budget for the Sahara province, excluding Ifni, remained fairly stable at about 320 million pesetas until 1965, when it began to rise rapidly, and in 1972 it totalled some 1,215 millions.[47] Liberally in Villa Cisneros and El Aaiun, and on a much smaller scale in the rural settlements, Spanish public funds were channelled into urban improvements, notably the distribution of water and electric current and the construction of hospitals, lodgings, schools and mosques, as well as in the form of subsidies for importing military equipment and, for both the Spaniards and the Sahraouis, consumer goods.

Because the government's aim was to stabilise and satisfy the Sahraouis, Spanish immigrants and the armed-forces personnel, apparently no effort was made to lighten the burden which Spain's west African dependencies represented for its taxpayers, whose contributions not only supplied budget funds but also made possible annual grants for special socio-economic projects. Labour was paid higher wages in Africa than in Spain, as were the armed forces, which played an important part in executing the development plan by digging wells, building roads, installing navigational beacons along the coast and the like. In 1966 it was noted that some 3,000 Sahraoui families had been settled in the towns and hamlets of the Sahara province,[48] but so limited a success numerically was hardly commensurate with the expenditure involved. Ironically enough, it was just when returns from phosphate-mining at Bu Craa promised to bring Spain some compensation for such expenditures, or at least to lessen the financial drain they represented, that Madrid was forced to withdraw from the Sahara.

Transport and Communications

The Spanish Sahara's orientation toward Spain and the Canary Islands could not have been more clearly illustrated than by the development of its sea and air communications with areas to the north and west, to the virtual exclusion of an internal transportation network. Until the Spaniards began expanding inland from the coast in the mid-1930s, the traditional caravan routes were the sole means of land communication in and with the hinterland. Impetus was given to improving this infra-structure, especially as regards airfields, by the joint Franco-Spanish military campaigns in 1957-8. The development plan launched in 1960 assured further progress, so that by 1963 there existed 19 tracks connecting the Spanish military posts with their nearest watering points, and these were rated 'more or less motorable over a total length of 3,320 kilometres or 5,495 kilometres, depending on the source consulted'.[49] By the time Spain withdrew from the Sahara, paved roads ran from the northern post of Tah to El Aaiun, from which branches led to Bu Craa and to Cape Bojador. A hard-surfaced road forked off from the latter branch to Smara, and shorter paved stretches connected Villa Cisneros and La Guera with their immediate environs. Elsewhere tracks linked Smara with Tindouf by way of Mahbes, and Bu Craa with Guelta Zemmour and points farther south.

Aviation facilities were better than land communications, and already by 1960 they consisted of airports at Villa Cisneros and El Aaiun and 29 landing strips in the hinterland. Air traffic was mainly military, but between Madrid, the Canaries and the Saharan coastal towns there were regular plane services that were expected to promote an embryonic tourist industry. Along the Sahara's rocky and desolate coast there were no natural harbours suitable for port construction except at Villa Cisneros.[50] Beginning in 1960, the coast was marked by beacons and lighthouses that reduced the hazards to navigation, and the main towns along the littoral were linked to the Canaries by regular if infrequent shipping services. In the mid-1970s sea traffic had declined to a few thousand passengers a year and travel by plane was growing rapidly. The port of Villa Cisneros was enlarged and improved, and the anchorage at La Guera was supplemented by a wharf, but the major innovation of those years was the creation of a great phosphate-loading port near El Aaiun. As to telecommunications, radio stations at Villa Cisneros and El Aaiun broadcast news, educational programmes and propaganda in Spanish and *hassaniya* Arabic, and in 1966 television was inaugurated by relaying telecasts from Madrid by way of the Canaries. Censorship of the press took the negative form of simply omitting news about the Sahara, with respect to both anti-Spanish activities and mineral-prospecting.

Trade

Until the mining of phosphates began in 1972, the Spanish Sahara's production for export was confined to fish, livestock and animal products. As regards domestic trade, the territory's few products were more often bartered than sold for manufactured imports (tea, sugar and cloth) or for locally grown foodstuffs (cereals, dates and salt). Such caravan trade as had survived the outlawing of slavery and the decline in gum-arabic exports was largely in the hands of Tekna tribesmen and confined to supplying nomad needs. Although the two main caravan routes of the Western Sahara passed through Spanish territory, where Smara was the most famous caravansari, the markets mainly frequented by the nomads were those of Tindouf and Goulimine for camels and Atar for dates. However, when the free-trade zone set up by the Spaniards in Rio de Oro offered imported commodities there at prices lower than those in surrounding countries, the focus of trade shifted somewhat to the south. Increasingly, the markets of Villa Cisneros and La Guera attracted nomad patronage from across the southern border, promoted dealing in cash rather than barter trade and above all gave rise to smuggling. In 1969 the value of goods smuggled between Rio de Oro and northern Mauritania was reportedly the equivalent of one-third of the Mauritanian budget for that year.[51]

Africa as a whole provided Spain with only 5 per cent of its imports, north and west Africa accounting respectively for 48 per cent and 19 per cent of that small total.[52] Yet on the other side of the ledger, Spain was by far the major source of its Saharan province's imports, which consisted mainly of foodstuffs, manufactured goods and fuel. During the first post-Second World War decade, imports were roughly double those of exports, but beginning in the late 1950s the trade imbalance was seriously aggravated as the consumer character of the province's economy became more accentuated. The increase in imports was due to the rapid growth of the Spanish civilian and military population, successive years of drought and above all a massive increase in equipment-goods imports for the development of mining at Bu Craa. Between 1960 and 1973 the exports officially listed were negligible, whereas in 1971 imports reached the record value of 1,618 million pesetas. Two years later, however, phosphate sales abroad began to redress the trade balance, and in 1974 they brought in 2,411 million pesetas, thus for the first time causing exports to exceed imports in value.[53]

Agriculture

In the Spanish Sahara, agriculture lacks everything it needs in sufficient quantity for its development except sunshine. The soil is poor and scanty, water very limited in quantity and permeated with salt and agricultural labour primitive in its techniques and practised only by black *harratin*. Moreover, droughts and locusts are recurrent, wind and sand storms strong and frequent and temperatures exceptionally high except in the more humid coastal region.

Small amounts of cereals (wheat, corn and especially barley), as well as some vegetables and fruit trees have been grown in the low-lying areas (*graara*), and date palms are cultivated in the oases of El Aaiun and Smara, but the central and eastern hinterland is almost totally sterile. Even in the best years, production has been so irregular and inadequate to meet the demand that large amounts of foodstuffs have had to be imported, and in drought years they were distributed gratuitously to the Sahraouis. A study of the province's agriculture in 1960 stressed the area's poverty. It noted that in an area half the size of France, there were cultivated only 2,000 palms, 300 fruit trees (in addition to 12 pomegranate and 20 fig trees) and one vineyard.[54] Four years later, however, the total area planted to cereal crops covered 2,750 hectares as compared with 187 hectares in 1961.[55]

Thanks to the discovery by Spanish geologists in October 1963 near Villa Cisneros of a subterranean lake 60,000 square kilometres in area, at a depth of 423 metres, agriculture expanded in the south, which until then had fewer known water resources than the Saquiet El Hamra. This additional water supply enabled the Spanish administration to promote irrigated cultivation and to create three model farms in the Villa Cisneros area where potatoes and tomatoes could be grown. At Daora, north of El Aaiun, the Spaniards experimented with irrigated farming. Between 1960 and 1970 Spain spent 170 million pesetas in drilling wells, and it maintained an anti-locust mission in conjunction with similar services in neighbouring countries, yet the output of 7,000 tons of barley and 210 tons of wheat in 1974 represented record crops. One fortunate aspect of the nomads' disdain for farming was the absence of landownership disputes such as those that plagued many other Third World countries.

Animal Husbandry

Most writers on the Spanish Sahara who note the wide fluctuations in the number of animals reported by the census-takers and their fairly even distribution among the tribesmen usually enliven their statistics with anecdotes that illustrate the unique and important role played by the camel in the Saharan way of life. Variations in the total animal population can be attributed to the insufficiency of pastureland, frequency of droughts, armed conflicts in the desert and the difficulties inherent in accurately counting the herds belonging to mobile tribesmen intent on disguising their number. The figures of camels, goats, sheep, donkeys and horses reported in 1952 bear a striking resemblance to the totals for 1971 — 220,000 and 231,000 respectively — although in the intervening years the sharp decline in their number, particularly between 1956 and 1968, does reflect the generally unfavourable climatic conditions and political unrest that characterised that period. The subsequent reconstitution of the herds can be attributed largely to the work of the Spanish veterinary service, and not to any increase in the rainfall and consequently improved pastures.

As of 1975, the herds in the Sahara province reportedly comprised 63,000 camels, 125,000 goats, 10,000 sheep, 1,600 donkeys and 350 horses.[56] Figures concerning the tribal ownership of the different breeds of animals are far older and appear to be even less reliable. Statistics dating from the early post-Second World War years attributed 14,300 camels to the Reguibat, 5,170 to the Tidrarin and 3,200 to the Ouled Delim[57] — unimpressive figures for the Reguibat, who were long reputed to be among the greatest camel-rearing tribes of all the Sahara. Yet almost overnight and very largely because of the current guerrilla warfare in the Western Sahara, the camel has been virtually superseded by the Land Rover as a means of transport for Polisario militants. Among the older generations of tribesmen, however, it will undoubtedly take longer to dethrone an animal that has always played a primordial role in their economy, psychology and way of life.

Fisheries

Spain's determination to establish fishing rights in the Atlantic off north-western Africa was the main motivation behind its early acquisition of footholds along the Saharan coast. The importance of the African coast fisheries to Spain's fishing industry has often been underestimated, for it has not usually been recognised as a primary objective of its Saharan policy. Subsequently, the history of the fishing industry in the Spanish Sahara bears a striking resemblance to that of Mauritania. Along with mining, fishing has been the most important economic activity in both countries, although the abundant resources of their coastal waters have been of little benefit to the indigenous population except for the Im-raguen and Chenagla tribesmen, and have been mainly profitable to foreigners, including Canary Island fishermen. Only some 5,000 tons of the annual catch — whose total volume is unknown — have been landed at the ports of La Guera and Villa Cisneros, where they were either mar-keted locally or salted for export to Equatorial Guinea. Paradoxically, the Spaniards, for political reasons, have been far more helpful in pro-moting Mauritania's fishing industry at Nouadhibou than they have been in developing La Guera as a processing centre. In their own territory, however, the Spaniards did form two fishing companies in 1948, sub-sequently built up and modernised the local fleet and canning industry, and in 1969 began to train fishermen in a school at Villa Cisneros.

Mining

Beginning in 1940, the mineral potential of the Sahara province aroused the Madrid government's active interest in geological research. Seven years later the discovery by Spanish prospectors of extensive phosphate deposits at Bu Craa, 70 kilometres inland from El Aaiun, was confirmed, and this encouraged the search for other minerals. Traces of iron were found in many places, especially in the Agracha region (which was be-lieved to contain 70 million tons of ore), but they were inaccessibly located and not on a scale comparable with the deposits of Gara Djebelit and Zouérate.

Inevitably, prospecting for oil was also undertaken in the 1960s. As this required more capital than was then available for that purpose in Spain, a liberal petroleum code was promulgated that opened the way for foreign companies to prospect and mine hydrocarbons for the first time in an overseas Spanish territory.

Attacks by the ALS in 1957-8, the kidnapping of foreign oilmen by self-styled Moroccan patriots in 1961 and the succession of dry wells during four years of drilling discouraged six of the foreign companies then working in Spanish territory. Early in 1964, therefore, they cancelled their exploration contracts and abandoned the area,[58] but the $50 million or so they had spent there by that time was a financial bonanza for the inhabitants of the Spanish Sahara.[59] An even more positive development related to this unsuccessful oil venture was the discovery of fresh water deep in the subsoil near Villa Cisneros, which made the residents of that town independent of the drinking water formerly imported from the Canary Islands and enlarged the area's agricultural potential. On the debit side of the ledger was the disruption of the economy caused by the rapid, large-scale recruiting of labour for the mining enterprises among the nomads and immigrant workers, followed by wholesale dismissals, for the jobless were reluctant to return to their former life. Enminsa (Empresa Nacional Minera del Sahara), the state oil company formed in 1962 by the Instituto Nacional de Industria (INI), inherited the abandoned concession, where it continued occasional and futile drilling.

As the prospect of an oil strike in the Western Sahara receded, Spain rekindled international interest in that area's mineral resources in June 1963 by dissipating some of the mystery surrounding its phosphate discovery because it needed to attract foreign capital for their development. The huge Bu Craa deposits were said to total between 1,400 and 1,700 million tons, covering nearly 1,200 square kilometres, and to mine and ship the ore abroad would require investments of some $100 million. Transporting the mineral to the coast involved construction of a 96-kilometre conveyor belt and of an ore-loading port near El Aaiun, because Tarfaya – the only port suitable for such a purpose in that area – was by then in Moroccan hands. A loan of $5 million to buy mining equipment was raised abroad.

In 1968, after several years of tortuous negotiations with various potential foreign investors, Fosbucraa (an Enminsa subsidiary) emerged in full charge of the Bu Craa operation. The withdrawal of American and European capital was attributed to the concurrent decline in the world price for phosphates, Madrid's insistence on processing the ore in Spain and the discovery of phosphate deposits in politically more stable Australia, as well as to the revival of Morocco's claims to the Spanish Sahara. Fosbucraa at once began building an ore-crushing and a desalination plant, a village for workers to house more than 1,200 persons, and port facilities capable of handling ships up to 100,000 tons.[60]

Obviously Morocco felt threatened by the competition that Bu Craa phosphates – superior in quality and easier to handle than those of

Morocco — would soon offer to its increasingly shaky position as the world's largest exporter of phosphates. World production of phosphates had more than doubled between 1959 and 1968, rising from 37.5 to nearly 82 million tons, but Morocco's output, albeit also growing, represented a declining share of the total, having decreased from 19 to 13 per cent. Moreover, the United States was not only the world's largest producer and increasing its output, but was finding new markets in Europe that had long been Morocco's main outlet. In the late 1960s the demand and price there for phosphates were declining, and because the American product was cheaper it was outselling its Moroccan counterpart. Yet Rabat twice rejected Madrid's offer to share in the development of Bu Craa in return for renouncing its territorial ambitions in northwest Africa at Spain's expense. The first exports from Bu Craa in 1972 coincided with the beginning of a spectacular rise in the world demand and price for phosphates. Consequently Morocco's determination to gain control of the Spanish Sahara hardened in 1973-4, as did Spain's resolve to keep its grip on that territory. Nevertheless, in 1975 Spain did turn over its western Saharan possessions to Morocco and Mauritania, as described below.

Hispano-Sahraoui Relations

Throughout the 1960s Spain seemed to be experimenting with various solutions to the Saharan problems raised by Third World insistence on the rapid decolonisation of Africa. For many years, Spain had eliminated competing claimants for the Sahraouis' loyalty, or at least won Sahraoui acquiescence, by combining largesse with an almost total lack of constraints on the nomads, and, more recently, by arousing their fears of communism emanating from neighbouring countries. Then in 1963, the Madrid authorities began setting up the apparatus for eventual Sahraoui self-government through the creation, first, of partly elected municipal councils and a provincial *cabildo*, and then through a wider-based assembly (*yemaa*) for the whole population. But all these were rubber-stamp bodies that did not impinge on the authority of the Spanish governor general. Nor did they alter the picture that Madrid tried to paint of the Sahraouis as contented and assimilated Spaniards living in a distant province, whose representatives asked for nothing more than to move gradually towards autonomy under Spain's protecting aegis. Participation by 95 per cent of the Sahraoui electorate in the plebiscite held on Spain's constitutional law of 13 December 1966 seemed to confirm the assimilationist thesis, as did the manifestos of support for Spain's Saharan policy submitted by Sahraoui Notables to the UN that same year.

In view of their long-standing good relations with the Sahraouis, the Spanish authorities were both astonished and shocked that the modest demonstration they had organised in El Aaiun on 17 June 1970 in favour of the Sahara province's continued association with Spain literally back-fired when a counter-demonstration against Spanish rule erupted into violence. The bloodshed during these riots and the nascent co-operation between Morocco, Mauritania and Algeria[61] in the Western Sahara forced Madrid to reorient its policy significantly in regard to the Sahraouis, as well as to reinforce considerably its troops stationed there.

The new image of the Sahraouis that Spain now tried to project to the outside world was that of authentic autonomists, free to choose the steps and the pace at which they would move toward control of their own destiny in collaboration with Spain. Madrid reiterated its willing-ness to grant them self-government if and when they said the word, and also stressed that the infrastructure for implementing this 'guided nationalism' stood ready to hand. Although the *yemaa* was still only an advisory body, its membership was appreciably enlarged so that it could serve as a forum for expressing the views of a larger number of Sahraouis. Time was to show the flaw in this argument, for violent demonstrations and sabotage, not the orderly processes of representative government, were the channels used by Sahraoui rebels to express their rejection of Spanish rule. To be sure, not all the tribesmen reacted in similar fashion, for an analysis of the signatures appended to the March and October 1966 manifestos to the UN showed that half of the Reguibat Lgoua-cem, the Tekna confederation, the Ouled Delim and even the Ma El Ainin gave the Spanish thesis their approval.[62]

Doubtless encouraged by this response, Spain persevered for five more years in seeking some more acceptable alternative to independ-ence than acceding to Moroccan and Mauritanian demands — one that would safeguard its phosphate investments, assure defence of the Canary Islands and preserve the Mediterranean *presidios* as well as its fishing rights in the area. With remarkable dexterity Spain managed to keep Morocco, Mauritania and Algeria at bay, and also to placate its critics in the UN and the OAU by repeated pledges to hold a referendum by means of which the Sahraouis could determine their own destiny when they so desired and when the conditions for doing so were propitious.

To substantiate the bona fides of such declarations, the *yemaa* was in-duced to make proposals to that effect, to which the Madrid government gave the appropriate responses. On 20 February 1973 the *yemaa* 'declared' itself by affirming the Sahraouis' right to self-government and asked the Madrid authorities to set in motion the procedures whereby the Sahraouis could attain self-government under circumstances that would guarantee their freedom of expression. Six months later, Generalissimo Franco responded by stating that the natural wealth of the territory belonged to the Sahraouis, who had the same rights as all other Spanish citizens. The *yemaa*, according to this statement, was to manage domestic affairs, albeit subject to the governor general's veto, while Spain would continue to respect the Sahraouis' traditions, assure the integrity and defence of their territory and represent its interests abroad. Naturally, the *yemaa* accepted these terms, adding that it would reject any attempt by outside forces to intervene in the Sahara's internal affairs — a resolution to which the Spanish embassies in Rabat, Nouakchott and Algiers gave considerable publicity.[63]

Nevertheless, by 1974 time was clearly running out for the Spaniards in the Western Sahara after 15 years of successful procrastination. The neighbouring nations not only were putting effective pressure on Spain to decolonise but were sponsoring 'nationalist' movements among the Sahraouis living on their soil in forced or voluntary exile. One of these, the Morehob, gave Spain special cause for alarm by establishing direct contacts with the Canary Island dissidents, but the strongest of Spain's local adversary forces proved to be the Mauritania-based Polisario Front, whose clashes with the Spanish troops grew in frequency and violence. (Morehob and the Polisario Front are treated in more detail in the next section.)

Late in the autumn, Spain announced that on 4 November the *yemaa* would elect four of its members to a council that would prepare the Sahraouis for what was officially defined as an 'independent Sahraoui state under Spanish guidance'.[64] At the same time, Madrid began preparations to update its electoral rolls by taking the first thorough census of its nomad populations. Some observers assumed that the nomads' well-known aversion to being counted would provide Spain with the alibi it was seeking for not consulting the Sahraouis as to their future status, but it was the sudden and drastic change in Morocco's strategy that gave Madrid the excuse it needed to postpone the referendum once again — this time, however, with international approval. In August 1974 King Hassan said that he would accept no referendum that raised the question of Sahraoui independence; in September he proposed consulting the International Court of Justice at The Hague as to Morocco's historic rights in the Western Sahara; in October he effectively ended the tripartite entente with Mauritania and Algeria; and in November he concluded a secret pact with Mauritania whereby he and President Daddah were to divide the Spanish Sahara between them. By the end of 1974, the three countries most directly concerned with the territory's future, as well as the UN General Assembly, had agreed to accept the arbitration of their dispute by the judges of the World Court.

Obviously the Madrid government had to be informed of the secret Morocco-Mauritania pact, Spain's approval being indispensable, but persuading the Spaniards to accept the partition of their Sahara province proved long and difficult. Already in July 1974 Madrid had apparently anticipated and tried to counter some such move by getting the *yemaa* to adopt a statute of autonomy, and then by following this up with preparations for a census and an administrative apprenticeship for selected Sahraouis. As the implementation of this policy required time, the prospect of a breathing spell, to be provided by consulting the World Court, was as welcome to Spain as it was to Morocco and Mauritania, and indeed also to the UN General Assembly.

Spain used the intervening months until the court's judgement was made known in October 1975 to assay Sahraoui reactions to the offer of a fictitious independence as an alternative more attractive to them than autonomy, and to prepare for its implementation in the event of what was expected to be an overwhelmingly favourable response in a referendum to be held early in 1975. Such a solution also promised to please Madrid as more likely to safeguard Spanish interests than would a 'government' emanating from the *yemaa* as then constituted. A warning of what Spain might expect had been issued by that body in September 1974, when two of its Sahraoui members — Ahmed Salia Uld Abeida and Obrahim Baschir — made what amounted to a Reguibat declaration of independence.[65] An even more aggressive note was struck a few months later when Khatri Ould Jamani, the Reguibat president of the *yemaa*, declared that after independence the Sahraouis would claim as their rightful heritage land then included within the frontiers of neighbouring countries.[66] Even the deputy mayor of El Aaiun, Ahmed Uld Brahim, after expressing gratitude to Spain for guiding the Sahraouis along the road to self-government, said that they should have been consulted before holding a referendum or before taking the Sahara question to the Hague court. 'In the mid-twentieth century,' he added, 'the Sahraouis will not accept the whole world speaking for them as if they were cattle.'[67]

To lend credibility to their new policy, the Spanish authorities in September 1974 created a Sahraoui Progressive Revolutionary Party whose role was to seek independence in collaboration with Spain, but so obvious was its origin that this so-called party was stillborn. Six months later, however, the Polisario Front had become so active that Spanish army officers revived the project. In March 1975 at El Aaiun, there was launched the Partido del Unidad Nacional Sahrui (PUNS), whose secretary general was Khali Henna Ould Rachid, an engineer trained in Madrid and Las Palmas. Not only did the PUNS also fail to win local support, but Ould Rachid promptly absconded with the party funds to Rabat, where in May he swore allegiance to King Hassan.[68] Not surprisingly, the PUNS fell apart, one element moving to Mauritania[69] while its members still loyal to Spain sought to organise during the summer of 1975 a counter-demonstration to the well-publicised Green March. This attempt brought the pro-Spanish PUNS element into conflict not only with Morocco but also with the Polisario, which violently opposed their holding meetings and sacked the PUNS office in El Aaiun.[70] PUNS members who refused to follow any of the proposed courses of action elected a new secretary general, Dueh Sidna, whose announced policies were virtually identical with those of the Polisario. In fact, before the year's end, the PUNS had virtually ceased to exist as a political entity,[71] and thus Spain's second attempt to create an 'independent' Sahraoui national party proved even more disastrous than the first.

The PUNS's multiple defections and growing Spanish doubts as to the *yemaa*'s docility were but the culmination of a series of disheartening developments for Spain during 1975, played out against a background of more frequent and bloodier clashes with the Polisario and with Moroccan forces. In May the distribution of anti-Spanish propaganda by Sahraoui students in the Canary Islands led to their arrest and repatriation, and mutiny among the Sahraoui troops prompted the Spanish army command to pay off and disband 200 of those remaining in its service; the mission sent to the Western Sahara by the UN Decolonisation Commission was visibly impressed by the strength of the Polisario Front; and finally the Moroccans were allowed to name an *ad hoc* judge to counterbalance the presence of a Spanish judge on the World Court, then debating the Sahara question. By the end of May it became obvious that the Madrid government had decided to withdraw from the Sahara, whose mineral wealth, the Spanish Minister of Armed Forces declared, was 'not worth a Spanish tear or drop of blood'.[72] A few days later, on 29 May, the *yemaa* was officially informed that the Sahraoui people should prepare themselves for a 'precipitate' transfer of power — but to which of the forces disputing Spain's heritage was far from clear.

Until mid-November 1975, when the Spaniards finally charted their course in the Sahara, they pursued, seriatim or simultaneously, divergent policies in the area. By then the Polisario Front was their most likely successor, and throughout the summer of 1975 Hispano-Polisario relations grew closer. In July and August the Polisario refrained from attacking Spanish posts, and in September it released 14 Spanish prisoners, to which gesture the Spaniards reciprocated in kind. Moreover, in the late spring, when Khatri Ould Jamani met at Tindouf with the Polisario secretary general, El Ouali, Spain seemed to be encouraging an entente between the *yemaa* and the Polisario Front,[73] but two months later the Spaniards persuaded the *yemaa* to set up a mixed commission that could serve as an embryonic provisional government in the event of Spain's hasty withdrawal from the Sahara. Then, according to El Ouali, he met on 9 September with the Spanish Foreign Minister at the latter's request, 'in a small village in a foreign country',[74] and after negotiating all night reached agreement on independence for the Sahraouis on condition that Spain's economic and cultural interests would be safeguarded.

That there was reportedly no further discussion of a referendum at that time was perhaps a measure of the Polisario's belief that its leadership was acceptable to all the Sahraouis. It also showed the confidence of the Spaniards, who probably assumed that their technological skills, notably as regards mining, would make them indispensable to any 'independent' government created under Polisario auspices in the Western Sahara. Ironically, what finally ended Spain's long hesitation waltz was the ambiguity of the Hague court's decision in October 1975, which gave full satisfaction to none of the parties most directly involved in the dispute.

To understand Spain's volte-face in signing the agreement of 14 November 1975, which in effect divided the Saharan province between Morocco and Mauritania, requires analysis of the various pressures to which the Madrid government was subject in 1974 and 1975. Foremost among them were the complications created in this instance by Spain's long-term traditional policy of nondiscriminatory friendship with all Arab states, Morocco's aggressive attitude in regard to fishing rights and territorial claims, and Madrid's concern not to jeopardise the Canary Islands' defence, the future status of the *presidios* or its heavy investments in the Sahara, most notably at Bu Craa. A factor of considerable relevance was Franco's protracted terminal illness and the uncertainty as to his succession, which coincided with the negotiations that led to the November 1975 pact.

On the psychological level, too, was the bitterness generally felt by the Spanish military establishment toward Morocco.[75] There was also Generalissimo Franco's well-known sentimental attachment to the African dependencies, where he had spent his early years and which had long served as a base and training ground for much of Spain's armed forces.[76] Spanish army officers, still mindful of their defeat during the Rif war of the 1920s, felt frustrated by their government's successive cessions of Tarfaya and Ifni to Morocco, and now in 1975 they were being ordered not to resist Moroccan military infiltration and indeed to abandon the very territory which they had been assigned to defend. This was particularly humiliating in view of the steady increase in the number and equipment of the Spanish armed forces until they reached more than 50,000 on the eve of Spain's withdrawal from the Sahara — a force considered by their officers to be sufficiently strong to defend that province against invaders from neighbouring countries or any local uprising unless it was supported by some external power.

Proof of the importance attributed by the government to the army's attitude in handling the Saharan question could be seen in the surprise visit of Prince Juan Carlos to El Aaiun twelve days before the tripartite agreement was signed. Not only was he probably seeking the troops' support for his own succession to power but also their officers' approval of the concessions that the Madrid government was about to make to Moroccan demands.[77] Apparently by prearrangement, the prince announced his firm opposition to Morocco's Green March, to which King Hassan responded a week later by ordering his marchers to return home.[78] This strategy had the virtue of enabling Spain to save face, a factor of considerable importance to the Spanish army officers. They had no wish to die in the desert for an obviously hopeless cause, but they also felt that their government's vacillations had made less than honourable the decolonisation of a territory that had been at least nominally under Spanish sovereignty for nearly one hundred years.

To what degree Spanish public opinion, which had been kept inadequately informed about developments in the Sahara, was concerned or had views on the Saharan question is hard to judge. Presumably, the majority of politically conscious Spaniards wanted Spanish economic and cultural interests there to be preserved and also desired international approval by means of a withdrawal under UN auspices, and they welcomed the economies in budget expenditures that this would effect. Ultraconservative elements headed by José Solis Ruiz, long-time administrator of the Moroccan royal family's property in Spain[79] and leader of what was called the 'Moroccan lobby' in Madrid, naturally favoured reaching an understanding with Rabat. He argued that an independent Sahara would be dominated by Algeria, operating through the Polisario Front, would make common cause with the Movement for Self-Determination and Independence of the Canary Archipelago (MPAIAC), would nationalise the Bu Craa mining enterprise, and would ignore Spain's treaty fishing rights. At the other end of the spectrum, the liberal and left-wing groups in Madrid who supported the Polisario formed an association early in January 1976 called 'Friends of the Sahara', which was joined by distinguished scholars, artists and lawyers. For its part, the Spanish communist party, eager to use any means to attack the Franco regime, impartially issued a statement backing the anti-Spanish stand taken by the Front for Liberation and Unity (FLU)[80] and also sent a delegation headed by Santiago Carrillo to Boumediene's Polisario protégés.

Although the precise terms of the November 1975 pact were not made public, it was soon assumed that Spain would retain a large share of the Bu Craa enterprise as well as its existing fishing rights, and would be given Morocco's pledge not to press for the return of Ceuta and Melilla. Although no mention of a referendum was made, one of the few clauses in the agreement that have become known specified that 'the option of the Saharan people as expressed by the *yemaa* will be respected'.[81] The importance thus attributed to the *yemaa*'s role led to a meeting of that body two weeks after the Madrid pact was signed. It was held at Guelta Zemmour, an area 'liberated' by the Polisario, and was chaired by its vice-president, but neither the *yemaa*'s president, Khatri Ould Jamani, nor the PUNS general secretary, Khali Henna Ould Rachid, was present. Indeed, sources differ as to just who attended that meeting and what took place there. According to the semi-official Polisario version,[82] two-thirds of the *yemaa* membership attended, along with almost as many Sahraoui Notables and chiefs. Together they declared that they would make no decisions that would be binding on the Sahraoui people, dissolved their assembly, and called for the formation of a national provisional Sahraoui council in the interest of unity. Furthermore, still according to the same source, the signatories of that declaration proclaimed the Polisario to be the sole representative of the Sahraoui people and proceeded to set up a National Provisional Council on 3 December 1975. The Moroccan account, on the other hand, reported that the *yemaa* had ratified the Madrid pact and stressed the subsequent visit to Rabat by Khatri Ould Jamani to swear allegiance to King Hassan. Rabat also claimed that on 12 December, the day after Moroccan troops had taken over El Aaiun, 85 members of the *yemaa* met there in regular session, having been joined by ten of those who had participated in the Guelta Zemmour meeting.[83]

Liberation Movements

None of the self-styled liberation movements, whether promoted by external or by indigenous forces, antedated the late 1960s. Their late start and almost simultaneous burgeoning differentiated them from the independence movements in nearby African countries. Given the superficial character of Spanish rule in the Western Sahara and the absence of any sense of nationhood among the scattered and disparate tribes, the existence of such movements could be attributed to no spontaneous upsurge of collective resentment against an oppressive foreign government.

Although their origin was obscure, all of these movements apparently were formed outside the Spanish Sahara – in Morocco, Mauritania, Algeria and perhaps even Egypt. Their belated and concurrent flowering suggests that they owed their existence to the publicity given in the early 1960s to the extent of the Western Sahara's mineral wealth. Its existence whetted the appetites of Spain's three African neighbours, who for a time could dissemble their predatory ambitions under the widely acceptable guise of encouraging anti-colonial movements. But Spain's imminent withdrawal from the disputed area brought into the open the artificial and competitive nature of those organisations. At the same time, the realisation that Bu Craa's phosphate reserves could make an independent Western Sahara economically viable accounted for the development of the first authentically Sahraoui movement – the Polisario Front.

The strength of the Polisario Front has been due to its concentration on the one objective deeply rooted in Western Saharan traditions, that of total independence from foreign controls – although for foreign consumption this was later somewhat overlaid by Marxist-nationalist verbiage. This was the only goal that could bind together and maintain discipline among the Western Sahara's bellicose and mutually antagonistic, anarchic tribes. The hit-and-run tactics of guerrilla warfare come naturally to the Sahraouis in general and to the Reguibat in particular, armed raids having been the breath of life for the latter tribe less than fifty years ago, before France pacified the western desert. Today, the modern weapons and Land Rovers with which Algeria and other 're-volutionary' states have lavishly provided the Polisario have revived moribund nomadism in the Western Sahara, so that the stability of any future government in that area seems dubious. In the meantime, however, the Polisario, albeit fighting on its own terrain and for its own goals, has become dependent for arms and funds on Algeria (and to a lesser degree on Libya), which has access to the sea and is the only nearby country able and willing to supply them, for motives combining both ideology and the hope of economic gain.

The Madrid pact of November 1975 and the departure of the last Spanish troops early in 1976 ended the period of shadow-boxing by the area's major opponents, Morocco and Algeria, and at the same time thwarted the repeated attempts made by international organisations and individual mediators to conciliate those *frères-ennemis* in the name of African or Arab unity. With the occupation of the former Spanish coastal towns by Morocco and Mauritania, the battle was now joined between them and Algeria, operating through the Polisario Front, for by this time the ersatz liberation movements had simply vanished from the scene. The strikingly similar history of the Morehob (referred to below) and the PUNS illustrates the hazards run by foreign governments in creating out of whole cloth so-called indigenous national movements under handpicked leaders who represented no interests other than their own.

As for Algeria, which had the good fortune to back the only Sahraoui organisation capable of holding its own against the Moroccan army, the Boumediene regime seemed to run no serious risk in intervening actively in the Saharan war, despite protests by some outstanding Algerian individuals. However, the steady flow of arms and funds (even with Libyan help) to the Polisario represents a considerable drain on Algerian resources, to compensate for which only the development of its vast iron deposits near Tindouf could turn Algeria's Saharan gamble to profit. Should the Polisario succeed in establishing an independent state in the former Spanish Sahara, Algeria would need its co-operation to mine and export that ore. In that event it is questionable whether the Polisario's sense of gratitude to Algeria for services rendered would prevail over the Reguibat's deep-seated resistance to acknowledging dependence in any form, as shown by their history of broken alliances and unabashed self-interest.

The confusion concerning the evolution of the many anti-Spanish movements formed during the 1965-75 decade was caused by their ephemeral nature and their puzzling changes of name, membership and even political orientation. Perhaps the least relevant of them was an Arab organisation created in Cairo in about 1970 to free all of Spain's

African dependencies, but the first movements more directly related to the Sahara were the Nidam, a vague name simply denoting an organisation, and the Mouvement de Libération du Sahara, which were formed respectively in 1968 and 1969. Both demanded independence for the Spanish Sahara, held unauthorised meetings in El Aaiun, claimed 'credit' for the June 1970 riots there and may have been forerunners of the Polisario Front. The severity of the subsequent Spanish repression led to the disappearance of those movements or, more likely, to their metamorphosis. The latter was suggested in an interview with two former members of Nidam published in the Oran newspaper, *La République*, early in January 1971, indicating that that organisation now advocated gaining independence by negotiation and using armed force only as a last resort.

More is known about the birth and demise of Morehob (Resistance Movement of the Blue Men), whose name indicates a Ma El Ainin origin. It was formed in January 1972 at Rabat, its goal from the outset was the Sahara's independence from Spain, and its leader, Eduardo Moha, was an enigmatic Sahraoui who had early adopted a European name. One source[84] asserts that Moha was a Reguibat born in 1943 near Smara and educated in France and Morocco, where he formed his anti-Spanish resistance movement among young Sahraoui students in Rabat. Another authority,[85] however, describes him as a native Moroccan who was employed at various times by the police services of Spain, Morocco and Algeria, and who recruited his followers in Spanish territory. Both sources, however, agree that in 1972-3 Moha was politically very active, appealing for support to a wide range of world celebrities, including the Pope and Kurt Waldheim, and travelling in Eastern Europe as well as in Africa, during which time he successfully publicised his Morehob party. His strong advocacy of independence for the Western Sahara, however, was unacceptable to his Moroccan hosts, so in March 1973 he shifted his base to Algiers. There he also soon became *persona non grata* because of the Algerians' growing doubts as to his honesty as well as to the sincerity of his political commitment. By the end of 1973, therefore, he again moved on, this time to Brussels, where he apparently remained quiescent for more than a year. After the pro-Moroccan members of the Morehob elected to return to Rabat in June 1973, Moha seems to have toyed with the possibility of transferring his allegiance to Mauritania, and in preparation for such a move he held a meeting that same month in the southernmost Spanish settlement of La Guera. There Moha's only known accomplishment was to have selected a flag for the future 'Republic of the Arab Sahara'.[86] His denunciation a month later of Nouakchott's annexationist aspirations in the Spanish Sahara indicates that the Mauritanians were unresponsive to his overtures.

By mid-1973 the Morehob had in fact ceased to exist in all but name, for despite its consistently anti-Spanish position it had never succeeded in winning international acceptance, and by then virtually all its members had either joined the Polisario or created a short-lived 'Movement of August 21' at Rabat. Early in 1975 Moha tried once again to stage a comeback, this time by rallying with fanfare to King Hassan, but this had minimal effect. In May Moha's pleas for recognition by the visiting mission of the UN Decolonisation Committee went unanswered, he was not allowed to present his case to the International Court at The Hague, and, left with no other alternative, he returned to live in obscurity at Rabat.

The disappointing performance of the Morehob left Morocco without any strong Sahraoui organisation that could substantiate the king's claim to the loyalty of the Western Saharan tribesmen. Consequently, on the eve of the UN mission's visit in May 1975, Hassan formed a Front for Liberation and Unity (FLU), composed of a congeries of pro-Moroccan refugees at Tantan, Sahraoui soldiers recently demobilised from the Spanish army and Moroccan irregulars, reminiscent of the ALS. Rumour had it that the FLU also included 500 regular Moroccan troops directly responsible to Col. Ahmed Dlimi, commander of the royal armed forces in southern Morocco,[87] but naturally such a rumour concerning what was billed as a spontaneous organisation could not be acknowledged as fact. The task allegedly assigned to the FLU was not so much that of forcing the Spaniards to depart as of disproving the Polisario's contention that it alone could speak in the name of the Sahraouis.

Terrorist attacks by the FLU along the southern Moroccan frontier and in the *presidios* certainly contributed to the rising tension throughout the summer of 1975 that, in part, caused Spain to decide to get out of the Sahara as soon as it had made the best possible deal with those of its adversaries most likely to preserve Spanish interests there. The FLU did not, however, persuade the UN visiting mission in May that it was as representative of Sahraoui aspirations as the Polisario, nor did its formal organisation as a fully fledged party the following September at Agadir improve its international standing.[88] At this constituent meeting a central council of 79 members and an executive committee of 17 were elected. The FLU's goal of liberating the Sahara so that the people of that area could return to the mother country, Morocco, was likened to the aims of the Palestine Liberation Organisation. The movement's ultimate gestures in 1975 consisted of organising a demonstration of left-wing Dutch militants in front of the International Court building in October and joining with the 'Movement of August 21' in urging the non-aligned-nations conference in Lima to prevent Spain from setting up a puppet state in the Sahara.[89]

The Front for the Liberation of Saquiet El Hamra and the Rio de Oro, known successively as the Frelisario and the Polisario Front, had a mixed parentage. Outstanding among its founders was Mohammed Said Brahim Bassir, born in 1944 into a Sahraoui maraboutic tribe, who attended the Koranic school in El Aaiun, received his secondary education in Morocco and went on to higher studies in Damascus and Cairo.[90] On returning to the Sahara in 1967 he founded a journal, *Al Chibah* (The Torch), and, while teaching in the mosque at Smara, organised an Islamic anti-Spanish movement called Mouslim, or 'Fighters for the Purity of Islam'. Although Bassir advocated gaining autonomy from Spain by peaceful demonstrations, his was one of the groups responsible for the riots of June 1970 in El Aaiun, following which he was arrested and never surfaced again.[91] Bassir was the catalyst of the Sahraoui liberation movement, and time has transformed him into a folk hero about whom ballads are composed and sung in the refugee camps, whose political colouration changes with the character of the particular nomad encampment.[92] In song and written propaganda, Bassir is pictured by the pro-Polisario Sahraouis as having fought the Spaniards for the independence of his country, whereas among the pro-Moroccan Sahraouis, Bassir is regarded as more of a martyr to Spanish colonialism because he tried to reintegrate his fellow-countrymen into the Moroccan motherland.

The loss of the movement's leader, as well as the severity of the Spanish repression, caused Bassir's followers to be more discreet in their tactics and propaganda, as well as more inclined to favour union with Morocco. The bases for what eventually became the Polisario Front were laid in Rabat by about a dozen Sahraoui students attending the universities there in the late 1960s, who met to discuss means of freeing the Sahara from Spain. Among their leaders was a 22-year-old Reguibat law student, El Ouali Mustapha Siyed, who was described as being then 'under the spell of the Egyptian Brotherhood movement . . . and for whom the liberation of the Sahara meant a return to the sources of Islam'.[93] Like Bassir, El Ouali and his companions in Rabat were initially more Muslim than Marxist, and they temporarily gravitated toward the Istiqlal and the Union Nationale des Forces Populaires (UNFP), whose leaders rather patronisingly welcomed the Sahraouis as 'provincial

Moroccans'. They insisted that the Sahraouis should seek liberation from Spain as junior members of their organisation — a proposal rejected by the El Ouali group, who now drew closer to those other Sahraoui students who were more nationalist than Muslim and who advocated a direct armed struggle for independence against Spain.[94] The June 1970 riots at El Aaiun marked the turning-point in this evolution.[95]

Late in 1970, the student militants began seeking contacts among the Sahraoui refugees living in Tindouf, Tantan and Zouérate. The older members of those colonies were either veterans of the ALS or former residents of the Spanish settlements who had fled from their homes during the bombardments of 1957-8. As they were in the process of being assimilated into their new milieux, they were indifferent to the students' militant propaganda, whereas it was welcomed by the younger generation who had fled from Spanish territory after the riots of 1970-1.

In 1972 began the tentative search for foreign aid, both directly by El Ouali, who toured European capitals, and indirectly through contacts made at the *mouggar* (annual fairs) at Tindouf. The Polisario emissaries sent to Libya, Algeria and Egypt met with encouragement but only at Tripoli received substantial pledges of aid. It was, however, in Mauritania that the movement's leaders decided to establish their base, owing to its proximity, ethnic and cultural affinities, and above all the support proffered by the Zouérate workers and the MDN.[96] On 10 May 1973 there was formally constituted at Zouérate the Frente por la Liberación de Saguia el Hamra y Rio de Oro (whose cumbersome name was later reduced to the Polisario Front), its stated objective being independence through armed struggle. Just ten days later and almost by accident, the Polisario captured the isolated Spanish post of Khangla, the first of a series of such successful assaults. Throughout 1973 and 1974 the Polisario proved to be the most effective of the anit-colonial movements, not only in terms of Spanish losses in men and material, but in those of propaganda as well. Because Algeria offered better facilities and more aid than Mauritania, the Polisario's headquarters were moved to Tindouf in 1975, only an office for disseminating propaganda being kept at Algiers, where it could not operate officially because it was not yet accredited to the FLN.

In its early stages the Polisario compensated for its comparative military weakness after Spanish troop reinforcements arrived by stressing party organisation and public relations. The extent of its propaganda activity was illustrated in November 1973 by the arrest in El Aaiun, following a demonstration, of some Sahraoui workers found to be in possession of Polisario tracts printed in Algeria. The themes then stressed by the Polisario – total Sahraoui independence and Arab unity, support for Third World liberation movements, nationalisation of the country's mineral resources, industrialisation and the development of agriculture and fishing – reflected more a nationalistic than a revolutionary ideology, as well as the decline in its earlier strongly Islamic orientation. The tone of the party's second congress, held near the oasis of Ben Tili in August 1974, was shriller in its insistence on being recognised as the sole movement representing the Sahraoui people and in its criticism of Morocco as being tepid in its opposition to Spain and annexationist in its ambitions. In an open letter of 9 September 1974 which the congress addressed to Hassan II and also sent to foreign news agencies, the king was denounced for 'claiming rights' in the Sahara that he did not possess, for establishing military bases there and for 'stifling the Sahraouis' national dignity' as well as every evidence of their Islamic identity.[97]

Anti-Spanish attacks were stepped up in the weeks that followed the Polisario's second congress. They were triggered by evidence that Spain was at last preparing to hold the long-heralded referendum and even to transfer some administrative responsibility to handpicked Sahraouis who were members of the *yemaa*. The most spectacular Polisario attack thus far occurred in October 1974, when the phosphate conveyor belt was sabotaged. During the first months of 1975 terrorist activities accelerated to such a degree that Spanish troops were withdrawn to the coastal towns from outlying posts, except Smara, and the repatriation of Spanish families was begun after the capture of two patrols, including six Spanish officers, and 14 motor-vehicles. In April the Polisario enjoyed minor propaganda successes in staging pro-Sahraoui demonstrations at Las Palmas and Barcelona, and in effecting the desertion of some Sahraoui soldiers from the Spanish army, as well as that of the announcer for Radio El Aaiun, to swell the Polisario ranks. In May, however, harassment of the Spanish military and civilians took second place to creating a favourable impression upon the visiting mission from the UN. In that endeavour, the Polisario proved to be eminently successful and also focused the world's attention on itself for the first time, arousing the sympathy of liberal opinion and winning the Arab League's approval.

As the Polisario's hostility to Spain diminished during the summer of 1975[98] and as its fear and resentment of Morocco's policy grew, its leaders turned briefly to Mauritania as a counterpoise. This was evident during the Hague court's hearings on the Saharan question when the evidence presented there corroborated Nouakchott's insistence on the close ethnic and cultural ties existing between the Moors and the Sahraouis.[99]

Although Mauritania also voiced its claim to the Spanish Sahara, that country had been the site of the Polisario's constituent congress, it was Mauritanians who had provided the Polisario with some of its earlier recruits, and Moorish leaders harboured latent suspicions of Moroccan designs on their country.

The Polisario command was unable to head off the negotiations leading up to the Madrid pact of 14 November, and Mauritania for its part was most reluctant to take up arms against its erstwhile friends and allies until it was forced to do so by the Polisario's seizure of La Guera as soon as the Spaniards had abandoned it. Spanish troops left La Guera a week before they were pledged to do so, in order to avoid becoming involved in the battle they foresaw between the Polisario and first the Moroccan and next the Mauritanian troops seeking to take over that town.[100] Reportedly, the Polisario intended to use La Guera as a base for Sahraoui refugees from the north and as the site for declaring itself the Arab Democratic Sahraoui Republic, and to facilitate that operation Colonel Khadafi of Libya urged the Mauritanians to delay their takeover of the Rio de Oro. Only the timely arrival of Moroccan troops at La Guera prevented this plan from succeeding.

Two days after the Madrid pact was initialled, Mauritania announced the formation of a Front de Libération et de Rattachement du Sahara à la Mauritanie, whose nucleus was 13 Sahraouis who had come from Villa Cisneros to Nouakchott to declare their allegiance to President Daddah.[101] The timing of this belated effort by Mauritania to form its own supportive Sahraoui party indicated that Nouakchott was not trying to compete with analogous groups sponsored by Spain, Morocco and Algeria. Rather it was an attempt to offset the recent defection to the Polisario of two outstanding Moors — Ahmed Baba Miske, former general secretary of the Nahda and Mauritanian ambassador to the UN, and Brahim Ould Darouich, a labour leader in charge of relations between the PPM and the country's sole trade-union organisation.

As of early November 1975 Spanish troops occupied only the main towns, or 10 per cent of the province's area, and the race was on between Morocco and the Polisario to take over the abandoned posts. Polisario militants were concentrated in the northeast, trying to encircle or at least to stem the advance of the Moroccan soldiers who were accompanying the Green Marchers on their way to El Aaiun and were also trying to prevent any Algerian infiltration. By 26 November, Morocco seemed to be in control of the Saquiet El Hamra, having taken charge of the radio station and airfield, and had installed a governor at El Aaiun, whose Spanish and Sahraoui population had largely deserted that town.

As the year ended, Rabat appeared to have won the first or military round, but the formation of a Sahraoui provisional national council by the anti-Moroccan members of the defunct *yemaa* on 3 December gave the Polisario an edge in the realm of public relations.

The Role of the Sahara in Spain's Foreign Relations

Until the mid-1970s, Spain was able to outstay the stronger powers of France and Britain in west Africa thanks to the modesty of its ambitions there, the absence of even the semblance of a centralised authority among the tribes that roamed its desert wastes and the apparent worthlessness of its hinterland. When the last-mentioned assumption was shattered in the mid-1960s by reports of valuable mineral resources there, the days of Spanish rule in the Sahara were numbered, although by adroit diplomacy, piecemeal concessions to its opponents and a minimal show of force, Madrid was able to postpone its withdrawal for more than a decade.

Of the three claimants disputing the Spanish heritage, Morocco was the most aggressive and dangerous from the Spanish viewpoint. Not only did Morocco covet the Western Sahara to protect its own phosphate revenues from competition, but in order to fulfil its national dream of *le Grand Maroc*[102] it also had to absorb the *presidios* – settlements that had been Spanish for four centuries and which no Spanish government could consider yielding to a foreign state. Until the extent of Bu Craa's phosphate resources was realised, Madrid had been willing to surrender its Saharan territory in return for Rabat's recognition of Spain's sovereignty over the *presidios*. Fishing rights off the coast of northwest Africa and Morocco's support for Spanish claims to Gibraltar were other factors determining Spain's relations with Rabat, and to improve them Madrid successively threw sops to the Moroccan Cerberus – Tarfaya in 1958 and Ifni in 1969 – but to no avail.

Mauritania proved relatively easy to mollify with economic and technical aid, for its claims to Spain's Saharan province were moderate and backed by no significant armed force or diplomatic clout. Algeria's demands fell into still another category, for they included no territorial claims but were based on principles whose validity had won widespread international acceptance and which Spain did not dispute. In its dealings with Madrid, Algiers held two trump cards: one was its encouragement of persons or groups considered subversive by the Franco government and the other, more important, was its capacity to export hydrocarbons badly needed for the industrialisation of northern Spain.

So long as Morocco and Mauritania were at loggerheads (1960-9) and Algeria's conflict with Morocco remained unsettled (1963-70), the pious resolutions passed by the UN General Assembly, beginning in 1965, could be safely ignored. And even after those differences between the three contenders had been papered over by a tripartite front, Spain might still have weathered the diplomatic storm, for it had earned the goodwill of the Third World by its grant of independence to Spanish Guinea on 12 October 1968 and by its unequivocal support of the Arabs against Israel in 1967 and 1973. Furthermore, the Western Sahara posed a problem that could be contained because of its geographical isolation, the lack of great-power involvement there and the overshadowing significance of concurrent events in Angola, southern Africa and Ethiopia. Probably no single factor was responsible for Spain's decision to withdraw from the Sahara in February 1976, but contributing to its formulation were the agreement reached with Morocco and Mauritania on 14 November 1975 in regard to a partition of the Sahara province and shares in the Bu Craa enterprise; Morocco's sovereignty over the *presidios* and Spanish fishing rights; the fear lest a Polisario-controlled Western Sahara might unite with the Canary Island dissidents of the MPAIAC; the increasing attacks by the so-called liberation movements against Spanish nationals and property; and finally, the death of Generalissimo Franco and uncertainty as to his succession.

If Spain's hasty retreat from the Western Sahara was to some degree lacking in dignity and a sense of responsibility, at least it did not precipitate a blood bath. Given the mutually contradictory objectives of the Moroccans, Mauritanians, Algerians and Sahraouis, and the divisions in Spanish public opinion as to if, when and how Spain should leave the area, no Spanish government could have failed to give offence to at least two of them. Under these difficult circumstances, further complicated by the imminent change of regime in Madrid, the most that could be done was to satisfy two of its would-be successors and to safeguard Spain's *presidios* and economic and cultural interests in the region as far as possible. As the time drew near for Spain's formal departure from the last of its Saharan strongholds, the government of King Juan Carlos and liberal opinion in Spain began to have second thoughts about the Madrid pact. These were reflected in a message sent on 26 February 1976 to the UN secretary general, in which the Spanish government stated that it had handed over its administrative functions to Morocco and Mauritania but was awaiting the outcome of a consultation of the Sahraoui people on their future status before deciding where to transfer its sovereignty. At the time this was widely considered to be a disclaimer — a move by Madrid to exonerate itself from any responsibility for the gathering storm — but in the summer of 1977 the statement was revived by the Polisario and Algeria as 'proof' of the illegitimacy of Moroccan and Mauritanian claims to sovereignty over the Western Sahara.

Mauritania

The protection of fishing rights of Spaniards and Canary Islanders off the coast of Mauritania has been the only constant factor in Spain's relations with that country. It was to strengthen the Spanish fishing industry that Spain asserted control over the coast from Cape Blanc to Cape Juby, and it was in hope of acquiring the best natural harbour there that in 1900 Spain vainly tried to wrest from France the site of what became the town and port of St Etienne (now Nouadhibou).[103] More than fifty years later, Spain set up there the Imapec, a huge fish-processing firm[104] that represented the largest single Spanish investment made until then in Mauritania (1 billion CFA francs as of 1965).

Aside from fisheries, Spain's interest in Mauritania *per se* was very limited. In the mid-1950s, after five years of negotiations, Madrid refused the Miferma company[105] permission to build a railroad through Spanish territory to carry its iron ore from Fort Gouraud to the coast unless Miferma would improve facilities at Villa Cisneros for use as its rail terminus and loading port. This refusal, however, reflected Spain's overall mercantilist policy *vis-à-vis* a foreign private company rather than its attitude toward Mauritania or its people. Indeed, except in the case of Spain's treaty of 1886 with the emir of Adrar, its relations with Mauritania until 1960 were necessarily determined by those between Madrid and Paris.

After Mauritania became independent, Spain used the conflict between Nouakchott and Rabat to play their governments off against each other and to neutralise their respective claims to the Spanish Saharan province. Madrid spared no effort to win over the Moorish leaders, providing capital and technology to develop Mauritania's economy during the 1960s. Spain operated a low-rate air service between Nouakchott and Las Palmas to carry passengers and foodstuffs between those two towns. Scholarships and youth hostels in Spain were provided for Mauritanian students, and in a co-operation agreement of 1967 Spain promised to build a radio station, a cement plant, oil-storage facilities and a generating plant to provide electric current for some Mauritanian towns. In the psychological domain, Spain flattered Mauritania by posting a diplomat of ambassadorial rank to Nouakchott, frequently exchanging official visits, and agreeing to rename Rio de Oro 'Spanish Mauritania'.[106] Then, in 1968, Madrid not only acknowledged that Mauritania had a 'vocation' to supply the Sahraouis with teachers and judges of Islamic law, but also discussed the practical ways to meet those needs.[107] Indeed, so cordial did Hispano-Mauritanian relations become that Spain's Foreign Minister, when he inaugurated the Imapec plant in 1970, stated that the only point in dispute between the two countries was the future of the Spanish Sahara.[108] From the Mauritanian viewpoint, however, that issue was crucial to Hispano-Mauritanian relations. Nouakchott would have preferred to settle its claims to the Spanish Sahara through bilateral agreements with Spain, but realised that in view of Rabat's demands this was impossible.

Three years before Mauritania attained independence, Mokhtar Ould Daddah voiced the first of his country's repeated demands for the Rio de Oro. The motivation for these claims, as well as the circumstances under which they were made, changed with the passage of time but, curiously enough, were rarely based on the Almoravid early conquests.[109] Quite consistently, Daddah's pleas were based on the undeniably close ethnic and cultural ties between members of the tribes whose trek areas straddled all of the Western Sahara's frontiers. After independence, Mauritania's concern to cultivate good relations with Spain developed more positive aspects than it had during the last years of French rule, although at the outset its motivation was as negative as that of Spain. Essentially, if Madrid was trying to win Mauritanian goodwill in order to block a pooling of claims to the Spanish Sahara by Nouakchott and Rabat, Daddah aimed to prevent Spain from ceding that province to Morocco lest it give Mauritania a long, indefensible common frontier with the latter country, especially near the vital centres of Fort Gouraud and Port Etienne. In a modified form, this dog-in-the-manger attitude on the part of Mauritania was reminiscent of the motivation behind Spain's early occupancy of the Western Sahara.

In the history of the Spanish Sahara, 1968-9 was a memorable period during the course of which all the main protagonists changed their previously held positions. It marked Morocco's formal acceptance of Mauritania's sovereignty (in part through Algeria's good offices) and Spain's cession of Ifni to Rabat, as well as the grant of independence to Spanish Guinea — the latter two moves marking a departure from Spain's generally inflexible policy in Africa. Those steps opened the way for the three Arab states bordering the Spanish Sahara to join forces in international organisations and among themselves to oust Spain from its Saharan dependency. The prospect of losing Spain as a buffer between

Mauritania and Morocco could not but have given Daddah pause. Yet Mauritania, as a former French colony, could not afford to invite Third World opprobrium by supporting the status quo in the Sahara.

Algeria

The history of Hispano-Algerian relations illustrates the predominance of economic interests over ideology on the part of both governments. Just as the importance of fisheries has been fundamental in Madrid's continuing interest in Mauritania and to a lesser extent its relations with Morocco, so the role of hydrocarbons is the key to Spain's courtship of Algeria. Similarly, political considerations have been transcended by Spain's importance to Algeria as a nearby source of technology, a trading partner outside the European Economic Community and the means of access to sharing in the Bu Craa mining enterprise. To be sure, politics have played some part in this relationship, for Franco's ultraconservative dictatorship could hardly approve of Boumediene's revolutionary creed, and especially of the refuge he offered to Spanish and Canary Islands dissidents. On the other hand, friendship with Boumediene offered certain advantages. Algeria had no territorial claims to the Spanish Sahara, it was the most effective nearby check on Morocco's irredentism there, and it was an increasingly influential member of the Arab world that Spain had been assiduously cultivating since the Second World War. Reciprocally, and for practical reasons, an understanding with Madrid would be desirable for the export of Gara Djebilet's iron-ore from a port on the coast of the Spanish Sahara.

Six months after Algeria became independent in 1962, Spain named its first ambassador to Algiers, and the next year air services between the two countries were established. Soon Spain initiated negotiations to purchase Algerian oil and natural gas for industrial purposes. Agreement in principle was reached in 1966 for the sale by Algeria of 50 billion cubic metres of gas over a 15-year period, and for Spanish financial and technical aid to carry out 14 projects for developing Algerian fisheries, textile industry, geological research, irrigation and the like. The timing of this agreement was not without relation to Algeria's recent decision to restrict the importation of French consumer goods because France had failed to honour its commitment to purchase Algerian wine, and it was related as well to Spain's failure to find and arrest the murderer of Mohammed Khider, a political refugee from Algeria living in Madrid.

Trade between Algeria and Spain grew so rapidly that by 1971 its value had increased tenfold and amounted then to nearly $60 million annually.[110] Because Spain could buy Libyan gas for less than that of

Algeria until 1969, the gas contract negotiated in 1966 had not yet been entirely fulfilled. Consequently, the trade balance was unfavourable to Algeria until a new economic and financial agreement was signed on 20 June 1972, whereby Spain agreed to purchase 25 billion cubic metres of gas annually for a 20-year period beginning in 1974.[111] The 1972 agreement not only promoted Spain to third rank among the buyers of Algeria's natural gas but also made Algeria the biggest market in Africa for Spanish exports, and a Hispano-Algerian Chamber of Commerce was established in 1974.

The intrusion of a political issue, specifically the future of the Spanish Sahara, into what was in 1966-7 a mutually satisfactory, if incipient, trading partnership, seemed gratuitous, inasmuch as there was then no discernible crisis in that area. It coincided, however, with the launching of Fosbucraa,[112] which set in motion a chain reaction that was potentially alarming to the Algerian leaders, and it was clearly related to their declaration in the UN that Algeria was an 'interested' party in the Saharan issue. The development of the Bu Craa deposits had already revived Morocco's determination to control that mine's output, lest its production in Spanish hands undermine Morocco's status as the largest exporter of phosphates. Furthermore, a Moroccan takeover of the Spanish Sahara would probably eliminate the possibility of Algerian participation in the Bu Craa enterprise, as well as that of shipping out Gara Djebilet's ore through the nearest Atlantic port. It is therefore not surprising that Boumediene consistently strove to 'internationalise' the Spanish Sahara question, and to bring it before the UN General Assembly and the Organisation of African Unity (OAU) on every possible occasion.

Boumediene rightly attributed the anachronistic survival of a Spanish territorial dependency in the Western Sahara to Madrid's successful application of the old imperial policy of divide-and-rule. In this instance, however, ruling meant not 'dominion over palm and pine' or over tribes for that matter, but simply remaining in control of the three coastal settlements that it had founded and developed and of the phosphate deposits that it had discovered and was in the process of mining. Spain's strategy of negotiating separate economic and financial agreements advantageous to each of the countries bordering on its Sahara province, and of exploiting the conflicts between them, worked admirably so long as their governments remained mutually suspicious and jealous or had something to gain by Spain's continued presence in the area. Such was no longer the case after the extent of Bu Craa's phosphate resources became public knowledge, and there was the possibility that other equally rich discoveries might follow.

Although in the long run the drive to possess such a source of wealth aggravated the competition between Spain's three Arab neighbours and budding Sahraoui nationalists, in the short run they came to agree that Spain's elimination from the Western Sahara was the indispensable preliminary to any radical change in that area's government and, consequently, in the ownership of its mineral resources. Initially, Morocco and Mauritania used the UN as the major agency in which to press their respective claims to the Spanish Sahara, and although Algeria also used the same forum it was mainly to assure its inclusion in any settlement of those claims. At the UN, all three governments stressed the Sahraouis' right to self-government and denounced Spanish colonisation in Africa, assured of the backing of Third World countries, whose number was being steadily increased by the admission of many former colonies to membership in that world body.

In the debates leading up to passage of UN General Assembly resolution No. 2229 on 20 December 1966, in which Spain was asked to accord the right of self-determination to the Sahraoui people, Algeria's spokesman in that assembly stressed for the first time the importance that his government attached to a solution of the Spanish Sahara problem, which he called the key to peace in that region.[113] Preparatory to its campaign for decolonising the Spanish Sahara, Algeria warmed up its relations with Mauritania to such good effect that in March 1967 Mauritania came out in favour of Algeria's right to be consulted regarding the future of the area.[114] Mauritania also confirmed its support for Algeria in the latter's difference with Morocco, and in return Boumediene later was instrumental in reconciling Daddah with King Hassan.

Settling the Algero-Moroccan frontier conflict in the Western Sahara inevitably proved far more difficult for Boumediene. By 1972 he seemed to have resolved the problem insofar as presenting a united anti-Spanish front in the UN and the OAU was concerned, but not as to the terms or the significance of the referendum that they all advocated, or as to precisely who would be qualified to vote. Apparently Mauritania and Morocco expected that Sahraoui voters would include not only the transfrontier tribes but Sahraoui 'refugees' living in their countries, and that the majority of the Sahraoui electorate would support their respective claims to sovereignty over them. Algeria, on the other hand, seems to have assumed that independence would be an alternative offered to all the Sahraouis and preferred by them, and that a nominally sovereign Saharan state would not only check Moroccan expansionism but also prove to be clay in Algerian hands. As to the Bu Craa deposits, Boumediene envisaged their exploitation as a joint enterprise in the context of a united Arab Maghreb, leaving little or no place for Spanish participation. These basic differences in outlook and goals, albeit obvious from the outset, were publicly ignored by all three parties in their zeal to maintain a united anti-Spanish front. Periodically, however, they surfaced, as in the sponsorship of rival nationalist Sahraoui movements, and ultimately caused the break-up of the tripartite entente.[115]

In regard to the bilateral relations between Spain and Algeria, which were founded on mutual economic benefit, the Saharan question was extraneous. Actually, in September 1970, when the tripartite agreement was made, Algeria's position was closer to that of Spain than to Morocco's, and approached Mauritania's to a lesser degree, for both Boumediene and Franco were willing to recognise an 'independent' Sahraoui state but not to accept a partition of the Spanish Sahara. When, however, Boumediene, by threatening economic blackmail, tried to force Spain to oppose Hassan's Green March in November 1975, he failed. To Madrid the problems of the *presidios* and the fisheries in particular, and the proximity of Morocco in general, were primordial considerations, whereas Algeria's leverage was limited because there were other attractive, if less convenient, sources of gas and oil. Indeed, Boumediene's attack on what he described as 'Spain's pure and simple capitulation to pressure' was so vehement that it was censored in the Spanish press.[116]

Boumediene vented his indignation at Madrid's policy decision by allowing the MPAIAC to broadcast anti-Spanish propaganda over Radio Algiers. Yet Hispano-Algerian economic co-operation was not only resumed but strengthened. After Franco's death, Boumediene sent his condolences to the Spanish people, and a year later, to show his displeasure with King Juan Carlos's policy, praised the generalissimo as a friend of the Arab nation to a visiting delegation of Spanish communists and socialists.[117] Then in 1977, Air Algerie inaugurated a weekly service between Algiers and Barcelona. The Hispano-Algerian rapprochement noted during the summer of 1977 was related to Boumediene's hope that pressure exerted by the Spanish left-wing parties would lead the Madrid government to reconfirm its statement on the Spanish Sahara on 26 February 1976 to Kurt Waldheim, notably denying that it had transferred sovereignty over its Sahara province and declaring that it was still awaiting the outcome of a referendum on self-determination from the Sahraouis to do so.

Relations between Madrid and Algiers continued to blow hot and cold throughout 1977. Their sudden deterioration in December was related to the inability of the OAU to hold the long-planned conference on the question of the Spanish Sahara and to violence instigated by the MPAIAC in the Canary Islands, which was presumed by Spain to have been engineered by Algeria and the Polisario. In order to discredit the legitimacy of the Madrid pact of 14 November 1975, Algeria wanted Spain to play host to such a conference. The Polisario stepped up its pressure on the left-wing Spanish parties, with which it had developed close relations, to influence the Madrid government to reopen the transfer-of-sovereignty issue, and the MPAIAC renewed its efforts to tie independence for the Canary Islands to that of the Sahraouis, and thus as an 'African liberation movement' to win the support of the OAU.[118] A crisis was triggered by an inflammatory article published on 19 December in the semiofficial Algerian newspaper, *El Moudjahid*, which accused Spain of exploiting intensively the economy of the Canary Islands and tolerating two American bases there that were linked to installations in Morocco. In that article also, the MPAIAC was strongly supported in its claim that the Canaries were the last colony in Africa and as such had the right to independence. Madrid at once protested sharply to the Algerian government and recalled its ambassador, but stopped short of breaking off diplomatic relations because of the importance to Spain of its economic ties with Algeria.[119]

This attack on Spain's policy in the Canaries proved to be a tactical error in Algero-Polisario strategy, for it served to rally Spaniards of all political stripes behind the government so strongly that on 26 January Radio Algiers abruptly ceased broadcasting MPAIAC propaganda. This in turn prompted the Spanish Socialist Workers party to take up the cudgels again for the Polisario, and by the end of January it had succeeded in getting the foreign-affairs committee of the Cortes to pass a resolution designed to force revelations about the conditions under which the 14 November 1975 pact had been negotiated. Should they also confirm the existence and, above all, the content of secret clauses included in that agreement, there would doubtless be serious repercussions on the Spanish political scene and possibly on the course of events in the Western Sahara as well.

Morocco

After nearly a millennium of close association, Spain's relations with Morocco are unique, as well as the most important of all those it has with any country in Africa. Long duration, however, is not their only claim to distinction: periods of Moroccan predominance alternating with those of Spanish ascendancy, religious motivation with that of military conquest, national prestige with that of economic gain — all these have given variety and colour to a relationship that has left mutu-ally profound influences but neither victor nor vanquished.

Morocco's Role in Hispano-French Rivalry. In 1492 Spain ended the Moroccan occupation of southern and eastern Spain, but its acquisition of Ceuta and Melilla, also in the fifteenth century, and its later settle-ments along the Atlantic coast, prolonged its ties with northwest Africa. A brief war in 1859-60 ended with a Moroccan defeat by the Spaniards, and a further weakening of the cherifian realm in the late nineteenth century enabled the Spaniards to gain more ground at the expense of the sultan.[120] It was, however, the extension of French power in the region that, while reducing still further the sultan's domain, gave Spain a more formidable opponent in northwest Africa. Between 1904 and 1907 Spain and France were covert adversaries in the Sahara, although their respective areas of influence were delimited by the agreements of 3 October 1904 and 27 November 1912. Spanish policy toward the nomad desert tribes was the antithesis of that of France, in whose efforts to 'pacify' the Sahara Spain would have no part. That policy, moreover, by its very passivity, offered shelter and a base of operations in Spanish-controlled areas for the activities of anti-French tribesmen.

Events in the 1950s further aggravated Franco-Spanish tensions. Allal El Fassi, leader of the Istiqlal party that advocated independence and territorial integrity for Morocco, fanned the flames of Moroccan nationalism by campaigning for the restoration of *le Grand Maroc* in its historical boundaries.[121] According to his thesis, Greater Morocco was a vast area reaching as far south as the Senegal River and southeast to Timbuctu, and in the west it included Tindouf and the Saoura valley. As *le Grand Maroc*, thus defined, comprised all of Mauritania, Rio de Oro and southwestern Algeria, it naturally aroused strong resentment in France and Spain, not to mention opposition from Mauritanian and Algerian nationalists. Yet their common response to the Istiqlal chal-lenge did not lead to improved relations between France and Spain, notably between 1953 and 1957, for the Franco regime, in an apparent effort to assume championship of the Arab cause in Western Europe, backed the local nationalists seeking independence from France in the Maghreb. In 1953 Spain flatly refused to accept the replacement of Sultan Ben Youssef by Ben Arafa at Rabat, about which it had been given little prior notice. Because the exiled sultan was still regarded as the spiritual and temporal overlord of all Moroccans, prayers in the mosques of the Spanish protectorate continued to be said in the name of Ben Youssef.[122] The Algerian revolt against France that began the next year elicited Spanish support in international forums, if not in more tangible form locally.

This latent Franco-Spanish antagonism burst into the open as soon as Morocco gained independence in 1956, for Spain lost no time in retroceding the northern part of its protectorate to Morocco and in making agreements with the new government at Rabat that, in the eyes of Paris, were deliberately detrimental to French prestige. Even before the grant of independence, Spain issued a communiqué on 14 January 1956 promising to return all of its protectorate to Moroccan control and also to 'protect' its own interests there as well as 'Moroccans from the dangers of communism and other forms of subversion'.[123] In the joint Hispano-Moroccan declaration of 1956, Spain recognised Morocco's sovereignty, promised aid to Ben Youssef (who became King Mohammed V on 15 August 1957), and confirmed its respect for the territorial integrity of the cherifian empire.

Supplementary agreements signed at Madrid on 4 April 1956 laid the bases for new Hispano-Moroccan relations in the economic and, especially, cultural domains, for which Spain allotted ever-larger funds.[124] By February 1957 Spanish relations with Morocco had become so competitive with those of France that Rabat was able profitably to play the one off against the other. A case in point occurred that month when Morocco requested Spain to look after its interests in those Latin American countries where it had no separate diplomatic representation, and Rabat rejected a protest by France, which claimed it had been assigned that function in recent Franco-Moroccan agreements.[125] The nadir in Franco-Spanish relations *vis-à-vis* Morocco came in April 1957, when the Istiqlal indirectly proposed that Rabat grant Spain special economic concessions in Morocco itself in return for Spanish recognition of Moroccan rights over Rio de Oro, including those of using that territory as a base of operations against Mauritania.

Nevertheless, by mid-1957 Spain was beginning to have second thoughts about yielding to the escalating demands of the Istiqlal and its supporters, especially regarding the Ifni enclave. There Istiqlal agents were preparing a revolt against Spain by the indigenous Ait Ba Amrane tribesmen, in conjunction with an attack by Moroccan irregulars calling themselves the Army for Liberation of the Sahara (ALS). The latter were remnants of the army of liberation which had not been incorporated into the royal army after Moroccan independence, and which were now attacking French and Spanish military posts deep in the Western Sahara. Although the net cast by the Istiqlal leadership was so wide as to include Algerian territory, the ALS was content for the time being to give the FLN free rein there and to concentrate on Spanish territory and Mauritania.

Obviously the French and Spanish governments had every interest in joining forces against their common adversary, and at a secret meeting in San Sebastián in August 1957 the French and Spanish Foreign Ministers tried to lay the bases for co-operation in defence and economic development in the Western Sahara.[126] They failed to agree on boundaries between their respective dependencies and Morocco, or on Spanish participation in the mining enterprises at Fort Gouraud and Gara Djebilet, but they did succeed in solving their immediate practical problems. This meeting marked a turning-point in the history of the Sahara as well as in Franco-Spanish relations: it represented the final attempt by the colonial powers in that area to regulate its future solely among themselves,[127] and at the same time it opened the way for highly successful if temporary Franco-Spanish joint military operations there early in 1958.

Late in November 1957, while Mohammed V was on a state visit to the United States, the ALS attacked the Ifni enclave, driving the Spanish troops out of all but its town and port, where they were eventually rescued by paratroopers flown in from the Canary Islands. During the next few weeks the ALS carried out harassing operations in the frontier zone between Algeria, Mauritania and the Saquiet El Hamra, until the Franco-Spanish campaign called *Opération Ecouvillon* (mop-up) eliminated that threat in February-March 1958. The widespread bombing carried out during that campaign caused the first mass exodus of Saharan refugees, most of whom gravitated to Hassi Tantan and to Goulimine in southern Morocco.

Upon returning to Morocco, the king was faced with a hard choice between the risks of disavowing the Istiqlal's nationalistic demands and — if he showed himself incapable of controlling the ALS — those of alienating the United States and France, the countries most likely to promote Morocco's economic development. Furthermore, the activities of the ALS, if unchecked, might simply lead to another setback at Ifni or, worse, precipitate a Spanish naval bombardment of Agadir. The king resolved his dilemma by announcing his approval of the Istiqlal thesis and by also agreeing to negotiate with Spain regarding the return of the southern Spanish protectorate. In February 1958 the king went to Tagounit and Mhamid, which he called the gateway to the desert and where in widely publicised speeches he asserted Morocco's historic rights to the Western Sahara. He also saluted his 'faithful Sahraoui subjects' — that is, the assorted tribesmen of the area who 'wanted to return to their mother country'. This was the climax of a propaganda campaign which began in 1956 and in which petitions from, and personal appearances by, various tribal chiefs and Notables from the Western Sahara claiming Moroccan nationality were played up in the Istiqlal press. Furthermore, Radio Rabat began broadcasting a special programme to Morocco's 'Saharan brothers' in September 1958.

Spanish Concessions to Independent Morocco. The negotiations that culminated in the Cintra agreement of 1 April 1958 were the result of unpublicised compromises on the part of both Spain and Morocco in respect to the Spanish protectorate. Its southern or Tekna region — Cape Juby and the two towns of Hassi Tantan and Villa Bens — was restored to Morocco and renamed the province of Tarfaya. The Ifni enclave, however, although it remained formally under Spanish control, was in fact taken over by the royal Moroccan army, except for Sidi Ifni and its immediate environs, which continued to be occupied by Spanish troops.[128] To stress Spain's determination that the foregoing represented the ultimate concessions that it would make to Moroccan nationalist demands, Ifni was made a province of Spain, but this distinction between *de jure* and *de facto* ownership was considered irrelevant by the Moroccan hardliners. To them, the Spanish gesture did not spell generosity but only simple justice, and they regarded it as but the first step in recuperating a much vaster region.[129] Furthermore, in Moroccan eyes the Cintra agreement represented only the Spanish terms of a settlement, and the Foreign Minister, Ahmed Balafredj, made it clear that in signing the agreement his country was not bound to respect the line of 27°40' north latitude as its southern boundary.

These conflicting interpretations of the Cintra agreement of 1 April 1958 could not have been better illustrated than by the botched takeover of the new province of Tarfaya. A battalion of the royal army, commanded by Crown Prince Moulay Hassan, who was accompanied by four ministers, was stopped by the Spanish army when it tried to take a short cut through Spanish territory to reach Villa Bens from Goulimine. This caused a great outcry in the Moroccan press about Spanish 'duplicity' and an even stronger protest from the Madrid-based media against Morocco's breach of the Cintra agreement. Spanish grievances also included Morocco's nomination as governor of Tarfaya of Bou Aida, 'a dishonest merchant known for his anti-Spanish activities in Ifni', and of a Ma El Ainin sheikh, who had left a job with the Spanish government, to become his deputy.[130]

Inasmuch as neither side wanted to use force, the situation was

eventually smoothed over. Spain was above all eager that Ifni should
not serve as a precedent for a surrender of the *presidios* in any form.
Although Morocco was still eager to recuperate Rio de Oro and Saquiet
El Hamra, its efforts were now focused on trying to prevent Mauritania
from being recognised as a sovereign state and being granted a World
Bank loan to help finance the Miferma company's operations. By the
end of 1960, however, Morocco had lost out on both counts, and its
sense of frustration was further sharpened by the possibility that oil
might be found outside Moroccan boundaries in the Western Sahara,
prospecting permits in the area having been granted that year by Mauritania and Spain to several foreign companies.

Not only was no oil discovered in that area, but early in 1961 eleven
European prospectors were kidnapped at gunpoint by Moroccan irregulars, or 'patriots fighting for their country's freedom', as they were
described by the king when he handed the prospectors over, unharmed,
to their respective consuls in Rabat.[131] Spain, for its part, charged that
the kidnappers were members of the royal armed forces, and reinforced
its garrisons at El Aaiun and Smara, lest such attacks be the prelude to
a Moroccan campaign to take over the Spanish Sahara by force. Once
again, however, this failed to materialise for reasons that were, paradoxically, largely negative. Most important among them was the sudden
death of Mohammed V in February 1961, followed by the accession to
the throne of his little-known son, Hassan II; the slow disintegration of
the Casablanca bloc formed the month before by Mohammed V with
Ghana, Guinea, Mali, the UAR and the GPRA to rally African support
for Morocco's territorial claims; and above all the failure to discover
hydrocarbons in the Western Sahara. At the same time, Spanish policy
seemed to be taking international opinion more into account, judging
by the somewhat defensive tone adopted by Spain in submitting the
first report on its African dependencies in May 1961 to the UN Committee on Non-self-governing Territories. Three months later the new
Moroccan king displayed a strong hand at the helm when he formed a
National Resistance Bureau to exert control over those members of the
Army of Liberation who had not been absorbed into the royal armed
forces.

The year 1962 brought both renewed aggressiveness and defensive-
ness on the part of Morocco and Spain respectively, but ended on a
conciliatory note. In June relations became strained when Rabat claimed
and tried to blockade Ceuta and Melilla, unilaterally extended its territorial waters to twelve miles, and threatened punitive action against
trespassing Spanish fishermen. Spain indignantly rejected Moroccan

claims to its *presidios* and protected its fishermen by a display of naval strength in September. This show of force on both sides gave way to negotiations in the late autumn, and the Spanish and Moroccan Foreign Ministers exchanged visits which led to mutual concessions regarding trade and travel. In July 1963 the king's visit to Franco was marked by a display of Spanish cordiality, which observers attributed to the generalissimo's desire to establish friendly relations with a new Arab potentate. During those high-level visits, Morocco reportedly again turned down an offer said to have been first made in 1956, when Spain proposed ceding all its Saharan territories to Rabat in exchange for Moroccan recognition of Spanish sovereignty over the *presidios*.[132]

In the Maghreb the autumn months of 1963 were dominated by the inconclusive Algero-Moroccan *guerre des sables*. As regards Morocco, that brief war had the dual effect of deflecting Rabat's territorial ambitions from the southern to the Western Sahara and of making its leaders less prone to resort to armed force. Franco's manifest sympathy with Morocco in its trial of strength with Algeria derived in part from his vain hope that Rabat's recovery of Tindouf might divert its attention from the Spanish Sahara. In the UN General Assembly debates during October 1964 on the status of Gibraltar, Morocco reciprocated by supporting the Spanish thesis.[133]

The 'era of good feeling' from mid-1963 to mid-1965 in Hispano-Moroccan relations was notable for the priority given by both sides to economic over territorial issues, and perhaps significantly it coincided with Morocco's brief experiment in parliamentary democracy. In June a Spanish-Moroccan Friendship Association was formed in Madrid 'to prepare the Spanish public for the probable cession of its territory in Africa to Morocco'.[134] The Foreign Ministers of Spain and Morocco met again in July, negotiated a new trade agreement and laid the basis for technical co-operation and joint ventures. Trade between the two countries had not only grown appreciably since 1958 but was increasingly favourable to Morocco's exports of foodstuffs, phosphates and iron-ore. Although in the economic sphere most of the concessions were made by Spain, including permission to ship Moroccan oranges through that country to European markets, where they competed with Spanish oranges, Madrid stood firm on the issue of sovereignty over all its African dependencies. Franco's trump cards in dealing with Hassan were the surrender of Ifni, a share in developing the Bu Craa phosphate deposits, a nearby market for Moroccan exports and a source of technical expertise. In Spanish eyes, Morocco's assets were its conservatism and relative stability as a buffer state against inroads from revolutionary

Algeria, as well as a source of raw materials and of labour for the *presi-dios*, and as a model of Arab support for Franco's campaign to oust the British from Gibraltar. Inside Morocco, the king's failure to win any territorial concessions from Spain was so effectively exploited by the parties opposing the government that in mid-1965 Rabat forsook bi-lateral negotiations with Spain in favour of internationalising the Sahara issue. By representing the Western Sahara's future as the penultimate stage in the decolonisation of Africa by a European power, Rabat was guaranteed the votes of a majority in the UN General Assembly and the unanimous support of the OAU.

In the General Assembly of 1965-6, the question of Spain's African territories and the claims against them were for the first time linked together on its agenda. But in the resolution of 16 December asking Spain to take the steps required to decolonise its African territories, no choice was made between the claims of Mauritania and those of Morocco. Because of Madrid's failure to make any significant headway in carrying out that resolution during the next nine months, Morocco's attitude hardened, especially as Mauritania was then pressing its case and American interests were becoming involved in the Bu Craa mining operations. In October 1966, therefore, Morocco's delegate to the UN demanded that Spain withdraw its troops and administrators from the Sahara and permit the return there of Sahraoui refugees living in neigh-bouring countries. This was followed the next month by the OAU's in-sistence on Spain's withdrawal, and by a more forceful General Assembly resolution on 20 December urging Spain to acknowledge – and take steps to implement – the Sahraouis' right to self-government.[135] As time seemed no longer to be on Spain's side, Madrid accepted the principle of Sahraoui self-determination, but not that of independence or Spain's total withdrawal, 'lest the western Sahara become a *casus belli* between Mauritania and Morocco'.[136]

Because a referendum was to be the means by which the Sahraouis were to choose their future status, it behoved both Spain and Morocco to elicit, or at least offer, evidence of the maximum tribal support. This was, of course, a game at which all the contestants could play, and it was the main stimulus for the formation of such nominally spontaneous movements as the Morehob, PUNS, FLU and others.[137] On the Spanish side, creating the *yemaa* was Madrid's most generous gesture thus far to the principle of Sahraoui representative government. Morocco, for its part, stepped up the parade of Sahraoui chiefs coming to Rabat to swear allegiance to the king, and in August introduced a radio programme in Arabic and Spanish beamed exclusively to the Western Saharans. In

April 1967 the installation of the former head of Morocco's national-security police as the governor of Tarfaya (which at the same time was made a free-trade zone), as well as the king's sharper insistence on the 'restoration' of Ifni in his speech from the throne, were not unrelated to his reminder that the 'liberation' of Tarfaya had been preceded by the threat to use force.[138]

By mid-summer of 1967 Madrid had decided to surrender Ifni to Morocco and, in retrospect, it is hard to understand why Spain had not done so earlier, for by this time Ifni had lost most of its value as a bargaining counter. With the development of missiles, Ifni no longer had the same strategic importance for defending the Canaries, and it had no economic assets beyond the revenues derived from a small fish catch and the issuance of postage stamps and of remittance payments to their families by the Spanish soldiers and officials stationed there. It is equally difficult to grasp why the 40,000 or so impoverished members of the Ait Ba Amran confederation, who barely survived in the enclave by small-scale farming, fishing and animal husbandry, should choose to forgo the benefits they derived from Spanish rule. To be sure, Spain had done little or nothing to develop the enclave economically, but the tribesmen did receive free medical care and were exempt from taxation. Moreover, they had occasional employment on public works at relatively high wages, a modest share in the municipal government, and fairly ready access to Morocco, to which from one-third to one-half of the Ba Amran tribesmen seasonally migrated each year.[139] The only publicised Ba Amran grievances were the requirement that they carry an identity card denoting the bearer's Spanish nationality, and 'excessive fines' for crossing the Moroccan frontier without official permission.[140]

Except for the loss of what were largely sinecures for some 5,000 resident Spaniards and Canary Islanders, Spain had more to gain than to lose by the treaty signed at Fez on 4 January 1969 which restored Ifni to Morocco. Spain was thereby relieved of the burden of subsidising that enclave, gained the right to fish in Moroccan territorial waters and earned some goodwill in the Arab world, especially as relinquishment of Ifni coincided with the grant of independence to Spanish Guinea. On the other hand, while the treaty also guaranteed Morocco's continued support of Spain on the Gibraltar issue, it did no more than placate Rabat and only temporarily deflected Moroccan irredentism from the *presidios* to the more pressing question as to which country would control the output of the Bu Craa mines. The contrast between the increasingly friendly economic relations between Spain and Morocco on the one hand and, on the other, the stiffening of their respective stands concerning sovereignty over the *presidios* and the Spanish Sahara in the period between 1963 and 1970, suggests that the differences be-tween the two countries were less acute than official statements and press reports indicated. Their long historical associations and proximity, their common fear of revolutionary socialism, and their partially com-plementary economies were conducive to a *modus vivendi* which, how-ever, neither public opinion nor the military establishment in either Spain or Morocco was as yet willing to accept.

An example of the lengths to which Madrid was willing to go with-out legal sanction to please Rabat occurred in February 1970 when Spain repatriated to Morocco two members of the major opposition party, the UNFP,[141] who were then in Spanish jails, although there existed no extradition treaty between the two governments. As even this conciliatory gesture failed to silence or reduce Morocco's strident territorial demands, Foreign Minister Lopez Bravo, on his first official visit to Rabat in six years, brought with him in June 1970 a tempting offer for the joint Hispano-Moroccan exploitation of the Bu Craa de-posits. This, too, Morocco rejected, but this time its intransigence was caused by a drastic change in its relations with Mauritania and Algeria, as well as by a certain disillusionment with Spain, which had recently imposed a blockade on Gibraltar. Apparently the king had been led by some Spanish leaders to believe that the problem of the *presidios* would be settled to his satisfaction once the fate of Gibraltar had been decided in Madrid's favour.[142]

Hassan Mobilises International Pressure on Madrid. Although Boumed-iene was instrumental in bringing Daddah and Hassan together in 1969, a reconciliation between them would have been impossible had not the king by then become convinced that he could not conquer and keep all of the Western Sahara. Nor would the Tlemcen agreement with Algeria[143] have been reached on 27 May 1970 if Hassan had not come to believe that Algerian aid was indispensable to persuading Spain to withdraw peaceably from the western desert, even at the price of post-poning the settlement of his claims to Tindouf and the Saoura. Thus when they first met together at Nouadhibou on 14 September, the three heads of state quickly set up a committee[144] to co-ordinate their strategy for a trilateral diplomatic offensive in the UN General Assembly session beginning that month, with the aim of forcing Spain to comply with that body's resolution of December 1965 — that is, to hold a referendum under international auspices in the Spanish Sahara. By then Madrid had also accepted the necessity of formally consulting the Sahraouis about their future status, and set February 1971 as the time for so doing. However, Madrid laid down the conditions that the referendum be held under Spanish auspices, that the electorate be limited largely to sedentary tribesmen in Spanish territory, and that the choice offered them be restricted to independence under Spanish tutelage or the status quo.[145]

Because Spain subsequently continued to evade complying with the UN and OAU resolutions despite prodding by Algeria, Morocco and Mauritania during this period, Rabat largely by default won a relatively free hand to deal with Spain bilaterally. Thus Morocco maintained political pressure on Spain concurrently with the development of increasingly close economic and cultural relations. Moroccan students were welcomed in Spanish universities, a permanent committee for economic co-operation was set up in March 1971, and three months later a new agreement on trade, tourism and industry was reached, in which a joint venture in fishing figured prominently. Simultaneously with these developments, and to all appearances unrelated to them, Moroccan and Mauritanian claims to the Spanish Sahara were put forward more strongly than ever in the media and in international forums, and Spain remained unyielding on the sovereignty issue and on safeguarding its investments at Bu Craa. Both parties ignored the most significant new element that would eventually break the current stalemate — the rising power of the Polisario Front. The outbreak at El Aaiun on 17 June 1970 was the first public manifestation of that Sahraoui force, which, however, would take three more years to gain significant organisational and military strength.

In that interval, the only sign of life given by the tripartite allies as such was the meeting of the co-ordinating committee in January 1972 at Algiers. Its composition had changed and its size was reduced, but its concrete accomplishments were no greater than those of the Nouadibou conference to which it owed its existence, because the three member governments still could agree on no course of action beyond easing Spain out of the Western Sahara. In pressing for an internationally supervised referendum, each head of state seemed to believe that the Sahraouis would vote in accordance with his government's wishes. Of the three member countries, only Morocco had vital interests at stake in the Spanish Sahara — primarily economic ones, but those of national prestige as well. The abortive Moroccan *coups d'état* against the monarchy in 1971 and 1972, and the king's failure in the latter year to wrest Tindouf from Algeria by negotiation, reinforced the determination of Hassan — then also president of the OAU — to win an outstanding victory in the Spanish Sahara. For every reason, the king could not afford to risk the referendum's being determined by those Sahraouis who had benefited by Spanish rule and might therefore vote for either autonomy under Spanish guidance or a nominal independence that would primarily benefit Algeria. So Rabat, prodded by the Istiqlal, insisted on the enfranchisement of the thousands of Sahraoui refugees living in southern Morocco and on eliminating independence as a choice open to Sahraoui voters in the forthcoming referendum.

In such an electoral popularity contest, Nouakchott seemed to be counting on the Sahraouis' overriding desire to be reunited with their tribal relatives now separated from them by the Hispano-Mauritanian frontier, but to most foreign observers it seemed unlikely that the Sahraouis would choose to join so poor a country as Mauritania. Subsequently, Daddah somewhat diffidently proposed dividing the Spanish Sahara so that Mauritania could take Rio de Oro, in the belief that half a loaf was better than none. Boumediene, for his part, was strongly opposed to any partition of the Spanish territory that might isolate it from Algerian influence and block access to the Atlantic for Gara Djebilet's iron-ore. In any case, he could not imagine that any Sahraouis, inside or outside the Spanish area, would choose continued association with a European colonial power over independence at no matter what price. Finally Spain, which by now had come to prefer a nominal independence for its Sahara province as the least distasteful of the possible solutions, found itself more aligned with Algeria (on whose hydrocarbon exports it had come to rely heavily) than with Mauritania or Morocco.

With minor variations, 1973 brought a repetition of the pattern of growing Moroccan intransigence *vis-à-vis* Spain in regard to its sovereign rights on land and on sea, followed by a reinforcement of their bilateral economic relations.[146] Much the same could be said of Madrid's offer to hold a referendum in its Saharan province on the issue of internal autonomy, the novelty in this instance consisting of Madrid's acting as the spokesman for what purported to be a proposal made by the *yemaa*. This stratagem gave Rabat the chance to denounce as simply a modified form of colonialism the embryonic structure of representative government that Madrid had installed in the Sahara. It also prompted Mauritania to revive the tripartite alliance by convening a conference of its foreign ministers at Nouakchott on 8 May to prepare for a meeting of the three heads of state at Agadir on 23 July. Because of the contradictions between their ultimate objectives, this second summit meeting, like the first, was productive of little more than rhetoric.

Nevertheless, two elements that entered the picture in early 1973 did exert a decisive influence on the events of 1974-5. These were the formal constitution of the Polisario Front and the attempts made by both Spain and Morocco to widen the bases of their external support. Whereas in the spring of 1973 Madrid had shown exemplary patience in the face of Morocco's constant harassment of Spanish fishermen and of its extension of Moroccan territorial waters to 70 nautical miles, not to mention Rabat's bickering over payments to evicted landowners in the former Spanish protectorate, Madrid's determination to maintain its sovereignty in the Sahara was fast undermined by the violence of the Polisario's attacks on Spanish lives and property. The second new element was the appeals openly made to the United States and the Soviet Union by Moroccans for support against Spanish colonialism in northwest Africa. It was quite logical for Rabat to solicit Washington's pressure on Madrid to induce Spain to evacuate the Sahara, but it was a new departure that moves should be made, first by Spain and then by Morocco, to draw the major communist powers into the Saharan arena. Within two days after Franco had surprisingly given full diplomatic recognition to the Peking government, King Hassan successfully appealed to Moscow for moral support against Spain in northwest Africa.[147] Neither of those moves, however, had more than a transient bearing on the situation, and it was Morocco's despatch of troops to fight Israel in October 1973 that earned the king more enduring gratitude from Arab radicals and conservatives alike. In its relations with the Arabs, Spain could cite only its largely negative record of being the one Western European power never to have extended formal recognition to the Jewish state.

The year 1974 opened propitiously for Hispano-Moroccan relations with a settlement of their long and bitter fishing dispute, and a few months later the repatriation of many Spaniards who had been living in the former Spanish protectorate reduced the litigation resulting from expropriation of their property and 'Moroccanisation' of their activities.[148] In May the political feud between the two countries was revived by a pamphlet entitled 'The Moroccan Western Sahara', probably inspired by the Palace but written by the Communist Party leader, Ali Yata, who had now become acceptable to the government as head of the Parti du Progrès et du Socialisme (PPS). Moved by the ferment developing in the former Portuguese colonies, the author called for the recruitment in Morocco of volunteers who could liberate both the *presidios* and the Western Sahara.

This was the opening gun of an official campaign for a rapid solution of the Saharan problem, into which a sense of urgency had been injected by the sharp rise in the price of phosphates, and in which recourse to military means had not been ruled out. In June the death of Allal El Fassi, the oldest and most ardent champion of Greater Morocco, instead of damping down the fire added fuel to the flame. Furthermore, the attendance of President Bourguiba of Tunisia at the memorial service in Allal's honour was interpreted in Rabat as a significant change of front on the part of a leader who had been an opponent of Moroccan irredentism since 1960.[149] At the end of that month the formal opening of a road from Ifni to Tiznit offered a well-publicised opportunity for Sahraoui tribesmen to demonstrate their loyalty to King Hassan.

Despite their record of immobility, it was the Spaniards who were to trigger the militant phase of the long-simmering Hispano-Moroccan dispute over sovereignty in the Sahara. On 3 July 1974 Spain informed the ambassadors of Morocco, Algeria and Mauritania at Madrid that their governments should expect a change soon in the status of the Sahara province, which was to be made in response to the *yemaa*'s request for an acceleration of the procedures leading to internal autonomy, in accordance with the UN resolutions. To this the king promptly replied in a message to Franco, which he himself publicised on 8 July in a broadcast to the nation. In it, Hassan disclosed that when he met Franco in 1970 he had offered Spain the temporary use of Villa Cisneros and El Aaiun as military bases for defence of the Canary Islands in return for Spain's acknowledgement of Morocco's sovereignty over the entire province. To this and to a concurrent proposal to extract and sell the output from mineral deposits on land and offshore on a co-operative basis, the king had received no reply or indeed any encouragement to work toward a solution based on compromise.[150] In conclusion, he said, Morocco would still prefer to remain on friendly terms with Spain but would not hesitate to use force, if necessary, should Madrid try to set up a puppet state in the Sahara. Foremost among the king's unexpressed fears of such an outcome were that it would give Algeria an opportunity to extend its hegemony over the Western Sahara, as well as an opening to the Sahraoui leaders who had already announced their intention of reclaiming the ancestral lands which they alleged had been taken from them by their neighbours.

Obviously, Hassan's broadcast was intended primarily to win support at home and abroad for a policy that might culminate in armed conflict. After warning his listeners against being taken in by Madrid's apparent compliance with the UN's successive resolutions, the king also used the occasion to defend himself against accusations made by domestic and foreign foes alike. He denied that he was using the Sahara issue to divert his political opponents from their just grievances against his regime or to enhance his personal power by foreign conquests. And it was precisely the king's 'premeditated annexationist ambitions' that was charged by Madrid against Hassan in a letter addressed to Kurt Waldheim on 13 July, wherein the UN secretary general was reminded that Morocco's representative in that body had consistently voted in favour of a referendum by the Sahraouis on their future status. On 20 August Spain announced that it would hold that referendum early in 1975, despite — or perhaps because of — the presence in Madrid during the five preceding days of Morocco's premier and its foreign minister. The outcome of this hasty visitation was not publicised, nor was the gist of the talks that went on at about the same time between the king and Daddah. Probably all these developments contributed to some degree to the king's decision, announced on 24 August, that Morocco would reject a referendum if independence was to be one of the options offered to the Sahraouis. By implication, the king warned Mauritania that this would be that country's last chance to jump on the Moroccan bandwagon.

Rabat was the centre of intense diplomatic activity in the late summer of 1974, when Hassan initiated a crash campaign to win world support for the Moroccan cause. On both the domestic and the international front the timing for such a campaign appeared to be favourable. The break-up of Portugal's African empire made Spain even more conspicuous than in the past as European imperialism's sole survivor in west Africa. And at the next UN General Assembly session that began in September, Morocco did not fail to remind Spain that in 1973 it had abstained from voting the resolution recalling the UN's recommendations for a decolonisation of the Western Sahara. To carry Morocco's case to world capitals, the king lined up some 50 emissaries, among whom were such erstwhile domestic opponents as Ali Yata and Abderraham Bouabid, leaders of the PPS and the UNFP respectively. Indeed, foreign observers of the Moroccan scene were surprised to see how many of the king's former sworn enemies now flocked to his standard, once it had been raised on behalf of a highly nationalistic, if non-ideological, cause. To be sure, before doing so they had exacted their pound of flesh, in this instance a renewed pledge by the king to restore parliamentary government and to hold elections — a pledge that Hassan would not be allowed this time to ignore.

On the domestic scene, the unknown quantity was the loyalty of the army, many of whose top-ranking officers had been liquidated after their abortive attempts at regicide in 1971 and 1972. To restore the army's shaken morale, an exceptionally warm welcome was accorded in June to the troops returning from the Syrian front. In August the king named the army's controversial strongman, Col. Ahmed Dlimi, as governor of Tarfaya province, thus making him the only Moroccan official to exercise both civilian and military authority in what was an especially sensitive region.[151] This appointment, followed by the calling up of Moroccan reservists and military doctors, prompted a review of Spanish troops in the Sahara province by Spain's defence minister — who reconfirmed his government's pledge to defend the territory — now referred to as the Western Sahara and no longer as a province of Spain.[152] King Hassan then felt constrained to warn 'potential trouble-makers' in a speech delivered soon thereafter at Agadir to keep their hands off the Western Sahara. The practice of one-upmanship by both the major parties to the dispute not only contributed to heightening the tension between them but also implied a belief (or assumption) on the part of the king in the wholehearted support of the Arabo-African-Asian Muslim world, which he did not then have.

So long as Morocco's policy had been oriented exclusively to elimi-nating Spanish colonialism, Hassan received the unconditional backing of the Third World, the USSR and liberal opinion elsewhere. Less generally acceptable, however, was his more recent contention that the Western Sahara was historically, geographically, ethnically, linguistically and politically an integral part of the Moroccan nation. Moreover, his warn-ing to treat those unwilling to subscribe to that thesis as 'dishonest' or as 'avowed enemies' of Morocco was hardly endearing.[153] Mauritania, in particular, held sharply differing views, and to give them wide publicity Daddah sent his own spokesmen to world capitals, although not on so lavish a scale as had Hassan. As for Algeria, Boumediene at that time was still upholding Mauritania's claims, and although he did not publicly take issue with the king, the Algerian president reiterated his customary denial of territorial ambitions and his support for the 'just cause of an Arab nation seeking to free itself from Spain'. Obviously, the tripartite alliance had now simply fallen apart.

The army's dubious loyalty, the lukewarm reception given to Moroc-co's envoys around the world, Mauritania's obstinacy in maintaining its claims and the ambiguity of Algeria's attitude — all gave the king pause. Although his domestic political foes had been transformed almost over-night into loyal subjects, the price that he had had to pay for this in-dispensable support was very high in terms of his future authority. Another *guerre des sables* — and Morocco was far better prepared for it in 1975 than in 1963 — was what his military command had been clamouring for, but might not a clear-cut victory in the desert tempt its officers to try staging another *coup d'état*? — presumably with a greater chance of success than before.

Because of the principles professed by all the governments concerned in the Saharan question, Morocco realised that Mauritania's claim had to be defused, for on historical, geographical, ethnic and linguistic — but not political — grounds the evidence scarcely supported the thesis defended by Rabat. As regards Mauritania, this difficulty was resolved reportedly by a secret deal between the king and Daddah in October 1974, whereby Mauritania would be allotted Rio de Oro and a share in the output of Bu Craa in return for relinquishing its claim to Saquiet El Hamra. Obviously this arrangement required not only Spain's consent but also its withdrawal from the Sahara before carrying out the long-discussed referendum.

In the bilateral agreement reached between Mauritania and Morocco no provision apparently was made for giving Algeria any share in the spoils, but as Boumediene had expressed no territorial demands it was hoped that he would accept the *fait accompli* and be satisfied with the elimination of Spain from the Western Sahara. Nor was any notice seemingly taken of the goals announced by the Polisario Front, which had yet to show itself as a force to be reckoned with. As matters worked out, the Polisario's attacks on Spanish strongholds were highly effective in persuading the Spaniards to leave the Western Sahara in short order, and the Polisario's teaming up with Algeria — the other contestant left out in the cold — threatened to make a shambles of the structure that Hassan had so carefully contrived. Even without taking the last-mentioned factors into account, so great and incalculable were the risks, so delicate were the negotiations involved to carry out his plan, and so eager was the king to avoid an armed conflict with the superior Spanish forces, that he decided to play for time. This he did by proposing in September that the dispute over the Spanish Sahara be referred to the International Court at The Hague. Although at first blush this move seemed decidedly anticlimactic, by the year's end it had been approved by Spain, Mauritania, Algeria and the UN General Assembly, either because they, too, wanted a breathing spell or because they preferred any solution other than that of armed force, towards which Moroccan policy until then had seemed to be heading.

Ideologically speaking, none of the major parties to the Saharan dispute could boast a simon-pure record of consistency. Although all of them officially favoured the self-determination of peoples and had voted accordingly in the UN, none of them held out for a referendum in the Western Sahara before committing themselves to one or another of the groups or governments that claimed to represent the will of the

Sahraouis. Morocco was probably the most, and Algeria the least, in-consistent of them all, supporting or rejecting the principle of self-determination of peoples according to the shifting winds of national self-interest, such as it was perceived by their leaders at a given time.

Until the end of Spanish rule in the Sahara, Daddah favoured self-determination for the population of Rio de Oro, convinced that its tribes would vote to merge with Mauritania, but he finally took his slice of the pie rather than let Morocco swallow it all. Spain, like Morocco and Algeria, drew a distinction between legitimacy as defined by terri-torial integrity and legitimacy as determined by popular vote in the contested area. The Spaniards accepted the latter principle wherever they formed a numerical majority as in the *presidios*, but refused to acknow-ledge the validity of Britain's 1967 plebiscite in Gibraltar, the strategic promontory that Madrid regarded as part of Spain's national heritage. Similarly, Algeria supported Morocco wholeheartedly in the latter's insistence on taking over the *presidios* and opted for a referendum in the Spanish Sahara, but never considered applying that principle to the Tindouf area. Indeed, a proposal to hold a referendum in the Algerian Sahara put forth by the French government during the Evian negotia-tions in the early 1960s was vigorously opposed by the GPRA, and its refusal was supported by Morocco.[154]

International Opinion and the World Court

During the nine and a half months preceding the World Court's advisory opinion in October 1975, which was recognised — by all the parties des-cribed as either 'interested' or 'concerned' in the future of the Spanish Sahara — as a watershed in the history of that region, Morocco stepped up its campaign against Spain in Africa.[155] In the press and in radio broadcasts, as well as at the UN, Rabat challenged Madrid's rights to fish and to prospect for oil and other minerals in the waters east of the Canary Islands and, above all, to exercise sovereign rights over the *presidios*. In response, Spain felt constrained to put on another display of naval strength offshore from Ceuta and Melilla, as well as to post Foreign Legionnaires along the conveyor belt from Bu Craa to the sea to protect it against sabotage. Morocco, for its part, sent 17,000 troops, or about one-third of its ground forces, to points along its southern fron-tier. These developments indicated the tension between the two main protagonists in the Western Sahara when a fact-finding mission of the UN Committee on Decolonisation arrived at El Aaiun on 12 May, to be greeted by cheers alternating with violent anti-Spanish demonstrations on the part of a third and relatively new belligerent, the Polisario Front.

In conformity with the UN General Assembly resolution of 5 December 1974, the secretary general, Kurt Waldheim, had appointed Ambassador Simeon Ake of the Ivory Coast as leader of a three-member mission sent to ascertain on the spot the current state of Spanish Saharan affairs. In short order, the mission visited Madrid (three times), Rabat, Nouakchott, Algiers and even Paris, as well as refugee camps in southern Morocco and in the Tindouf region of Algeria. Early in their itinerary, the mission's members were clearly impressed by the Polisario's organised strength, representativeness and fervent advocacy of independence, and the seal of their approval was probably of greater significance than the report favouring self-determination for the Sahraouis which they submitted to the General Assembly in October. Not only did the mission's favourable reaction give the Polisario publicity and the semi-official credentials that it had theretofore lacked, but it may well have contributed to Spain's decision on 23 May to abandon the area as soon as was feasible.[156] Indeed, the mission's report to the General Assembly simply corroborated − without the legal substructure − the opinion expressed at about the same time by the World Court, which had a far greater impact as a catalyst on the evolution of events in the Western Sahara.

The court had agreed on 9 January 1975 to submit an advisory opinion on certain questions based on the General Assembly resolution of 14 December 1974, which, as before, asserted the right of colonial peoples to self-determination. Was the Western Sahara ownerless (*terra nullius*) prior to the Spanish occupation? What bonds, if any, existed between it and Mauritania and it and Morocco? If the answer to those questions was in the affirmative, would this justify modifying the UN demand that the Sahraouis be consulted about their future? And if the answer was negative, what were the judicial ties between the Western Sahara, the kingdom of Morocco, and the area now called 'Mauritania'? In the preliminary public hearings, in which all four countries pleaded their case, two basic issues arose. One concerned the rejection of Mauritania's plea that an *ad hoc* judge be named, on the ground that no juridical dispute existed between it and Spain, whereas a similar request by Morocco was granted largely to provide a counterbalance to the Spaniard who was one of the court's 16 judges sitting on the case. The second issue, which was raised by Madrid, concerned the court's competence to deal with a case that was not exclusively judicial in character. Although this objection was overruled by the court, Spain raised it again in August when it proposed that a conference of the four governments involved be convened to settle the question, but this once more proved unacceptable to the court and to both Morocco and Mauritania.[157]

The Case for Each Party to Dispute. Not surprisingly, Morocco's case rested mainly on historical evidence of the sultan's sovereignty over the Western Sahara, in part as confirmed by international law, and to a lesser degree because of ethnic and cultural affinities between the Moroccans and the Sahraouis, notably the Tekna. In arguments set forth at The Hague, many acts of allegiance by Sahraoui chiefs were cited, especially that of the *caid* of El Aaiun at the end of 1974, as well as the military and tax-collecting expeditions sent by past sultans to defend the Sahraouis at their request against Spanish and French encroachments.[158] The Act of Algeciras of 7 April 1906 recognising the sovereignty of the sultan and the integrity of his state in west Africa, which was signed by 13 countries, had greater international validity than did the later Franco-Spanish bilateral treaties that divided the area between them. In any case, so the Moroccan argument ran, Spain in recognising Moroccan independence in 1956 had formally acknowledged the unity of the Moroccan kingdom, of which Madrid gave further proof by retroceding Tarfaya and Ifni to Rabat. Initially, Morocco had agreed to a referendum of the Sahraoui people, feeling certain that they would choose to return to their motherland when the only alternative was to remain colonial subjects. Spain, however, by its prolonged procrastination, had either created or permitted to develop an ersatz national movement, which Algeria was now supporting instead of helping Morocco to liberate the Western Sahara from Spain and to build a united Maghreb. Mauritania, on the other hand, was collaborating with Morocco, and in accordance with UN objectives it was seeking a solution to the Western Saharan problem by negotiating with Spain as the power administering that area.

During the Hague court debates between 25 June and 30 July, the long-standing contradictions between the goals set by Rabat and Nouakchott almost miraculously disappeared, for the former was restricting its claims to Saquiet El Hamra and the latter to Rio de Oro. Yet there was a fundamental difference in the approach of the two governments to the basic problem. Whereas Morocco stressed mainly territorial integrity, Mauritania continued to emphasise the wishes and the cultural unity of the Sahraoui and Moorish tribesmen. Nouakchott argued that the desert, by imposing a common way of life on its inhabitants, was responsible for the development of similar customs and institutions in the area known formerly as Chinguitt. Mauritania contended also that this had made them one people, and that only the advent of European colonisation had prevented that people from forming a nation. Chinguitt could not be properly termed *terra nullius* for, although it had had no central government, it had been governed by local emirs, with one of whom – the emir of Adrar – Spain had negotiated in 1886.

The Algerian argument inevitably ran counter to that of Morocco, but in general did not take serious issue with that of Mauritania, and it treated the Spaniards fairly gently. Algiers held that the sultans' forays into the desert had been infrequent and inconclusive because the Alaouite dynasty had never firmly established its authority over the desert tribes. After chiding Rabat for reneging on its early advocacy of a referendum in the Sahara, the Algerians vaunted the purity of their own motives in insisting on Sahraoui self-determination. They denied any interest in acquiring a Saharan port for Gara Djebilet's iron exports, inasmuch as under Algeria's current development plan the ore was to be shipped by rail to Mostaganem to promote the industrialisation of that area. Algeria's main concern, its spokesman maintained, was to insure that the Western Sahara should again become a free Arab and Muslim entity, whereas the aim of the king of Morocco was to contain if not to destroy the Algerian revolution.

In the eyes of Boumediene, highly conscious of his role as champion of revolutionary Africa, Spanish colonialism must be extirpated as an evil compared with which other considerations were subsidiary. As his conviction grew that Morocco and Mauritania had secretly agreed to divide the Spanish Sahara between them, Boumediene's concern for that area's future became more practical and less theoretical. Although his foreign minister, Abdelaziz Bouteflika, during a visit to Rabat on 2-4 July 1975, reportedly expressed his satisfaction with the understanding reached between Morocco and Mauritania, Algeria's arguments voiced at The Hague became increasingly an indictment of Moroccan duplicity and greed in the Western Sahara. Similarly, Morocco's defence of its own policy turned more and more into an arraignment of Algeria's motivation in supporting the Polisario Front as a means of establishing its hegemony over all the Maghreb. In the course of the debates at The Hague, old wounds were reopened on both sides. Morocco accused Algeria of ingratitude for the services Rabat had rendered the FLN during the Algerian revolt, to which Algiers responded by denying any debt to its neighbours and even reproaching them for having failed to take up arms on behalf of Algerian independence.

Spain was the last of the governments to be heard by the International Court judges. After again expressing his country's doubts as to the

court's competence in this matter, Spain's advocate argued that before
the Spanish occupation the Western Sahara had been *terra nullius*, never
subject to either Morocco or Mauritania but inhabited by politically
independent tribes. Now, because of the violence perpetrated by both
the guerrillas and the Moroccan army, Spain had already given notice
that it might have to leave the area precipitately should the situation
get beyond its control.

The Court's Ambiguous Opinion. The lengthy and enigmatic opinion
delivered by the court on 16 October 1975 was a masterpiece of pru-
dence and compromise, designed to give some satisfaction to each of
the contestants but a decisive endorsement to none of them.[159] In addition, it reflected differences of opinion among the judges, nine of whom
made individual statements and one of whom expressed overall dissent.
By 14 votes to two, the court decided that before the Spaniards came
the territory had had juridical ties with the kingdom of Morocco, and by
15 to one that it had also had ties, albeit of a tribal and not a territorial
nature, with the Moors living in what is now Mauritania. Only in regard
to the answers to two questions were the judges unanimous. These were
that prior to Spanish colonisation the area had not been *terra nullius*,
and that no evidence had been offered that would justify the area's
annexation by neighbouring powers or a further delay in carrying out
the UN resolutions on the right of its peoples to self-determination.
As part of the UN's peacekeeping apparatus, the court had succeeded
admirably in temporarily defusing an emotion-charged issue, but all the
time, energy and talent expended to that end did nothing to settle the
fate of the region at stake.

   If the king's purpose in referring the Sahara dispute to the Hague
court had been to gain time in which to prepare for a rapid annexation
of the Saquiet El Hamra, he succeeded. If, on the other hand, he had
hoped that the court would clearly confirm Morocco's sovereignty over
the Spanish Sahara and thereby liberate the Morocco-Mauritania tandem
from further subjection to UN resolutions recommending a referendum,
he failed, largely because he had underestimated the tenacity of the
Polisario and its Algerian backers. In any case, the reaction of all the
parties involved in the dispute was immediate and various, although
publicly the spokesman for each of the contestants presented the court's
opinion as a victory for his country's thesis.

The Green March. The Spanish and Algerian governments seemed
genuinely satisfied with the outcome as the best possible under the

circumstances, and Mauritania accepted it, although with some misgivings. Rabat, insisting that the court had vindicated its claim under the Islamic law to sovereignty over the Western Sahara, announced immediately that it would organise a people's pacific march of 350,000 unarmed volunteers to the Western Sahara. To this appeal, made on the same day as the court's opinion became known, the response was overwhelming[160] on the part of the population and the opposition parties alike. The fact that special trains and trucks were immediately available to carry the thousands of volunteers to Tarfaya, where the march was to begin, showed a long and meticulous preparation for this event, and the king himself moved first to Marrakech and then to Agadir so as to supervise personally the start of what he named the Green March.[161] As commander of the faithful, the king on 23 October sent greetings to his loyal Sahraoui subjects, to whom he also promised a general amnesty, and to the 50,000 or so volunteers already assembled at Tarfaya. As talks were going on at the same time between the Moroccan and Spanish Foreign Ministers, the date for the start of the Green March was postponed, reportedly until an agreement was reached between the two countries as to their joint development of the Bu Craa deposits.

At the UN General Assembly being held at that time, and also at Madrid, this was a period of intense diplomatic activity related to the Spanish Sahara, although in New York it was overshadowed by the problem of Angola and in Spain by the death-watch on Franco. As soon as Hassan had announced his Green March, Madrid had asked the UN Security Council to prevent this invasion of its Saharan province, and in the meantime bent every effort to dissuade the king from undertaking it. Hassan agreed to delay the march until the end of October, by which date he had received assurances of support from eleven countries of the Arab League and the general secretariat of the Islamic Conference. Concurrently, Kurt Waldheim engaged in some shuttle diplomacy between Madrid, Algiers, Nouakchott and Rabat; the French Secretary of State for Foreign Affairs paid a hasty visit to the Moroccan capital; and at Nouakchott the Moroccan Foreign Minister conferred with his Mauritanian counterpart.

Undoubtedly the most significant move in all this beehive activity was the delivery by the Algerian Interior Minister of a message from Boumediene to the Spanish government on 29-30 October, to which was attributed the suspension on the following day of negotiations that had been going on between Spain, Morocco and Mauritania. Presumably this was due to a threat made by Boumediene to cut off the flow of Algerian oil and gas to Spain, and perhaps also to default on repayment of the 1975 Spanish loan to Algeria of some 2,800 million pesetas. On 21 November Prince Juan Carlos made a surprise visit to the Spanish armed forces stationed in the Sahara, during which he spoke strongly in favour of a referendum there and denounced Morocco's Green March. Observers speculated about whether these statements were made out of personal conviction, or to win favour with the army officers, or to mislead Boumediene, but they may also simply have reflected the indecision of a government in disarray over the uncertain prospects following the Caudillo's imminent demise. In any case, by 3 November negotiations had been resumed between the Spaniards and Moroccans, and Algeria had sent troop reinforcements to the posts along the Moroccan frontier.

In the meantime, at Tarfaya, water was running short, there was some danger of an epidemic breaking out among the several hundred thousand recent arrivals, and the authorities were beginning to fear that they might not be able to control the volunteers, increasingly impatient at the protracted delays in receiving their marching orders.[162] These were finally given on 6 November by the king, who showed himself undeterred by Algerian threats and the Security Council's request to cease and desist. The marchers were to be accompanied by 20,000 troops of the royal army for their 'protection' in an area where the Polisario was fighting the FLU to take over the posts and settlements being abandoned by Spanish garrisons. Late on 7 November, the first contingent of marchers arrived opposite the line still held by the Spanish army, which had withdrawn 20 kilometres to the west of the Saquiet-Moroccan frontier so as to avoid a confrontation with unarmed civilians, and there they waited to be joined by another contingent of marchers the next day.

The marchers were a motley and picturesque crowd composed of old and young men and a few women, several wealthy businessmen and two royal princesses, peasants, unemployed youths and wage-earners, including some flown in from Paris, and token delegations from seven Arab countries. It was a cross between a jumbo-scale outing and a Muslim pilgrimage or crusade that fascinated the world press.[163] According to the journalists' reports, 5,813 buses and trucks had brought along with the marchers some 15,000 tons of foodstuffs, 63,000 tons of water, 379 doctors and nurses, 220 ambulances and 2,590 tons of gasoline. Although some of the equipment was contributed by foreign firms based in Morocco, this was obviously a very costly operation, even though less expensive than a war, which it was then hoped that the march would obviate. Moreover, it lent itself to ridicule, especially when Hassan, on 9 November, ordered the marchers to return home because their 'objectives have been attained'. (No reactions on the part of the marchers themselves to this stillborn excursion were publicly expressed. For the great majority among them it was a stirring experience and a break in their harsh and monotonous existence, but the desolation of the desert — their 'promised land' — could not but have been bitterly disappointing.) What the king described as a dignified and symbolic manifestation of national solidarity and religious zeal was interpreted by some observers as an extravaganza and a poorly disguised diplomatic defeat — the king had ordered his men to march up the hill only to march them down again.[164] This was not, however, the view of Boumediene, who on 10-11 November made a last ditch attempt at Béchar to dissuade Daddah — whose compatriots had not participated in the Green March — from jeopardising Mauritania's future by linking it with Morocco.

The Madrid Pact and its Repercussions. On 14 November, the day on which the Algerian president personally warned the Spanish premier that his country would not accept any solution of the Sahara problem in which Algeria as a concerned and interested party was not associated, an agreement between Spain, Morocco and Mauritania was signed at Madrid. According to its publicised terms, Spain agreed to decolonise the Sahara and leave the area before 28 February 1976. In the interim, the territory would be administered by the Spanish governor general, assisted by two Moroccan and Mauritanian deputy governors, who would respect Sahraoui public opinion as expressed through the *yemaa*. The vague terminology of this last-mentioned provision was responsible for the tug of war that ensued between rival *yemaas*, each claiming authenticity as representatives of the Sahraoui people.[165] As to the Bu Craa deposits, Spain would retain 35 per cent of the shares in the Fosbucraa company, and a portion of the 65 per cent that would go to Morocco would presumably be allotted to Mauritania. Reportedly there were unpublicised agreements among the three signatories that gave satisfaction to Spain as regards its fishing rights and included a postponement of further Moroccan demands for the *presidios*, as well as compensation for repatriated Spanish and Canary Islands civilians. Five days later, this pact was ratified by the Cortes, and on 18 November King Hassan announced that 'the Sahara question has finally been settled'.

Superficially, Hassan's strategy appeared to be an unqualified success in winning almost wholehearted domestic support and also some international approval. Without bloodshed and by bluff and astute diplomacy, he had gained substantial economic concessions from Spain and had accomplished the ending of Spanish rule in the Western Sahara without causing Madrid to lose face. Furthermore, he had made a collaborator out of his erstwhile opponent, Daddah, by granting Mauritania a substantial if lesser share in the spoils. Now he faced Algeria with a *fait accompli*, thus forcing Boumediene either to engage in a trial of military strength with Morocco or to carry its case once more to the international forums, which had thus far shown themselves incapable of taking forceful action. This again proved to be the case when Secretary General Waldheim on 20 November, after reporting to the Security Council on his unsuccessful mediation efforts during the preceding month, merely asked the Committee on Decolonisation to express its views on the pact of Madrid.

Algeria, in the meantime, vented its resentment of the Madrid pact and of Morocco's initiative by acts of economic retaliation. The employees of Air Algérie refused to service Moroccan planes landing at Algerian airfields, the government began expelling the 25,000 or so Moroccans living in Algeria, and Radio Algiers started to broadcast two new programmes, the 'Voice of the Free Sahara' and the 'Voice of the Free Canaries'. Nor was all quiet on the Saharan front during this interregnum. Against strong Polisario opposition, the Moroccan forces occupied Smara on 27 November, and in early December they replaced Spanish troops which had pulled back to the coastal settlements in accordance with Spain's established policy of gradual withdrawal from Africa. On 11 December some 4,000 Moroccan soldiers, accompanied by several hundred civil servants, entered El Aaiun, took over the Spanish radio station and inaugurated regular flights between El Aaiun and Rabat. A week later Mauritanian troops occupied La Guera, where they joined the Moroccan forces who had been fighting the Polisario commandos installed there following its sudden abandonment by the Spaniards.[166] On the other hand, Villa Cisneros, one of the earliest Spanish settlements along the Saharan coast, was the last to remain under Spanish control, and it was not until 12 January 1976 that it was occupied by the Mauritanians and given the name of Dakhla.

Against this background of violence and rapid change, two contradictory proposals were laid before the UN General Assembly on 10 December, and both were endorsed by that body. The first, proposed by Tunisia, Senegal and Zaïre, took note of the tripartite agreement of 14 November and asked its signatories to respect the wishes of the Sahraouis, whose freedom of expression should be guaranteed by an observer responsible to the UN secretary general. It received 88 affirmative and no negative votes, but 41 countries abstained. The second proposal, which emanated from Algeria, ignored the Madrid pact and called for the replacement of the Spanish administration by a four-member supervisory council, representing Spain, Morocco, Mauritania and Algeria, that would hold a referendum of the Sahraoui people on their future status. It polled 56 favourable and 42 adverse votes, with 24 nations abstaining. As these proposals neutralised each other, and as neither of them censured Morocco or Mauritania for sending troops into the disputed territory, the General Assembly in effect if not formally accepted the *faits accomplis*.

By taking no clear-cut stand based on principle, the UN General Assembly, like the World Court in handling the Sahara question, lost some of its prestige and effectiveness, and the same was true of the OAU and the Arab League. Because they were dealing with countries all of which were African, Muslim and governed by Arabs, those two organisations had no common adversary against which they could take a united stand. And because the great majority of their member states were already shaken by internal dissensions, they preferred to sidestep an issue that was potentially divisive and had no immediate or practical interest for them. To be sure, the Arab League as such did not attempt to cope with the Sahara question, but the individual governments, in trying to mediate the conflict, showed a partisanship that in general was based to varying degrees on national interests, geographical proximity and ideology, and in particular on the attitude of each of them toward Morocco and Algeria. Thus the conservative-to-moderate Arab states, such as Saudi Arabia, Jordan, Kuwait and the Gulf emirates, tended to line up behind Morocco, whereas the so-called revolutionary nations like South Yemen, Somalia and Mali were inclined to support Algeria and the Polisario Front.

Nevertheless, it should be noted that Syria and the PLO were in a quandary because their normal propensity to undermine King Hassan's regime was mitigated by their gratitude for the troops he had sent to fight Israel. Libya was similarly divided between its admiration for the Polisario desert fighters and its disapproval of their carving another small unviable state out of what should be a single united Arab nation. Powerful Algeria's weaker neighbours, Tunisia and Mali, were also split on the issue, albeit for different reasons. Ideologically and economically, Moussa Traore's Mali was close to Algeria, but in the days of Modibo Keita and the Casablanca bloc it had received appreciable aid from Morocco, and currently Mali did not want to alienate Mauritania, with which it shared a long frontier and membership in the OMVS. Tunisia, for its part, charged Boumediene with ingratitude for not acknowledging Tunisian aid to the FLN during the Algerian war for independence. Bourguiba was particularly resentful of Boumediene's adamant refusal to share with Tunisia the hydrocarbon resources found along their common southern frontier, and although in the years 1957-69 he had actively opposed Morocco's campaign against Mauritania, he now gave his blessing to the division between those two countries of what had previously been no more than a European colony.

Even more than the Arab League, the OAU was paralysed by the divisions among its members, but it did have the courage to address itself as an organisation to the issues raised by the conflict in the Western Sahara. In the mid-1960s the OAU seemed to be the logical intergovernmental agency for mediating the Sahara dispute, because it had been fairly successful in halting the hostilities between Algeria and Morocco in 1963. And the OAU was in fact charting the path which the UN General Assembly was later to follow, for in its 1966 session Algeria for the first time explicitly stated its interest in the Sahara question and the OAU endorsed the principle of self-determination which the General Assembly adopted in its resolution of 20 December 1966. Within a few years, however, the OAU lost its leadership role, for in 1971 and 1972 alphabetical order brought the rotating presidency first to King Hassan and then to Mokhtar Ould Daddah. During their incumbency it was neither expedient nor diplomatic to bring up the problem of the Western Sahara, and so the OAU lagged behind even the General Assembly's ineffectual efforts to decolonise the Spanish Sahara.

The eclipse of Spain as a colonial power in the Sahara deprived the Arab League and the OAU of the one common adversary against which they could take a united stand, and the great majority of their members were relieved not to have to commit themselves further by a public vote. As for the great powers, they remained discreetly in the background, considering that other problems in Africa deserved priority consideration. Nevertheless, the different sources and volume of the combatants' military equipment have provided a clue as to where the shifting sympathies of the United States, the Soviet Union and France have been directed at one time or another during the protracted Saharan conflict.

Notes

1. The *presidios* include also Alhucemas, Penon de Valez and the Chafarinas Islands.

2. In using the term Sahraoui, the authors are simply distinguishing the Western from other Saharans without attributing any political connotation to that term.

3. Rio de Oro was the name by which all of Spain's Saharan dependencies were known until the 1960s, when it was applied only to the area south of Saquiet El Hamra.

4. *Les Territoires Espagnols d'Afrique* (La Documentation Française, *Notes et Etudes Documentaires*, No. 2951, 3 Jan. 1961).

5. J.L. Miège, 'Les Origines de la Colonie Espagnole du Rio de Oro' in *Le Sahara: Rapports et Contacts Humains* (7ème Colloque d'Histoire, Faculté de Lettres d'Aix-en-Provence, 1967).

6. *Maghreb*, no. 22 (July-Aug. 1967).

7. See pp. 216, 315-17.

8. J. Mercer, *Spanish Sahara* (Allen and Unwin, London, 1976), p. 117.

9. Capt. P. Azam and J. Cauneille, 'L'Afrique Occidentale Espagnole' (CHEAM, Mémoire No. 1009, July 1946).

10. Ibid.; A. Gaudio, *Le Sahara des Africains* (Julliard, Paris, 1960), p. 19.

11. C.C. Stewart, 'Much Ado About Nothing', *West Africa*, 3 Nov. 1975.

12. Mercer, *Spanish Sahara*, pp. 220-4.

13. See B. Fessard de Foucault, 'La Question du Sahara Espagnol', *Revue Française d'Etudes Politiques Africaines* (Dec. 1975).

14. R. Rezette, *Le Sahara Occidental et les Frontières Marocaines* (Nouvelles Editions Latines, Paris, 1975), pp. 101-4.

15. Mercer, *Spanish Sahara*, p. 199.

16. *Maghreb*, no. 22 (July-Aug. 1967).

17. Some authorities cite 40 as the number of seats for elected candidates, but this does not take into account the government's gerrymandering tactics.

18. Rezette, *Le Sahara Occidental*, p. 106.

19. R. Pelissier, 'Territoires Espagnols d'Afrique', *Le Monde*, 24-5 Oct. 1967.

20. Mercer, *Spanish Sahara*, p. 225.

21. *Les Territoires Espagnols d'Afrique*.

22. Mercer, *Spanish Sahara*, p. 203.

23. Ibid., p. 204.

24. A. Dahmani, 'Aux Portes du Sahara Espagnol', *Jeune Afrique*, 19 Oct. 1974.

25. *Maghreb*, no. 22 (July-Aug. 1967).

26. *Jeune Afrique*, 10 June 1977.

27. Ibid.

28. According to *Censo/74*, there were 59,000 Sahraouis in the Moroccan zone and 14,000 in the Mauritanian zone.

29. *Les Territoires Espagnols d'Afrique*.

30. Mercer, *Spanish Sahara*, p. 130.

31. F.E. Trout, *Morocco's Saharan Frontiers* (Droz, Geneva, 1969), and 'The Return of Ifni to Morocco', *Genève-Afrique*, vol. IX, no. 1 (1970).

32. A. Gaudio, 'L'Autoroute du Sahara', *Jeune Afrique*, 27 July 1971; Pelissier, 'Territoires Espagnols'.

33. See pp. 107-8, 140.

34. P. Oliva, 'Notes sur Ifni', *Revue de Géographie du Maroc*, no. 19 (1971).

35. I.W. Zartman, *Morocco: Problems of New Power* (Atherton Press, New York, 1964), pp. 82-3.

36. See pp. 155-6.

37. Gaudio, *Le Sahara des Africains*.

38. See pp. 172-5, 242.

39. *The Economist*, 17 Oct. 1964.

40. See M. Vieuchange, *Smara, Carnets de Route* (Plon, Paris, 1932).

41. Z. Daoud, 'La Bataille du Sahara', *Lemalif* (Aug-Sept. 1970).

42. According to *Censo/74*, Guelta Zemmour and Aousserd had populations ranging from 2,440 to 3,000; Tifariti 1,778; Bir Enzaren 1,398; Mahbes 1,396; five other settlements from 500 to 1,000; and the remaining four listed, from 100 to 300.

43. *Jeune Afrique*, 10 Oct. 1974.

44. As of 1970, US $1 = 68.91 pesetas.

45. *Les Territoires Espagnols d'Afrique*.

46. Mercer, *Spanish Sahara*, p. 197.

47. Ibid., p. 117; *Europe-France-Outremer*, no. 449 (June 1967).

48. *Marchés Tropicaux*, 17 Dec. 1966.

49. *Les Territoires Espagnols d'Afrique*.

50. *Industries et Travaux d'Outremer* (Oct. 1971).

51. Rezette, *Le Sahara Occidental*, p. 31.

52. *Marchés Tropicaux*, 12 Oct. 1968.

53. *Jeune Afrique*, 9 March 1976.

54. *Les Territoires Espagnols d'Afrique*.

55. *Marchés Tropicaux*, 26 Dec. 1964; *Maghreb*, no. 22 (July-Aug. 1967).

56. *Jeune Afrique*, 5 March 1976.

57. Gaudio, *Le Sahara des Africains*, p. 57.

58. *Petroleum Press Service*, March 1964.

59. *New York Times*, 20 Jan. 1964.

60. Mercer, *Spanish Sahara*, pp. 184-7.

61. See pp. 130, 160-1, 236.

62. Mercer, *Spanish Sahara*, p. 235.

63. *Christian Science Monitor*, 4 Oct. 1973.

64. Fessard de Foucault, 'La Question du Sahara Espagnol'.

65. Agence France Presse despatch from Madrid, 1 Oct. 1974.

66. *West Africa*, 24 Feb. 1975.

67. Ibid., 21 Oct. 1974.

68. *Marchés Tropicaux*, 30 May 1975.

69. See p. 142 and note 101 below.

70. 'La Marche Verte' (CHEAM, anonymous typescript, 15 Dec. 1975), p. 16.

71. M. Barbier, 'L'Avenir du Sahara Espagnol', *Politique Etrangère*, no. 4 (1975).

72. General Coloma-Gallegos's statement to the press, *Afrique Nouvelle*, 10 June 1975.

73. *Marchés Tropicaux*, 6 June 1975.

74. *Le Monde*, 2 Dec. 1975.

75. One exception, however, was the chief inspector of the Spanish armed forces, who was promptly dismissed for coming out in 1969 in support of Morocco's claim to the Western Sahara. See Mercer, *Spanish Sahara*, p. 236.

76. According to René Pelissier (*Le Monde*, 24 Oct. 1967), some Spaniards claimed that Spain clung so long to its African dependencies solely to enrich its officer corps, whose members automatically received a 180-per-cent pay increase if they were sent to Ifni or to any of the Spanish garrisons spread over 20 posts in the Sahara province. If the maintenance of Spanish rule in the Sahara was a burden for Spanish taxpayers, it was certainly profitable for the military.

77. B. Crimi, 'Le Dernier Quart d'Heure', *Jeune Afrique*, 28 Nov. 1975.

78. See pp. 174-5.

79. *Le Monde*, 30 Oct. 1975.

80. The FLU was a mixed bag of Sahraouis demobilised from the Spanish army, refugees at Tantan and Moroccan irregulars, probably remnants of the ALS.

81. *The Times*, 14 Jan. 1976.

82. A. Ben Miske, *Front Polisario, Ame d'un Peuple* (Editions Rupture, Paris, 1978), p. 208; *El Moudjahid* (Algiers), 9 Dec. 1975.

83. *Afrique Nouvelle*, 9 March 1976.

84. Mercer, *Spanish Sahara*, p. 228.

85. 'La Marche Verte', p. 13.

86. *West Africa*, 2 July 1973.

87. 'La Marche Verte', p. 24.

88. *Marchés Tropicaux*, 26 Sept. 1975.

89. *West Africa*, 8 Sept. 1975.

90. *Jeune Afrique*, 19 Oct. 1974; Ben Miske, *Front Polisario*, pp. 118 et seq.

91. Nevertheless, later that year he sent a warning to President Richard Nixon on the eve of his visit to Spain that 'another Sirhan' would kill him if he tried to establish NATO bases in Spain. Agence France Presse despatch from Madrid, 31 Oct. 1970.

92. *Jeune Afrique*, 14 May 1976.

93. Ibid., 26 Dec. 1975.

94. *Le Monde*, 27-8 Nov. 1975.

95. See E. Assidon, *Sahara Occidental: Un Enjeu pour le Nord-ouest Africain* (Maspéro, Paris, 1978), p. 40; Ben Miske, *Polisario Front*, p. 113.

96. See pp. 64, 68.

97. *Marchés Tropicaux*, 13 Sept. 1974.

98. *West Africa*, 8 Sept. 1975.

99. Ibid., 25 Aug. 1975.

100. *Jeune Afrique*, 13 Feb. 1976.

101. Eight of them were former members of the PUNS, three were Ouled Delim tribesmen, including the new party's president, Mohammed Lamine Ould Houroumtallah, and two were Reguibat.

102. See pp. 215-23.

103. See pp. 78-80, 85-6.

104. See p. 85.

105. See pp. 79, 81-2.

106. A.G. Gerteiny, *Mauritania* (Praeger, New York, 1967), p. 199.

107. Fessard de Foucault, 'La Question du Sahara Espagnol'.

108. *Le Monde*, 14 June 1970.

109. See pp. 33-4.

110. *Marchés Tropicaux*, 10 March 1972.

111. *Industries et Travaux d'Outremer* (April 1972).

112. See pp. 126-7.

113. *El Moudjahid*, 9 Nov. 1966.

114. *Le Monde*, 29 March 1967.

115. See pp. 128, 135-9, 166, 236-7.

116. *New York Times*, 28 Nov. 1976.

117. *Jeune Afrique*, 5 Nov. 1976.

118. *Christian Science Monitor*, 27 Dec. 1977; *Le Monde*, 23 Dec. 1977.

119. In 1974-5 Hispano-Algerian trade had greatly expanded, and in the latter year Spain made a loan of 2,800 million pesetas to Algeria and agreed to buy from it 4,500 million cubic metres of natural gas annually.

120. C. Gallagher, *Morocco and its Neighbors* (American Universities Field Service Reports, April 1967).

121. In addition to the party organs *Al Alam* and *L'Opinion*, the Istiqlal began publishing two other journals to promote Morocco's claim to the Sahara; these were *Sahara El Maghrib* (beginning in 1957) and *Perspectives Sahariennes* (1958).

122. *Marchés Tropicaux*, 12 Sept. 1953.

123. *New York Times*, 15 Jan. 1956.

124. *Europe-France-Outremer*, no. 449 (June 1967).

125. *New York Times*, 24 Feb. 1957.

126. *The Economist*, 30 Nov. 1957.

127. *La Vie Française*, 30 Aug. 1957.

128. Gallagher, *Morocco and its Neighbors*; M.R. Thomas, *Sahara et Communauté* (Presses Universitaires de France, Paris, 1960), p. 13.

129. *Le Monde*, 23 March, 4 April 1958.

130. Ibid., 19 April 1958.

131. *New York Times*, 5 April 1961.

132. I.W. Zartman, 'The Sahara: Bridge or Barrier?', *International Conciliation*, no. 541 (Jan. 1963).

133. S. Schaar, 'Hassan's Morocco', *Africa Report* (July 1965).

134. *New York Times*, 23 June 1964.

135. P.A. Dessens, 'Le litige du Sahara Occidental', *Maghreb-Machrek*, no. 71 (Jan.-March 1976).

136. *New York Times*, 18 Nov. 1966.

137. See pp. 131, 135-9.

138. *Le Monde*, 14 Jan., 10 May 1967; *Marchés Tropicaux*, 19 Aug. 1967.

139. V. Monteil, 'Notes pour Servir à un Essai de Monographie des Tekna du Sud-ouest Marocain et du Sahara Nord-occidental' (CHEAM, Mémoire No. 1232, Sept. 1945).

140. *New York Times*, 20 Dec. 1958.

141. See pp. 189-90.

142. *The Economist*, 20 June 1970.

143. See p. 236.

144. After a meeting that lasted only an hour and a half, Hassan, Boumediene and Daddah agreed that the committee should be composed of four Moroccans, two Algerians and two Mauritanians, thereby reflecting the view they held at that time of the comparative strength of the national interests involved.

145. *Ya*, 11 June 1970.

146. Morocco's imports from Spain in 1973 were valued at 233 million DH, compared with 138 million DH in 1972; Moroccan exports to Spain in those years were valued respectively at 180.8 million DH and 163.6 million DH. *Marchés Tropicaux*, 16 Aug. 1974.

147. *Christian Science Monitor*, 9 April 1973.

148. *Le Monde*, 22 March 1974.

149. *Marchés Tropicaux*, 19 July 1974.

150. *Le Monde*, 10 July 1974.

151. *Jeune Afrique*, 5 Oct. 1974.

152. *Christian Science Monitor*, 10 Oct. 1974.

153. R. Pelissier, 'Sahara Espagnol: L'Escalade', *Revue Française d'Etudes Politiques Africaines* (Sept. 1974).

154. *Le Monde*, 3 March 1976.

155. A minor but telling episode was the king's despatch of his son and heir in January 1975 to tour Tarfaya province, where he was hailed as Prince of the Sahara.

156. See pp. 163-4.

157. *Afrique Nouvelle*, 27 May 1975; Fessard de Foucault, 'La Question du Sahara Espagnol'.

158. Dessens, 'La Litige du Sahara Occidental'.

159. C. Vallée, 'L'Affaire du Sahara Occidental devant la Cour Internationale de Justice', *Maghreb-Machrek*, no. 71 (Jan.-March 1976).

160. For a vivid first-hand account of the march, see Thierry Desjardins, *Les Rebelles d'Aujourd'hui* (Presses de la Cité, Paris, 1977), pp. 89-100.

161. The descriptive adjective 'green' was said to denote the march's peaceful and Islamic character, as well as to suggest the fertility that the Western Sahara would acquire under a Moroccan government.

162. 'La Marche Verte', p. 30.

163. Desjardins, *Les Rebelles*, pp. 63-126.

164. *West Africa*, 17 Nov. 1975.

165. See pp. 110-11, 130.

166. See pp. 120, 142, 269.

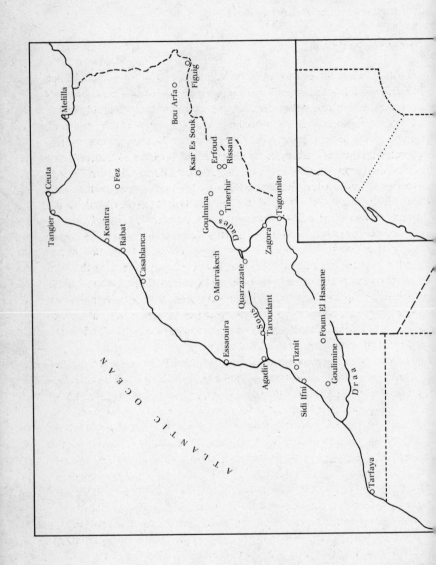

PART III: MOROCCO

The Deep South

Only a very small portion of the Sahara lies within Morocco if Oued Draa is assumed to be, as it was under the protectorate, that country's southern boundary. Although the oases of Jebel Bani, Mhamid, Ktoua, Tafilalet and the Guir-Zousfana have a truly desert setting, the great bend to the west taken by the Draa below Zagora marks the limit of permanent human habitation. This immense sector of Morocco's pre-Saharan region extends for more than 1,200 kilometres from Tarfaya to Figuig and covers about one-third of Morocco's total surface. The plentiful rainfall and snows of the eastern High Atlas give birth to the Dadès River, which joins with Oued Ouarzazate to form the Draa, and to the Rheris, whose tributaries are the Ziz and the Tadra. Farther to the east is Oued Guir, which after being united with Oued Bou Anane and the Zousfana forms the Saoura. These rivers, which flow through-out the year in the mountains, begin to be utilised beyond the foothills to irrigate the most northerly date-palm groves. By the time they reach Ksar Es Souk and Goulmina their flow has become intermittent, so that farther downstream the groves are irrigated only by flood water, *rhettaras* (underground canals) and wells.

South of Oued Draa and of the juncture of Oued Ziz with Oued Rheris are the rocky *hammada* (plateaus) of the Draa and the Guir that form the northern rim of the Sahara, and beyond them lie the dunes of Erg Iguidi and Erg Chech. Those *hammada* block the southward flow of the rivers originating in the Atlas Mountains, which create a formidable barrier to communication with northern Morocco and account for the area's aridity, but which are also the source of the surface and sub-terranean waters that make possible irrigated farming in the Jebel Bani and in the valleys of the Draa, Rheris, Ziz and Guir. The existence of those waterways, supplementing the fitful and insufficient rainfall (54 to 99 millimetres a year), has permitted a large and heterogeneous population to survive in this remote region for several thousand years.

Neither the western nor the eastern part of pre-Saharan Morocco has permanent surface water. The string of oases bordering Jebel Bani from Foum El Hassane to Foum Zguid depend on water pumped from underground rivers originating in the Anti-Atlas. Figuig, Morocco's most easterly group of oases in the pre-Saharan zone, is dependent on springs whose water is unevenly distributed among the seven *ksour* (hamlets or fortified villages) by gravity and according to highly complex local customs. Elsewhere absolute priority is given to the upstream users of *oued* water, unless some agreement has been reached among the tribes living at different topographic levels along the river banks. Consequently, the villagers who have access to the least regular water supply are those living in the plains, which is the area most often threatened by famine and therefore most given to emigration.

Until the French protectorate in the 1930s, both by force and by modern technology, brought the peoples of the southern mountains and oases, known as the *blad es siba* (dissident territory), under the control of the *makhzen* (central government), they were largely cut off from contacts with northern Morocco and were therefore oriented by trade and topography to the south and the east. In Tafilalet, Sijilmassa was founded in 757 AD, and for centuries it was the capital of an independent kingdom that extended from the High Atlas to the Draa valley,[1] and was equally important as a commercial and religious centre. After an eclipse, Sijilmassa revived in the seventeenth century as the political and military base for the indigenous cherifian dynasty of the Alaouites. It also managed to survive as a trading centre until the early nineteenth century, when it was finally abandoned about 1818 after being destroyed for unknown reasons — variously attributed to a local feud, an earthquake and the sinfulness of its inhabitants.

In the latter half of the nineteenth century, after the abolition of the slave trade and the capture of Timbuctu by the French in 1894, the nature and routes of the trans-Saharan commerce underwent marked changes. Sugar and tea succeeded slaves and gold as the merchandise most highly valued by both nomads and sedentaries. And the military posts set up by the French and Spaniards became important markets, contributing to a shift in the desert trade routes to the north and to the west. Tindouf and Tabelbala in Algeria, and Figuig and Goulimine in Morocco, drew the caravans away from the old trans-shipment relay points of the Draa, Tafilalet and Jebel Bani. By the early twentieth century those old entrepôts had become moribund as commercial centres but remained locally important for their agricultural production. Moreover, Tafilalet continued to be a hotbed of political intrigue and of resistance to French encroachments from Algeria. Because the Atlantic regions of the Moroccan southwest were more accessible to European conquerors and merchants than was south-central Morocco, they were subjected to modernising influences that largely bypassed the peoples of the Draa and Ziz-Rheris valleys. At the same time, the isolation as well as the ethnic diversity of the latter gave birth to and preserved an original socio-political structure there.

Political Evolution

As a frontier region inhabited by aggressive nomadic tribes, Morocco's deep south has been subjected to military rule in one form or another throughout the protectorate and again after independence. It was not until 1938 that the Ait Khabbache finally surrendered to the French, only to find themselves once again relatively free of France's control during the Second World War and the years immediately thereafter.[2] France's defeat in 1940, followed by the ascendancy of the Vichy regime, demoralised the French officer corps in Morocco and depleted their numbers to the point where the country's most distant regions were left almost without any effective administration. Then, in 1955, the jubilation occasioned by the return of the sultan from exile in Madagascar to Morocco revived anarchic conditions in southern Morocco, where Mohammed V had to put an end to the violence resulting from the ALS's operations in the border area. And finally, Morocco's acquisition of the Spanish territories of Ifni, Tarfaya and Saquiet El Hamra (1958-75), and the ensuing guerrilla warfare conducted by the Polisario Front, required enlarging the range of the military command and strengthening it not only in Morocco's deep south but throughout the northwestern Sahara.

With significant changes in nomenclature and, more particularly, in personnel, the administrative apparatus bequeathed by the protectorate was taken over in 1956 and subsequently expanded and reorganised by the newly independent state. The modifications in the French protectorate system were made with a view to strengthening the nation at the expense of tribal and local institutions, prominent among which were the *caïdat*, the *djemaa* and Berber customary law. Thus the administrative units grew markedly in number and shrank in area, and the rural and urban communes created by the protectorate in 1954 as a more modern version of the tribal *djemaa* decreased within the span of twenty years from about 1,000 to fewer than 750. The overall trend was towards total 'Moroccanisation' and greater centralisation, for the announced official policy of regionalisation was largely confined to increasing the powers of the provincial governors (*dahir* of 16 March 1977) and to programmes for economic development. This reorganisation enabled the sultan-king as head of the state and government, commander-in-chief and *imam* to keep the reins of power in his own hands. The crown prince was entrusted with reorganising the army, and the king himself took charge of the police and exercised close control over the ministry of the interior. Under that department was erected a pyramidal structure reminiscent of, but markedly different from, the network of officials who had served under the protectorate.

At the base of the new local-government administration was the village headman (*moqqadan*), the only authentic holdover from the traditional system, but he enjoyed little prestige and influence, and for lack of formal education he could not aspire to rise in the administrative hierarchy.[3] He took orders from the sheikh who administered the rural commune for the *caïd*, or *amal*, who headed the next highest administrative unit, the *cercle*. A variable number of *cercles* were comprised in the province, which was in the charge of a governor named by the king and responsible to the minister of the interior. The governor became the keystone to the local administration, but the *caïd* was downgraded for, as a bureaucrat, he no longer represented his tribe or had the judicial authority that his predecessor had enjoyed. Moreover, he had to share the executive power in his circumscription with a *cadi*, or judge. Newcomers to Berber regions, the *cadi* were professional magistrates who administered the national Islamic law (*sharia*), from which the Berbers had been exempted by the *dahir* of 1930, designed by the French to promote Berber autonomy in Morocco.

The *djemaa* as the tribe's administrative body was another casualty of the political and economic changes that took place in Morocco following the Second World War. Its authority declined partly because of the creation of elective rural communes, but even more as a result of its own inherent weaknesses. Of these the most patent were its domination by local vested interests and its failure to represent the most dynamic elements among its constituents in the south. The *harratin* who farmed the land and repaired the irrigation canals were excluded from its membership, which was now composed largely of elderly and influential Arab and Berber proprietors of palm groves and water rights. The administrative work of the *djemaa* was handled by the *caïd* and his entourage, who took their most difficult problems directly to the *amel* who occupied the next higher rung in the bureaucratic structure. The post of *amel* was created on the eve of Morocco's independence, at which time it had become clear that the *djemaa* was moribund as an institution because it reflected the social and economic inequities that could no longer be justified by the services rendered by its privileged members.[4]

At first glance it seems surprising that except for the brief revolt by Adi Ou Bihi in Tafilalet,[5] there was little organised resistance or even adverse reactions on the part of Berber traditionalists to the eclipse of their ancient institutions.[6] To be sure, the Berbers have rarely presented a monolithic front when faced with strong opposition or even distasteful innovations, but in this instance their apathy was probably due to their being outmanouevred, though not outnumbered, by the increasing number of Berber officers in the Royal Armed Forces (FAR) and of educated young Berber bureaucrats appointed to administrative posts in the south.[7]

Certainly the main beneficiary of the foregoing developments has been the king, the base of whose support is traditionally the army and the rural population. Inasmuch as the largest *ksour* in Morocco's deep south have no more than 10,000 inhabitants, the king's loyal supporters there are proportionately more numerous than in the more populous settlements farther north. The infrequent tours of the deep south made by the king, usually to inaugurate a dam or a road, have elicited popular enthusiasm[8] but no sustained political action to bolster the throne. Nor did either the Istiqlal or the UNFP, when they were the main opposition parties, take root there, because they represented, respectively, the goals of the upper bourgeoisie and of the urban radicals — hardly the desiderata of the oasis-dwellers in the Saharan borderlands.

Southern Moroccans are fully aware that the Alaouite dynasty had its origins in their region, and Hassan II's survival of two attempts to assassinate him (in July 1971 and August 1972) seems to them clear proof that he possesses the *baraka*. Only the pro-government, moderate Mouvement Populaire may be said to have acquired an appreciable following among the Berbers in Morocco's deep south, but in that area its support for the throne is passive rather than active. The only political activists among the southern Moroccans seem to be the *harratin* who have emigrated to the big coastal cities.[9] Those at Agadir and Tiznit are said to account in part for the USFP's domination of those towns' municipal councils. At Casablanca, emigrants from the Saharan regions, as members of a large and growing proletariat, are naturally attracted to one or another of the three radical parties, the UNFP, the USFP and the PPS. Consequently such party allegiances perpetuate in an urban setting the cleavages that have long existed between the haves and the have-nots in the oases of the Draa and Tafilalet.

The aggressive policy adopted by the king in 1974 in regard to the future of the Spanish Sahara marked a turning-point in the history of the throne's relations with Moroccan political parties. Except for Abdallah Ibrahim of the UNFP, all the party leaders in Morocco rallied behind the royal diplomatic campaign to support the king's decision to take over the Saquiet El Hamra,[10] and in November 1975 the Green March gave proof of a spectacular unity in Morocco's body politic. Consequently all the parties, again excepting the UNFP, participated in the three-tiered elections of 1976-7,[11] and the success at the polls registered by the pro-government candidates clearly showed how effective had been the king's policy in unifying his country. In all the elections the massive return of candidates running without a party label has been variously interpreted as evidence either of the depth of royalist sentiments among the Moroccans or of the lack of party organisation among the rural element that even today makes up 61 per cent of the country's total population.[12] As applied to Morocco's deep south, both interpretations of the election returns seem valid.

The Economy

In Morocco's last three economic and social-development plans, top priority has been given to agriculture, with tourism and mining in second and third places. As all those sectors of the economy are of primary importance to southern Moroccans, a marked increase in their revenues should logically have ensued from application of the official programmes. Yet in the pre-Saharan regions, the production of dates is generally stagnant, tourism has suffered since 1975 from the insecurity engendered by the Polisario's guerrilla raids, and mining has yet to become a major occupation in Morocco's deep south.

Southern Morocco has a showcase of miscellaneous minerals, but most of the deposits are small, their quality is mediocre, and their location is inaccessible. Some of the manganese, cobalt, gold, copper, lead and zinc deposits found in the centre and east of the Saharan borderlands have long been worked by a few thousand non-professional miners, but some of the most important companies there have ceased operations, either because the deposits were near exhaustion or world market prices for their zinc and manganese output collapsed in the late 1960s. In Tafilalet, which is the area best endowed with minerals, the government in 1960 established an agency, the Centre d'Achat et de Développement du Tafilalet (CADET), to purchase and sell local zinc and lead ores, but this monopoly was unpopular with the miners, and could not solve the problem of transporting their production.[13] The long search for hydrocarbons carried out by some of the big petroleum companies in the deep south proved unrewarding, but in a speech on 3 March 1974 the king announced the recent discovery in Tarfaya and the Middle Atlas of 'sufficient reserves of oil shale to meet Morocco's oil needs for centuries to come'. If the techniques for processing oil shale should be further developed and made less costly, thanks to American aid, the improvements that have been carried out in the transportation system of the coastal region should appreciably reduce production costs for Tarfaya's oil shale, which is located near Tantan.

Animal husbandry is of major importance only for the nomads, who are fewer than the sedentaries, and the latter cannot increase their small herds of cattle, sheep and goats because they lack pastureland and propitious climatic conditions. Fisheries are of economic significance off Morocco's northern coasts, and they should certainly become more important in the south if Morocco retains control of Tarfaya, Ifni and the Saquiet El Hamra.

Since drafting its first development plans, the government has focused on increasing agricultural production through extending the irrigated farming area. This is being done by a big dam-building programme, which began during the French protectorate and has been expanded by independent Morocco and reoriented in its objectives.[14] Whereas the French army engineers were primarily concerned with generating electricity for developing the northern and northwestern areas of the country, in the south they simply carried out improvements in the age-old network of dams and of the surface and subterranean irrigation canals (*seguias* and *rhettaras* respectively) and drilled new wells. Their work did promote a better utilisation of flood water and rainfall, but failed to add appreciably to the area under cultivation or to markedly improve crop yields. Nor did the French authorities make much headway in discovering the cause, let along the cure, for *bayoud*, a plant disease that was decimating the palms of Tafilalet.[15] However, in the 1940s and 1950s they had greater success in limiting the damage caused by recurrent locust invasions.

In the first post-independence years, changing circumstances required the rethinking of Morocco's irrigation policy. The south's increasing aridity, as shown by the greater frequency of droughts, the very rapid growth of the population (averaging about 3 per cent a year), the progressive fragmentation of land holdings,[16] which was stimulating the rural exodus and an excessive urbanisation, as well as the ever-greater cost of food imports and the expansionist dream of a Greater Morocco — all these factors requiring placing a fresh emphasis on effectively and quickly augmenting Morocco's agricultural output, particularly in the south. To increase the farm land under irrigation, a new dam-building programme was formulated by the newly created Office des Irrigations, which by 1976 had built dams on Oued Draa and on Oued Ziz.

The major obstacles to revising land and water rights in the south have been the diversity and tenacity of local customs and the government's ignorance of their precise nature. In certain areas and among some tribes, notably the Ait Atta, water rights are collective, whereas in others they are individual, and they may or may not be related to the land through which the water flows. Apparently the only uniform custom in this respect is the priority given to upstream farmers, who may use as much water as is available without concern for the needs of those living downstream. In view of the confusion and contradictions arising from the mixture of French, customary and Koranic law, it is not surprising that the central government has hesitated to apply fully its own legislation guaranteeing existing water rights, pending completion of a detailed study of the tribal and communal customs prevailing in the different southern farming regions.

It is easy to exaggerate the size of Morocco's palm groves, as their enumeration is often subject to fantasy, but it would be hard to overestimate the importance of the date palm for southern Moroccans. Its fruit is their basic food and only commercial crop, aside from small quantities of henna and tobacco; barley and wheat, the only supplementary food crops, are grown in the shade of palms, all of whose produce from leaves to trunk is essential to the villagers' existence; and as recently as 1949, dates were still being used as currency by tribes practising a barter economy.[17] The alternation of droughts with inundations invalidates any serious forecast of crops and yields, but even in the most productive years and since the new dams have helped to stabilise production, Morocco's output, averaging some 95,000 tons a year from about 4.5 million palms, does not meet the demand. About a fourth of the crop is exported, and to increase that percentage, the government has periodically organised date fairs in Tafilalet and has built several plants to process and package dates for shipment abroad. Although Tafilalet still possesses the largest groves in Morocco, the number of its palms is declining and will continue to do so until the *bayoud* disease is brought under control or the palms most vulnerable to it are replaced by hardier if inferior species.

Aside from large-scale dam-building and some improvements in tourist facilities, including more hotels and better road and air transportation, the economic resources of Morocco's deep south are so meagre that they have not attracted investments to any appreciable extent. To be sure, work has continued on paving the highway, 1,048 kilometres long, between Agadir and Figuig by way of Ouarzazate and Ksar Es Souk, a project begun by the French during the inter-war period; good roads link the two last-mentioned towns to the main centres under their administration; and airfields have been built for those two provincial capitals. But the mining operations in the south-central pre-Saharan region, except at Bou Arfa, are hampered by inaccessibility as well as by primitive techniques. As their deposits of lead, zinc and cobalt are so insignificant and as the few thousand miners constitute so small a part of the population, there is little likelihood that the funds required to remedy those defects will be forthcoming.

It is the Atlantic coastal region, particularly the territories acquired from Spain since 1958, that have benefited most from official benevolence. Among the projects envisaged in the 1973-7 development plan were new ports for Tantan and Tarfaya (where a radio-broadcasting station had already been built), and airports at Goulimine and Tantan. New roads between Tiznit and Ifni and between Tantan and Tarfaya were inaugurated in 1974 and 1975 respectively, and even more ambitious projects are being undertaken to develop Saquiet El Hamra.[18] As for the economy of the pre-Saharan region as a whole, the most promising outlook for it seems to lie in a greater development of tourism. In the meantime, as in the past, a solution for the major problems caused by overpopulation is being sought in emigration.

By the mid-nineteenth century, Casablanca was already attracting rural Moroccans, and as that town grew it became increasingly a more powerful magnet than Marrakech and Fez for emigrants from the south and central regions. Generally speaking, the northern cities of Morocco received most of such migrants, but many from Tafilalet and Figuig were drawn to Algeria before 1975. As soon as Morocco's deep south was pacified, the French began to encourage temporary departures from the densely populated and drought-ridden oases, where their number reflected the seasonal fluctuations in rainfall.[19] On the other hand, the nomads, albeit wanderers by their pastoral vocation, presented no such problem, for few of them were inclined to leave the spacious *hammada* even briefly.

Even more than did the protectorate, the government of independent Morocco has discouraged permanent emigration, both to keep the south agriculturally productive and to discourage any further influx of migrants into towns already overcrowded with a floating proletariat. In working toward that end, the authorities have been aided by the Saharans' inability generally to adapt themselves to urban life and to be assimilated into the local population. Their dark skin and different customs make it hard for northern Moroccans to accept them, and their lack of skills condemns them to humble occupations which in turn mean perennially low wages and living standards.[20]

The Peoples and Their Habitat

Until the twentieth century, the population of Morocco remained small and unevenly distributed, and as recently as 1960 that of the deep south probably numbered no more than 600,000.[21] In the oases of Rherir and Tadra the population density was 200 to 300 to the square kilometre, whereas in the zones of pastoral nomadism, such as Tarfaya and Jebel Bani, the average density was one inhabitant to the square kilometre. A long-standing characteristic of those peoples along the rim of the desert has been their constant spontaneous mobility, generated in modern times by the numerical increase in the human and animal population beyond the region's capacity to feed them. Necessity has driven an ever-larger stream of emigrants from the south, less to seek their fortunes elsewhere than simply to survive. Some tribes, such as the Reguibat and Tekna, moved south of what became Morocco, and other Sanhadja Berbers and Maql Arabs migrated northward, especially to Atlantic-coast pastures and towns.

Southern Morocco, with its entrenched peasantry, was a reservoir of manpower for the north, a great trading and religious centre in its own right, and also the birthplace of the Saadian and then of the more durable Alaouite dynasties. Its intensively cultivated and populous oases inevitably attracted the desert nomads, some of whom pillaged them while others came to profitable terms with their inhabitants, and eventually both nomad elements became semi-nomads or sedentaries. In general, the Arab nomads shunned contacts with Europeans and kept their base in the Sahara, whereas the more outgoing Berbers were transformed by their exposure to a more modern economy into semi-nomads and, for a price, became the sedentaries' protectors against even more predatory intruders.

Chronic warfare and political upheavals seem not to have greatly altered the socio-economic structure which the sedentaries had devised to assure their survival, nor did the nomads' suzerainty over them prove catastrophic.[22] It was rather the southward extension of the French protectorate in the early 1930s that caused a drastic change by upsetting the delicately balanced relationship among the oasis sedentaries, and between them as a group and their nomadic protectors, notably the Ait Atta confederation. By the eve of the Second World War, the protectorate had encouraged the sedentaries to shake off the nomads' domination, especially by supporting the former's refusal to pay tribute for a protection now assured by the French armed forces.[23] Having already impoverished the nomads by suppressing the slave trade and eliminating caravan transport, France, by depriving them of their last traditional source of income, indirectly forced them to renounce their wanderings in favour of more lucrative and stable occupations. The consequent increase in the sedentary component of the population created a new set of problems for the central government, first that of the protectorate and now that of King Hassan. The latter has had to combat centrifugal tendencies the while encouraging regionalism, and also to provide the sedentaries with means of livelihood sufficient to keep them on the land.

Nomads. Compared with the sedentary component, the nomads are few, and their proportion to the total population has been declining rapidly throughout the twentieth century. Because of the imprecision of official statistics, which do not distinguish between the nomads and other elements of the rural population, and the lack of a definition as to what constitutes a nomad, it is difficult to know to what degree. Captain Georges Salvy in the years after the Second World War believed that the nomads then in Morocco numbered some 100,000, but Professor Daniel Noin estimated that by 1964 their total had dropped to 40,000, which would mean that there was then one nomad to every 16 peasants.[24] Today these figures must be further revised downward, in view of the increasing sedentarisation of the nomads and because of the current war in the Western Sahara, of which they have been the main victims.

Nomad tribes, both Berber and Arab, are scattered throughout the western and central areas of southern Morocco. They are most numerous in the Atlantic regions, where there are few oases and the ocean fogs have preserved pastureland better than in the hinterland, where the rainfall is minimal. These western nomads are in the process of becoming sedentaries or semi-nomads practising transhumance. Increasingly they prefer to raise sheep rather than camels, and gravitate to such administrative, trading and military centres as Tarfaya, Tantan and Goulimine. To a lesser degree this is also true of the nomads in the centre and east of southern Morocco, which is dominated by the Ait Atta tribesmen. Indeed, the history of nomadism in Morocco's deep south is largely that of the Ait Atta, although it also concerns smaller Berber tribes such as the Ait Oussa and Ait Isfoul, as well as those of Arab origin, for example, the Aarib and Doui Menia. However, to such a degree have these nomads intermingled, the Arabs becoming Berberised and the Berbers claiming Arab descent and adopting Arabic customs, that in many cases the language they speak and the costume they wear provide no reliable clues as to their origin.

Invasions by the Maql Arabs in the thirteenth century defeated and displaced the indigenous Berber pastoral tribes. Those in Jebel Sarhro, however, remained in southern Morocco, unlike the Reguibat, although they became widely dispersed there. After the Arabs began to leave Jebel Sarhro, a local Berber warrior named Dadda Atta rallied resistance to Arab domination in the sixteenth century, and in so doing he organised the confederation that adopted his name. Some Ait Atta went as far afield as the northern slopes of the High Atlas, whereas others remained in the south-central areas. Of the two principal southern Ait Atta branches, the Ait Alouane and the Ait Khabbache, the former became semi-nomads after coming to an agreement with the oasis sedentaries of the Dadès and Draa valleys. By this means they acquired a portion of the crops and the right to graze their animals on certain *ksour* lands in return for their protection of the sedentaries' palm groves and irrigation canals. The Ait Khabbache, on the other hand, after making their main base in Tafilalet and dominating its most southerly oases, expanded southward and eastward in the nineteenth century. By becoming breeders of camels, the Ait Khabbache acquired a mobility and a militancy not shared by other Ait Atta tribesmen.

In both areas the Ait Atta's aggressiveness met with opposition from other nomads, not to mention the sedentary farmers. The Ait Alouane, based at Tagounite, competed with the Aarib and Ait Isfoul for the few areas of arable land and for tribute from the oasis-dwellers the length of Oued Draa. However, except for the Dadès valley, their way north to the green pastures of the Atlas mountains was blocked by the Ait Yafalman, a defensive coalition of their rivals.[25] To guard their vassals in the *ksour* and the oases, the Ait Alouane, Aarib and Ait Isfoul tribesmen installed themselves in a *bordj* (fort) or in a settlement which they dominated, each *fraction* developing such close relations with its villagers that the nomads eventually became sedentaries themselves.[26] These protectors, by driving a wedge between the Arabs in the oases and those in the Sahara, and by making individual and mutually advantageous contracts with their vassals, behaved toward their protégés in a way that contrasted greatly with the destructive practices of the early Maql Arabs.[27] The latter, after conquering an oasis or *ksar*, reduced its inhabitants to serfs and took all their portable resources back with them to the desert whence they came. The Berber conquerors, on the other hand, were careful to stop short of destroying agriculture and trade, and only in extreme cases did they kill resisting inhabitants.[28] Because they disdained farming and because the *harratin* were predominantly blacks, they never considered the sedentaries to be their political or social equals, although they were egalitarian among themselves. The *debiha*, the act of submission that they exacted from their vassals, was considered by the latter to be humiliating, but for both parties it proved to be a practical *modus vivendi*: the Ait Atta acquired dates and cereals without stooping to perform manual labour, and the sedentaries and their institutions survived very largely intact.

Until the mid-1930s the evolution of the Ait Khabbache followed a different course. As pastoral nomads on the Guir *hammada*, they did not have to compete initially with other nomads, for that area was vast and sometimes the various tribes nomadising there came to terms with each other for the use of its pastures in grazing their camels and sheep. When, however, they began to carry out raids deep into the desert and brought back slaves, camels and dates, they found themselves in conflict with the Doui Menia, Reguibat, and Berabech who were engaged in similar activities.

In their control of some south Moroccan oases and in their raiding and trading operations between Tafilalet and their base at Taghit in the Zousfana valley, the Doui Menia both resembled and competed with the Ait Atta. In the Draa oases, the Doui Menia clashed with the Ait Alouane to monopolise the tribute that the Drawa paid for their 'protection', and in the Saoura the Doui Menia came to blows with the Ait Khabbache in pillaging the Touat oases. France's penetration into southern Algeria threatened to terminate such lucrative activities, so that it was only natural that the Doui Menia and Ait Khabbache should band together to oppose the French advance. By 1903, however, France's military superiority and the new trading opportunities opened up by the French at Béchar together weakened the Doui Menia's opposition, with the result that they deserted the Ait Khabbache, and after their joint forces had been defeated at Boudenif in 1903 the Doui Menia accepted French rule. The Ait Khabbache, on the contrary, continued to fight on, with only the support of a minor tribe, the Bani Mhammad, and it was to forestall attacks by those two tribes that the French established a military post at Tabelbala.

Periodically the Ait Atta tribesmen joined forces to safeguard their fiefs against non-Berber opponents, and the main reason that the Ait Khabbache became and remained so powerful was that as nomads their tribal organisation had not disintegrated as did that of those Berbers who had moved into the oases and engaged in transhumance. The Ait Khabbache were divided into five primary sectors, or *khums*, which were subdivided into tribes and below that into clans.[29] Their supreme chief, the *amghar nufilla*, served as liaison between the Ait Khabbache subdivisions, and negotiated for them in their dealings with other tribes. The *amghar* was elected each year by the tribal *djemaa* from among the *khums* in rotation, and he had no powers other than those delegated to him annually as the federation's executive, spokesman and mediator. The democratic nature of this office and the absence of any permanent overall authority exemplified Berber strengths and weaknesses. Although the annual meeting of the *djemaa* as an electorate strengthened their unity as a tribe, it did not increase the Ait Khabbache's military effectiveness nor did it wholly obviate infighting among the clans. Nevertheless, thanks to the Ait Khabbache's domination of the area between the Ziz valley and Touat, and that of the Ait Alouane along Oued Draa, the Ait Atta confederation had become by the turn of the century the strongest, richest and largest tribal entity among the indigenous opponents of French rule in eastern Morocco and western Algeria.

Progressively, the Ait Khabbache were cut off from one after another of their sources of trade and booty until in 1933, the French forces, converging on Jebel Sarhro from across the Atlas and from the Ziz valley, decisively defeated them in their homeland at Bou Gafar. This put an end to what Professor R. E. Dunn has called the venture in Berber imperialism that might have carried the Ait Khabbache across Algeria had not the French intervened at the peak of their expansion. For some years before their final submission, the Ait Khabbache had been little by little pushed back into the Tafilalet area by political and physical restrictions that forced them to turn from camel-herding to sheep husbandry and to such supplementary sources of income as mining.

The ownership of camels had indeed conveyed prestige and provided the Ait Khabbache with mobility and with the most important element in their diet, milk, but it required more pastureland than was now available to them and had fewer practical advantages than did sheep-rearing. Although sheep needed more regular watering and guardianship, and thus limited the range of their owners' mobility, they did provide the Ait Khabbache with milk, wool and meat (in greater quantity than did camels because the nomads were less reluctant to slaughter them), and they also multiplied more rapidly. In fact, it was the rapid growth in herds and in the human population as a result of *pax gallica* and improved health conditions under the protectorate that caused what came to be called the 'crisis of nomadism' in the first years after the Second World War.[30]

Animal husbandry as practised in Morocco's deep south has been well suited to the terrain and to Berber mentality. Among the great desert nomads it was egalitarian in that pastureland on the *hammada* was limited only by climatic conditions, the movement of herds was organised in such a way as to respect the tribe's individualism, and the booty netted by raids was shared by all the participants.[31] Among the semi-nomads, the trek areas of transhumance had long been established by custom or through agreements among the pastoral tribes, and because sheep ate the natural grass that grew spontaneously on land generally unsuited to farming, rearing livestock was independent of agriculture. Its weak points, however, were that animal husbandry in Morocco's deep south demanded almost unlimited space, and this was not available in the oases, where, moreover, the humidity and the presence of a parasitic fly were unhealthy and even fatal for some breeds of animals. To reach the more plentiful and better-watered pastures of the Atlas, the nomads had to have the consent of the mountain tribes that controlled them.

In the mid-1940s, successive dry years, the rapid growth in the human and animal population, and wartime restrictions combined to create the adverse conditions that brought about a crisis for the southern nomads. When they tried to drive their herds north from the *hammada* earlier in the summer than usual, they found their way barred by both the sedentary farmers and the mountain tribes. The former wanted to keep more of the grazing land for their own use, and the latter insisted on waiting for the grass in their pastures to reach maturity, knowing from experience how the southern nomads allowed their sheep to consume all the available vegetation without concern for the future or for the herds of other tribes. Because of the havoc such practices wrought and because the mountain tribes had long since accepted French rule, the protectorate authorities supported their stand and utilised access to the northern pastures as the most effective means for disciplining the dissident Ait Atta.

This policy proved successful insofar as it served to keep most of the southern nomads in the deep south, for they tended to emigrate far less than did the sedentary component of the population, notably the oasis-dwellers. At the same time, the protectorate's policy was certainly a major factor in restricting the growth of herds, although other causes of their stagnation or decline were periodic droughts, inundations, diseases and more recently the war in the Sahara. To just what degree the animal population of southern Morocco has been affected by these hazards is hard to assess, for official statistics simply enumerate the number and breed of animals on which taxes are paid. Such figures even under peacetime conditions were notorious underestimates, were subject to incredible annual fluctuations and failed to distinguish regional variations.

Apparently the number of sheep in Morocco during the last few years has remained fairly stable at about 14 million head, but that of camels (which are almost wholly concentrated in the deep south) declined from 115,000 in 1972 to 81,000 in 1974-5. The most valid single explanation for the sharp fall in southern Morocco's camel population is that the rapid decline of nomadism and the development of modern technology have made camels obsolescent in contrast to their former role as almost the sole means of mobility and as beasts of burden. Motor-vehicles, first the truck and more recently the Land Rover, have replaced the camel caravans and the *mehara* for trans-Saharan transport. As more and more nomads become sedentaries by stages, the ever-fewer camels they still breed are used now mainly for meat or for access to those desert areas that are impassable for motor transport.

Sedentary Groups. The *ksour* is the basic community in Morocco's deep south, and it varies in size from a few hundred to some thousands of inhabitants. Excepting small groups of Arabs living in Tafilalet and the Draa, most of the white *ksour*-dwellers are Berbers. The great majority of their inhabitants, however, are blacks and mulattos.

In principle, the *ksour* owed allegiance to the sultan, either directly to the *makhzen* or through the *pasha* of Marrakech, represented in the area by a deputy (*khalifa*). In reality, however, this region was the *blad es siba*, a land of miniature Berber republics, which managed their own affairs and dealt directly with their nomad overlords, on whose protection they depended for survival. When the *ksour*'s suzerains were Berbers, the contract negotiated with them by the *ksour djemaa* was subject to annual revisions through hard bargaining on an individual basis. On the whole, the symbiotic relationship between nomads and sedentaries worked out to their mutual advantage, and from it there developed a curious informal alliance. This was between the sheep-herding nomads and the sedentary farmers, who shared the belief that the land should be preserved intact and be made to produce. This conflicted with the views of the camel-rearing nomads, who regarded the oases as sources of wealth to be exploited to the maximum and then abandoned when they ceased to be productive.[32]

Of the four groups of oases in Morocco's deep south that bordered on the desert, those in the more or less isolated regions of Oued Draa and Tafilalet are of greater economic and sociological interest than are the peripheral oases of the Atlantic area and of Figuig, which have been modified by their longer exposure to external influences, both commercial and political. At no time in recent history has this whole region been valued for its own resources, except as a limited source of dates and cereals for the local nomads and sedentaries. Such importance as it has attained derived from its situation, either on a great trade route or as a refuge for rebels, hence after it became a commercial backwater and the area was pacified, Morocco's deep south was ignored and left to fend for itself.

The Dadès and Draa Valleys. Prehistoric remains in the Draa valley show that it has been inhabited since ancient times. In the ninth century, Islam infiltrated from Tafilalet into the Draa, whose fertile fields bordering on the *oued* attracted farmers and craftsmen, including Christianised Berbers and Jews. The northward expansion of the Almoravids, Sanhadja Berbers from Mauritania, was unsuccessfully opposed by the Zenata Berbers, who then occupied the Draa valley, Tafilalet and the eastern slopes of Jebel Bani. Other Muslim Berbers, the Almohads, succeeded the Almoravids, but in the thirteenth century southern Morocco was invaded by Maql Arab bedouins who laid waste to the land. They ruled Morocco until the sixteenth century, which witnessed a resurgence of the Sanhadja Berbers. The great Ait Atta confederation established itself in the Tafilalet and Draa valley areas, and the *cherifian* Saadi tribesmen, native to the Draa, gained control of southern Morocco and established their capital at Marrakech. It was a Saadian ruler, Ahmed El Mansour, who sent his army across the desert to capture Timbuctu in 1591. Saadian caravans plying between that town and the markets of Mhamid and Sijilmassa brought merchandise from the sudanese zone to the northern rim of the Sahara for transshipment to Marrakech and Fez. And it was another desert dynasty, the Alaouites, who conquered Fez in 1666 and who are still the rulers of Morocco today.

Under the Saadi and Alaouite sultans, forays into the Sahara were motivated primarily by their need for slaves, camels, salt and gold. Yet those rulers never succeeded in making their Saharan caravan routes secure by fully subduing the anarchic desert tribes. At its apex, Moroccan domination of the western desert as far as the Touat oases lasted only a quarter-century at the most, and it was never more than largely nominal and sporadic. Only in their acknowledgement of the sultan's religious leadership as *imam* did those nomadic tribesmen accept his authority.

The valleys of the Dadès and upper Draa are 'casbah country', whose *ksour* are the main tourist attraction in southern Morocco.

Their crumbling walls resemble those of medieval castles, perched on the heights overlooking the river or built in the cultivated fields on which their inhabitants depend for their food. There and in the oases to the south live the Drawa, as the Arabised Berbers, Berberised Arabs, blacks and mulattos, and some Jewish residents, are called. Cast up on the banks of those remote rivers by external forces, the Drawa live side by side in a relatively harmonious *modus vivendi* that they have worked out over the centuries as the sole means of assuring their survival. Thanks to the Draa's brief and violent floods, only slightly controlled by primitive dams and a network of irrigation canals, the Drawa have been able to grow dates, small quantities of barley and wheat, and minute amounts of henna and tobacco. Of southern Morocco's river valleys, the Draa has the most abundant, albeit poorly utilised, water supply and also the smallest amount of usable land in relation to the size of its population.[33]

Access to those valleys from the north is limited to two passes through the eastern slopes of the High Atlas, at Tichka in the west and at Ksar Es Souk in the east. Midway between those passes flows the Dadès, whose main tributary is the Mgouna and whose source lies among the snowiest peaks of the High Atlas. The waters of the Dadès are joined with those of Oued Ouarzazate to form Oued Draa, downstream from the region's capital and communications centre of Ouarzazate. The oases along the lower reaches of the Draa are open to the desert, but their position on the border of the nomad world and their smaller share of the Draa's inundations make their inhabitants more vulnerable to predators and to climatic vagaries than are the more northern Drawa.

The *ksour* of the narrow Dadès valley are small settlements compared with those of the middle Draa. They are separated from each other by hedges of rose bushes, especially abundant at El Kelaa-des-Mgouna, where an ancient industry, recently modernised, produces an essence, used for perfume and in medicine, from the more than 700 tons of roses annually grown in the valley. The valley's inhabitants concentrate on utilising to the maximum its limited arable land, which cannot support any appreciable increase in its present population of some 80,000. That number has remained fairly stable in recent years, thanks to the steady flow of emigration. The Mansour Eddahbi dam at Zaouia N'Ourbas, completed in 1974, should make Dadès valley crop yields less precarious, but obviously it cannot increase the planted area.

Of the 311 *ksour* in the Draa valley, which extends for 150 to 200 kilometres along the middle course of Oued Draa, those of Zagora and Ktoua are the most important. Zagora marks the dividing line between the Berberised area farther south and the Arab-dominated region to the north. It is the administrative, medical and educational centre for the whole Draa valley and also the turntable for communications with the main towns of Morocco's deep south. Since 1965 the government has made a big effort to provide schools and improve health conditions in the valley. A single doctor is stationed at Zagora, which has an 80-bed hospital but no operating facilities, and 18 nurses are posted among the main villages. To improve literacy among the Drawa, of whom only 6.4 per cent can read and write and 1 per cent have gone through grammar school, the number of schools has been doubled in the past decade, but the difficulty of staffing them with qualified teachers has not been resolved. As of 1972 there were fewer than 5,000 students attending elementary school and 487 in Zagora's sole secondary school, and 71 Drawa were receiving university education.[34] Paved roads connect Zagora with Ksar Es Souk (480 kilometres), Marrakech (374), Agadir (331) and Ouarzazate (171), and tracks lead to Rissani (250). At Tamgrout, 22 kilometres from Zagora, is situated a renowned Qadriya *zaouia*,[35] which was the most famous centre of religious learning after Smara was destroyed and which still attracts students of Muslim law and literature from all parts of Morocco. Mhamid El Ghazlan, 88 kilometres by track from Zagora, is of limited interest except historically. It was the point of departure for the Saadian army that crossed the Sahara to destroy the Songhay empire, and it became the first customs post in southern Morocco for caravans bringing salt from Taoudenni for Marrakech. So it was not by chance that in February 1958 King Mohammed V chose Mhamid as the place to announce his support for the Istiqlal's claims to the desert between Oued Draa and the Senegal River. Today Mhamid is once again in the military limelight, for it has become a garrison town and rear base for the royal Moroccan army and therefore a prime target for attacks by the Polisario Front.

Because of the Draa valley's geological compartmentalisation and the limited area of arable land, it has been a melting pot for its heterogeneous residents. Although the members of a tribal fraction or ethnic group have always lived in separate districts in a *ksar*, they are so closely packed together and share so many common objectives and dangers that their origins and ethnic characteristics have become blurred. Observers have often noted that among the *ksour* sedentaries, most Arabs have adopted Berber customs, and many Berbers have taken over the Arabs' traditions and dress along with their language. In the Draa valley, Berbers and Arabs belong to the same *leff*, the ancient Berber system of alliances whose origins are unknown. Elsewhere, and notably in the Atlas and Kabylie mountains, ethnic and other traditional divisions among members of a *leff* are much more rigidly enforced.

Nevertheless, to some extent the social hierarchy prevalent through-out the Sahara has survived among the Drawa in attenuated form. White Arabs and Berbers, albeit not warrior or marabout tribesmen, form the aristocracy; landowning blacks and mulattos are the Notables who used to dominate the *djemaa* and consequently chose its chief; the black and mulatto farmers (*harratin*) are the backbone of the farming community, along with the former slaves who stayed on with their erstwhile masters despite being legally emancipated in 1933. This socio-political pattern typical of Saharan oases developed new forms in the Draa valley, thanks to its isolation, compactness and greater residue of Berber customs, particularly in its southernmost oases. The integration of the Draa valley into Morocco, which began under the French protectorate and acceler-ated since 1958, has modified a structure that took centuries to evolve, and in such a way as to deliberately enhance the authority of the central government at the expense of unique local institutions.

In 1933 France extended to the Draa valley the same administrative system as prevailed in northern Morocco. Initially, a new element in the form of a bureau of native affairs was superimposed, whose officers were instructed to maintain the existing social structures of the Drawa. Then the protectorate applied to them the policy of governing through outstanding tribal chiefs, in this instance the powerful *pasha* of Marra-kech. He was represented locally by the *khalifa*, who was chosen from among his servitors and ordered to destroy every regional obstacle to Glaoua rule.[36] Such obstacles included the traditional *leffs*, whose partisanship eventually became identified with opposing Moroccan political parties in some cases. Overall, the protectorate indirectly and inadvertently undermined the bases on which Drawa society rested, mainly by assuming responsibility for maintaining order, settling local disputes, suppressing slavery and to a limited degree opening up the valley to the outside world by building roads and a modern hydraulic system. The royal government, by pursuing more diligently and directly the policy it inherited of integrating the Drawa into the Moroccan nation, has further weakened their distinctive institutions, notably that of the *djemaa*.

Traditionally, each *ksar* has had two *djemaas*, in both of which every *fraction* or ethnic group was represented and elected its own chief. Members of the smaller *djemaa* were the most important Notables, who supervised the activities of the larger assembly, particularly as they related to the *ksar*'s day-to-day administration and its farming opera-tions. They also laid down guidelines for the negotiations carried on by their elected chiefs with the suzerain nomadic tribe whose protection had been solicited by or imposed on the *ksar*. The terms of this peculiarly Berber form of 'social contract' usually included the payment of tribute in local produce and the provision of pasture for their overlords' herds in return for the nomads' guarding the *ksour* from attacks by other predatory tribes. As the *ksar* was free to choose from among competitive suzerains, its chief periodically renegotiated the terms of this contract, and as he could be dismissed only by the unanimous vote of the *djemaa* that had elected him, he enjoyed considerable power.[37] This procedure changed after France had pacified the whole area in 1933, and even more after Morocco became independent in 1956. Because the central government assured all the population's security, there was no further need to negotiate with the nomads or to pay them tribute. Consequently the chief's authority declined, as did that of other officials similarly elected, such as the guardian of the *ksar*'s granaries and the supervisor of water distribution, who were thenceforth paid a small monthly wage by the state. Furthermore, the central government set up a pyramidal structure in which local officials were placed under the orders of a *caïd*, who himself was named by and made responsible to the minister of interior. The three *caïds* appointed to represent the *makhzen* in the Draa valley were the subordinates of a regional senior *caïd* stationed at Zagora, who in turn was himself directly answerable to the provincial governor at Ouarzazate.[38]

Nearly 1.8 million date palms grow on some 22,000 hectares in the Draa valley. Its largest groves are still those of the Ktoua and Mhamid oases, although the increasing aridity of the climate and the priority given to upstream users of the river's flood waters have caused many of the trees to be abandoned or neglected.[39] Custom regulates minutely the time of distribution and the partition of irrigation waters under the supervision of agents chosen by the *djemaa*, as it does the planting and cultivation of the crops growing in the shade of the palms. As regards the repair of *seguias* and *rhettaras* (surface and subterranean canals respectively), customs vary from one *ksar* to another. In the *ksour* where water rights are not a resource belonging to all the residents as a community, each family is required by custom to provide one or more of its members for the repair of canals, in proportion to the amount of water to which it is entitled.

Although date production likewise fluctuates from year to year and from grove to grove, depending on the age and species of palm and the volume of water available for irrigation, it averages some 32,000 tons annually, of which at least half is locally consumed and the rest shipped by truck to Marrakech.[40] Proceeds from the date sales are used by the growers to buy such necessities as sugar, tea, oil and occasionally meat, but it is as food, fodder, firewood and building material that date palms are vital to the Drawa. Virtually all activities in the valley revolve about date culture, which has acquired an almost sacrosanct character in the southernmost oases. In that area the tombs of saints are located in the groves, the *bayoud* disease is treated by magical rites, and the selection of palms to be cut down is regulated by time-honoured religious traditions. Local custom does not sanction the sale of date palms, but they may be used as collateral for a loan.

The chief crops associated with date culture are wheat and barley in winter and corn and sorghum in summer. In a favourable year, 11,000 hectares may be cultivated, principally for food crops, and of these 2,200 hectares are planted to wheat, 6,000 to barley and barely 100 to corn and sorghum. Vegetables occupy 300 to 400 hectares, henna 100 to 150 and lucerne (alfalfa) about 1,500 — the last-mentioned being a crop that is increasing with the development of cattle husbandry in the valley and the shortage of agricultural labour.[41] The Mansour Eddahbi dam, intended to irrigate 18,000 hectares when fully operative, should not only stabilise crop production but also generate 8 to 10 million kilowatt hours of electric current. This current could be used to fuel a processing industry, but the dam's main purpose is to obviate such agricultural disasters as resulted from the *oued* floods in 1965.

A survey conducted in the late 1960s[42] among 12,732 Drawa families living on 10,549 hectares showed that 69 per cent of them owned parcels covering only from one-half to one hectare. Of those that owned no real property, 21 per cent were *khammes* (sharecroppers), labourers, craftsmen or government employees, many of whom were peasant farmers. Much of the rented land was inalienable *habous* property, that is, owned by *zaouias* or held in trust for religious purposes. Of all the arable land in the Draa valley, about one-fifth was *habous* property and more than half was worked by the families that owned it, 30 per cent by *khammes*, 15 per cent by tenants, and 5 per cent by 'associates'. The contract between landowners and workers called 'association' was becoming increasingly popular, as it was a more flexible formula and gave to the associates a larger share in the land's produce than did the traditional *khammesat* relationship. Under that system, the *khammes* worked for large property owners who supplied seed, equipment and water, and in return was entitled to receive only one-fifth of the fruit of his labours. Furthermore, the big landowners dominated the valley's economy by their quasi-monopoly of moneylending and of the transport and sale of dates in the Marrakech market. Their stranglehold on the valley's economy, combined with the area's overpopulation, was driving the small property owners as well as the *khammes* away from the palm groves to seek labour for wages in the public-works programme or by emigration.

Small-scale seasonal emigration from the Dadès and Draa valleys probably began in the interwar period. Later it gathered momentum and changed its orientation, but its temporary character has not been altered, nor has it changed the basic imbalance of those valleys between a growing population and the area's limited resources.[43]

A survey conducted in the years 1945-50 indicated that emigration involved one-third of the able-bodied males in the Draa's upper valley, one-half of those in its central section, and two-thirds of those in its lowest reaches. A second survey, in 1966, noted that altogether 2,900 emigrated that year, but not all at the same season, and usually for not more than six months, sometimes less. *Khammes* and peasants holding only very small plots of land accounted for the bulk of such emigrants.

After the Second World War, Drawa emigrants went mainly to the western coastal regions of Morocco, then in the process of rapid economic development, and most of them were employed in agriculture. By the late 1960s, however, more than half of the Draa emigrants gravitated to the towns, especially Casablanca, where they got jobs mainly as watchmen, masons and butchers;[44] the percentage of those going to rural regions had markedly declined; and barely a fifth of the total were miners in the Ouarzazate area. By mid-1969 the impending exhaustion of mineral deposits in southeastern Morocco was having serious repercussions on the local labour market. The closing of the Bou Arfa manganese mines in 1968 was followed by that of the lead and zinc mines at Bou Beker the next year, resulting in the dismissal of at least a thousand workers, who had little prospect of finding alternative employment. Yet late in 1971 the miners' union was strong enough to call three successive strikes in the Ksar Es Souk region, which led to a 29-per-cent increase in their pay – the first wage rise for workers in the private sector for ten years.[45] Generally speaking, the wages earned by Drawa were low because they were unskilled, and the remittances sent by emigrants to their families barely sufficed to keep them alive. Indeed it was the inability of the Drawa to command high pay that prevented the wave of emigration from assuming large proportions or becoming permanent, and it was sheer necessity that forced the Drawa to leave again after each return trip to their valley.

By initiating a public-works programme in the Draa valley to provide a cash income for the unemployed, notably work on construction of the Mansour Eddahbi dam, and by encouraging a tourist industry there, the government has tried to stem the rural exodus from the Draa and Dadès valley before it becomes excessive.[46] Furthermore, by reducing the locally available labour supply, a new class of wage-earner has emerged — the agricultural worker who insists on being paid in cash and no longer in kind. His advent has changed relations among the Drawa far more rapidly than the region's overall economy has been modified. Agriculture provides the income for two-thirds of the valley families; 91 per cent of the Drawa are still engaged in farming and only 7 per cent in trade; and 0.1 per cent work in hotels and restaurants. Some landowners deprived of their *khammes*'s services have preferred to cultivate their groves themselves rather than abandon them, but even their attachment to the soil is undergoing a change. The prospect of improved money revenues because of better irrigation facilities and wage-earning opportunities cannot appreciably raise the population's low living standard. About 68 per cent of the Draa families spend 80 per cent of their income on food, and have no hope of being able to loosen the grip on the valley's economy now held by the big landowners.

Tafilalet. As the repository for archaic customs and institutions that have evolved over the centuries in a virtually closed socio-economic circuit, the Draa valley has been the subject of many studies. The Tafilalet province, on the other hand, has not attracted as much scholarly attention. This neglect may be due to the fact that few vestiges of Tafilalet's past glories remain, or because it has been and still is a confusing and amorphous area that has been perennially disputed first by tribal and more recently by nationalistic forces. Nevertheless, historically, politically and economically Tafilalet is more important than the Draa valley, although they share much of the same geology, ecology and economy.

At the time France established its protectorate over Morocco, Tafilalet's population consisted chiefly of sedentary Arabs in the oases, surrounded by far more numerous Berbers, whose trek areas extended as far east as the Guir *hammada*. Tafilalet's sedentary inhabitants were more homogeneous than were those of the Draa and Dades valley, and even more rigidly stratified socially. Obviously the top Arab echelons were *chorfa*, descendants of the Prophet, among whom the Alaouites were outstanding, and the *mrabatin*, who claimed descent from holy men and were thus qualified to mediate local disputes. Below this elite came the landowning white farmers, who formed a majority of the sedentary population and who regarded their black and mulatto *khammes* as socially beyond the pale. But it was the Berber nomads, particularly the Ait Khabbache branch of the Ait Atta confederation, who were the real masters of Tafilalet.

The Tafilalet basin with its long chain of palm groves extends over 24,000 hectares and provides a livelihood for some 80,000 sedentaries.[47] Concentrations of the population inhabit the *ksour* bordering on the Rheris and Ziz rivers, which periodically inundate the plain that contains the great oasis of Tafilalet. Eight of the *ksour* in the Erfoud region have more than 1,000 inhabitants, and one of them, Jorf, with its 6,200 residents, is among the largest villages in all southern Morocco. The *ksour* near Rissani, on the other hand, are very small, some of them sheltering fewer than 100 persons.[48] Population density in Tafilalet, as in the Draa, is directly related more to the regularity of its water supply, both from floods and from wells, than to its volume. Rainfall and snow are plentiful in the High Atlas, from whose southern slopes flow the Rheris, Ziz and Todhra, and farther to the east, Oued Guir. The Rheris and Ziz follow an almost parallel course until below Rissani, where they join together to form Oued Daroua, which eventually is swallowed up by the desert.

To regulate the brief and violent floods of the *oueds* so as to irrigate the palms and cereal crops, the inhabitants of the Rheris and Ziz valleys centuries ago built mud retaining walls and underground canals. As of 1965, there were eight dams and five *rhettaras* on the Rheris, and ten dams and seven *rhettaras* on the Ziz.[49] Although these hydraulic works made Tafilalet the region of irrigated agriculture *par excellence* in Morocco's deep south, so erratic and insufficient were the floods that the oasis-dwellers were periodically threatened with famine. Although French army engineers strengthened and modernised the existing dams and canals and dug new wells in 1953, 1954 and 1957, an especially disastrous flood in November 1965 left 25,000 homeless and uprooted 75,000 olive trees and 12,000 date palms.[50] This catastrophe, combined with the fear lest another heavy flood might change the course of the Ziz and deprive the whole area of water, thereby accelerating the decline in Tafilalet's date production, gave urgency to the projects being drafted by the newly created Office des Irrigations. Among them was construction of the Hassan Ad Dakhil dam on Oued Ziz, ten kilometres upstream from the provincial capital of Ksar Es Souk, to improve irrigation in an area of 15,000 hectares. Building of the dam began in 1968 and was completed in 1971, and it was inaugurated by the king three years later. Constructed wholly by Moroccan labour and financed by a tax on sugar, this dam was the most important undertaking by the

Moroccan government on behalf of a long-neglected area — an oversight difficult to reconcile with Tafilalet's strategic importance as a frontier and trading zone and its long history of revolt and warfare.

Throughout most of the nineteenth century, the Ait Khabbache's *drang nach osten* had brought that tribe into chronic conflict with the sultan of Morocco, who claimed suzerainty over the Touat oases; with rival nomads, mainly the Doui Menia; and above all with the French, then in the process of conquering Algeria. To forestall what he feared might be French plans to take over Tafilalet, Sultan Moulay Hassan decided in 1892 to prove that he was master of the area by putting down the Ait Khabbache's dissidence. After leading his army and his court across the Atlas from Fez to Tafilalet, the sultan found that his *khalifa* in the latter territory was a weak reed on which to lean and that the second-ranking power there, as in the Draa valley, was the virtually autonomous *djemaa* of the *ksour*.[51] Because he obviously could not impose his will on those *djemaa* nor contain Ait Khabbache expansionism, the sultan decided to reverse his previous policy of aiding the enemies of the Ait Khabbache by identifying his own interests with theirs — that is, by blocking the French advance. The sultan's change of policy preceded his death by a few years, but neither event could alter the course of events that led inexorably to France's takeover of the Touat oases at the turn of the century and the establishment of a French post at Erfoud in 1905.

After independence, Morocco lacked the personnel and armed forces needed to assert the king's authority throughout the country, particularly in the southeast, which was undergoing a severe drought and where the ALS were then co-operating with the FLN. The first FAR troops did not reach Tafilalet until early in 1957, and the transfer of power was not completed there until the French garrison left Ksar Es Souk in mid-1958.[52] In the meantime, the Berber governor of Tafilalet, Addi Ou Bihi, had led a brief revolt against the new Moroccan government, but not against King Mohammed V. Indeed it was to defend the king and the throne which he believed to be in danger that Addi distributed rifles to his followers after arresting the *caïds*, judges and police chief appointed to serve in Tafilalet by the minister of interior. The crown prince, in the absence of the king, broadcast an appeal for national unity, and by a combination of force and ruse he persuaded the recalcitrant governor to come to Rabat. There Addi was placed under arrest, tried two years later and condemned to death, and he died in prison of dysentery in January 1961.[53]

This small-scale, highly localised uprising has been variously interpreted as the revolt by a Berber chieftain against Arab domination, a hostile reaction on the part of southern Moroccans against rule by the traditionalist elite of Fez, a manoeuvre by activist elements of the PDI against the recently installed, Istiqlal-dominated national government, and finally as an attempt by some French officers to create trouble indirectly for newly independent Morocco and also for the FLN.[54] It was certainly the gesture of a traditionalist and high-handed Berber tribal chief who felt personal loyalty to the sultan but no allegiance at all to the politicians who ruled in his name. It was indicative of widespread Berber resentment that the Mouvement Populaire, founded as the party of rural Berbers in October 1957 and almost immediately banned as subversive, should have adopted Addi posthumously as a folk hero. Furthermore, the action taken in 1957 by the crown prince revealed the decisive and ruthless character of the future King Hassan II and justified his concept of the FAR as the most effective agency for asserting the authority of the national government over the tribes throughout Morocco.

Until the early 1970s the FAR duly played their assigned role of bolstering the royal authority, and until then there were no reports of further tribal rebellion in Tafilalet, which suffered from neglect rather than from interference by an over-zealous government. To be sure, the Hassan Ad Dakhil dam was built at great public expense, a regional development programme was launched and low-cost housing was constructed at Ksar Es Souk, where the stationing of some FAR troops gave a stimulus to the Tafilalet provincial capital, and fairs were periodically organised at Erfoud to promote the sale of local dates and craft wares. But during the years when the dam was under construction, Rissani was so seriously deprived of water that almost all the food required for its inhabitants' survival had to be brought in by truck, and some observers predicted that it would soon suffer the same fate as nearby Sijilmassa. Considering the intrinsic and strategic importance of Tafilalet and the Alaouite dynasty's sentimental attachment to its birthplace, it was ignored by the royal government to a surprising degree until the war with the Polisario Front, beginning in 1975, reawakened Rabat to its vulnerability in that area.

The Bani Oases. West of Zagora, a little-travelled and poorly surfaced road parallels the course of the Oued Draa as far as the small administrative centre of Foum El Hassane (421 kilometres), after which it turns north to join the main coastal highway at Bou Izakern. To the south of Bou Izakern lies Goulimine, a great camel market that is linked by road to the former Spanish territories of Ifni and Tarfaya.[55] The eastern portion of the road from Zagora to Foum Zguid gives access to the widely spaced and relatively populous *ksour* of Jebel Bani, the most important of which are Tissinnt, Tata and Akka. All of them are situated at the juncture of two or more *oueds* which provide water from the Anti-Atlas to the Bani area's million or more palms by means of a network of *rhettaras*. The outstanding groves are those of Akka, which is also a crossroads for tracks leading north to Irherm and south to Tindouf.

The oases of Jebel Bani are more dispersed than elsewhere in Morocco's deep south, and some are so densely populated that a *caïd* may administer as many as 10,000 sedentaries and semi-nomads. The demography of the Bani *ksour* resembles that of southern Algeria more than that of the Draa and Tafilalet. All the Bani oases were formerly slave markets, where the blacks who survived the desert crossing were sold to agents of the rich merchants of Fez and Marrakech. The most miserable specimens, however, remained in Jebel Bani, intermarried with the indigenous *harratin*, and together they cultivated the palm groves and repaired the *rhettaras* on behalf of their Berber and Arab nomadic proprietors. Thanks to the latter's dispersal and isolation, the sedentaries managed to gain a degree of independence from those great Saharan nomads and from the *caïds* appointed by the northern *pashas*.[56]

The abolition of slavery under the protectorate had little immediate effect on the status of the blacks and *harratin*, most of whom remained with their former masters for lack of any alternative. Gradually, however, the latter's authority weakened, and after France pacified the area an ever-larger number of serfs and slaves gained their freedom, mainly by emigrating to the northern towns. The remittances sent by those emigrants to their families enabled them to buy some of the groves and water rights formerly monopolised by the nomads, and within a span of twenty years there took place a marked change in the ownership of groves and of water rights, without a corresponding alteration in the size or composition of the oases' ethnic groups.[57] In Tata oasis, for example, one-eighth of the groves in 1935 belonged to blacks and *harratin*, but by 1955 that proportion had risen to one-half. Furthermore, the blacks and *harratin* now refused to repair the *rhettaras* unless the Arab and Berber proprietors performed an equal share of that dangerous work.

The evolution of the Bani oases has followed much the same pattern as in other parts of the pre-Saharan region, and they failed to develop the distinctive characteristics that have made the Draa and Tafilalet *ksour* attractive to scholars. In respect to the important role played by emigration in Jebel Bani, that region has affinities with the Figuig oases of Morocco's eastern border region.

Figuig. On a small scale, the group of seven *ksour* collectively called Figuig resemble Tafilalet in their vulnerability to external attack, an economy narrowly based on date-palm monoculture, and official neglect due to their isolation from the central Moroccan government. Like Sijilmassa, Figuig's importance as a market place and caravansarai was sapped nearly a century ago by the shift in trade routes and commerce of the Sahara,[58] but its pious, xenophobic and tradition-bound inhabitants can boast of no analogous past glories as a religious and cultural centre. Although Figuig has not been reduced to ruins as has Sijilmassa, its unenviable present status is deteriorating still further, and there is little likelihood of any marked improvement in its future economy such as is envisaged for Tafilalet and the Draa valley when their new dams will have stabilised crop yields.

Geographically and demographically, Figuig is so much an enclave of Algeria that it has sometimes been described as 'a Berber island in an Arab sea'. Situated in the eastern extremity of Morocco, 300 kilometres from the high plateaus, Figuig has been both ignored and cherished by Rabat, not for its intrinsic value but for its strategic situation. This outpost was the first settlement in southeastern Morocco to be administered by the French and to be analysed demographically by them.[59] In 1959, dissension between the Ben Barka militants of the UNFP and the *caïd* of Figuig gave rise to frequent and violent incidents in those oases.[60] Later, during the Algero-Moroccan war in 1963, and also in 1975-6, Figuig was again on the firing line.

The uniform appearance of the Figuig *ksour* is deceptive in that it masks their marked diversity and the conflicts between neighbouring villagers, whom only the threat of an enemy attack can temporarily unite. Zanaga is by far the richest and most dynamic of the *ksour*, accounting for half of Figuig's population and a preponderance of the rights to Figuig's water supply, and providing the smallest quota of emigrants from any of Figuig's component villages. To the solidly Berber basis of the oasis inhabitants have been added Algerian Arabs, Jews and semi-nomads, who make up a floating proletariat which lives in tents dispersed among the villages and remains unassimilated with the oasis sedentaries. Figuig's trade, which in the nineteenth century had depended on trans-Saharan caravans, was drastically altered in 1903 by construction of the railway from the Mediterranean coast to Beni

Ounif, directly opposite Figuig, and by its extension to Béchar two years later. This caused trade to bypass Figuig, making its oases economic backwaters, museums of obsolete customs, and almost wholly dependent for survival on their 150,000-odd date palms and the remittances sent by a growing number of emigrants. Lacking surface water in any appreciable amount, Figuig depends on the flow of twenty springs to irrigate its palm groves and vegetable gardens from a complex network of *seguias* and *rhettaras*. Without them Figuig would not exist, and even with them it barely survives. Geography and custom combine to make Figuig's water distribution not only subject to minute regulations but also inequitable, for the palms growing on the plateau receive less water than those on lower ground. Varying according to custom from one village to another, water rights may be collectively or individually owned, and they are so complex as to have defied official efforts in the 1960s to define and simplify them.[61]

The decline in Figuig's trade, along with the lowering of its water table, account for the increasing emigration that has been Figuig's hallmark during the post-Second World War years. Between 1914 and 1949, Figuig's population more than doubled, but during the last five years of that period wartime privations followed by a prolonged drought began to reverse the trend. On a small scale and for short periods, emigration had begun during the inter-war years, but from an annual average of 1,000 seasonal absences at that time, the number of young men leaving Figuig permanently has grown to some 4,000 a year. These departures have largely offset the population's natural growth, so that the number of its inhabitants has remained fairly stable at some 13,000 persons. In past years more than half of Figuig's emigrants have gone to work in Algeria or stopped there en route to France, and many of those who emigrate to other parts of Morocco have become miners, notably in the Bou Arfa manganese mines, which are only 120 kilometres from Figuig.

Figuig's plight epitomises the dilemma of southern Morocco in the late twentieth century. To an increasing degree, its population is outstripping local resources, both current and potential, and the absence of any compensatory influx of immigrants reflects a widespread lack of confidence in its future. There are already not enough known sources of water to maintain an economy reduced to date monoculture. Emigration, the only solution found thus far, has reduced Figuig's population to the old and the very young, and they lack the cohesion and dynamism required to surmount the oases' adverse circumstances caused by forces beyond their control.

Le Grand Maroc

The Western Saharan oases formed part of the dissident area known in Morocco as the *bled es siba*. Although nominally under the sultan's rule, the degree to which the central government (*makhzen*) exerted its authority in the outlying zones varied with the individual sultan, the strength of the tribes opposing him, and, in the nineteenth century, the inroads made by the European colonial powers. After France began its conquest of Algeria in 1830, the French military command there encroached increasingly on the *bled es siba*. It was not until more than half a century later that similar but less intense pressures began to build up south of Oued Draa.

In negotiating the treaty of Lalla Marnia on 18 March 1845, which first delimited the coastal region between Algeria and Morocco, the French aimed at halting the support then being given by the sultan to the chiefs opposing them in the Oranais and, more important, at forcing him to acknowledge France's control over the west Algerian Tell, which the sultan claimed as part of his empire.[62] France claimed that Morocco's eastern boundary should extend to the limits established by Turkey when the Sublime Porte ruled Algeria, but made no attempt to demarcate the frontier south of Teniet El Sassi, on the ground that that area was a waterless void unsuited to human habitation. Tafilalet, the birthplace of the Alaouite dynasty, was the southernmost region in which the *makhzen* was represented on a permanent basis, but even such relatively fertile fringes of the desert suffered from neglect, except when tribal revolts required sending there punitive or tax-collecting military expeditions.

The last years of the nineteenth century were marked by the consolidation of French rule in the Gourara-Tidikelt-Touat area, despite the opposition of such transfrontier tribes as the Doui Menia and the Ouled Djerir, and despite considerable infighting among the French military authorities in Algeria for control of the newly acquired territories.[63] Responding to each expansionist thrust by France, or trying to anticipate such moves, Sultan Moulay Hassan attempted to assert more control over the outlying settlements nominally subject to his rule by legally investing tribal *caïds* or by sending troops, or both, to the desert regions of the Atlantic coast and to the more easterly Saharan oases during the years between 1882 and 1890.[64] In 1883, however, the sultan committed a serious tactical error by imposing a tax for the first time on the oasis sedentaries so as to demonstrate his sovereignty over them, which aroused their deep resentment.

Moulay Hassan's attempts to control the regions south of Agadir were sporadic and were not even as effective as those he made among the more settled and productive inhabitants of the Zousfana and Guir valleys. Two military expeditions in the 1880s enabled the sultan to establish military posts at Tiznit, Kasbah Ba Amrane and Goulimine, but he failed to coerce certain Tekna tribes into submission.[65] He did, however, confer investiture on many local *caïds*, possibly including the leading marabout of Tindouf, but the farther south he tried to penetrate the less successful he became, for the emirs of Trarza, Adrar and Brakna preferred coming to terms with the French. Apparently the sultan made no attempt in 1896 to prevent the Reguibat from driving the Tadjakant out of Tindouf, nor did he respond to Timbuctu's plea for aid against the French two years later. On the other hand, he was spectacularly successful in enlisting the support of Ma El Ainin and his son El Hiba,[66] who acted as the sultan's delegates throughout the Spanish Sahara and in northern Adrar. It was thanks to Ma El Ainin that Morocco consolidated its hold on the region south of Oued Draa and especially on Oued Noun. The year 1910 marked the apex of Moroccan influence in the Atlantic coastal area, but even then it was far weaker than that the sultan exercised — with sharp fluctuations — in the Gourara-Tidikelt-Touat region.

In the first years of the twentieth century, French troops were moving erratically north from bases in French West Africa through Mauritania, eastward from Casablanca, and southwest from Oujda and Béchar, thereby virtually encircling the area still controlled by the Moroccan *makhzen*. In the diplomatic domain during that period, France managed to get a free hand from Great Britain, Spain, Italy and finally Germany to deal with the sultan, either by making concessions to each of them or by playing one government off against another. This process culminated in the treaty of Fez, signed 30 March 1912, in which the sultan's preeminence and Morocco's territorial integrity were recognised, but the reality of power passed to the protectorate administration installed by France. The Franco-Spanish treaty of 27 November 1912 recognised northern and southern Spanish protectorates and Spain's sovereign rights over the Ifni enclave,[67] but the border between the most easterly point of the southern Spanish protectorate and Ifni was left undefined. After France gained control of both Morocco and Algeria, the long-standing rivalry between their respective French officers and officials intensified rather than abated, and it increasingly focused on the undefined border between those two French dependencies. Widening their own spheres of influence in that area tended to preoccupy powerful elements among the French in both territories, including leading military and civilian personalities and conflicting economic interests, that gained strength by espousing local particularisms. In these protracted trials of strength, the Paris government was loath to intervene, and the sultan's authority, except in the religious domain, was royally ignored. The area most acutely in dispute, then and later, was the triangular wedge between the Saoura-Touat region to the east, the lower course of Oued Draa to the north and the northern border of French West Africa as defined in the Niamey convention of 1909.

The competition to control this huge, almost waterless, and uninhabited region was not due to its inherent value but to its use as a transit area for ever-larger bands of nomadic armed raiders. During the 1920s they inflicted increasing damage on the borderland peoples of the sahel who had accepted French rule. These raids (*rezzous*) originated in both the Atlantic coastal zone and southeastern Morocco. Bands of 200 to 250 Reguibat, Ouled Delim, Ouled Bou Sba and Ait Oussa Tekna preyed upon the Mauritanian settlements to the south, and smaller groups, composed of Ait Khabbache, Doui Menia, Ouled Djerir, Berabich and Kounta tribesmen from Tafilalet and the Draa valley, raided the central Niger River villages. The French West African authorities, unable to cope with these attacks, became increasingly dependent on the aid provided by the Territoires du Sud administration, especially its camel corps (*méhariste* platoons), in the central Sahara. Considering the frequency and scale of the aid given by the Algerian authorities to Mauritania and Soudan, and the ineffectiveness of Rabat's attempts to prevent the raiders from leaving southern Morocco, it was only natural that the French in Algeria should insist that the northwestern Sahara should come under their control.

Advocates of expanding Algeria's domain westward cited the impracticality and the heavy cost in money and manpower to its resources of policing a huge area not under the control of Algiers. The French in Morocco, for their part, knew that their troops were inadequate to patrol its share of the western desert, let alone cope with the chronically dissident tribes of the Atlas mountains. During and after the First World War, Lyautey's few troops were spread so thin throughout the protectorate that he was barely able to quell a serious revolt by the Ait Atta in Tafilalet (1918-19) and that of Abd El Krim in the Rif (1924-6). Nevertheless, rather than accept Algerian expansion in the Western Sahara, Lyautey preferred to risk encouraging the Berber Glaoua *pasha* of Marrakech to take over the Tafilalet and Draa Bend as a means of subduing the revolt there and of freeing his own troops for the protection of the country's more productive regions. Yet in 1922, when those tribes on the fringes of the Moroccan desert appealed to the Algerian administration for aid in resisting the *pasha*'s heavy fiscal levies, there was no response. Finally, the Tafilalet sedentaries, supported by the Ait Khabbache, joined together and evicted the Glaoua from the Mhamid oases.

Since neither Algeria nor the protectorate had the force or the authority to keep the Western Saharan tribes from feuding and raiding and the Paris government was reluctant to intervene, a series of north African conferences was held during the 1920s to discuss ways to pacify their respective desert areas and to eliminate the disparities between them in respect to taxation and customs. During these meetings, the boundary issue between Algeria and Morocco was debated inconclusively until the fifth conference, in July 1928, when the 'Vernier line', which favoured Algeria, was accepted by both administrations as their common border from Teniet El Sassi to Figuig. Yet within six months after that conference, the continued lack of co-ordination between the Algerian and Moroccan forces, as well as the inability of either to operate effectively alone in the Western Sahara, was demonstrated by the attack made from Tafilalet by raiding tribesmen on a French convoy in the Zousfana-Guir region, in which the general commanding the Ain Sefra territory was killed.

This incident caused a great outcry in Algeria and prompted the French government to intervene directly in a situation that had now obviously become impossible to resolve at the local level. In February 1930 a new military area called the Confins Algéro-Marocains was established under the resident-general of Morocco, inasmuch as most of the dissidence in the northwestern Sahara originated in the protectorate. Responsibility for security and supplies in the Confins rested with that French official until a decree of 4 June 1949 created the unified military command for the Confins Algéro-Marocain-Mauritaniens. As the years passed, the area included within the unified command diminished, its name was changed several times and its authority was progressively reduced, yet in one form or another it survived until Morocco became independent in 1956.[68] Thanks to this organisation, the problem of determining the frontier between Algeria and Morocco was sidestepped and the pacification of the Western Sahara was expedited, but it had two long-term drawbacks. The first was bequeathing a *de facto* boundary to Algeria and Morocco that was unacceptable to the latter when it became a sovereign state. The second was perpetuating the competition between Rabat and Algiers for control of the pacified areas as they were progressively placed under civilian administration.

In 1933 the capture of Tindouf marked the end of the *bled es siba* and of the dissidence of the Western Saharan tribesmen, but the control of that town became a major issue between the protectorate and Algeria. It was settled in March 1934 by the Paris government in the latter's favour, as had been many previous territorial disputes between the authorities in those two countries. The recency of the protectorate's establishment (1912) compared with the century-old French adminis-tration of Algeria (since 1830), gave the latter an undeniable advantage in any contest between their respective regimes. During the 1930s and early 1940s reorganisations of the military command reduced the area under the control of the Confins in the Saoura valley and in southern-most Morocco. Later, the discovery of vast iron deposits in the Tindouf region and the disputes over granting prospecting permits in the northern frontier zone sharpened the rivalry between Morocco and Algeria, as well as the former's sense of grievance. This legacy of bitterness which Moroccans inherited from the colonial regime was further complicated by the wartime roles played respectively by Rabat and Algiers, the per-sonal rivalries there between French officers and officials at the highest level, and their conflicting ideologies. In the case of the Moroccan nationalist movement, it contributed the element of irredentism to the platform of the Istiqlal, Morocco's first and most important party to demand the country's independence.

The rifts in Morocco's fragmented society, its predominantly rural and traditionalist character, the lack of a strong industrial and mercantile class, and the assumption of its leadership by the small Fassi bourgeois elite, deprived the Istiqlal of the organisational strength that was shown by a mass party such as the Neo-Destour of Tunisia.[69] The Istiqlal proved unable to control the more extreme nationalist elements, who organised urban violence and formed the Army of Liberation, and eventually also of a new political party, the Union Nationale des Forces Populaires (UNFP). Nor could the Istiqlal, despite its early call for in-dependence and the undeniable appeal of its claims to all the adjoining lands that at one time or another had accepted the sultan's suzerainty, compete with Sultan Ben Youssef's popularity as his nation's leader. His exile by France to Madagascar in 1953 automatically exonerated him from any possible charge of being a French puppet, and after his triumphant return to Rabat in 1955 his leadership and popularity were undisputed. In Africa, Morocco was unique, not in owing its present geographical boundaries — or lack of them — to a colonial government, but in being indebted to that same power for inadvertently building up national unity behind its hereditary sovereign. It was King Mohammed V who as Sultan Ben Youssef gave Moroccans their first sense of nationhood in a political framework that had existed in one form or another since Roman times.

When Sidi Mohammed Ben Youssef became King Mohammed V in August 1957, he inherited an administration that had become centralised in the late nineteenth century, had then experienced a pseudo-indirect rule under Lyautey (1912-25), and had finally been reduced to virtually the status of a colony under the marshal's successors. The *makhzen* — with its premier (Grand Vizir) and ministers of justice in charge of the Islamic law courts (*sharia*) and of religious establishments (*habous*), as well as its local *pashas* (urban governors) and *caïds* (tribal chiefs) — remained nominally intact under the sultan's authority. In practice, however, he was deprived of the substance of power, except in the religious domain and in retaining a veto power over all decrees (*dahirs*), by a parallel apparatus of French administrators, officers and technicians.

In the 1930s, and even more after 1945, progress toward greater autonomy was seemingly made in the form of municipal councils and tribal *djemaas*, which sent their representatives to the council of government in which the country's budget was discussed. Furthermore, an increasing number of indigenous civil servants were being trained, so that by 1954 about 26,000 out of a total of 54,000 functionaries were Moroccans. Although, in many cases, *makhzen* and protectorate officials worked together without friction, French district officers sometimes surreptitiously cultivated the clandestine maraboutic brotherhoods and the *pashas* and *caïds* who opposed the *makhzen*. In fact, the protectorate's policy favoured the Berbers, whose autonomy was promoted by a *dahir* of 1930 at the expense of the Arab *makhzen*. By encouraging Berber separatism as a means to damp down nascent Arab nationalism, French policy boomeranged against the protectorate, just as the similarly motivated measure of exiling Sultan Ben Youssef backfired 23 years later.

The Berber *dahir* of 1930 had the effect of fusing two hitherto distinct nationalist movements which had opposed the protectorate's increasingly direct rule in the 1920s. One was an orthodox Muslim reform group under Allal El Fassi and the other an association of university students in Rabat, led by Ahmed Balafredj and Mohammed Ouazzai, who had contacts in Paris with Moroccan students and the French Socialist Party. During the 1930s the protectorate turned a deaf ear to their pleas for democratic reforms, which resulted in the protests' being transformed into violent anti-French demonstrations. These led to the arrest of some of their leaders and the exiling of others, including Allal El Fassi, as well as further governmental repression and finally a split in the nationalist movement. The Second World War, however, revived the nationalists' hopes and self-confidence, proportionately to the weakening of the protectorate's authority following the fall of France in 1940 and the ensuing profound division in the large French resident community between Gaullists and Pétainists.

Sultan Ben Youssef gained stature internationally by his refusal to meet any German representatives in Rabat and to apply Vichy's anti-semitic laws in Morocco, and his sympathy for the Allies was rewarded by the personal endorsement of Churchill and Roosevelt in their meeting with him in January 1943. Perhaps for that very reason, the protectorate authorities, once again with unerring misjudgement, failed to undertake the needed reforms and continued their repressive policy *vis-à-vis* the nationalists. Convinced now that the drastic changes they demanded could be carried out only after independence was achieved, a cross-section of Moroccan nationalists formed the Istiqlal Party in January 1944. Its programme called for total independence, a democratic constitution and national reunification − the last-mentioned goal being concerned with recuperating portions of the Western Sahara that were then under French and Spanish administrations. Reportedly, the sultan approved the Istiqlal platform but the resident-general, backed by settler opinion and vested French interests in Morocco, rejected any basic alteration of the protectorate structure and shortly thereafter arrested 18 of the Istiqlal leaders on trumped-up charges. With the eclipse of the Istiqlal, other parties were formed in the early post-war period, of which the more moderate Parti Démocratique de l'Indépendance (PDI) perpetuated the division in the nationalist ranks. It became increasingly apparent that only the sultan could become the instrument for creating national unity.

The first post-war decade was marked by riots in Casablanca (1947 and 1952), which had become Morocco's economic capital and the birthplace of its trade-union movement and Communist Party. They took place against the background of a prolonged struggle between the ultraconservative resident-general (Alphonse Juin) and an equally intransigent sultan (Ben Youssef), who used his power to veto *dahirs* so as to foil French attempts to reduce his authority as laid down in the treaty of Fez. By humiliating and then deposing Ben Youssef in 1953, the protectorate created such a wave of anti-French violence and upsurge of support for Ben Youssef that it was forced to yield step by step to the nationalists' demands.[70]

On 7 December 1953 an all-Moroccan government headed by Si Bekkai was formed, which included the Istiqlal and the PDI as well as independent nationalists. The two major parties, albeit competitive in seeking power, were nevertheless agreed on the goal of a Greater Morocco for their country. And although the Franco-Moroccan declaration of 2 March 1956 ended the French protectorate, recognised Morocco's independence and proclaimed Ben Youssef to be full sovereign over Morocco, France was pledged simply to respect the integrity of Moroccan territory as guaranteed by international treaties, and French troops continued to be based temporarily in Morocco.

Before the sultan's return to Morocco, the Army of Liberation was created by mid-1955 under Istiqlal auspices. That army was composed of volunteers from the Rif, the Atlas mountains and tribes of the Draa area, and it operated mainly from bases in Agadir province. By early 1956 it had become known as the Army for Liberation of the Sahara (ALS) and had taken over much of southern Morocco to the detriment of the sultan's authority there, and it was active as far south as the Tindouf region.[71] Nominally, the ALS operated under directives of the Istiqlal, whose leader, Allal El Fassi, had returned to Morocco from his long exile abroad armed with maps and documents purporting to justify that party's goal of restoring Morocco's 'natural and historic frontiers'.[72] To the Istiqlal leadership, realisation of Greater Morocco took priority over achieving a union of the Maghreb countries.

Within a month of the Franco-Moroccan declaration, Spain surrendered control over its northern Moroccan protectorate, and in October 1956 Tangier and its immediate environs were similarly restored to Moroccan rule. Although these territorial gains were far from negligible, and although by mid-1956 most of the Army of Liberation had been integrated into the Royal Armed Forces (FAR), there remained a hard core of ultranationalists among its troops who continued to support actively the Istiqlal's entire irredentist programme. Inevitably that element sympathised and co-operated with the Algerian Front de Libération Nationale (FLN) in its revolt against French rule, and consequently desisted for the time being from pressing Moroccan claims to the indeterminate border area between their two countries. The ALS hardliners therefore concentrated their attacks in the south, against both the Spaniards in the coastal area and the French in northern Mauritania.

Throughout 1957, while Rabat's attention was distracted from the Sahara by uprisings in the Rif and the Middle Atlas, the combined Istiqlal-ALS offensive in the southwestern desert was stepped up as regards both propaganda and guerrilla warfare. In March of that year Allal El Fassi toured southern Morocco, where he told tribesmen there that 'the battle for the Sahara has just begun'.[73] The next month he founded an Arab-language newspaper, the *Moroccan Sahara*, to help 'our Mauritanian brothers to free themselves and rejoin Morocco, our common fatherland'. Mehdi Ben Barka, then president of the Moroccan national advisory assembly and still a member of the Istiqlal (from which he broke away in September 1959 to form the left-wing UNFP), supported Allal's thesis, as did both the Bekkai and Balafredj governments, albeit in more moderate terms. In that assembly, Sheikh Ma El Ainin represented Chinguett, as the Moroccans called Mauritania, and by anticipation also all the Western Saharan populations.

Initially, the king neither condoned nor condemned Allal's Sahara campaign. However, he was careful to disclaim responsibility for the military attacks made by ALS dissidents — estimated to number between 4,000 and 5,000[74] — claiming that they were out of the *makhzen*'s control, especially after the failure of the revolt inspired by the ALS against Spain in Ifni late in 1957.[75] Nevertheless, the possibility of a joint Franco-Spanish military operation against the ALS alarmed the king into creating, under his ministry of interior, an office — later a ministry — of Saharan and frontier affairs on 13 November 1957. This office was designed to be a counterpoise to the Organisation Commune des Régions Sahariennes (OCRS), an economic and administrative unit formed by the French at Algiers a few months before for development of the Saharan areas still under French control. The purpose of the office was to hasten the long-delayed negotiations for demarcating Morocco's western and southern frontiers, and to co-ordinate oil-prospecting activities in that area.

Moroccan-Mauritanian Relations

It was not until early 1958 that Mohammed V officially espoused the Istiqlal's Saharan objectives, with the notable exception of the Gourara-Tidikelt-Touat area. During a visit to Morocco's deep south, the king made a highly publicised speech on 20 February at Mhamid, in which he stressed the claims to the region between Oued Draa and Saquiet El Hamra, stating explicitly that 'We have decided to so orient our activities as to integrate that province into the national territory.'[76]

What induced the king to reach his decision at that time was the subject of speculation. He must have been aware of the weakness of Morocco's historical claims to an area in which prayers had never been said in the name of the Moroccan sultan, Rabat had never named *caïds* or collected taxes there, and the sultan had never arbitrated quarrels among the local tribes.[77] The king's need to retain the Istiqlal's political support was certainly a cogent factor, and another was the imminent defeat of the ALS by the Franco-Spanish forces, which had already caused an influx of refugees from Saquiet El Hamra into the Goulimine area,[78] leaving the former region devoid of supporters for Moroccan claims to sovereignty there. Other considerations of a more psychological nature were the arrival at Rabat of Horma Ould Babana and some tribal chiefs from the Sahara, as well as the prospect of even more eminent Moorish defectors to the Moroccan cause.[79]

The foregoing developments may well have led the king to overestimate the popularity of a union with Morocco among the Mauritanians, or to have misjudged its motivation. Although for eight years the conflict in Algeria was a *drame de conscience* for the francophone black African leaders, it was Morocco's determination to take over Mauritania in the name of 'national reunification' that created the first tension between the peaceful sub-Saharan countries still under French rule and the turbulent Maghreb, already well on its way to freeing itself politically from foreign control and to expanding or consolidating the territories it had inherited. The Moors who defected to Rabat, as well as such reputedly pro-Moroccan Mauritanian parties as the Nahda, seemed moved more by fear of a black federal executive at Dakar replacing the French West African Federation than they were spontaneously attracted to a merger with recently independent Morocco. This became more apparent in 1959, when leaders of the new-born Mali Federation tried to induce the black tribes living along the north bank of the Senegal River to join their organisation. The Moors' fear of black imperialism was not laid to rest until mid-1960, when the Mali Federation broke up and all the French West African countries, including Mauritania, became independent. But even after the disruptive forces from the south and east had lost their momentum, pressure from the north was still exerted for some years longer, though it took a different form. Morocco's military threat to Mauritania was replaced by a diplomatic offensive, in which appeals to Arab solidarity alternated with propaganda depicting Morocco as the standard-bearer of Islam in the desert and chief Arabic francophone leader to protest against French nuclear experiments in the Sahara — themes popular with many Third World countries, including Mauritania.

With Mauritania's admission to the UN in October 1961, Morocco's campaign to deny it international recognition failed, and the backing for Moroccan claims to sovereignty over Mauritania dwindled rapidly.

King Hassan II, who had ascended the throne at Rabat eight months before, had a less imperialistic concept of Moroccan-Mauritanian relations than had his father, Mohammed V, and beginning in mid-1960 he made direct overtures to Daddah. In a speech delivered in June of that year, he said that it was not in the interests of either country for Moroccan *caïds* to administer Mauritania: 'What we want is a kind of personal union, an association of state to state, on the level of religious and blood ties . . . They [the Mauritanians] have their traditions and customs and we ours, but I believe that if they were given the chance they would choose to walk the same road with us.'[80]

In the early 1960s Daddah, too, came to alter his view of Mauritania's relations with its neighbours, first by envisaging his country as a bridge between black and white Africa and then, after 1965, by moving clearly into the Arab orbit. He frequently and without animosity reiterated his desire for fraternal relations with Morocco, but remained adamant about requiring Rabat's prior recognition of Mauritania's sovereign status. Hassan II accepted that precondition only after a series of events in the 1960s — a brief, inconclusive war with Algeria, Morocco's isolation in Africa following his refusal to attend the OAU constituent congress because of Daddah's presence there, the disclosure of the extent of Saquiet El Hamra's phosphate resources and the return to Mauritania of three of the four outstanding émigrés. Only then was the focus of the king's Sahara strategy shifted from Mauritania to Spain's desert province. Those events marked the peak of Morocco's intransigence, and they also precipitated its tortuous search for a *modus vivendi* with Mauritania. King Hassan realised that he must escape from what had become an embarrassing and even dangerous impasse, but without alienating the Istiqlal nationalists, whose continued loyalty was vital to the Alaouite dynasty. Gradually and almost imperceptibly, Rabat gave Nouakchott *de facto* recognition at international meetings, ceased to press its claims abroad against the Daddah government, and slowly dismantled the ministry of Saharan affairs.

In September 1969 Daddah accepted in the name of Muslim unity the king's invitation to attend the Islamic conference then being held at Rabat. For that meeting, the stage had been set at Dakar in exploratory talks held under Senghor's aegis, and the two men's reconciliation was inconspicuously effected at Rabat, in part through the good offices of Boumediene of Algeria.[81] What Daddah conservatively described on his return to Nouakchott as the 'normalisation' of Moroccan-Mauritanian relations was confirmed by the exchange of high-level missions at the end of 1969. They rapidly burgeoned into fully fledged diplomatic missions (in April 1970) and economic and cultural agreements (June 1970), and six years later agreed on a common frontier, initiated closer economic co-operation and signed a mutual-defence agreement. However, in the September 1969 meeting it was significant that there was no discussion of the Spanish Sahara, which both countries continued to claim, lest it delay or even disrupt the conciliation process. Yet the need to win Mauritania's consent to at least a division of the Spanish province was paramount, for it was the key both to placating the Istiqlal irredentists and to negotiating a peaceable settlement of the issue with Spain.

If Hassan's recognition of Mauritania's sovereignty represented a triumph for Daddah's patient and skilful diplomacy, the king's subsequent handling of Mauritania was no less conspicuous a success. A series of developments, largely the outgrowth of Hassan's strategy, served to bring Mauritania into his orbit: through its participation in the tripartite meetings beginning in 1970,[82] Mauritania aligned its policy with that of Morocco and Algeria, and by accepting a Moroccan loan of the funds needed to buy off the Miferma shareholders in February 1975,[83] Nouakchott became financially obligated to Rabat. Then, by the conclusion of the Madrid pact of 14 November 1975, Mauritanian rivalry for the control of the Spanish Sahara was transformed into a partnership for the division and development of that territory. Finally, in the ensuing undeclared war with Algeria, Mauritania's very vulnerability to armed attack drew the Polisario's fire away from Morocco, and this in turn forced Daddah to seek Morocco's aid in bolstering Mauritania's defences against the Polisario raiders. Thus not only by peaceful means but even at Daddah's request, Hassan was able to station troops in Mauritanian towns and, in effect, to occupy the country militarily, the goal that Morocco had been unable to reach by force or by diplomacy during the preceding twenty years.

Close Morocco-Mauritania relations lasted for four years, but they could not survive the military *coup d'état* at Nouakchott in mid-summer 1978 and, even more, the peace that Mauritania made with the Polisario Front a year later. However, the parting of the ways was not marked by violence or recriminations, and subsequently both sides have obviously tried to remain on as good terms as is compatible with their altered status.

Morocco's relations with its neighbours have always been stormy, for its tradition of expansionism into the Sahara has inevitably brought Moroccan leaders into conflict with rival claimants to that region. In its struggles against French colonialism, Morocco was steadfastly supported by its fellow Arabs, Muslims and black Africans, but when its aggressiveness was turned against Mauritania, black Africa withdrew its endorsement and the Arab nations, beginning with Tunisia, gradually followed suit. Similarly, the king's campaign to oust Spain from the Sahara (and the *presidios*) was applauded by all of the Third World, including his neighbours, but when he seized the mineral-rich Saquiet El Hamra against the armed opposition of local tribesmen who claimed that territory as their own, he lost the backing not only of black Africa but that of the Arab states — except for Egypt — as well.

The governments opposing Hassan's policy denounced it as being inspired by sheer greed or as breaching the then sacrosanct principle of respecting inherited colonial frontiers. Those states that continued more or less covertly to back his venture, either militarily or financially, did so mainly for reasons other than those by which Hassan sought to justify his aggression. Such motivation fell into three general categories: one was disapproval of creating still another small, non-viable state that could further fragment the 'Arab nation'; another was the more widespread opposition to disseminating Algeria's revolutionary creed; and still another, the fear of indirectly helping Boumediene thereby to establish hegemony over the area.

Moroccan-Algerian Relations

During the 1930s and the Second World War, the French officials administering the protectorate and Algeria respectively extracted portions of the Confins from the unified military command so as to bring the Saoura valley directly under the control of Algiers and the Oued Draa oases under that of Rabat.[84] However, no resident-general of Morocco, including even Lyautey, was able to persuade the *makhzen* to renounce its claim to the Zousfana and Guir valleys and to Tindouf. Consequently, by 1956, there had been no settlement of the claims by Morocco and by the Provisional Government of Algeria (GPRA) to the same land in that border region. After Morocco became independent the Franco-Moroccan commission that was to have settled the frontier question failed to materialise because both parties, for different reasons, favoured procrastination. The delay in appointing its Moroccan members was due in part to Mohammed V's expectation that a grateful GPRA would be more compliant with his wishes than would France. The Paris government, for its part, realised the imminence of Morocco's independence but not the long-term significance of the Algerian revolt, and therefore sought more time in which it might bring as much of the borderland area as possible under the control of what it expected would remain *Algérie française*.

Morocco's Role in the Algerian Revolt. By 1962, when both Algeria
and Morocco had become sovereign states, there was little hope that
the frontier question would be resolved in a Maghrebian context, for
both countries had already developed incompatible nationalistic goals
and had become involved to differing degrees with Pan-Arabism in
general and Nasser in particular.[85] During the Algerian revolt, it had
been obviously to the FLN's interest to cause trouble in that borderland region, both to diminish Moroccan authority there and to create
friction between Paris and Rabat. It was hoped that if Franco-Moroccan
relations deteriorated far enough, Rabat might permit the FLN to
establish a larger organisation and supply base in the frontier area, and
perhaps eventually join the Algerians in their guerrilla operations against
the French. Yet by no means all the agitation that occurred in the
borderland zone during the late 1950s could be attributed to either
the FLN or Istiqlal provocation, and among the supplementary causes
for the worsening of Franco-Moroccan relations were the nuclear-arms
tests being held at Reggane, which were the object of six protests by
Rabat to Paris and to the UN. Furthermore, those tests offered the
opportunity to reassert Morocco's title to the whole area running from
Béchar to Tindouf, and in his speech from the throne on 8 December
1959, Mohammed V officially voiced Morocco's claim to the Saharan
nuclear-testing area.[86]

In the Western Sahara, Morocco's rivalry with Algeria, which dated
from the colonial period, as well as Rabat's relations with France in the
first post-independence years, were not the only factors influencing
Morocco's attitude towards the FLN. Inevitably, the Moroccans sympathised with the Algerians' struggle for freedom, but their support was
never so wholeheartedly demonstrated as in October 1956, when the
plane carrying Ben Bella and his companions from Rabat to Tunis was
hijacked by the French. In the late 1950s the Moroccan Army of Liberation's raids in the region from Béchar to Tindouf were co-ordinated
with the FLN's operations so as to tie down French forces defending
the military posts there, and they also forced France to repatriate some
of the oil prospectors working in that region. Then in 1960, the outcome of Mohammed V's first attempts to hold democratic elections
greatly increased the king's fears of a left-wing opposition to his rule,
with the result that he drew closer to the GPRA.

To help the Algerian rebels, the Moroccans deliberately caused
trouble for France in the Oujda and Figuig regions, and at the UN

Prince Moulay Hassan sought to make Algerian independence an issue deserving international support. Until then, such aid as had been given the Algerian rebels by the Moroccan government and political parties had been restricted to the civilian refugees living in eastern Morocco, and to tolerating FLN political activities there, albeit under police surveillance. Moreover, some of the arms for the FLN guerrillas unloaded at Casablanca had been seized by the Moroccan authorities to prevent their falling into the hands of their local left-wing adversaries.[87] In July 1961, relations between Morocco and the GPRA seemed to have reached a more stable and constuctive level when the GPRA 'recognised' the territorial problem posed by the unmarked Algerian-Moroccan border and when Hassan II and Ferhat Abbas signed an agreement of co-operation which, in effect, postponed settlement of the frontier question until after Algeria had become independent.[88] Yet relations between the two regimes never became so informal and cordial as those between the FLN and the Tunisians, for the Moroccan *makhzen* was too authoritarian and too steeped in its own national and religious traditions to accommodate itself for any length of time to the views of such parvenu revolutionary leaders as Ben Bella and Boumediene.

As negotiations between Paris and the GPRA-FLN moved haltingly toward France's recognition of Algeria's independence, the Sahara became a major stumbling block to their conclusion, as well as a bone of contention between the Maghreb countries. The French believed that the Sahara should be developed as a distinct entity for the benefit of all its borderland states, and had set up the Organisation Commune des Régions Sahariennes (OCRS) accordingly. On the other hand, the Algerians, Tunisians and Moroccans demanded portions of it as integral parts of their national territory. President Bourguiba took the precaution of moving troops into the Saharan area claimed by Tunisia, but the Istiqlal supported the king in his postponement of negotiations on all frontier questions until such time as they could be carried on with an independent Algerian government and without French participation.[89] The king's stand on this issue, as well as his consistent support for the imprisoned Ben Bella, were interpreted at the time as being motivated largely by his determination to place the Algerian leadership under obligation to him and thus influence the course of Algeria's evolution in a more conservative direction.[90]

The Moroccan strategy became more obvious in March 1962 when Ben Bella and his companions were sent from their prison in France to Rabat on their way to Algeria, and the Moroccans wanted to welcome them as exiles and then ceremoniously return them to their compatriots.[91]

The Algerians, for their part, insisted on their leaders returning home as free men, indebted for their liberation solely to the FLN. Yet they refrained at that time from showing their resentment of what seemed to them Moroccan paternalism, for the GPRA realised that Algeria would continue to need Moroccan aid and trade for some years to come. Just twelve months later Hassan II became the first head of state to be welcomed in independent Algeria, but in the interval the ambivalent and fluctuating relations between the two countries had clearly deteriorated despite the efforts still made by both sides to maintain a show of cordiality. The king's goal of a Greater Morocco was the major cause of discord between him and the Algerians, and it was a measure of its importance to Hassan II, as well as of his opportunism, that he seized upon the power struggle that occurred among the Algerian leaders, immediately after their country became independent in July 1962, as his chance to press his country's claims to the areas lying to the south and east of Morocco.

The Border War. Clashes in the Béchar and Draa regions between the armed forces of the two countries were marked by charges and counter-charges of aggression on the part of both Rabat and Algiers, but the major contest between them was centred in and around Tindouf, where the vast iron deposits of Gara Djebilet were at stake. It was triggered by the arrival in Rabat of a delegation said to represent all the Tindouf tribesmen and Notables who had signed a declaration of their allegiance to the king. The climax to the dispute over Tindouf came to a head early in October 1962, when about a dozen persons were reportedly killed there after the Algerian officer in command at Tindouf had ordered the *caïd* to lower the Moroccan flag, which he had raised over the casbah, and to surrender his arms. Soon, however, talks at Rabat between high-level officials of the two governments papered over their dispute, as did the state visit of Hassan to Algiers in March 1963, during which a series of economic co-operation agreements were signed. Nevertheless, a lessening of the tension did not eliminate the basic dispute between the two countries, for it went deeper than the ownership of vast stretches of sand punctuated by a handful of watering points and oases. The fundamental differences concerned ideological issues, the prestige based on being recognised as the dominant power in the Maghreb, and the wealth that would accrue from development of the disputed areas' known or potential mineral resources.

A statement in *Al Ahram* attributed to Colonel Boumediene at about the time of the king's visit to Algiers, to the effect that the revolution in Algeria would spread beyond its frontiers, was hardly reassuring to a monarch already concerned about the support allegedly being given by Algerian sympathisers to Morocco's left-wing opposition parties.[92] His suspicion of such support was soon strengthened by a last-minute request from Algiers for postponement of the Casablanca-bloc conference due to be held at Marrakech on 3 May 1963. As the members of that bloc were the heads of such radical African governments as the UAR, Ghana, Mali, Guinea and the GPRA, Hassan had been counting on their presence at Rabat — especially that of Nasser — to calm down the left-wing adversaries of his regime, to whom it would appear to give the stamp of approval. In particular, the king attributed Nasser's belated refusal to attend the conference to Algerian pressure, and as the Egyptian president found the time a few days later to spend a week in Algiers, the snub administered to Hassan by both Nasser and Ben Bella was unmistakable. So when, in July, a plot allegedly hatched by Moroccan radicals was discovered in Morocco, where Fakih Al Basri and other close Moroccan friends of Ben Bella were arrested, Algerian connivance was confirmed in the eyes of officials at Rabat. As the Algerian leaders moved closer to Egypt and adopted a more revolutionary stance both at home and abroad, the Moroccan leaders became more conservative and postponed carrying out liberal domestic reforms.

Moroccan propaganda organs went into action, spreading rumours of an Algerian invasion and reviving claims to the border area between the two countries. The Algerian response to Moroccan allegations was not slow in coming. In August 1963 Moroccan nationals were forbidden to circulate in the Béchar region, and there ensued a series of frontier incidents that unleashed a virulent Algerian press campaign directed against the Moroccan monarch and his ministers.[93] Then when the *guerre des sables* started in earnest the following October, the Algerians stressed that 'the king's offensive coincided' with the first Kabyle uprising against Ben Bella's government, and also accused him of mistreating the Algerians then living and working in Morocco.

'The war of the sands', more poetically than realistically named, lasted only three weeks, not because either Morocco or Algeria conceded defeat but because both countries were materially unable to prolong the fighting because of lack of adequate equipment and logistics. This conflict, which was not deliberately provoked by either country but into which they drifted, developed into a more intense version of the frontier clashes that had been taking place since before Algeria became independent in the huge region between Béchar, Figuig, the bend of the Draa and Tindouf. As before, it was accompanied by rival historical claims to that area, reciprocal charges of aggression and of the maltreatment of nationals living in the other country's territory, and accusations of the offer of aid to the opponents of the enemy government for the purpose of undermining that regime. Yet this brief war had several unique features worth noting. It was the first open confrontation in north Africa between two Arab countries which had only recently become independent, thanks in part to their collaboration against their common colonial ruler. Then the attempt by both Algeria and Morocco to utilise for their own ends the domestic opponents of the adversary regime backfired, inasmuch as the war heightened the spirit of nationalism in both countries and thereby consolidated support for their existing governments. Furthermore, while the Western powers maintained a neutral attitude toward the belligerents, the USSR discreetly sent arms to the Algerians aboard Cuban freighters. And finally Egypt, by sending first military advisers and then troops to bolster the Algerian army, was able both to head off a Moroccan victory and, thanks to Nasser's great influence, to line up most of the Arab League states behind Algiers.

Inconclusive in every way as was the *guerre des sables*, and perhaps for that very reason, it proved to be a curtain-raiser (with significant variations) for the far longer and more violent conflict that occurred twelve years later between the same adversaries. Although their junior partners, the Polisario Front and Mauritania, had an important stake in the outcome of this war, the former served as surrogates for the Algerians, and the latter acted in part as decoys to draw the Polisario raiders away from the more strongly defended Moroccan posts in the Saquiet El Hamra. By 1975 the Moroccan and Algerian armed forces were roughly of equal strength, and they were better equipped and provisioned from external sources than in 1963. The Polisario troops were openly given generous support by Algeria and Libya from their oil revenues, and the Moroccan and Mauritanian armed forces received more or less covert aid from some Western powers and conservative Arab governments, more with the aim of 'containing' the Algerians than of achieving the belligerents' own objectives.

Militarily as well as financially, Algeria's Polisario allies were in a more favourable position than the Algerians themselves had been in 1963, when the latter proved ineffective in fighting a classical type of open warfare for which the Moroccan army had been better trained and organised. The Moroccans, by getting off to a fast start in 1975, had been able to occupy the Saharan military posts as soon as they were abandoned by the Spaniards, but the Moroccan garrisons there, once entrenched, were subjected to armed raids by the Polisario forces. Morocco's ultranationalists and its army high command wanted their troops to exercise the right to hot pursuit and to bomb the Polisario sanctuaries in Algerian territory. The king, however, was unwilling to incur international opprobrium and the risk of transforming the Algerian public's reaction to the war, thus far tepid, into a national crusade. As matters turned out, the Algerians did almost none of the actual fighting, and the Moroccans at first comparatively little, and it was the partners of both countries that bore the brunt of the attacks in the case of the Mauritanians, or who took the offensive in that of the Polisario.

As regards mediation of the frontier conflict, both in 1963 and in 1975, many Arab and African leaders offered their good offices. Logically, in 1963, the Arab League should have been the mediating agency to which two Arab member countries should turn to help settle their dispute, but the League's domination by Nasser, who was aiding the Algerians, made it unacceptable to Morocco.[94] Similarly, Bourguiba's proposal of himself as honest broker was rejected by Ben Bella because of Tunisia's claim at that time to ownership of the Edjeleh oilfields. As an international body that might resolve the conflict in an all-African context, there remained the OAU, founded just five months earlier and committed to the principles of the territorial integrity and sovereignty of its member states and of the inviolability of inherited colonial frontiers. And it was on the initiative of two of its founding members, Emperor Haile Selassie of Ethiopia and President Modibo Keita of Mali, that a conference was hastily called at Bamako to end the hostilities, determine their cause and propose a solution acceptable to both belligerents. There a four-member commission was appointed to arrange a ceasefire and the withdrawal of all troops from the combat zones, and this was finally accomplished on 4 November 1963 under the supervision of Ethiopian and Malian officers.

At an OAU meeting at Addis Ababa in mid-November 1963, Algeria refused to negotiate directly with Morocco, so a seven-member committee was formed, composed of the foreign ministers of Ethiopia, Mali, Ivory Coast, Nigeria, Tanganyika, Sudan and Senegal, to work out a long-term solution. At the time, the stopping of further bloodshed between Morocco and Algeria was considered a promising show of strength on the part of the fledgling OAU, and indeed for some years it was the only success that could be credited to it. In April 1964 the military committee was disbanded two months before diplomatic relations between Morocco and Algeria were restored and their frontier was reopened. No progress had been made in demarcating the frontier, however, and within a few weeks renewed agitation in Kabylie and at Casablanca revived the mutual charges by Algiers and Rabat of each other's responsibility for the unrest. As to the *ad hoc* committee that succeeded the seven-man committee, its members early recognised the impossibility of carrying out their assigned tasks of ascertaining the facts behind the 1963 war amid the welter of mutual recriminations and the futility of proposing solutions that they could never impose. The best that the committee could do was to attempt to lessen the tension between Morocco and Algeria by postponing positive action.

Both Morocco and Algeria seemed to recognise the folly of resorting again to force and the need to take time to reach some *modus vivendi*, hence the status quo was maintained for nearly two years.[95] Then Hassan took the initiative and arranged a meeting with Ben Bella at Saidia near the Algerian frontier on 12 May 1965, during which the two leaders worked out some economic agreements. Nevertheless, a new setback occurred the next month when Ben Bella was ousted by Colonel Houari Boumediene, who since 1963 had succeeded in building up the Algerian army with Soviet help. Boumediene proved to be less conciliatory than Ben Bella, refusing to accept Ferhat Abbas's commitment to Morocco[96] and declaring that 'Algeria's frontiers are not negotiable'. In May 1966 his intransigence took a more concrete form when he deployed troops throughout the disputed frontier area and nationalised all of Algeria's mines, including the controversial Gara Djebilet iron deposits. At Hassan's request, the OAU *ad hoc* committee was reactivated and once again its members were able to reduce tensions but sidestepped dealing with its basic cause, when the rapid political and economic evolution of the Spanish Sahara and Israel's victory in the six-day war — external events, in which Algeria and Morocco shared common interests — provided diversions that temporarily overwhelmed their frontier quarrel.

Conciliatory Moves. In September 1968 the king's presence at the OAU summit meeting in Algiers marked his first move toward reconciliation with Boumediene. Despite continued political sniping, the year 1967 had brought promising economic agreements between the two countries. In March their governments contracted to process in Morocco some of the lead and zinc mined in northwestern Algeria, using the Algerian port of Ghazaouat (formerly Nemours) for their export, and in August they widened the scope of a trading agreement that had been concluded on 25 November 1964. The former arrangement was the continuation on a smaller scale of a French project in the 1950s to install an industrial complex in the Béchar region as the first step towards creating a 'Saharan Ruhr'. As to the trade agreement, it aimed to enlarge the exchanges of Moroccan agricultural and manufactured products for Algerian hydrocarbons and industrial goods.

Both developments underscored the growing importance of economic issues in the area's evolution and particularly in that of Moroccan-Algerian relations, as well as the complementary nature of their economies,[97] but not to the point where they transcended or modified their respective political and ideological differences. By 1968 Algeria had become Morocco's chief trading partner in Africa, holding fifth place as its provisioner and ranking sixteenth as its client, but because the African trade as a whole accounted for only 6.1 per cent of all Morocco's foreign commerce, the trade with Algeria was not vital to its economy. What was of great concern to both Moroccan and Algerian leaders was the maintenance of the exclusive right to develop, process and dispose of their country's resources in what they deemed to be their national interest, and they were not disposed to share such enterprises with other countries except in return for very substantial concessions.

No north African government has long maintained cordial relations with its neighbours, but since 1974 those between Morocco and Algeria have been consistently and conspicuously bad. In particular, Morocco's attitude towards Algeria combines fear with envy and disdain, resulting in a sense of frustration and isolation. Fear that Algeria's revolutionary doctrines might be contagious or deliberately propagated in Morocco was heightened by the former country's rapid military build-up with Soviet aid beginning in 1964.[98] To cope with what King Hassan regarded as a military threat, he bought arms from the United States, and also proposed to the UN secretary general in March 1967 that the latter appoint a military commission charged with checking the growth of armaments in the Maghreb. As for the element of contempt-cum-envy in Morocco's attitude toward Algeria, it was the disdain felt by Hassan — heir to an ancient monarchy claiming descent from the Prophet and to an empire, albeit shrunken — towards an upstart 'artificial nation' like Algeria, mingled with jealousy of the latter's mineral resources and Boumediene's growing international prestige.

Algeria, for its part, was still smarting under its quasi-defeat by Morocco in 1963, and was determined not to yield a centimetre of its hard-won land, particularly to a monarch so 'reactionary' as Hassan II, or to let him take over unopposed the iron-ore of Gara Djebilet and the phosphates of Bu Craa. To thwart the king from achieving those objectives, as well as to support Mauritania's claim to the Spanish Sahara,

Boumediene invited Daddah to make a state visit to Algiers at the height of the Moroccan-Algerian tension in March 1967. Morocco retaliated by promptly giving encouragement to Boumediene's domestic opponents, as symbolised by the ceremonial burial at Rabat accorded to Mohammed Khider, who had been mysteriously assassinated in Spain. Within a few months, too, the king ordered the dismissal of the hundred-odd Algerians who were still employed by the Rabat administration.[99]

The Tripartite Front and the Tlemcen Agreement. Nevertheless, by the late 1960s Madrid's obvious intention of transforming its Saharan province into an autonomous territory under Spanish tutelage had awakened Morocco, Algeria and Mauritania to the need for joint action if Spain were to be eliminated from the western desert. As a preliminary step, Boumediene made a state visit to Morocco in January 1969, and at Ifrane he and the king signed a treaty of co-operation and good neighbourliness. Nine months later he helped to end the long feud between Daddah and Hassan, thereby laying the foundations for the tripartite entente that materialised in September 1970 at Nouadhibou.[100] On 27-8 May of that year, Boumediene and Hassan met at Tlemcen, where they announced that, *inter alia*, they had reached an agreement in principle on their frontier dispute. Although the terms of this accord were not then divulged because of anticipated Istiqlal opposition, it was known that in general terms Morocco had thereby accepted Algerian sovereignty over the Saoura and Tindouf in return for a share in the development of Gara Djebilet's iron, its export through a Moroccan port, and limited Algerian support for Morocco's claims to the Spanish Sahara. This Tlemcen agreement was widely hailed at home and abroad as a giant step towards building a united Maghreb, and also as proof that Africans could settle their disputes among themselves. The terms of the Tlemcen agreement were spelled out in a treaty signed by the two heads of state on 15 June 1972. It was ratified by Algeria on 17 May 1973, but not by Morocco, on the ground that there was then in existence at Rabat no body authorised by the constitution to take such action.

Between 1970 and 1974 trade between Morocco and Algeria increased and many economic projects were planned jointly by their governments. Moreover, the personal relations between Boumediene and Hassan developed in an atmosphere of unwonted cordiality. After the king escaped assassination in July 1971, Boumediene immediately telephoned his congratulations. Yet observers noted that the Algerian press and radio at that time remained noncommittal, in contrast to the enthusiasm they had displayed in 1969 when Colonel Khadafi had overthrown King Idriss in Libya.[101] A year later, in August 1972, just after the attempt had been made to shoot down the king's plane carrying Hassan home from France, rumours began to circulate in Morocco linking that action with Moroccan exiles living in Algeria as well as in Libya. Then confirmation of the active role played by Colonel Khadafi in the attempt to oust Hassan came in March 1973, when an armed band of Moroccans (reportedly backed by the UNFP leader, Mohammed Basri), financed and trained in Libya, was intercepted by the Moroccan police at Goulmina in the Middle Atlas, whither they had infiltrated by way of Algeria for the purpose of stirring up a popular uprising against Hassan. Despite denial of reports that the Algerian government, alerted by Rabat, had arrested hundreds of Moroccans living in Algeria, the suspicion remained that Algeria, as well as Libya, had aided the Moroccan guerrillas in their attempt to stage a *coup d'état*.[102]

The trial at Kenitra of the Moroccan officers accused of attempted regicide, the king's failure to attend the conference of non-aligned nations in September 1973, and his general neglect of the OAU even during the year when he was president of that organisation, did not contribute to Hassan's popularity. Yet he proved to be a good host to Boumediene and Daddah during the tripartite meeting held at Agadir in August 1973, and the Algerian president warmly praised his hospitality. In October 1973 Hassan recovered much of his prestige in the Arab world by sending Moroccan troops to fight Israel on the Golan Heights, and in consequence even the Libyan broadcasts temporarily suspended their anti-Hassan campaign. Encouraged by this break in his isolation, the king in December 1973 left his country for the first time in eighteen months to visit Algiers.

In view of these developments, the question naturally arises as to why King Hassan believed in August 1974 that he could permanently and with impunity exclude Algeria from participating in the negotiations he was carrying on with Spain and Mauritania for the legal takeover of the richest and largest portion of the Spanish Sahara. He may well have been convinced that by formally renouncing Morocco's claims to Algeria's far west in 1972, and by peaceably terminating Spain's colonial rule in the Western Sahara, he had satisfied Boumediene's main desiderata there. Furthermore, he may well have believed that without Algerian interference he could duplicate the successes he had had in negotiating bilaterally with Madrid for the return of Ifni, and with Daddah for renouncing his claim to all the Spanish Sahara in return for Rio de Oro and a share in the Bu Craa enterprise. Another cause for his optimism was Algeria's absorption in developing closer relations with Libya and black Africa and, even more, in its involvement in Middle Eastern affairs. Moreover, Algeria's expenditures to carry out its ambitious development plans seemed likely to discourage its leaders from undertaking costly military ventures in an area where Algeria had no interest directly at stake. Hassan may also have counted on the indifference of the Algerian public in regard to the Sahraoui cause so long as no attack was made on national territory, as well as on the reluctance of all the Arab states except Libya to take sides in a remote quarrel between fellow-Arabs over land whose resources, actual and potential, were apparently of direct interest only to its immediate neighbours.

As events were to prove, the king had gravely underestimated the tenacity of Algeria and its Polisario partners, but he had also underestimated the enthusiasm aroused at home by his own irredentist policy. By tapping the rich vein of Moroccan nationalist sentiments among radicals as well as among conservatives, peasants and bourgeois alike, not to mention the armed forces, Hassan won such widespread popularity for the first time in his reign that he risked being pushed too far and too fast into war. And because of his standing as a bulwark against the spread of the Algerian revolution, the king received discreet pledges of substantial financial support from the conservative world capitals to which he had sent envoys to plead Morocco's cause during the summer of 1974. Furthermore, the spectacular rise in Morocco's revenues from its phosphate exports in that year, as well as the prospect of cornering the output of Bu Craa, doubtless elated Hassan to the point where he would risk a limited war for such high stakes.

In the debates that took place in 1975 before the World Court at The Hague, sparring between Morocco and Algeria was couched in legal language and continued to be moderate at international gatherings wherever Algeria succeeded in getting the Spanish Sahara question placed on the agenda. Algeria consistently stressed its disinterestedness in that area and its advocacy of the principle of self-determination as laid down in the UN resolutions that had been endorsed by all the parties involved in determining the future of Spain's Saharan province. Morocco just as consistently upheld the principle of territorial integrity and its historical rights to the region. Only through the propaganda media of those countries did the basic issues between them surface. These were the ideological incompatibility between regimes based respectively on revolutionary socialism and on liberal capitalism as interpreted by a conservative autocratic monarchy; hegemony in the Western Sahara; and, in the practical domain, the ownership of the Gara Djebilet iron deposits.

It was Algeria's recognition of the RASD on 28 February 1976 that caused Morocco (and Mauritania) to break off diplomatic relations with Algiers on the following 7 March. That step in turn provoked Algerian retaliation, which took the form of closing the frontier with Morocco, refusing to service Moroccan planes flying between North African cities and repatriating from 25,000 to 40,000 Moroccans living in Algeria. In terms of economic warfare, Algeria had the upper hand, for Morocco was more dependent on imports of Algerian oil than was Algeria on Moroccan exports.

At various times during the winter of 1975-6, armed conflict between the two countries seemed inevitable, and indeed the propagandists on both sides appeared to be taunting the adversary into declaring war.[103] In the summer of 1975 Boumediene was said to have told Bourguiba that no Algerian soldier would fight outside the boundaries of his own country,[104] and indeed only in the two bloody battles for Amgala (in January and February 1976) did Algerian troops actively participate. Inasmuch as the Algerians did not then win control of Amgala, and as a few weeks later the Polisario declared the independence of the RASD, it was obviously to Boumediene's advantage to operate militarily through an organisation that now claimed to be a sovereign state. Indeed, both he and Hassan were basically prudent men loath to risk open war between two evenly matched forces. Moreover, by early 1976 the war in the Saquiet El Hamra had reached a stalemate; the Moroccans could not patrol the desert or cut off the Polisario's supplies from its Algerian bases; and the Polisario guerrillas could not drive the Moroccans out of the coastal settlements or military posts. Subsequently the battleground shifted to the south, whither Moroccan troops soon had to be sent to shore up the Mauritanian defences.

Although it had become increasingly improbable that the Saharan dispute could be settled by wholly military means, the two main protagonists continued to be adamant in refusing the offers of mediation repeatedly made by Arab and black African leaders. Apparently the Moroccans and Algerians still believed their own propaganda – to the effect that international pressure and especially subversive action could bring about the adversary's downfall or withdrawal – which was based on surprising misconceptions. Neither regime understood the power base of its rival or credited the latter with reflecting the will of the population it governed. Each government has seemed convinced that under pressure from internal opponents and from the economic hardships imposed by the war, the people of the other country would rise up and drive out their oppressive leaders.

Apparently the Algerian leadership assumed that the Moroccans, appalled by the casualties inflicted by the Polisario and exasperated by the fast-rising cost of living and their government's arbitrary actions and corruption, would overthrow the monarchy and support the Sahraoui RASD.[105] Obviously the Algerians underestimated the depth of rural Moroccans' veneration for their *imam*-sovereign, as well as their national pride and their resentment against Algerian presumption. Similarly, the Moroccans were misled by the hostility of some Algerian exiles and native bourgeoisie to the Boumediene government's nationalisation programmes. They seemed to believe reports that Boumediene was suffering from such delusions of grandeur that he planned to colonise Niger as well as the Sahara. What was more serious was that they apparently thought that the manifesto issued in March 1976 by four prominent former leaders of the Algerian revolt reflected popular discontent with the government's policy *vis-à-vis* Morocco.[106] In 1976-7 the Moroccan leaders discounted the Algerians' hearty endorsement of their National Charter and of their government at the polls, just as, conversely, the Algerians would not accept evidence of the king's popularity as indicated by the parliamentary mandate given by the Moroccan electorate to his supporters.

Perhaps the most striking paradox of the Moroccan-Algerian relationship — one that has been caused or exacerbated by the Sahara dispute — has been the misunderstandings and mutual mistrust that have developed between the left-wing opposition parties of Morocco and the socialist government of Algeria. In principle they should be allies, given the similarity of their doctrines and their common commitment to a united Maghreb, but in practice they have diverged increasingly in their respective concepts of the scope and governance of that Maghreb which both desire to build. According to Abderrahim Bouabid, leader of the major Moroccan opposition party, the UNFP, the Moroccan left wing as of 1976 had been repeatedly rebuffed by both the Algerian government and its domestic opponents when it proposed a partnership in developing the Western Sahara in a Maghrebian context, because the Algerians insisted on its division by national frontiers.[107] Perhaps inevitably, competitive nationalisms were the rock on which their potential partnership foundered.

Initially, the UNFP leaders' argument ran as follows: in a few years the monarchy would surely be swept away and Algeria, which already had the lion's share of the Sahara, should help Morocco to attain economic independence by helping it to develop the western part of that desert. As for the proposal to create a nominally sovereign state there, this would only contribute to Balkanising the area, and the Sahraouis' clamour for independence could be discounted as merely the desire of some of their leaders to gain access to a consumer society. On the charge of Algerian ingratitude for services rendered by Morocco during the 1954-62 revolt, and of Algeria's duplicity in negotiating secretly with Spain to set up a puppet state in the Sahara that would eventually give Algeria access to the Atlantic, Bouabid was echoing the Moroccan nationalists' accusations. But the Saharan issue also brought to the fore the special grievances felt by Moroccan radicals against the regime of Boumediene (and Ben Bella), as well as their denunciation of the Algerian leaders' 'ideological hypocrisy'.

When the Moroccan left-wing parties were undergoing a severe repression by the royal government, the Algerians, Bouabid complained bitterly, had made no effort to help them. As to Algeria's brand of socialism, it was flawed by its government's close ties with capitalist countries and multinational companies, and its advocacy of self-determination for the Sahraoui was hardly consistent with its recognition of the RASD without a prior referendum and with its failure to grant such a right to the Touareg within its own borders. Bouabid wound up his diatribe by suggesting that 'sooner or later the Moroccan army may have to respond [to Polisario harassment] by attacking the commando bases in Algeria', and he added that 'to my knowledge there are no Moroccans who support Algeria's stand on the Sahara except some extremist groups, and even they have their reservations'.[108]

From the Algerians has come no response comparable to Bouabid's lively attack, although the official *El Moudjahid*, beginning to heat up in October 1975, devoted every day a column and sometimes a page to publicising the Polisario's exploits and the justice of its cause, with only brief respites during the National Charter and electoral campaigns. The Algerian government and its spokesmen clearly preferred international forums in which to denounce Morocco and Mauritania for reneging on their approbation of Sahraoui self-determination and for their self-serving expansionism.

Until late in 1975 a rupture between Algeria and its fellow-members in the tripartite entente seemed not to be inevitable, for Boumediene needed and, it appeared, sincerely wanted good relations with his neighbours and a united Maghreb. He, like Ben Bella before him, was understandably jealous of Algeria's mineral wealth, for which their compatriots had fought at great sacrifice. They were also highly conscious of the vulnerability of their country's frontiers with seven states, all of which had attained independence earlier than had Algeria. Boumediene envisaged the north African union, which he first called a People's Maghreb in June 1975, as a Maghreb of national states demarcated as they had been in colonial days and amenable to Algerian leadership. Not only did he resist the claims asserted by Bourguiba and Hassan to 'Algeria's Sahara', but he opposed any merger or alliance between neighbouring states, such as those proposed between Tunisia and Libya in 1974 and realised between Morocco and Mauritania in 1976. In the spring of 1975 Boumediene had reportedly approved of Moroccan-Mauritanian moves to force Spain out of the Western Sahara, and he seemed also to have accepted their plan to divide the Spanish Sahara between them after his foreign minister, Abdelaziz Bouteflika, had talked with Hassan the following July.[109] But in November came the Green March and then the Madrid pact that marked the turning-point in his attitude, which thereafter became openly hostile. Apparently Boumediene had come to believe that the Moroccan-Mauritanian alliance in respect to the Spanish Sahara was but the first step in an irredentist scheme that included the eventual absorption at Algeria's expense of Tindouf and Touat.

For two countries so well balanced as Morocco and Algeria in human and natural resources, and sharing many international goals as well as a common colonial heritage, a united Maghreb seemed obviously the framework in which they could achieve co-operation and settle their differences. Yet since independence their governments responded so aggressively to the 'territorial imperative', either by provocative, predatory moves as in the case of Bu Craa, or by a dog-in-the-manger attitude as in the development of Gara Djebilet's mineral wealth, as to risk plunging them into a mutually destructive war which neither of them could win. In the process of trying to resolve their rivalry by force, both Morocco and Algeria were wasting resources that they needed for their economic development, Mauritania jeopardised its survival as a nation, and thousands of Sahraouis became miserable refugees, either voluntarily or perforce, having exchanged their freedom as nomadic herdsmen for a nominally sovereign status.

Notes

1. For much of the material in this section the authors are indebted to the work of Ross Dunn. See Bibliography.

2. F.E. Trout, *Morocco's Saharan Frontiers* (Droz, Geneva, 1969), p. 352.

3. E. Gellner, 'Patterns of Rural Rebellion in Morocco during the Early Years of Independence' in E. Gellner and C. Micaud (eds), *Arabs and Berbers*.

(Duckworth, London, 1973), pp. 368 et seq.

4. A. Hammoudi, 'L'Evolution de l'Habitat dans la Vallée du Draa', *Revue de Géographie du Maroc*, no. 18 (1970).

5. See pp. 210-11.

6. A. Coram, 'Note on the Role of the Berbers in the Early Days of Moroccan Independence' in Gellner and Micaud, *Arabs and Berbers*, pp. 260-76.

7. O. Marais, 'The Political Evolution of the Berbers in Independent Morocco' in ibid., pp. 277-84.

8. D.E. Ashford, 'Politics and Violence in Morocco', *Middle East Journal* (Winter 1959).

9. A. Adam, 'Les Sahariens à Casablanca' in *Le Sahara* (Septième Colloque d'Histoire, organisé par la Faculté de Lettres d'Aix-en-Provence, 1967).

10. See pp. 30-1, 165, 175, 238.

11. Municipal and communal elections were held on 12 November 1976, those for provincial assemblies on 25 January 1977, and the final legislative elections on 3 June 1977.

12. As of 1976, there were 10,869,000 persons living in rural areas as against 6,956,700 urban residents.

13. *Marchés Tropicaux*, 24 Dec. 1960, 22 July 1961.

14. P. Roché, 'L'Irrigation et le Statut Juridique des Eaux au Maroc', *Revue Juridique et Politique* (Jan.-March, April-June, Oct.-Dec. 1965).

15. D. Jacques-Meunié, 'La Vallée du Draa au Milieu du XXe Siècle' in *Maghreb et Sahara* (Société de Géographie, Paris, 1973), pp. 163-86.

16. According to Adam, 'Les Sahariens', 'it is not unusual to find a date palm whose produce is divided among ten owners'.

17. *Marchés Coloniaux*, 10 Dec. 1949.

18. See pp. 293-5.

19. Lieut. Henriet, 'Un Problème de l'Extrème-sud Marocain' (CHEAM, Mémoire No. 6, Oct.-Nov. 1937).

20. An analysis of the population of Casablanca, which numbered some 960,000 in 1960, showed that most of the newcomers to that city were southern Moroccans, of whom the Saharans accounted for 13 per cent, and of that percentage only 0.2 per cent were Ait Atta tribesmen. As to their occupations, 18.2 per cent were employed as gardeners, 14.6 per cent in the sanitation service, 12.3 per cent in industry and 6.2 per cent on public works. Employers were said to favour Saharans because of their docility and comparative stability, despite their tendency to return home at least once every two years. Adam, 'Les Sahariens', pp. 169-92.

21. D. Noin, *La Population Rurale du Maroc* (2 vols., Presses Universitaires de France, Paris, 1970), vol. 1, p. 183.

22. Ibid., vol. 2, p. 272.

23. Capt. de Saint-Bon, 'Les Populations des Confins du Maroc Saharien' (CHEAM, Mémoire No. 27 bis, 11 May 1938).

24. Noin, *La Population Rurale du Maroc*, vol. 1, p. 189.

25. R.E. Dunn, 'Berber Imperialism: the Ait Atta Expansion in Southeast Morocco' in Gellner and Micaud, *Arabs and Berbers*, p. 104.

26. Saint-Bon, 'Les Populations'.

27. A. Gaudio, *Les Civilisations du Sahara* (Collection Marabout-Université, No. 141, Paris, 1967), p. 19.

28. G. Spillman, 'Districts et Tribus de la Haute Vallée du Draa' in *Villes et Tribus du Maroc* (Rabat, 1931).

29. See Trout, *Morocco's Saharan Frontiers*, p. 218; Dunn, 'Berber Imperialism'; Gaudio, *Les Civilisations*.

30. G. Salvy, 'La Crise du Nomadisme dans le Sud Marocain' (CHEAM, Mémoire No. 1563, May 1949).

31. J. Couleau, *La Paysannerie Marocaine* (Conseil National de Recherches Scientifiques, Paris, 1968), p. 89.

32. Capt. P. Azam, 'Sedentaires et Nomades dans le Sud Marocain: le Coude du Draa' (CHEAM, Mémoire No. 1009, 1946).

33. C. Lienz, 'Vallée du Dadès', *Encyclopédie Mensuelle d'Outre-Mer* (July 1955).

34. G. Toutain, 'Sur une Evolution de la Vallée du Draa' (CHEAM, Mémoire No. 4428, 1972).

35. Gaudio, *Les Civilisations*, p. 308.

36. Capt. P. Azam, 'La Structure Politique et Sociale de l'Oued Draa' (CHEAM, Mémoire No. 2039, 1947).

37. Saint-Bon, 'Les Populations'.

38. On 23 June 1971, seven economic regions were created, the first of which comprised the provinces of Ouarzazate, Agadir and Tarfaya and the seventh those of Meknes and Ksar Es Souk. Each of the regions was endowed with a directorate and a regional assembly, which advised the government on economic projects for developing its area. A decade earlier, in October 1961, Morocco had been divided into six military regions, one of which was that of Agadir.

39. Roché, 'L'Irrigation'.

40. Toutain, 'Evolution de la Vallée du Draa'.

41. As recently as the late 1960s, a prosperous Draa family might own one or two cows, three or more sheep, and a mule, and families in the poorest *ksour* had only goats and donkeys. The Draa valley is reputedly unhealthy for camels.

42. See Toutain, 'Evolution de la Vallée du Draa'.

43. Noin, *La Population Rurale du Maroc*, vol. 2, pp. 183-91.

44. Adam, 'Les Sahariens'.

45. *Marchés Tropicaux*, 21 June 1969, 30 Oct. and 27 Nov. 1971.

46. In early 1970 the government payroll comprised 300 to 500 Drawa locally employed in the building industry, 700 to 3,000 in the 'national promotion' programme, and 2,000 to 3,000 in the regional-development bureau. Between 1,000 and 2,000 other Drawa were working on government jobs outside the valley.

47. J. Cazaunau, 'Le Relèvement du Niveau de Vie dans les Régions Sahariennes et Présahariennes au sud de l'Atlas', *Encyclopédie Mensuelle d'Outre-Mer* (Jan. 1957).

48. Noin, *La Population Rurale du Maroc*, vol. 1, p. 186.

49. Roché, 'L'Irrigation'.

50. *New York Times*, 21 Jan. 1966.

51. Dunn, 'Berber Imperialism', pp. 99 et seq.

52. I.W. Zartman, *Morocco: Problems of Power* (Atherton Press, New York, 1964), pp. 79-94.

53. Ibid., p. 79.

54. J.K. Cooley, *Baal, Christ, and Mohammed* (John Murray, London, 1965), p. 289.

55. See pp. 117-18, 154, 159.

56. G. Salvy, 'Le Sahara du Nord-ouest' and 'Le Sahara du Nord et Rédaction d'Ensemble' in *L'Economie Pastorale Saharienne* (La Documentation Française, *Notes et Etudes Documentaires*, No. 1730, 21 April 1953).

57. Capt. Moreau, 'Les Sociétés des Oasis. Une Race de Bani: Les Harratins' (CHEAM, Mémoire No. 2431, Jan. 1955).

58. R. Gromond, 'Le Particularisme de Figuig' (CHEAM, Mémoire No. 215, April 1937).

59. M. Bonnefous, *La Palmeraie de Figuig: Etude Démographique et Economique du Sud Marocain* (Service des Statistiques, Rabat, 1952).

60. Agence France Presse despatch from Algiers, 10 April 1959.

61. Roché, 'L'Irrigation'.

62. The writers are indebted to Trout, *Morocco's Saharan Frontiers*, for much of the material in this section.

63. To solve the problem, the Paris government created the Territoires du Sud between 1903 and 1905, and placed that area directly under the governor-general of Algeria, who was also given responsibility for policing the new unit's frontier.

64. Trout, *Morocco's Saharan Frontiers*, p. 26.

65. Ibid., pp. 152-6.

66. See pp. 315-17.

67. See pp. 105, 117.

68. See Trout, *Morocco's Saharan Frontiers*, pp. 287 and 384; E. Méric, 'Le Conflit Algéro-Marocain', *Le Monde Diplomatique* (Nov. 1963).

69. C.H. Moore, 'Political Parties in Independent North Africa' in L.C. Brown (ed.), *State and Society in Independent North Africa* (Middle East Institute, 1966), p. 24.

70. 'In the two years of the sultan's exile, 6,000 acts of terrorism were committed and over 700 persons killed.' *Area Handbook for Morocco* (The American University, Washington, DC, 1972), p. 58.

71. M.R. Thomas, *Sahara et Communauté* (Presses Universitaires de France, Paris, 1960), p. 69.

72. A. Gaudio, *Allal al Fassi, ou l'Histoire de l'Istiqlal* (Paris, 1972).

73. M. Howe, 'Oil and Politics Mix in the Sahara Desert', *Mainichi Daily News*, Osaka, 15 March 1957.

74. G. Chaffard, *Les Carnets Secrets de la Décolonisation* (Calmann Levy, Paris, 1965), p. 265.

75. See p. 118.

76. *Le Monde*, 25 Feb. 1958.

77. G.M. Désiré-Vuillemin, *Les Rapports de la Mauritanie et du Maroc* (Service des Archives Nationale de la Mauritanie, St Louis-du-Sénégal, 1960), p. 30.

78. See pp. 153-4, 162, 253-4.

79. In March 1958 the emir of Trarza and three ministers in the Daddah administration came to swear allegiance to the king at Rabat. Soon they were given ambassadorial or high civil-service posts. Eventually the emir himself became minister for the Sahara in the Moroccan government. *Le Monde*, 9 Nov. 1960.

80. *Le Monde*, 10 June 1960.

81. During the Islamic conference all issues of *Al Alam* and *L'Opinion*, the Istiqlal organs, that contained any reassertion of Morocco's claim to Mauritania were confiscated by the government. *West Africa*, 4 Oct. 1969.

82. See pp. 160-1.

83. See p. 83.

84. Trout, *Morocco's Saharan Frontiers*, p. 354.

85. J. Recoules, 'Notes sur la Frontière Méridionale du Maroc', *L'Afrique et l'Asie*, no. 64 (1963).

86. *Marchés Tropicaux*, 12 Dec. 1959.

87. Ibid., 4 June, 12 Nov. 1960.

88. *Maghreb*, no. 6 (Nov.-Dec. 1964).

89. P. Maillot, 'La Politique Marocaine de Non-dépendence', *Revue Juridique et Politique d'Outre-Mer* (Jan.-March 1963).

90. *Marchés Tropicaux*, 2 Dec. 1961.

91. Ibid., 11 March 1962.

92. E. Méric, 'Le Conflit Algéro-Marocain', *Revue Française des Sciences Politiques* (Aug. 1965).

93. See *El Moudjahid*, 8 Sept. 1963.

94. N. Boyer, 'Le Problème des Frontières du Maroc' (CHEAM, Mémoire

No. 4237, 1968).

95. J. Woronoff, 'Différends Frontaliers en Afrique', *Revue Française d'Etudes Politiques Africaines* (Aug. 1972).

96. See p. 229.

97. A Tiano, *La Politique Economique et Financière du Maroc Indépendant* (Presses Universitaires de France, Paris, 1963), p. 146.

98. By 1967 Algeria's armed forces, numbering some 60,000 men, were estimated to be better equipped, especially as regards planes and tanks, than was Morocco's 45,000-strong military force. See A. Pautard, 'Frontière Algéro-Marocaine: Le Conflit Reste Ouvert', *Revue Française d'Etudes Politiques Africaines* (April 1967), and C. Gallagher, 'Morocco and its Neighbors', *American Universities Field Staff Reports*, part II (March 1967).

99. *Marchés Tropicaux*, 19 Aug. 1967.

100. See p. 160.

101. *Marchés Tropicaux*, 31 July 1971.

102. *Le Monde*, 17 March 1973.

103. At his press conference on 25 November 1975, the king said that 'logically I expect Algeria to make war on us'.

104. 'La Marche Verte' (anonymous typescript, 15 Dec. 1975); *Révolution Africaine*, 26 Feb. 1976.

105. See *El Moudjahid*, 7 May 1976.

106. *L'Opinion*, 24 May 1976.

107. Interview with Bouabid, *Jeune Afrique*, 11 June 1976; *Afrique-Asie*, 1 Nov. 1976.

108. Mahdi Takhdan, spokesman for such a group, writing in *Afrique-Asie*, 1 Nov. 1976, attacked the government's domestic, not its Saharan, policy, when he asserted that because of economic exploitation, 'the area from Agadir to Taroudant is ripe for revolt'.

109. *Marchés Tropicaux*, 11 July 1975.

PART IV: THE POLISARIO FRONT AND THE PARTITION

The Polisario Front, '1975 model', was better organised and more Marxist and publicity-oriented than any of the movements from whose ashes it had risen, and it placed less stress than its predecessors on Islamic orthodoxy. Thanks to the support in funds and arms that it had begun to receive from Algeria and also sporadically from Libya, it was also far better equipped in weapons and vehicles. In 1973 the Polisario Front had looked primarily to Mauritania for backing, in proportion as its hostility to Spain diminished and its suspicion of Moroccan intentions grew. Although Mauritania was too poor a country to provide the Polisario with material aid, it offered a handy base from which to operate, the Moors were ethnically and culturally related to the Sahraouis, and the youthful radicals who opposed the Daddah regime might qualify as allies. Furthermore, a merger with Mauritania was advocated by Colonel Mouamar Khadafi, president of Libya, who gladly financed the Polisario so long as it fought against Spain but who could not, as a proponent of the concept of an Arab nation, approve the creation of an independent Sahraoui state. Algeria was the only remaining alternative, but the initial contacts were not promising in view of President Boumediene's distrust. This was based on his recent disillusionment with Eduardo Moha and the Morehob, which he had earlier sponsored as an authentic liberation movement.[1]

Nevertheless, by late 1974 the rumours circulating about a Moroccan-Mauritanian deal to divide the Spanish Sahara between them brought together the Polisario command and the Algerian leadership out of mutual need. The Polisario had to have such a base as Tindouf, not only for its military operations but also for the Sahraoui refugee camps it was organising, and Boumediene wanted a reliable and tough fighting force that would effectively combat the Moroccan army without requiring direct Algerian military intervention. Furthermore, Boumediene's belief that Madrid would never yield its Saharan province to Mauritania and Morocco was being fast undermined, and he was now less afraid to lose Spain's economic co-operation should he permit the Polisario to attack the Spaniards from an Algerian base.[2] With objectives more practical than those of Khadafi, Boumediene was now willing to endorse the Polisario's proposal for a non-aligned, socialist-oriented Arab republic

247

in the Western Sahara, and by 1975 was giving it appreciable aid.[3] Before such a plan could be carried out, however, certain changes had to occur. To create a legally recognised political vacuum into which the new republic could step, it was necessary that Spain withdraw from the Sahara. Moreover, the disorganised refugees fleeing before the Moroccan onslaught had to be securely placed in camps, either in Algeria or under the protection of the Polisario, before the latter could move to the offensive. The times were not ripe for such developments before the end of 1975.

The République Arabe Sahraouie Démocratique

Two days before Spain formally terminated its rule in the Sahara, the forty-odd local and foreign journalists then in Algiers were invited by the Polisario Front to fly south in a chartered plane to cover an 'important' but unspecified event. In the late afternoon of 26 February 1976, the plane landed at Tindouf, where the journalists were taken to the refugee camps and makeshift hospital to see and hear evidence of Moroccan brutality and the refugees' pitiable plight. At nine that evening they boarded Land Rovers and trucks and were driven into the desert for about two hours. According to an eye witness,[4] the convoy suddenly came to a stop beside a large camp near Bir Lahlou, in front of which some thousands of women and children formed a wide circle around a flagpole. A guerrilla unit lined up at the foot of the pole, saluted the new Sahraoui flag, and everyone present joined in singing the Sahraoui anthem.[5] Then at midnight in this dramatic setting and by the headlights of the convoy's motor vehicles, M'Hamid Ould Ziou, president of the provisional Sahraoui council, with some 40 of its members as well as the deputy general secretary of the Polisario Front, Mafoud Ali Baba Laroussi, moved to the centre of the circle. There Ould Ziou read the Sahraoui Arab Democratic Republic's declaration of independence in Arabic, each sentence being translated into Spanish and French. Rockets and guns were fired, the women emitted the traditional ululations, and the Westerners applauded.

After the ceremony, El Ouali,[6] as the Polisario's general secretary, gave a press conference – an event noteworthy in itself, as reportedly he had been dismissed from his post early in February because of infighting in the Polisario high command and had been reinstated only at Khadafi's urgent behest.[7] El Ouali stated that the RASD's declaration of independence was in conformity with the resolutions of the UN, the

OAU and the Arab League, and that its structure would consist of a council of the revolution, a people's congress and a ministerial cabinet.

Between May 1973 and September 1978 four people's congresses were held at two-year intervals. They confirmed the proposals made by the nine-man executive council of the congress — successor to the provisional national Sahraoui council set up at El Guelta Zemmour in late 1975[8] — and a 21-member Polisario politburo. At each step in this political process, the position of the Polisario as the republic's sole political party was strengthened, so that its general secretary was authorised to appoint all ministers of the RASD government, which was first formed in March 1976 so as to offset the administration appointed by the Moroccans at El Aaiun. Three other members of the politburo became *ex officio* heads of the mass organisations of workers, peasants and women, and as a unit the politburo formed the majority of the forty-member national council. Its other members were elected by local-government bodies ('people's base committees') which met every eight months.

The local-government bodies are made up of representatives elected by the party cells of eleven members, organised in each refugee camp. These camps or *daïras* (communes), named for the villages from which their inhabitants had fled, are the units by which the Polisario leaders hope to perpetuate such community life as had existed in the Western Sahara prior to the diaspora. They are to be situated in what might be called the three 'anticipatory' *wilayas* (provinces) of El Aaiun, Smara and Dakhla, into which the RASD intends to divide its territory after winning independence.[9] As every adult cell member can vote at the local level and all members belong to one or more functional committees, such as those for education, transport, supplies and the like, and as each child over the age of ten receives some elementary military training, this organisation might be considered to reflect participatory, if not Western-style, democracy.

Not surprisingly, the personnel of the RASD cabinet, the Polisario politburo, the army command and various councils have overlapped because of the paucity of qualified Sahraouis and the rarity of defections from the Polisario ranks. The Polisario general secretary, El Ouali, was killed in June 1976, as was the RASD minister of education and health, Bouela Ould Ahmed Zine, and they had to be replaced. Occasionally portfolios changed hands in the three government reshuffles, but there have been few changes in the cast of characters. Among the Polisario leaders who have remained prominent in its operations are Mahfoud Laroussi, Hakim Ibrahim (alias for Brahim Ould Derouiche),

Ibrahim Ghanli Ould Mosefa, Mohammed Abdelaziz Mahfoud, Ahmed Ben Miske and M'Hamid Ould Ziou. Virtually all the RASD's ministerial appointees were unknown outside the Western Sahara, with the exception of the handful who had studied or worked abroad. Although their names are generally *noms de guerre* and their tribal affiliations are politically and socially more significant than their places of birth, the number of Mauritania-born Sahraouis holding high rank in the RASD and Polisario is striking.[10]

As to the Sahraouis' ideology, their spokesmen's policy statements and the resolutions passed at their congresses suggest that it is in short supply. The Polisario Front's constituent congress placed the stress on the Arab character of its movement, and advocated the use of violence as the proper means of freeing colonies from imperialism. A more positive programme was adopted by the second congress in late August 1974, which announced its members' intention of setting up a non-aligned sovereign state on the principles of scientific socialism, and supported land reform, the mobilisation of the masses, as well as other admirable objectives unrelated to the Sahraouis' current state of politico-economic development. Major events, notably the Madrid pact of 14 November 1975, the El Guelta conference a few weeks later, and the proclamation of the RASD in February 1976, occurred before the third congress, held six months later, laid down policy and practice for the two years to come.

In general terms, the RASD's constitution and the party's policy statements proclaim Islam to be the religion of the state, social justice its ultimate goal, and the individual's right to the vote, to schooling and to medical facilities. Among the constitution's 31 articles there is provision for a judicial system including a state security court, sanctuary is pledged to political refugees, and slavery as well as the inferior status of women is denounced. Natural resources will be nationalised but the right to hold private property, provided it is not exploitive, is guaranteed, as is freedom of expression on condition that it does not run counter to the law or harm public interest. These principles are strongly reminiscent of those of other 'revolutionary' African governments, for there is a striking contrast between the militant Marxist vocabulary and goals as expressed by the Polisario leaders to visiting journalists[11] and the more moderate statements made in official documents and by RASD spokesmen. Ahmed Ben Miske's description of the Polisario as a liberation movement that is neither socialist nor fascist, but a democratic and social revolution at home and non-aligned abroad,[12] seems nearer the mark.

The overall impression created more by their words than by their deeds, is that of inexperienced, naive and determined leaders who have adopted a doctrinaire creed largely to gratify their Algerian and Libyan mentors and benefactors. In reality, they appear concerned solely to win and consolidate their independence, and are apparently groping for some pragmatic solution to the problems of tribalism and regionalism that are especially resistant obstacles to the development of nascent Sahraoui nationalism. Historically speaking, independence and Islam are the only two themes that have consistently rung true for the tribesmen of the Western Sahara. In terms of nation-building, their strongest moral assets are courage, austerity and self-reliance, whereas their main liabilities appear to be a tendency to anarchism and inconstancy in alliances, the absence of any central authority, and the lack of realism in their claims and avowed aims.[13] Nevertheless, the internal dissensions among the Sahraoui leaders have not been permitted to surface, let alone to disrupt the Front's unity as has been the fate of the analogous Frolinat movement in Chad.

The need for international support is recognised by the combatants and their sponsors and it can be seen in the extraordinary efforts put forth by the RASD and the Polisario Front in the field of public relations. So remote is the conflict from the main international currents and so unknown is the whole Western Sahara to the outside world, that the Polisario leaders have missed no opportunity during the period of guerrilla warfare to invite delegations from friendly countries to attend celebrations of the party's many anniversaries and to induce visiting journalists to accompany a Land Rover convoy patrolling the 'liberated' areas of the desert. Without exception, what became a routine excursion into the Sahara was highly successful in terms of favourable reporting. Even the veteran correspondents who drew parallels between the Vietcong or the Palestine Liberation Organisation and the Polisario expressed admiration for their hosts' tenacity and endurance, and noted their mastery of the milieu and their ability to disrupt the mineral production and exports of Morocco and Mauritania, as well as to keep the latter's troops harassed and holed up in their isolated desert blockhouses. The image of the guerrilla warrior presented by the generally romantic Western journalists has been that of the noble nomad fighting to remain free against desperate odds, while his equally intrepid family has chosen to live under exceptionally harsh climatic conditions and without sufficient food in the refugee camps rather than remain under alien masters in more comfortable and safer surroundings.

Quite different, in timing and distribution, has been the propaganda

directed by the Polisario to the enemy leaders and soldiers. The outstanding examples of Polisario propaganda to the enemy leadership
were the letters written in the name of El Ouali to President Daddah
and King Hassan on the eve of the RASD's declaration of independence.[14] The familiar and almost insulting terms in which Daddah was
addressed reflected the Polisario's estimate of Mauritania's subordinate
position, and contrasted sharply with the extremely courteous, even
obsequious, tone of the letter sent to the king of Morocco, who at the
time was trying to persuade Khadafi to stop supporting the Polisario.
As to the Polisario's propaganda to enemy soldiers, they were assured
of a warm welcome if they would turn against their oppressive governments and join the ranks of the freedom fighters.[15] Mauritanians were
warned against being dupes of the imperialistic Moroccans, who, under
guise of helping their military defence, were taking over the country.
The Moroccans, for their part, were assured that their losses at the
hands of the Polisario were so staggering that their ruthless government
dared not publish the casualty lists lest this lead to a mutiny.[16] To drive
this point home, the Polisario made a practice of displaying to foreign
visitors and television cameramen their war prisoners along with captured enemy equipment. In September 1977 it added a convincing
refinement to this ploy by grouping the prisoners on display according
to the place and date of the battles in which they had been captured.[17]

In contrast to the data publicised by the Polisario organs and *El
Moudjahid*[18] concerning the Front's victories, the lack of precise information as to the number and origin of those who make up the rank and
file of its troops and of the Sahraoui refugees is striking. This is due in
part to the Polisario's dispersion throughout a vast region and to its
claim to areas inside the boundaries of neighbouring countries as established when they became independent, and in part to the same obstacles
that hampered the Spaniards in their attempts to define and enumerate
the Sahraouis living in their Sahara province.

Historians of the Western Sahara and observers of the current scene
agree that the bulk of the Polisario's fighting forces between 1973 and
1975 was made up of Reguibat tribesmen, with a lesser admixture of
Ouled Delim, numbering in all about 800 men. Late in October 1975
a considerable proportion of the 3,000-odd nomad and other troops
demobilised by Spain reportedly offered their services to the highest
bidder.[19] Because the Algerians were believed to have outbid the Moroccans and, in addition, allocated weapons more generously, most of the
former Spanish *harkis* (indigenous auxiliary forces) joined the Polisario.
In any case, the numerical strength of the Reguibat and Ouled Delim

and their renowned physical endurance, martial traditions and intimate knowledge of the desert all supported the view that those two tribes predominated both in the fighting forces and in the Polisario leadership.

The round figure of 10,000 men has been widely accepted since 1977 as the total force that the RASD could put in the field, despite the changes that have occurred since then in the scale and locale of the fighting. Initially, 90 to 100 men, operating in units called *katiba*, had been trained and equipped with modern weapons by Algerian officers, and fully motorised in convoys of Land Rovers, and they were provisioned in food and fuel from bases hidden in the desert. By these means they were able to carry out hit-and-run attacks, notably on the railway in Mauritania and on the conveyor belt at Bu Craa, in line with the overall Polisario strategy of crippling the main economic resources of Mauritania and Morocco. Kidnapping Europeans (including Spanish fishermen caught in 'Sahraoui coastal waters') was a by-product of these raids, but one that proved to be counter-productive as regards formal international recognition of the RASD, albeit productive of much publicity for the Polisario. It took the *coup d'état* in Mauritania in mid-1978 for the character of the war to change from guerrilla operations to large-scale attacks against strongholds inside Morocco by far stronger Polisario forces. The timing of each strike was co-ordinated with some outstanding political or diplomatic event, such as the sessions of the OAU or the UN General Assembly, and, in particular, the death of Houari Boumediene. Reportedly as many as 5,000 Polisario troops were committed to the battle for Smara in September 1979.

The Polisario's casualty lists, the size of its armed forces, and even the number of refugees in the Western Sahara again raise the vexed questions of who and how many are the Sahraouis, and what constitutes a refugee. These questions are also basic to the carrying out of the UN and OAU resolutions for a referendum of the Sahraouis in regard to their future status. As to where the Sahraoui refugees are located, one source, two years after the Madrid pact of 1975, gave the number of those living in Morocco as 59,000 and in Mauritania as 14,000.[20] On the other hand, the Polisario leadership has maintained that of a total of 750,000 to 800,000 Sahraouis, 400,000 are living in Morocco and Mauritania and 150,000 in the refugee camps.[21] In analysing such estimates, one should remember that 'refugee' is a blanket term that has often been used by promoters of liberation movements so as to swell the ranks of their followers or to include inhabitants of the areas to which they lay claim. For example, the handful of Sahraouis living in the Canary Islands, who were described by Eduardo Moha as refugees wanting to return to their homeland,[22] were almost all individuals who had gone there seeking opportunities for study or economic gain not available in the Spanish Sahara. Elsewhere others similarly designated as refugees were simply seasonal nomads driven out of the Spanish Sahara by adverse climatic conditions to seek pastures in neighbouring countries. Those who could be called refugees in the sense of persons fleeing from conditions they considered to be physically or psychologically intolerable can be divided into two major groups. Both are composed largely of sedentary persons who had left their homes to escape bombing or subjection to foreign invaders. Inconsistencies and disparities seem evident in the time lag of nearly two decades between the three exoduses, the numbers involved and the calibre of the migrants.

The 25,000 to 30,000 Sahraouis who emigrated from Saquiet El Hamra in 1957-8 to escape aerial bombing during *Opération Ecouvillon* included *caïds*, merchants and 'intellectuals', who doubtless were also attracted to Morocco because it had recently become independent.[23] That they nevertheless intended to remain in that country only until the Spanish Sahara should itself become free was indicated by their continuing to live in temporary camps set up in the Goulimine and Tantan areas even after Tarfaya was restored to Morocco in 1958. Apparently they made no effort to be absorbed into southern Moroccan society, and indeed their rootlessness after 17 years of exile was considered by some observers to have been a factor in causing King Hassan in August 1974 to reverse his previous endorsement of a referendum in the Spanish Sahara if independence were to be one of the options offered to Sahraoui voters.[24]

The second group of refugees comprised only a few hundred young Sahraouis who feared reprisals after their instigation of and participation in the anti-Spanish demonstrations at El Aaiun and Tantan in 1970-2. The third wave, however, was a mass exodus that began in 1975 and was composed of destitute families as well as a bigger nomad component. The great majority of these refugees fled during the severe fighting that occurred between November 1975 and April 1976 in the frontier zone between Morocco, Algeria and Mauritania, and the flow, albeit diminished, received additional recruits after each of the increasingly frequent attacks by the Polisario. If the estimated total of 73,500 Sahraouis living in Spanish territory, as recorded by *Censo/74*, is compared with the figure of 130,000 refugees in the Tindouf area and of 10,000 men fighting in the Polisario ranks, it seems evident that the earlier statistics were grossly distorted or that there are nearly twice as many 'refugees' as there were Sahraouis living in the Spanish Sahara in 1974.

Moroccans and Mauritanians fleeing from Polisario attacks deep inside their country's internationally acknowledged boundaries could certainly account for some, but not all, of the additions to the refugee ranks. Rabat and Nouakchott attributed this accretion in part to the influx of Touareg nomads seeking better living conditions in the Tindouf region than those prevailing in the Sahel refugee camps of Niger and Mali,[25] but even more to the pressure exerted by the Polisario and Algeria on the Sahraouis to force them into their camps and keep them there. If such was the motivation, the refugees could serve as hostages or bargaining counters in any eventual negotiated agreement on the future of the territory.[26]

To what degree the advent of 'refugees' from Mali, Algeria and Niger has altered the composition and orientation of the Polisario forces and command has been the subject of conjecture. By actions and by implication, both President Traore of Mali and President Kountche of Niger have expressed their concern lest the propaganda and recruiting by the Polisario revive dissent among the nomads in their respective areas of the Sahara.[27] There seems little doubt that by 1978, the Sahraouis — that is, natives of the former Spanish Sahara — had become a minority in the top echelon of the Polisario command and perhaps in its army as well.[28]

Inasmuch as the majority is now apparently composed of Saharans from Mauritania, Mali, Morocco, Algeria and perhaps Niger, it is no wonder that the Polisario is not a monolithic organisation and that, despite a seemingly solid united front, its various factions or leaders have shown a certain flexibility in their demands. At different times and places, negotiations have been carried on secretly by one or another of them with Mauritania and even Morocco, not to mention more openly with Spain and France. In the case of Mauritania, negotiations alternating with threats of renewed warfare culminated successfully in the peace treaty of 6 August 1979. As regards Morocco, the biggest stumbling block has been the Polisario's insistence on Rabat's recognition of the RASD's sovereignty over land that the Moroccan people almost unanimously consider to be their national heritage. Obviously, a nation of landless nomads is a contradiction in terms, so no compromise in this matter is conceivable for the Polisario Front.

To date there have been few indications as to precisely how the Sahraoui leadership as a whole envisages the future Sahraoui Arab Democratic Republic. Indeed the very existence of any concrete programme

is open to doubt, perhaps because the Polisario leaders fear the serious
repercussions that a centralised governmental authority would have on
the Sahraoui socio-economic structure. To its neighbours' apprehension,
the Polisario command has never placed any exact geographical limits
on the area to which it lays claim. Nor has it indicated what would be
the future state's economic base. Given the Sahraouis' long-standing
distaste for farming and fishing and for cohabitation with the black
sedentaries who practise those occupations, the difficulties of recon-
stituting their cherished camel herds, which have been virtually ex-
terminated by warfare and drought, and finally their inexperience and
ignorance of the phosphate industry, it is difficult to envisage how such
an entity as the RASD could survive except in some form of dependent
association with one or another of its Arab Muslim neighbours. Such
dependence, as well as the type and level of productivity required to
make the Sahraoui state viable, would undermine the mobility and
autonomy which have always been the essence of a patriarchal and
archaic society based on pastoral nomadism. Furthermore, the indispensable cultivation of a sense of nationhood among the Sahraouis
would necessarily destroy the tribalism and regionalism that have always
been their strongest bonds.

Already these processes are going on in the refugee camps of the
Tindouf area, where by force of circumstances and by their leaders'
directives the Sahraoui tent-dwellers are becoming self-disciplined,
industrious communities of sedentaries. Living under extremely adverse
and primitive conditions, and dependent as they have been since 1976
on international and especially Algerian charity,[29] the Sahraoui leaders
are trying to create a tightly knit socio-political organisation for each
camp, and one that is adapted to transplantation as an almost self-
sufficient community to the settlement whither they expect to return
after their territory is liberated. So active are all the refugees, children
as well as adults, in carrying out the task assigned to each member by
the elected cell leader, so closely supervised is the distribution of supplies, and so rigorous is the training given every child ten years of age
and older, that the Sahraoui refugee camps have been considered by the
UN Commission for Refugees to be models of their kind.[30]

The Polisario Front's Foreign Relations

By forcibly occupying the coastal settlements and the military posts
abandoned by Spain against the organised opposition of the local tribesmen, Morocco and Mauritania forfeited the well-nigh universal approval
that had been given them so long as they were apparently only helping

to free the colony of a European power. Similarly, in setting up the RASD with the trappings of a sovereign state the Polisario lost the chance of being recognised by the OAU as a liberation movement, while not improving the prospect of its being admitted as an independent nation to membership in that body.[31] The Polisario thus added a disruptive political dimension to what until then had been applauded as the challenge by an African David to a European Goliath. By early 1976, therefore, the stakes in the Western Sahara had been so altered by both parties to the dispute that the Third World in general and the Polisario in particular were cast into disarray. The new 'imperial powers', Morocco and Mauritania, as well as their opponents and the latters' sponsors, were all Arabs and Africans. Each of the contenders professed to believe in the principle of self-determination for the Sahraoui people, but they differed as to how it should be expressed. National political and economic objectives masked as 'territorial integrity' or as a 'people's right to choose their own future form of government', brought Algeria and Morocco, the two almost equally matched major powers of the Maghreb, into covert conflict.

The tangle of ideologies and realities, as well as the irrelevance of both to the immediate interests of the nations not directly involved in the Western Sahara, tended to isolate further the remote area under dispute. Not that there was any lack of mediators, black as well as white, all of whom vainly tried throughout 1976 to negotiate a compromise between the disputants. Among the latter, only Mauritania, initially the most reluctant to engage in armed combat, seemed at all likely to accept a negotiated solution, for it was militarily weaker and economically more vulnerable than either Algeria or Morocco, and was consequently the main target for increasing military and propaganda attacks by the Polisario. By its raids on Nouakchott (8 June 1976 and 3 July 1977) and on Zouérate (1 May and 16 July 1977) the Polisario hoped to overthrow the Daddah regime, or at least to cut off the lifeline of Mauritania's economy by stopping iron-ore exports. The Polisario also taunted the Mauritanian army with its inability to protect the country from guerrilla attacks, reminded young Moorish radicals of their ideological kinship with the RASD's objectives, and tried to reawaken the long-standing fears of all Mauritanians concerning Morocco's irredentism and its *de facto* occupation of Mauritanian bases.

Although the Polisario placed most of its hopes for victory on the battlefield, where its guerrillas excelled, it also followed Algeria's lead in working to develop external support. In so doing, however, the RASD leaders laboured under the serious handicaps of their own inexperience and the world's unawareness of their existence. Except for El Ouali, who had gained some fame as a picturesque desert fighter and mystic, the Polisario leaders became known outside the Western Sahara only when they began to travel between the capitals of 'friendly brother peoples' and from one international conference to another. Even those governments most sympathetic with the Polisario's objectives found it hard to take seriously 'ministers' from a vast ill-defined area composed of rock and sand which called itself the Sahraoui Arab Democratic Republic, and whose only settlements were simply camps made up of hundreds of tents pitched around water points.

Cut off from the Atlantic seaboard by the Moroccan and Mauritanian garrisons stationed in the coastal towns, the landlocked RASD had perforce to rely almost wholly on Algeria, and to a lesser degree on Libya, for funds and supplies of food and armaments. (Given the growing rivalry between Libya and Algeria for the priority position as the Polisario's principal patron, there can be little doubt that the close ties between the Front's leaders and Tripoli have been maintained with an eye to the future. Should Algeria become too demanding and domineering after the RASD shall have defeated Morocco, the Polisario's leadership could turn to Libya with an assurance of generous support.) Although Boumediene proved to be a good provider and freely used his personal prestige on the Polisario's behalf, and although the use of an office in Algiers and of its radio station was invaluable to the RASD leaders, they found their almost total dependence on Algeria galling. Moreover, as time went on they learned that Algeria's sponsorship had drawbacks as well as advantages, depending on such factors as the fears or the admiration inspired by that country's revolutionary regime, its policy in Africa and the Middle East, and its attitude towards neighbouring states to the south and the east. In particular, moderate and conservative governments were hardly reassured as to the future of northwestern Africa when Polisario leaders stated that 'the liberation of the Sahara is only a beginning, and we ask the patriotic forces in Morocco and Mauritania to join us in overthrowing their regimes'.[32]

The Polisario leaders came to realise that to widen the base of their external support they must establish their regime's legitimacy as the prerequisite to recognition by international organisations. Under existing conditions in the Western Sahara, there could no longer be any question of holding a referendum to legitimise the RASD, hence the most that could be expected was acceptance as a member by at least one of the three concentric international bodies for which it might qualify. Initially, the Arab League, the smallest and most homogeneous of those bodies, seemed the most promising, but after its general secretary became the first outstanding Arab League official to talk with the Polisario leaders, the League's mediation became unacceptable to two of its members, Morocco and Mauritania.

Inside the League, the main dividing line separated the conservative from the radical Arab states, but aside from that ideological division, individual member countries had their own relations with Morocco and with Algeria. (This was less true of Mauritania, as Daddah was a favourite with virtually all his Arab and African peers.) In general, individual country-by-country relations were determined by such factors as geographical proximity and whether a government had old scores to settle, favours to repay or trade to promote with one or the other of the main adversaries. The case of Libya illustrates the complexities of an Arab country's reactions to the Western Sahara conflict because of its geographical and cultural ties to all the belligerents and because of its leader's extreme views as to the universality of Islam and his own role in building the Arab nations and extending Libyan influence into black Africa.

Libya has been unique in maintaining close relations with both the Polisario and Mauritania, despite the latter's withdrawal from the war and the drastic change in its government. Beginning in 1976, Colonel Mouamar Khadafi has used his country's vast oil revenues to finance, *inter alia*, many of Mauritania's cultural and economic development projects through both official and individual channels. Specifically he urged first President Daddah and then the military junta to achieve some kind of union with the Polisario by ceding to it the Tiris El Gharbia. Khadafi has calculated that the creation of such a buffer state might block the territorial expansionism of Morocco's conservative monarchy and would punish King Hassan for supporting Sadat's negotiations with Israel. At the same time, Khadafi's continuing close ties have enabled him to compete with Saudi Arabia as protector and patron of Mauritania, a weak biracial but wholly Islamic state, and to challenge both Algeria and Morocco for potential leadership of the united Arab Maghreb which all the states of northwest Africa claim they want to create.

As for the Polisario, Khadafi's attitude toward that movement has been highly ambiguous. On the one hand he has been pleased to aid 'rebels against Spanish colonialism and French neocolonialism', but he balks at recognising the RASD, which he believes would be economically unviable as a state and politically would 'balkanise the Arab nation'. He has long aspired to mediate the whole Sahara conflict in the near future; he evidently hopes to prevent Algeria from winning all the credit for the Polisario's recent military and diplomatic successes, and in the long run to mediate dissensions throughout all the Sahara. Like other would-be honest brokers in this inter-Arab imbroglio, Khadafi is less concerned about the state of the Sahraouis themselves than about the conflict's repercussions on the overall situation in northwest Africa. However, contrary to the policies of the black leaders of the Saharan borderland countries who fear Arab progress in Africa at the expense of the negro world, and unlike those of the Western powers which aim to preserve the status quo in the Maghreb, Colonel Khadafi aspires to promote the southward advance of Islam in general and that of Libya in particular. It is in the light of such goals that his aggression in Chad and his creation at Tripoli of the newborn Mouvement Berbère and the Front de Libération du Nord Mali should be viewed.

The far-reaching implications of Libya's recent policies would have been of themselves sufficient to involve the OAU deeply, but in addition that organisation's aid in solving the Saharan problem has long been solicited by the UN. Initially and quite logically, the Saharan issue was carried before the UN, but after passing a pair of contradictory resolutions in December 1975 and confirming its support for the principle of self-determination for the Sahraoui people, the General Assembly was only too relieved to postpone the debate on its application for one year. It then decided to await the outcome of the extraordinary meeting on the Saharan conflict for which the heads of the OAU member states had voted six months before. Finally, at the Khartoum summit meeting in July 1978, just after the Mauritanian *coup d'état* and the Polisario's ceasefire order in the southwestern Sahara, the OAU achieved sufficient consensus to set up a five-member *ad hoc* committee (Comité des Sages), chaired by Mali and Nigeria, to analyse the Sahara situation and make recommendations to deal with it.

In both the UN and the OAU, Algeria kept vainly increasing its pressure (supported by equally assiduous Polisario lobbying) to force a vote by either of those bodies that would be tantamount to their recognition of the RASD, despite the obvious eagerness of almost all their members to be let off the hook. Of those two organisations, Algeria tended to prefer the UN as the forum more likely to supply the votes that would favour its cause, whereas Morocco until 1978 found more allies among the OAU members. For several years the OAU heads of state were too cautious to admit the RASD to its membership or even to permit its delegates to attend their meetings.[33] The basic reason that the OAU — like the UN before it — was unable to come to grips with the issue was that no African nation wanted to assume the responsibility either for breaking up the OAU or for condoning African imperialism, especially over such an issue as the future of the Western Sahara.

Of the 19 states that have thus far recognised the RASD, none except Algeria has a common frontier with any of the belligerents, and only a few have Arab governments. As of late 1979, the RASD had not yet been recognised even by such 'progressive' francophone neighbours as Mali, Niger and Guinea, although eight more countries had jumped on the Polisario bandwagon during the preceding eighteen months. After the coup of 10 July 1978 at Nouakchott, it was because of Mauritania's efforts to extricate itself from the desert war without mortally offending Rabat and because of the Polisario's military successes in late 1978 and early 1979 in southern Morocco that the tide turned, first in the UN General Assembly and then at the OAU summit in Monrovia.

The usual resolution endorsing self-determination for the Sahraouis was passed by the General Assembly in December 1978 with an even greater majority than before (90 votes to 10), and for the first time the Polisario was cited therein by name when being praised for its unilateral declaration of a ceasefire. When King Hassan, in March 1979, presented his official complaint against Algerian aggression in southern Morocco to the UN Security Council rather than to the OAU, and then, at the last minute, failed to attend the Monrovia conference where he could have fulfilled his expressed wish to meet with Algeria's new president, Chadli Bendjahid, Morocco's popularity fell to its lowest point.

The decline in support for the Moroccan cause among the king's peers in the OAU was clearly shown in July 1979 by the two-thirds majority vote[34] which they gave to the report by the *ad hoc* committee recommending an overall ceasefire in the Sahara and a referendum among the Sahraouis as to their future status. When the peace treaty between Mauritania and the Polisario, signed 5 August 1979, was swiftly followed by Morocco's seizure of Dakhla, Rabat's isolation in the international community became obvious. Among the African states in the OAU, only Senegal, Gabon, the Comoro Islands, Zaïre and Djibouti did not by implication condemn Morocco's action, while among the Arab countries that remained favourable to the king's cause, outstanding and unique was the support — both verbal and military — given the king by Egypt. Hassan's breaking off diplomatic relations with Cairo after Egypt had made its peace with Israel, followed by his joining the 'rejectionist front', neither won him a return to Arab good graces nor permanently alienated Sadat, who subsequently sent him arms and technical advisers. The king's diplomatic vacillations, which indicated a failing self-confidence in his dealings with the Third World opposition in the

UN and the OAU, also affected and altered his relations with the Western world.

From the outset of the Sahara conflict, it had been clear that neither superpower wanted a war in the Maghreb, either because their leaders considered the former Spanish Sahara a prize not worth a confrontation between them, or because the issues and loyalties involved were too confused and contradictory. In any case, they were far more concerned with other and − to them − graver African problems. Although the United States officially has been neutral in the Sahara conflict, its history of close military relations with Rabat since the Second World War suggested that Washington strongly favoured Morocco. That country's assets for the United States have been and still are its strategic location in northwest Africa and its political conservatism that has checked the westward push of Algerian and Libyan radicalism. In a wider context, Hassan's politically risky support for Sadat and his sending Moroccan troops twice to Zaïre to shore up the West's position in Shaba, as well as his hospitality to the self-exiled shah of Iran, for some time outweighed in American eyes the importance that Algeria had recently acquired as a trading partner and as a major source of natural gas. Early in 1978, however, congressional opposition aroused by Rabat's use of American military equipment to combat Polisario forces attacking posts in 'Greater Morocco' halted further sales of military aircraft to the king until the autumn of 1979. By then, however, the possibility that Morocco's military reverses in the south might lead to Hassan's overthrow and thus 'destabilise' the Maghreb reinforced the apprehension caused by the concurrent, fast-deteriorating position of the United States in Iran, following the fall there of another pro-Western monarch. The legalistic opposition to selling arms to Rabat was based on an international agreement of 1960 banning their use outside Morocco's internationally recognised frontiers. More cogent, however, was the emotional American resistance to their use against a small people fighting for their freedom, as well as the practical arguments that their sale to Rabat would surely alienate Algeria and that the very possession of more powerful weapons would increase the king's intransigence against making the concessions required of Morocco to achieve a durable peace treaty.

As for the Soviet Union, it too has had to make a difficult choice between supporting its ideological partner, Algeria, and its major external source of phosphates and fish, conservative and capitalistic Morocco. By discreetly supplying arms to the Polisario by way of Algiers, but resisting pressure to recognise the RASD and to sell to the Polisario the most sophisticated Soviet weapons, Moscow seemed to be more even-handed than the United States in supporting its traditional ally — until early in 1978, when economic interests won out over ideology. On 26 January 1978 there was initialled at Moscow what King Hassan described as 'the contract of the century', whereby the Soviet Union agreed to spend more than $2 billion over a thirty-year period to finance the mining of Meskala phosphate deposits and related industries in Morocco. Three months later, there was signed a fisheries agreement whose wording had been subject to prolonged negotiations so as to avoid any implication that Soviet vessels would be fishing in Sahraoui waters. Thus, by 1978, time was fast running out when the superpowers could safely supply their respective protégés with just enough support to maintain their own credibility in Third World eyes but not so much as to tempt either Morocco or Algeria to resort to open warfare. By not intervening decisively in the Western Sahara, the superpowers let the war run its course, thus enabling the Polisario to fight its way to a position of such strength that it can no longer be ignored in any long-term settlement of the future Maghreb.

France, like the United States and for many of the same reasons, has officially maintained a policy of neutrality in the Sahara conflict while in fact it long favoured the Mauritania-Morocco tandem. For obvious historical, economic and political reasons, France has continued to have close relations with all parties to the dispute, but has been careful to disclaim any role as mediator between them. Since the colonial era the limitation of Arab and Muslim influence south of the Sahara has been a long-term objective of all French governments, but the application of that policy in countries along the desert borderlands has become complicated by irredentist aspirations and the nationalist sentiments to which independence has given birth. Specifically, this has meant bolstering the unity and preserving the sovereignty of the biracial Saharan states, notably Mauritania and Chad.

In both countries Paris long supported the locally elected leaders — Daddah and Tombalbaye respectively — under whom those countries became independent, until their governments proved to be so ethnically biased, economically weak and militarily incompetent that domestic dissidents backed by self-interested neighbours put an end to their rule. In both cases, too, the kidnapping of French nationals interjected an emotional element — played up by the mass media — that was further complicated by internal political issues in France. It would be politically disastrous for any French government to choose openly between supporting either Algeria or Morocco. The one constant factor in France's policy in northwest Africa has been that of maintaining the independence and integrity of Mauritania, and at different times this has brought Paris into both physical and psychological conflict with Rabat and — through the Polisario — with Algiers.

In the UN, France has voted affirmatively on the various resolutions endorsing self-determination for the Sahraouis, and it has announced its willingness to sell arms to Algeria on the same terms as to Morocco. It was also careful to appear impartial in its dealings with both governments until the Polisario raid of 1 May 1977 on Zouérate, in which two French nationals were killed and six others taken hostage. Consequently French public opinion became incensed against both the Polisario and Algeria for treating those hostages as mercenaries, equating them with prisoners of war, and even refusing to give any information about them simply because they had been employed by a mining company in a country with which the RASD considered itself at war. Algeria, too, disclaimed any responsibility for the hostages' welfare or whereabouts, only offering to serve as liaison between the French government and the Polisario. Suddenly, in December 1977, the Polisario informed the head of the French Communist Party then visiting Algiers that the French hostages it had been holding incommunicado for seven months would be returned to their families before Christmas, and in a carefully prepared ceremony, the Polisario handed them over to the UN secretary general, who escorted them back to France.

It is not clear as to whether the Polisario's decision antedated or was the result of France's despatch of combat planes to help the Mauritanian army find and destroy the Polisario guerrillas raiding posts inside the country's 1960 boundaries. Insofar as the kidnapping of Europeans working in Mauritania's supposedly heavily guarded mining centre showed that the Polisario was a growing and formidable force in the desert war, and still had strong supporters among workers in the country's key industry, this episode might be termed a success. It failed, however, in its political and psychological objectives. These were to force Mauritania to list the Polisario prisoners it was holding, to compel France to cease giving military aid to Rabat and Nouakchott and, more important, to recognise the RASD as the sole legal representative of the Sahraoui people. Moreover, far from accepting the Polisario's release of the hostages as a humanitarian gesture, French public opinion remained alienated by an operation that it considered to be political blackmail.

Even if it had been the combination of diplomacy and armed force that finally effected the hostages' release, all the parties involved, including the French government, were left dissatisfied to varying degrees.

To be sure, France's military intervention had altered the character of the war from hit-and-run operations to one of aerial bombardments, which proved disastrous for the guerrillas and which they were not equipped to resist. But it had also proved costly to France in terms of money and international opprobrium, notably by undermining its pose of neutrality. Now convinced that military intervention alone would not solve the Saharan conflict, Paris redoubled its efforts to find a political solution. For some months it tried working through various diplomatic channels, and initiated the vain attempts at mediation made by the two black African presidents, Léopold Senghor and Félix Houphouët-Boigny.

Then on 10 July 1978 the *coup d'état* at Nouakchott coincided so neatly with France's diplomatic impasse that it aroused suspicions of collusion between Paris and the military junta that overthrew Daddah. In any case, the end of Mauritania's status as a belligerent caused a shift in the area of the war to the north, where King Hassan's position progressively weakened. Paris continued to send Morocco arms and technicians and also persuaded the king to withdraw his troops from Mauritania, whose independence France was more than ever determined to preserve. At the same time, the French government stepped up its diplomatic offensive geared to improving its relations with Algeria, whose deterioration had long been bewailed by both French business-men and French left-wing leaders, albeit for dissimilar reasons of trade and ideology.

At a press conference on 15 February 1979, President Giscard d'Estaing gave the public its first inkling of a gradual reorientation of his Saharan policy when he characterised the conflict there as a 'problem of decolonisation'. Then after his minister of co-operation a few days later spoke of the Sahraoui people's right to self-determination regard-less of their small number, the Polisario leaders prematurely concluded that France was drawing closer to the Algerian position.[35] Again it took developments at Nouakchott, first a mini-coup in April and later the peace treaty signed with the Polisario in August, for Franco-Mauritanian relations to achieve a firmer and more co-operative basis. Premier Hey-dalla's visit to Paris in September elicited pledges of substantial mone-tary and technical aid from France and of protection of his country's national frontier against all predators, including Morocco. The next month France posted 150 paratroopers to Nouadhibou.

Like France, Spain was reluctantly drawn back into the Sahara im-broglio after it had tried to extricate itself from its former colony's problems. In both instances, a combination of political and economic

interests required Madrid to pursue an even-handed policy towards
Morocco and Algeria, but circumstances — some of them extraneous
to the Sahara — caused Spain to tilt first one way and then the other.
Until late in 1977 the need to placate Morocco was paramount. That
country was considered to be a bulwark against Algerian radicalism,
and it held the key to control of the *presidios* as well as of the Bu Craa
mines — all of which were viewed as being of prime importance to
Spain. As the war continued, however, the Polisario attacks on the Bu
Craa conveyor belt brought phosphate exports almost to a halt and
led to the repatriation of most of its Spanish miners, while the Polisario's seizure of the crews of Canary Island fishing boats 'trespassing
in Sahraoui waters' harmed Spain's important fishing industry. Moreover, trade between Spain and Algeria was growing as Spanish industry
became increasingly dependent on Algerian gas and oil supplies.

Tension between Madrid and Algiers mounted after the Cortes in
February 1978 ratified new fishing agreements with Mauritania and
Morocco, which acknowledged those countries' sovereignty over Saharan coastal waters. While the Polisario continued to assault Spain's
economic strongholds in northwest Africa, Algeria attacked Spain's
political hold on the Canary Islands. By permitting Antonio Cubillo,
leader of the MPAIAC secessionists, to use Algiers radio for his broadcasts, and by urging the OAU foreign ministers' council in March 1978
to support independence for the Canarians as 'colonised Africans',
President Boumediene was holding a political club over Premier Suarez's
head. Furthermore, at the same time the Polisario and Algeria strove
to invalidate the Madrid pact of November 1975. By referring this
legal issue back to Spain, whose sovereignty as a colonial power in the
Western Sahara they had long denied, and whose creation of the *yemaa*
as a body representative of Sahraoui opinion they had derided, the
Polisario and Algerian leaders were apparently without conscious irony
laying the legality of their previous positions open to doubt.

With the aid of left-wing Spanish parties, whose ideology conformed
with that of the Polisario, and of conservative Spaniards, who favoured
closer relations with Algeria for business reasons or to expiate the guilt
they felt over Spain's abrupt abandonment of its 'Spanish province in
the Sahara' to Rabat and Nouakchott, the RASD and Algerian leaders
indirectly instigated a heated debate on the issue. It cast no new light
on the terms of the 1975 treaty and its disclosures were relatively insignificant.[36] Subsequently, the government simply reiterated its assurance
that it had merely bestowed administrative authority over its province
to Mauritania and Morocco in 1975, would welcome a referendum by

the Sahraouis as to their future status, and would then transfer sovereignty over its former colony in accordance with their decision. The party of Premier Adolfo Suarez did indeed send a delegate to attend the fourth Polisario congress in September 1978, but this was simply to secure the Polisario's release of Spanish fishermen and was not tantamount to an official recognition of the RASD by his government.

As of late 1979 Spain was still trying to walk the tightrope between the major combatants in the Western Sahara. Madrid showed itself willing to placate the Polisario, as in allowing it to open an office in the Spanish capital, but not to the point of renouncing Spain's preference for a referendum of the Sahraouis or accepting the Polisario as their sole legitimate representative. And Spain is now clearly determined to play a role in any final settlement concerning the region. As to the Polisario's policy in dealing with both Spain and France, its leaders miscalculated the strength of their left-wing allies in those countries. By encouraging the Canary Islanders to seek independence, and by holding French civilian hostages incommunicado for seven months in Algeria, they overplayed their hand. Even among their ideological sympathisers, the Spanish and French socialists and communists, nationalist sentiments transcended their Marxist ideology and they rallied behind their respective governments.

Notes

1. See pp. 137-8.
2. In the early 1970s Boumediene even confiscated arms and Land Rovers sent by Libya to the Polisario by way of Algeria. See *Le Monde*, 7 July 1977.
3. Ibid., 28 Nov. 1975.
4. Ibid., 29 Feb., 1 March 1976.
5. The anthem was based on a song from the Atar region, whose lines celebrating the beauty of the night are replaced by a paean to the Polisario Front's revolutionary sentiments.
6. See p. 139.
7. *Jeune Afrique*, 2 April 1976.
8. See pp. 134-5.
9. *Le Monde*, 24-5 May 1977.
10. Notable examples are El Ouali, Hakim Ibrahim, Ben Miske and Mansour Omar. On 14 August 1977 Daddah made one of his many appeals to all Mauritanian nationals who had been serving with the Polisario to return home to the 'motherland'. They, as well as the Mauritanians serving the Algerian government, he reassured them, would be 'treated fairly and without retaliatory measures for the rest of their days'. *Marchés Tropicaux*, 10 Aug. 1977.
11. J.P. Caudron, 'Huits Jours avec le Front Polisario', *Croissance des Jeunes Nations* (Feb. 1976).
12. See his *Front Polisario, l'Ame d'un Peuple* (Rupture, Paris, 1978).

13. See *Le Sahara Libre*, communiqués from Algiers and broadcasts of a programme entitled 'La Voix du Sahara Libre'.

14. See *Jeune Afrique*, 9 April, 25 June 1976 and 8 July 1977. The authors of the last-mentioned article believe that these letters were written without El Ouali consent by partisans who wanted to break with the Mauritanian president, and that differences over military strategy had put El Ouali at odds with Premier Mohamed Lamine, who advocated attacking Mauritania inside its 1960 frontiers.

15. See *West Africa*, 18 April 1977; *Le Monde*, 7 Aug. and 3 Sept. 1977.

16. *Le Monde*, 7 Aug. 1976; *El Moudjahid*, 4 Nov. 1976.

17. *Le Monde*, 15 Sept. 1977.

18. Since October 1975 that official organ of the FLN has regularly given a large coverage to Polisario military and diplomatic triumphs, either as front-page news or in a column headed 'République Arabe Sahraouie Démocratique'.

19. *New York Times*, 12 Oct. 1976. For another version of this phenomenon, see Ben Miske, *Front Polisario*, p. 206. Still other estimates of the number of Sahraoui troops in the early war years can be found in *Le Monde*, 6, 7 and 8 Aug. 1976; *Jeune Afrique*, 28 Nov. 1975; *New York Times*, 20 March 1977.

20. *Jeune Afrique*, 25 Nov. 1977.

21. In any case, the figures proposed vary as to their source and at best are valid only for a specific period of time, given the fluctuating fortunes of the desert war.

22. *West Africa*, 25 Dec. 1972.

23. *Le Monde*, 13 March 1957; N. Boyer, 'Le Problème des Frontières du Maroc' (CHEAM, Mémoire No. 4237, 1968).

24. 'La Marche Verte' (anonymous typescript, 15 Dec. 1975).

25. *Marchés Tropicaux*, 15 Oct. 1976.

26. The transfer in February 1977 of some 5,000 refugees from Tindouf to a camp 240 kilometres from Béchar was used to substantiate that argument. See *L'Opinion*, 18 Feb. 1977.

27. *Le Monde*, 10 July 1979.

28. D.L. Price, 'Morocco and the Sahara', *Middle East International* (Aug. 1978)

29. World philanthropic and church organisations, as well as the Algerian and Sahraoui Red Crescent Societies, have given food, funds and medicines. These gifts, however, largely supplement the aid proffered by the Algerian authorities, which has helped to train medical personnel and assure regular supplies of food and drugs. Reportedly the refugees' per capita diet has averaged some 1,700 calories a day. See *Le Monde*, 7 Aug. 1976 and 29-30 Jan. 1978.

30. *Jeune Afrique*, 23 Sept. 1977.

31. To become a member required a two-thirds affirmative vote by the OAU heads of state, whereas recognition by the OAU of the Polisario as a liberation movement needed only a simple majority.

32. *New York Times*, 27 June 1977.

33. At the time of the Mauritius and Gabon summit conferences in 1976 and 1977, the RASD delegation was not even permitted to enter those countries.

34. In the night of 20 July the Botswana delegate was said to have been routed out of bed so that he could cast the decisive thirty-third vote in favour of the committee's report. See *Jeune Afrique*, 1 Aug. 1979.

35. *El Moudjahid*, 4 March 1979.

36. This debate did bring out the fact that Algeria had asked Madrid to arm the Sahraouis so that they could oppose the Green Marchers in November 1975. It also showed that the Spanish military authorities in the Sahara had been deliberately kept in ignorance until the last minute about both the Green March and the terms of the Madrid pact. See *Le Monde*, 19-20 March 1978; P.A. Dessens, 'Le Litige du Sahara Occidental', *Maghreb-Machrek*, no. 71 (Jan.-March 1976), and 'Le Problème du Sahara Occidental Trois Ans après le Départ des Espagnols', *Maghreb-Machrek*, no. 83 (Jan.-March 1979).

PART V: THE WAR'S REPERCUSSIONS ON MAURITANIA AND MOROCCO

Tiris El Gharbia

The annexation of Tiris El Gharbia (the former Rio de Oro) proved to be more of a liability than an asset to the Mauritanian people. Contrary to the abundance suggested by its former name, River of Gold, Mauritania's new province cost it dear in terms of manpower, treasure and good foreign relations. Its acquisition also increased the area to be defended as well as the risk of absorption by one or the other of its more powerful neighbours. It contributed to internal disunity and undermined the civilian government by enhancing the power of the military. Offsetting these drawbacks were certain assets, of which some were unknown quantities and others proved to be of only temporary advantage. These assets included appreciable additions to Mauritania's natural resources, notably fisheries and minerals, an unprecedented influx of funds from conservative Arab sources and a transient gratification of national pride.

By precipitating a reversal of Mauritania's foreign policy, the conflict over the Western Sahara could hardly have come at a more crucial time in that country's history. Barely three months before the Green March, which forced Daddah's hand, a consensus among Mauritanians had been effected by Daddah on the basis of a platform calling for political, economic and cultural independence. Although there were revolutionary socialists on the left and orthodox Muslim traditionalists on the right, Daddah appealed to the nascent nationalism of both by terming his takeover of Rio de Oro a 'reunification of the fatherland'. The Polisario Front, however, did not see it in that light, and the fierce resistance that its guerrillas offered to the Mauritanian army's efforts to dislodge it from La Guera, Argoub, Tichla and Aousserd was the first shock that threatened to disrupt Mauritania's new-found unity. Mauritania was not only unprepared to defend its former frontiers against the Polisario's increasing attacks but was psychologically not yet ready to accept dependence on Morocco's (and much less France's) military protection and on the funds and arms provided by the conservative Arab states and capitalist countries as the price for its survival.

The Polisario's raids on Nouakchott and Zouérate, not to mention

269

the settlements of southeastern Mauritania, did cause a brief upsurge of Moorish patriotism as well as alarm, but it was Algeria's complicity in arming and supporting the guerrillas and, even more, the evidence that Boumediene aimed at overthrowing the Daddah government that caused deep resentment. (Reportedly, a blueprint for installing a puppet regime in place of the Daddah government was found among the documents carried by El Ouali at the time of his death during the June 1976 raid on Nouakchott.) On many counts the Mauritanians had become increasingly vulnerable to Polisario broadcasts from Algiers, whose overall goal was to sever Nouakchott's ties with Rabat and to instal a Mauritanian government that would be manned by Polisario leaders and be beholden to Algeria. Ideologically, the young Mauritanian radicals were sensitive to the charge that their country, in collusion with imperialists and capitalists, was fighting fellow Arabs and Muslim tribesmen struggling to be free. The Mauritanian army, recently enlarged greatly, was taunted for its inability to defend the national territory and to prevent its occupation by aliens. Finally, Daddah himself was accused of genocide, and warned in a letter, purportedly written by El Ouali, to 'fear God, Mokhtar, for you are sending your people to their death so as to drive your Sahraoui brothers from their land'.[1] Although Daddah came to denounce Algeria by name and refer to the Polisario as 'Algerian mercenaries', he continued to manoeuvre skilfully under very difficult circumstances to win the maximum support both at home and abroad. Saudi Arabia, Kuwait and Abu Dhabi, above all, were underwriting most of Mauritania's military expenditures and many of its third economic-development plan projects, and they were also among the countries most assiduous in offering their good offices to settle the Saharan dispute.

From the outset of his political career, Daddah voiced an irredentist policy with regard to the Western Sahara, with striking perseverance but also without flamboyance, with less than wholehearted backing by his people, and with smaller means at his disposal than those of Morocco. Realism having always characterised Daddah's appraisal of Mauritania's status, he progressively reduced his territorial demands from those of an area larger than the entire Spanish Sahara to what he called Western Tiris, or Tiris El Gharbia. That province, as delimited by the 14 April 1976 agreement with Morocco, had a northern frontier that generally followed the twenty-fourth parallel and covered about two-fifths (96,000 square kilometres) of the former Spanish Sahara province. Daddah's acceptance of a smaller share of the spoils than Morocco obtained was eased in December 1975 when Spain gave him confidential data as to the vast extent of fish resources off the coast between Dakhla and La Guera.[2] These data were contained in a report that had been kept secret till then lest it further inflame the Sahraouis' ardour for independence.[3] There were also grounds, if not equally hard evidence, for believing that Tiris El Gharbia possessed appreciable mineral resources. Furthermore, the inhabitants of Western Tiris were by their culture and blood ties closely akin to the Moors of Mauritania. Indeed, the Daddah government's foreign minister, Hamdi Ould Mouknass, belonged to the Graa tribe, most of whose members lived in Tiris El Gharbia; the family of Mauritania's 'strongman' and pro-Moroccan minister, Ahmed Ould Mohammed Salah, came from Aousserd; and the brothers of two high-ranking officials were the mayors of La Guera and of Dakhla.[4]

After fighting for control of Dakhla, the Nouakchott authorities strove to absorb and develop the new territory. Beginning in January 1976, the province (*wilaya*) of Tiris El Gharbia was named the Thirteenth Region and given the same administrative and party organisation as Mauritania proper. Then the following 8 August, over 90 per cent of its 10,071 registered voters actually went to the polls to elect the new province's seven deputies, who swelled the number of national assemblymen at Nouakchott to 77.[5] At the same time as these moves towards integration took place, many of the practices and policies initiated by the Spaniards, especially those favouring the indigenous population, were perpetuated. To meet severe shortages following the Spaniards' precipitate departure from Dakhla, food for its 4,000 or so residents had to be flown in, and, on a long-term basis, Nouakchott continued the gratuitous distribution of water and electric current, and renewed the status of a free-trading zone for all the coastal settlements. To meet the costs there of its civilian administration alone, Mauritania allotted 600 million *ouguiyas* in the two years 1976-7, or three times as much as it spent in the far more important Nouadhibou region, where the returns in revenues were appreciable.[6]

The grants made to Tiris El Gharbia represented a big investment by Nouakchott, but in comparison with the Spaniards the Mauritanian newcomers looked like poor relations. Although Mauritanians had generally a higher standard of living than did the inhabitants of Tiris El Gharbia, the upper strata in the latter region had been handsomely subsidised by Spain simply to remain quiescent, and in Dakhla alone there lived no fewer than 29 sheikhs.[7] To maintain the local elite in the style to which they had become accustomed, the civil servants employed by the Spaniards were retained, and the soldiers and gendarmes were integrated into the Mauritanian armed forces at their equivalent rank. In 1976 about 700 new jobs were said to have been created in the province, notably in the local bureaucracy, and the experimental farming of market-garden crops for Dakhla, initiated by Spain at nearby Touarta, was pursued. Moreover, at Tichla a co-operative society was formed in April 1976 to grow foodstuffs for the people of that region.

It was principally in the political and cultural domains, however, that the Nouakchott authorities tried to 'Mauritanise' the population of Tiris El Gharbia. By the end of 1977, for example, about 1,000 children were attending new primary schools in Dakhla, where a radio station had also been built to counter adverse enemy broadcasts, and regular weekly air services by Air Mauritanie linked the provincial with the national capital.[8] The more costly and technically demanding exploitation of the Thirteenth Region's only major economic resource of fishing, which had been expanding under Spanish rule, was left to the foreign fishing companies with which Mauritania negotiated new agreements. Similarly neglected by the Nouakchott authorities was the Spanish project for promoting Dakhla's urbanisation, although the influx of nomads driven into the comparative security of the coastal settlements from the war- and drought-ridden hinterland caused an acute housing shortage in the mid-1970s.

Nevertheless, observers who visited towns of the former Spanish Sahara in that period noted the contrast between the calm prevailing in Dakhla and Aousserd and the tension in the more highly developed urban communities under Moroccan rule.[9] In general, they attributed the differences less to the success of Mauritania's assimilationist policy than to its underadministration of the province. When within six weeks of the *coup d'état* at Nouakchott on 10 July 1978 it became clear that the military junta there would use the Tiris El Gharbia as a bargaining counter to secure peace with the Polisario, there was no evidence of trauma among either the Mauritanians or the Dakhla population, although the latter during the preceding four years had lived successively under the flags of Spain, the Polisario, Morocco and Mauritania. (Apparently much the same could be said following the takeover of that town by Morocco about a year later.)

Mauritania's Deteriorating Economy

Slight and ineffectual as was Mauritania's short rule over Tiris El Gharbia, it posed serious financial and military problems for the government. Even before the fighting for Dakhla began, a new national defence tax was levied early in November 1975 on Mauritanians whose monthly salaries exceeded 12,000 *ouguiyas*, to pay for the anticipated military build-up.[10] In April 1976 there was instituted a 'contribution to national solidarity' — the revival on a larger scale of the emergency tax that had been imposed on business turnover (*chiffre d'affaires*) and on workers' daily wages during the drought of 1973. By the spring of 1976 the size of Mauritania's armed forces had more than sextupled (from 2,000 to 12,000 men), and to pay and equip its soldiers Mauritania's defence budget had come to absorb 30 per cent of the country's expenditures. To placate local critics who complained that this 'fratricidal war' was undermining the country's 'revolutionary philosophy of development',[11] the government announced that the third development plan was being carried out on schedule.

Nevertheless, by the beginning of 1977 only 59 per cent of the plan projects had been completed, and the balance of trade had also become unfavourable to Mauritania. That deficit was caused not only by the increased cost of administering and defending Tiris El Gharbia and of the growing military establishment, but even more by the concurrent rise in the prices of imports and the decline in the national revenues derived from Mauritania's exports. Some of these unfortunate economic repercussions might have been mitigated by the choice of more financially viable programmes to be developed under the plan,[12] but they were due mainly to factors beyond Mauritania's control. Those were the climatic conditions consequent to Mauritania's geographical location and the steady fall in world prices for its iron and copper exports. Furthermore, the Polisario's attacks on the railway from Zouérate to Nouadhibou reduced the volume of ore transported, and by 1978 iron exports had shrunk from 8.4 million tons the preceding year to 6.5 million tons, and the shipment of copper concentrates had ceased entirely.

The resurgence of drought conditions in the Mauritanian sahel during 1977-8 caused such losses in Mauritania's herds and crops as to spell the end to extensive animal husbandry in the country, require phenomenally large food imports, and reverse the ratio of the sedentary to the nomadic components of the population.[13] These economic developments, together with the growing size and cost of the military establishment, caused the volume of the budget to increase to 10.2 billion *ouguiyas* in 1978, and with it the trade deficit and the foreign public debt. Of and by themselves, none of those adverse factors would probably have incited the Mauritanians to overthrow the Daddah regime, for the national currency was basically sound and the public debt, albeit large,

was tolerable, thanks to the continued generosity of the conservative
Arab states. There was also the prospect of far larger revenues to be
derived from completion of the Nouakchott-Néma highway, various
promising hydroagricultural projects underway in the south (notably
the OMVS), and above all mining of the *guelbs* iron deposits in the
north. The fall of the regime was due to the cumulative effect of all
the above-mentioned adverse circumstances, superimposed upon a basic
indifference and — as time went on — hostility to a war that had been
thrust upon the black Mauritanians, for it was they who bore its brunt
in terms of manpower and productivity. Not only did the war fail to
give them returns commensurate with the sacrifices it demanded, but
it threatened to break up the unity of the country and to destroy its
social order.

Daddah's Downfall

The war in the Sahara revealed how weak were the structures on which
Daddah had built Mauritania's independence and unity, and how in the
process of trying to reinforce them he lost the support of — or alienated
— the very groups on which his authority depended. The Polisario's
military success in attacking the Zouérate-Nouadhibou railway had
serious consequences both in indirectly causing French military intervention in the conflict and in precipitating the collapse, like that of the
proverbial house of cards, of one pillar of the Mauritanian body politic
after the other.

Certainly some of Mauritania's most serious weaknesses were due
to factors beyond Daddah's control, notably climatic conditions, the
world economic recession and the fall in market prices for Mauritania's
exports. It could also be plausibly argued that the fatal weaknesses were
already so built into the country's politico-economic structures that
they would have eventually surfaced had there been no desert war —
although doubtless not all at the same time or to the same degree. Had
Mauritania chosen to renounce the Spanish heritage in 1975, it would
probably have acquired Morocco as its immediate neighbour to the
north — a situation that it had striven to avoid throughout the 1960s
and which in any case has now occurred. This proximity may still make
Mauritania subject to Morocco's attacks as the rear base for the Polisario, which has never severed its close ties with northern Mauritania.
Be that as it may, by making the fateful decision to cast in his lot with
Morocco, Daddah incurred Boumediene's enmity, gained no large-scale

advantages for his country and lost his own power and freedom. By the end of 1977 the die was cast and the only uncertainty concerned who would be Daddah's successor and when.

Because the funds required to maintain Mauritania's government and modern economy depended very largely on the revenues from the iron-ore carried on the railway from the mine to the shipping port, the defence of that line was a major duty of Mauritania's armed forces. Time showed, however, that without outside support the Mauritanian army was not only unequal to that task but also unable to prevent the kidnapping of Europeans and Senegalese employed by the mine or railway. In turn those developments caused public opinion to lose confidence in the Mauritanian army's ability to defend the country and in its government's capacity to survive without French and Moroccan support.

The repercussions from these phenomena were both physical and psychological. Since it was black Mauritanian sedentaries who formed the bulk of the troops, it was they who suffered the most casualties and who stood to gain the least from a war waged to safeguard a territory far from their geographical base and inhabited by alien Arab and Berber nomads. As to the Moors, they were called upon to fight against tribesmen who were ethnically and culturally and — in some cases — literally their kin, and who were fighting for their freedom. To the youthful intellectuals of whatever ethnic origin, the policies of nationalising the Miferma company, breaking away from the franc zone and establishing state monopolies over the country's economy, which had only recently won their adherence to the PPM and support for Daddah, were now not merely in abeyance but actually being reversed under wartime pressures. That the conservative political and economic forces were gaining the upper hand, and that Mauritania was relapsing into dependence on alien capitalists and neocolonialists, was the message the intellectuals got from the PPM congress of January 1978.

Neither the atmosphere surrounding the PPM congress in Nouakchott nor the resolutions passed by its delegates betokened the significance which this meeting later attained as the turning-point in Daddah's 18 years of rule in Mauritania. It was preceded by none of the demonstrations of personal animosity toward Daddah, strikes or circulation of anti-government tracts that had been associated with the major political developments in 1972-3. Although the press in Mauritania was subject to discreet censorship and labour unions had been brought under the PPM's control, Mauritania was not charged with being a police state, nor was Daddah's claim that no political dissidents were in prison challenged.

Indeed, internal democracy seemed to prevail inside the party, and the acquiescence to its directives was so widespread that it was conjectured that the grievances formerly expressed by the Kadihines might have been deliberately siphoned off at the meeting held by the Conseil Supérieur de la Jeunesse held in mid-summer 1977.[14]

In retrospect, the very lack of any serious criticism by black Mauritanians of the government's policies was in itself portentous, for the congress had been billed as 'extraordinary', and because it was the first held since 1975 it had awakened keen expectations. It would seem to have provided an opportunity to discuss basic official objectives, the new defence agreements with France and Morocco, what measures should be taken to improve the management of state enterprises and to reduce the cost of living, unemployment and war profiteering, as well as how to improve the deplorable housing and sanitation conditions in overcrowded Nouakchott. To be sure, the delegates duly denounced Algeria and its 'mercenaries' as well as Sadat's visit to Jerusalem, but remained little more than a rubber-stamp assemblage. Unanimously the delegates expressed confidence in the government's conduct of the war and Daddah's personal leadership, and to give their approbation the widest possible base, representatives of the labour, women's and youth organisations were admitted to membership in the PPM politburo.

The congress also approved of official proposals to bring Mauritania's legal system into closer conformity with the *sharia*, and to restructure local government institutions so as to place the bureaucracy under closer control by party officials. Finally, to put into practice Daddah's insistence on greater economy in public expenditures, the number of ministers was reduced from 17 to 13. It was in executing that last-mentioned directive that there occurred the most significant accomplishment of the congress — the appointment of a pro-Moroccan civilian (Mohammeden Bobah) to replace Colonel M'Barek Ould Mohamed Bouma Moktar as minister of defence. At the time, Colonel M'Barek's dismissal was variously interpreted as due to Daddah's mistrust of his loyalty, intention to downgrade him so as to promote Colonel Mustapha Ould Ben Salek, or determination to exercise greater personal control over the conduct of the war.

Mauritania's Armed Forces

The great increase in Mauritania's armed forces from fewer than 2,000 men[15] to about 17,000 (including paramilitary units) between 1975 and mid-1978 had significant political as well as financial consequences, of which the PPM leadership was well aware. In particular, Daddah was highly conscious of the role played by the military in toppling the governments of many independent African states, and by frequently rotating senior officers in the different regions and even appointing some of them to managerial or ambassadorial posts, he vainly hoped to prevent the occurrence of such a *coup d'état* in Mauritania.

Never involved in politics or concerned with rank, Mauritania's armed forces had only a handful of professionally trained officers, of whom the four highest in rank were colonels. In 1975 the army was headed by a former ambassador to Zaïre (Colonel M'Barek), and the minister of defence was a civilian (Dr Abdellahi Ould Bah). If the Moorish contingent in the army had such assets as warlike traditions, familiarity with the terrain and the use of firearms, and some experience with military tactics and discipline as *goumiers* and *méharistes* in the French army, the same could not be said of the black conscripts. As the war dragged on, Mauritanians from the Senegal River valley formed an ever-larger percentage of the armed forces. Among them mutinies and desertions were periodically reported,[16] for they had no direct stake in a war that had little relevance to their interests.

The Polisario's surprise attack on Nouakchott in June 1976 made Daddah more aware of his country's military weakness. He not only reversed his previous policy by calling on France and Morocco for aid but also laid the basis for creating a professional army in Mauritania. A military academy was created at Atar, staffed by French instructors, the defence budget was rapidly increased to nearly 60 per cent of total national expenditures, and the garrisons at crucial military posts were enlarged. In March of that year Daddah went so far as to name Colonel M'Barek minister of defence, but three months later his renewed suspicion of the army leaders was indicated by his removing Lt Colonel Viyah Ould Mayouf, the popular 'victor of La Guera', from his command post to make him minister of construction. Again it took Polisario aggression, in the form of successive raids on Zouérate in 1977, to make Daddah fully realise to what extent his armed forces were undertrained, overmanned, equipped beyond their capacity to utilise and of dubious loyalty. He finally placed his country's three military zones directly under the highest-ranking officers, made the general staff responsible to the minister of defence, and granted full powers to Colonel M'Barek to organise the country's defence system.

These changes, however, did not deter the Polisario from continuing to attack the Zouérate-Nouadhibou railway, Mauritanian posts in the desert and coastal settlements so effectively that France and Morocco, at Daddah's urgent request, sent in military elements to shore up

Mauritania's crumbling defence. By an agreement with Rabat, a joint military command was created in northern Mauritania, in which Moroccan officers predominated, and by July 1977 the first 600 of a contingent of Moroccan soldiers – who eventually numbered some 8,000 – took up positions at Zouérate, Akjoujt and Dakhla. A few months later French combat planes flying missions from bases at Dakar and Nouadhibou introduced a new element into the conflict by bombing groups of Polisario raiders who were attacking Mauritanian posts. Militarily speaking, neither French nor Moroccan support proved to be decisive, but it did prevent the Polisario from overrunning Mauritania. From the political angle, such a humiliating revelation of Mauritania's inability to defend itself, and so complete a reversal of Daddah's vaunted policy of military independence from Paris and Rabat, certainly contributed to the widespread discontent that culminated in his overthrow by the armed forces on 10 July 1978.

Unlike similar *coups d'état* in francophone Africa, that of Mauritania was military largely in the sense that it was not engineered by civilians and that it expressed grievances that were by no means exclusively felt by civilians – that is, general war-weariness and frustration. Its leaders were officers who were bound together by no common ethnic or social background, or shared experience in the French colonial army, or belief in any positive programme. Although all the top leaders had been trained in France, they had attended different military academies, belonged to different generations and had served in different branches of the armed services. Moreover, Daddah had been at pains to see that his officers developed no solidarity but competed among themselves to earn promotion through his benevolence. Daddah's practice of assigning senior officers alternately to military or ambassadorial and even managerial posts had the advantage of broadening their experience and contacts, but at the expense of their professional competence and *esprit de corps*. A case in point was the rivalry that developed between the coup leader, Colonel Mustapha Ould Ben Salek, and Colonel M'Barek, who was not only excluded from membership in the Comité Militaire de Rénovation Nationale (CMRN) but briefly arrested along with the heads of the gendarmerie and air force.

Although the CMRN and the government that emanated from it on 12 July reflected to some degree a settling of personal accounts, their position was also to some extent fortuitous. Early in July certain officers of the general staff who had been summoned to listen to Daddah's litany of complaints about corruption in the armed forces were thereby given the unforeseen opportunity to plot his overthrow.[17] Within a week they had organised the agenda for their seizure of power, which was carried out with remarkable speed and efficiency and without bloodshed, but also without concern for achieving consistency in viewpoints or for representing all branches of the armed services. A case in point was that of Colonel Viyah, who was not included among the original conspirators but whose prestige subsequently won him a place in the junta.[18]

Given the circumstances under which the coup took place, the heterogeneous composition of the CMRN and its members' lack of commitment to any ideology or even to personal vindictiveness toward Daddah and his ministers, it is no wonder that for weeks after the coup occurred, Salek's policy was generally described as 'ambiguous'. In fact, it was positive and unanimous only in its goal of maintaining Mauritania's independence and unity, in extricating the country from the war without incurring Morocco's hostility, and in preventing civilian politicians from returning to power. In economic matters it was largely pragmatic, as it was also in cultivating or restoring close relations with those countries most able and willing to promote Mauritania's development.

The Comité Militaire de Rénovation Nationale (CMRN) and the Comité Militaire de Salut National (CMSN)

By unilaterally declaring a ceasefire in Mauritania, beginning in mid-July 1978, and subsequently by concentrating its attacks in southern Morocco, the Polisario leaders gave the CMRN time to consolidate its authority and to accept their terms for ending the war. The Mauritanians, however, failed to take seriously the Polisario's threats to resume military operations and they allowed old domestic quarrels to surface again, the army to be demoralised and demobilised and the economy to lapse into near bankruptcy. Only with respect to adopting *laissez-faire* as an economic policy and extricating their country from the Saharan conflict could Daddah's successors achieve a consensus, but they did not agree on the price they would pay for a lasting peace. After waiting vainly for some miracle unrelated to their efforts to settle the desert war, Mauritania's successive military governments placed their hopes for a solution in the recommendations made by the OAU *ad hoc* committee, but they were dashed by the Polisario's assault on Tichla exactly one year after its ceasefire had been declared. This effectively broke the deadlock inside the military junta, which on 6 August 1979 signed a peace treaty with the Polisario that ended Mauritania's belligerent status as well as its alliance with Morocco, and reinforced its dependence on the goodwill of its neighbours as well as on the conservative Arab nations and France.

Inside the CMRN, it was the problems posed by realpolitik rather than ideology, personal ties, or seniority in rank that accounted for the cleavages that soon developed between its heterogeneous members.[19] The most serious of these differences concerned the relations between the country's two major ethnic communities and between Mauritania and its immediate neighbours. Generally speaking, the principles involved in dealing with the country's administration or its economic problems seemed not to have greatly concerned the CMRN leadership. The constitutional charter which it gave the country a few days after the *coup d'état* simply abrogated the 1961 constitution, dissolved the national assembly and the PPM, and allocated legislative and executive powers to the CMRN until the new democratic institutions could be set up. Such an eventuality, Salek said, must await the peace settlement, and in the interval he saw no necessity for reviving political parties.[20]

Nevertheless, Salek did project a decentralisation of the administration so that the population could participate in the local-government process, and through councils at the regional and communal levels exert more control over local bureaucrats and socio-economic planning. The regions did, indeed, revert to their former names (and were no longer known by number) and to control by the minister of interior (and not the president of the republic), but it was the central government that continued to name the prefects for all the regions, with the notable exception of Tiris El Gharbia. The CMRN left the details of its proposals to be spelled out by a committee which would include a French expert, just as it did to other appointed bodies in preparing the even more sweeping reforms that it wanted to see carried out in the fields of education, justice and the rural economy. Like similar efforts to revise the administrative structure that had been undertaken by Daddah,[21] the CMRN reforms remained largely in the realm of theory.

It was in the domain of economic realities that the CMRN accomplished more because of the relative unanimity its members achieved as regards dismantling the apparatus by which the state controlled the economy. This trend was foreshadowed by a partial 'denationalisation' of the SNIM in April 1978, and was confirmed by the fact that the SNIM's director, Ismael Ould Omar, as well as the head of the Mauritanian businessmen's association, Sheikh Ould Laghdaf, supported the coup.[22] The stagnation, followed by the rapid deterioration, of the country's economy during the last year of Daddah's presidency convinced Mauritanian traders and industrialists that the war must be ended before work could be begun or revived on the major projects to which priority had been given in the 1976-80 development plan. These were the mining of the *guelb* deposits so as to relay those being exhausted at Kedia d'Idjil; completing the Nouakchott-Néma highway, to bring the Hodh region into closer contact with the capital and open up an area for nomad settlement; and promoting the industrialisation of the Nouadhibou region, so as to enhance the value of Mauritania's raw-material exports.

Accordingly, on 25 September 1978 the CMRN warmly endorsed a new plan based on liberal policies that stressed above all the revival of the rural economy; but disillusionment soon followed. Even though there were no further armed attacks on the railway, iron-ore exports failed to improve throughout the latter half of 1978, Nouadhibou's fishing port was still operating at only 30 per cent of its capacity and its related industries to merely 20 per cent of theirs, and the rural exodus continued unabated, as did the decline in agricultural output. To be sure, it was under the auspices of the military junta that the *guelbs* project received substantial funding (in January and July 1979), certain inefficient or bankrupt state enterprises were transformed into joint ventures, new fishing agreements were negotiated with foreign governments (and some of their provisions enforced), an investment code with appreciable fiscal concessions to large-scale investors was enacted (12 March), the cornerstone was laid for Nouakchott's deep-water port (10 April) and prices on some basic commodities were lowered (11 July). On the whole the balance was positive, and consequently the policy of economic liberalism has survived three changes of government and a mini-*coup d'état*.

The same continuity in regard to policy and personnel did not characterise the military government itself. The entente between soldiers and civilians and that among professional army officers themselves did not long survive the overthrow of the Daddah government which they had jointly engineered. To extricate Mauritania from the war, a policy on which they all agreed, proved more complicated than they had anticipated. To differing degrees, so did the division of personal power and that of collective power between the black and Moorish communities, which created a widespread instability whose end is not yet in sight.

In the first CMRN government, the portfolios of its 16-member cabinet were equally divided between civilians and military officers and fairly evenly distributed between pro-Moroccan and pro-Polisario ministers, but not as between the black and Arabo-Berber Mauritanians. This last-mentioned imbalance doubtless accounted for the measures taken by the government in November 1978 which, in essence, favoured Arabic as the sole linguistic vehicle in Mauritania's secondary schools. This was the same issue that had led in 1966 and 1971 to strikes, demonstrations and violence on the part of both blacks and government forces. The same scenario, with certain modifications and additions, was repeated in the first months of 1979, but with somewhat different results.

By the end of 1978, observers in Nouakchott noted that the blacks had become as critical of the CMRN as they had been of Daddah's government, and that the tracts they clandestinely circulated and meetings they secretly attended indicated a shift in their alignments and objectives. The black community's new-found allies were the *harratin*, who had theretofore aligned themselves with their former white masters,[23] and the new issues were Mauritania's membership in the Arab League and in the OMVS.[24] Even more divisive was the proposal to create some form of federation between the Polisario and Mauritania, because such a union would further weight the ethnic scales in favour of the Arabo-Berber community. When President Senghor of Senegal, at the OAU summit in July 1978, internationalised that issue by asserting that the right to self-determination on the part of the 500,000 or so southern black Mauritanians should be acknowledged as a counterpoise to application of the same principle to the Sahraouis of the former Spanish Sahara, he met with strong opposition from the Algerian delegation.[25]

Senghor's insistence was not unrelated to a progressive hardening of the terms demanded by the Polisario for making peace with Mauritania, and this in turn widened the gap between the pro-Polisario and the pro-Moroccan factions inside the CMRN led, respectively, by Major Jiddou Ould Saleck and by Colonel Viyah Ould Mayouf.[26] As the Polisario's terms came to include the recognition of the RASD as a sovereign state with control over Tiris El Gharbia (from which Mauritania must withdraw its administrators and troops), they were considered to be tantamount to unconditional surrender. As such they were unacceptable to a majority of the CMRN military officers, whose attitude toward Algeria, the principal Polisario supporter, cooled accordingly.

Colonel Salek's initial response to this development was to try to reconcile the opposing viewpoints, but when this failed he decided to offer greater satisfaction to the radicals. On 16 January 1979 he gave his conservative foreign minister, Laghdaf, a minor portfolio, and he promoted Major Jiddou to the sensitive post of interior minister, Brezilel to head the culture and youth ministry and Bneijara to the finance portfolio. Jiddou lost no time in applying the controversial linguistic school regulations, and when he rebuffed Ismael Ould Omar's request to form a liberal and democratic political party he announced that no elections would be held for another two years. Inevitably his attitude provoked so strongly adverse a reaction in the south that about a dozen black leaders were arrested in mid-March. Although they were quickly released, Senegal moved some troops up to its northern frontier in response to what it believed to be a threat to Mauritania's black tribesmen. At Nouakchott the tension increased so sharply that Salek, fearing a *coup d'état* at his own expense, abruptly changed course.[27] On 20 March 1979 Salek persuaded the CMRN to vote him full powers, which he promptly used to amend the constitutional charter, dismiss the leaders of both the radical and moderate factions[28] and form a national advisory committee that would reflect the country's ethnic composition and function until such time as democratic elections should be held.

These sudden shifts in personnel and his vacillating policies proved fatal for Salek's political survival. When it was learned that he had named 81 Moors and only 17 blacks to his new council, half of its appointed members decided to boycott its first meeting slated for 30 March. By that time it had also become evident that the 6,000 or so Moroccan troops, which were to have left Mauritania by the end of March, were still there. Yet other causes for the Mauritanians' exasperation with their government were the continuing deterioration of the economy and the malaise generated by the country's uneasy status midway between peace and war. Consequently few observers were surprised when on 6 April 1979 the moderate nationalists in the CMRN, headed by Colonel Ahmed Ould Bouceif and Colonel Heydalla, seized power and formed a Military Committee of National Safety (CMSN) to succeed the CMRN, although in a conciliatory move they named Colonel Salek honorary chairman of the new committee.

Superficially, membership in the CMSN and in the new cabinet resembled that of its predecessor, but with the significant omission of its civilian ministers and the addition of Premier Bouceif, himself a newcomer, Heydalla as defence minister, and Colonel Abdel Kader, a member of the government without portfolio. The CMSN's foreign policy was similarly oriented towards a negotiated peace with the Polisario, but now it was more frankly committed to surrender Tiris El Gharbia unconditionally. Mauritania was determined to extricate itself from the war but still was not ready in so doing to sacrifice its friendship with Morocco and France. Clearly the Moorish military officers who dominated the CMSN had run out of diplomatic options, and although they were not innovative in foreign affairs, they refused to accept collaboration with civilians and were actually retrogressive in domestic policy. Not only did they assert that the government's proper role was simply to execute the policy laid down by the CMSN but, more serious, they refused to share their power with the black component of the population.

In mid-April 1979 the CMSN leadership was alarmed by the enthusiasm generated by the liberation of some former ministers of the Daddah regime because it reflected a widespread disenchantment with military rule more than an upsurge of nostalgia for an administration which only a few months before had been denounced for its corruption and nepotism. Yet there was no doubt but that the officers who made up the hard core of both the CMRN and the CMSN were now largely discredited, for they had dissipated the good will they enjoyed in the wake of the *coup d'état* of July 1978 by fighting among themselves, and by their failure to end Mauritania's participation in the desert war and improve the economy. More significant in its immediate consequences was the military's intransigence in refusing to make real concessions to the black community's insistence on preserving its own culture and on being treated like first-class citizens. Of long-term significance was the CMSN's adoption of a new constitutional charter on 11 April that confirmed its collective authority and reduced the role of head of state to that of a figure-head.

Once again it was the government's insistence on using Arabic exclusively in secondary schools that in mid-April 1979 unleashed a new wave of student protests, followed by official repressive measures. In its use of force in this issue, the CMSN was supported by adherents of the old Mouvement Démocratique and Kadihine parties[29] whose Marxist radicalism was now submerged in the rising tide of Pan-Islamic Arabism. The intransigence of those elements may have been inspired, at least in part, by the formation earlier that month of the Front Walfougui by black Mauritanians.[30] According to a dispatch sent by its leaders to the secretaries general of the UN, OAU and Arab League, the Front would not hesitate to use armed force if need be to defend the black Mauritanians' right to self-determination. That this movement was founded in Dakar and was quickly followed by the official visit of President Senghor to Nouakchott — the first head of state to go there since the July 1978 coup — cast doubt on the authenticity of the Front as a spontaneous movement and substantiated the belief that it had been formed to serve as a Senegalese warning to the Moorish leaders of Mauritania.

On 27 May the death of Premier Bouceif in a plane accident further destabilised the already shaky Nouakchott government, thus forcing on the country a third change in leadership within one year. In the power struggle that ensued, Colonel Salek tried to make a comeback to centre stage, but he was finally eased out of Mauritanian politics and his place as head of state was taken by Colonel Louly.[31] And on 31 May Colonel Heydalla won the CMSN's nomination as prime minister, defeating his principal rivals for that post, Colonel Abdel Kader and Colonel Salem Ould Sidi.

The disappearance of Bouceif removed a major obstacle to improving ethnic relations in Mauritania, and the appointment of Heydalla as premier increased the chance for a negotiated peace in the Sahara. In the government that Heydalla formed on 3 June, he enlarged the number of portfolios allotted to the black community from four to five, although he penalised the two ministers in the Bouceif administration whom he held responsible for the school disorders in early 1979. Then, as a Reguibat born in the former Spanish Sahara, Heydalla was in a better position to deal with the Polisario than had been his predecessor, who came from central Mauritania. On the first anniversary of Mauritania's military coup, Heydalla proclaimed his support for the OAU resolution advocating the Sahraouis' right to self-determination and for the renewal of diplomatic relations with Algeria, while on the same occasion restating Mauritania's desire to remain on friendly terms with Morocco. Two days later, however, the Polisario ruptured its year-old ceasefire, and this forced Heydalla away from his neutral position and into making peace with the RASD largely, although not wholly, on its terms. The peace treaty signed on 6 August 1979 was applauded by all categories of Mauritanians, but it did not bring total reassurance because it failed to settle the fate of Tiris El Gharbia, whose takeover by Morocco a few days later threatened to disrupt Mauritania's hard-won peace.

On domestic issues, the CMSN's united stand *vis-à-vis* any challenge to its rule by civilian leaders was broken by the controversy that developed over liberating the former president of the republic and all of his ministers. Since his arrest during the July 1978 coup, Daddah had been held in various prisons in southeastern Mauritania and was in fast-failing health. Finally the pleas made on humanitarian grounds by foreign governments induced the CMSN to permit Daddah to be flown to France for medical treatment. The extreme precautions taken to keep his departure secret revealed indirectly how precarious was the balance thus far maintained between opposing forces inside the CMSN.

Nouakchott's Foreign Relations

The war wrought a profound change in the orientation of Mauritania's foreign relations, which had already undergone a volte-face during the last years of Daddah's rule. To the great regret of Mauritania's left-wing intelligentsia, the pendulum began in 1975 to swing away from the close ties which Daddah had been cultivating with such 'progressive partners' as Algeria, Cuba, North Korea and Vietnam in the early 1970s. It was above all with Algeria that the parting of the ways proved to be most traumatic, for Daddah could not forget the considerable aid that Boumediene had given him in moving Mauritania out of the French orbit, nationalising the Miferma and creating a national currency. Nevertheless, even at the height of their friendship, Daddah resented being ridiculed as the *'wali* of Algeria's sixteenth province', and found his benefactor's attitude sometimes overbearing.[32] The turning-point came in December 1975 when the Polisario, obviously armed by Algeria, attacked posts inside Mauritania's 1960 frontiers. Even after diplomatic relations were broken off following Algeria's recognition of the RASD on 6 March 1976, Daddah remained remarkably conciliatory. Reportedly, it was the Polisario raid of 8 June 1976 on Nouakchott and the capture of Algerian prisoners with documents proclaiming a new republic of Mauritania to be governed by the Polisario but under Algerian guidance that finally convinced Daddah of Boumediene's implacable enmity.

As the Polisario's attacks on Mauritania increased throughout 1976, Daddah's attitude towards Algeria progressively hardened, and after the Zouérate raid of 1 May 1977 he became almost vituperative when speaking of Algeria. It should be noted, however, that Mauritania's mounting hostility to Algeria was not balanced by a corresponding growth in enthusiasm for Morocco, its current ally. Relations between Rabat and Nouakchott, albeit correct, never became cordial, even after various agreements expanded the two countries' co-operation to economic and cultural as well as military matters. Because he found Mauritania's growing dependence on Morocco galling, Daddah strove to preserve his own freedom of action and cultivated assiduously his personal relations with the heads of many foreign states. In late 1976 and in 1977, Daddah's travels took him to China, Tunisia, Libya, Gabon and Zaïre, and, above all, to the Middle East Arab countries. His visit to Saudi Arabia was particularly rewarding in that he combined business with piety — gaining appreciable financial support for his country and visiting Islam's holy places. Daddah was especially active in maintaining close economic ties with Tripoli, which provided generous financial aid. He also found co-operation — though of a different kind — with Bamako rewarding, as did President Traore, who had every interest in collaborating with Nouakchott to stop the Polisario from using Malian bases to attack towns in southeastern Mauritania.[33] Less cordial were Daddah's relations with Senegal, whose president Léopold Senghor, openly championed the cause of black Mauritanians *vis-à-vis* the Moors.

During several weeks after the *coup d'état* of July 1978 and the Polisario's ceasefire, there was no apparent change in Mauritania's overall foreign policy. Indeed, the very lack of policy pronouncements by the CMRN created an atmosphere of uncertainty that was at first interpreted abroad as an astute manoeuvre by the new military authorities to disguise their long-term objectives. In time, however, it became clear that the CMRN had no objectives beyond its obvious desire to put an end to the fighting, live at peace with its neighbours and restore its shattered economy, and that its indecision was caused by divided counsels among its leaders as to the best means of achieving them.

The solution of buying peace with the Polisario by letting the RASD instal itself permanently in Tiris El Gharbia, long proposed by Libya, was acceptable to the CMRN but strongly rejected by Morocco and only partly satisfactory to the Polisario leadership. King Hassan proved 'understanding' of Mauritania's plight as regards ceasing its military operations, but was adamant in his refusal to accept the Polisario as permanent neighbours along Morocco's southern frontier, while the RASD would settle for nothing short of Nouakchott's recognition of its sovereignty, *de facto* as well as *de jure*, over all the former Spanish Sahara without the formality of holding a referendum there.

In the vague hope of finding some way out of this impasse, the CMRN used the breathing spell provided by the ceasefire to despatch successive high-level missions explaining Mauritania's position to all interested parties and soliciting aid from those most able and inclined to provide it — France and the conservative Arab states. The military junta also impartially used the good offices eagerly proffered by Algeria and Libya to drag out negotiations with the Polisario, but failed to obtain any significant concessions from either Morocco or the Polisario or to resolve the differences between its own pro-Moroccan and pro-Algerian proponents. Finally, the Polisario leadership, exasperated by the CMRN's delaying tactics, broke its self-imposed truce and forced Mauritania to face the immediate and unpalatable reality. This was to choose between resuming the war, which Mauritania was physically and psychologically incapable of doing, and accepting the Polisario's terms, which meant ending its fruitless attempts to placate all its neighbours and also its alliance with Rabat, as well as returning to the Algerian orbit. By accepting the OAU *ad hoc* committee's recommendations, the military junta avoided succumbing wholly to the Polisario ultimatum, and by protesting only *pro forma* against Morocco's takeover of the Tiris El Gharbia after Mauritania made peace with the Polisario, it escaped – at least temporarily – serving as the rear base for Polisario military operations and as a target for Moroccan reprisals.

In the long run, whatever government takes control of Mauritania must place its hopes for a lasting peace on the almost unanimous consent of all the foreign powers that are concerned for stability in the Maghreb and on maintaining that country's independence as a biracial sovereign political entity serving as a permanent buffer state between the black and Arab worlds. Its survival as such also depends on its own leaders' ability to counter the centrifugal tendencies of southern black Mauritanians by creating and maintaining unity between the country's two major ethnic communities.

Morocco's 'Lost Provinces'

Observers of the northwest African political scene continue to be astonished by the extent and depth of Moroccan feeling about its 'lost provinces', and by the king's refusal to make any significant concession that might achieve peace, lest it compromise his country's sovereignty over them. To understand the emotional aspect, one must view it from the perspective of Morocco's imperial past and its perennial rivalry with Algeria, and to grasp fully Hassan II's attitude one should fully appreciate his position as *imam* as well as king. No other country in the region combines such intense nationalist feeling with religious sentiments, or experiences so unifying a sense of nationhood, as does Morocco.

To be sure, the ardour arising from these unique phenomena, of which the world had its first inkling during the Green March, has been somewhat cooled during the years since 1976 by successive tax increases and a fast-rising cost of living for all Moroccans, and by the series of military setbacks since 1978 – but not yet to the point of causing challenges to the king's authority. Demonstrations and strikes by students and trade unionists for more democratic and agrarian reforms and for higher wages, which gathered momentum in 1979, have brought about some improvements but have also met with severe police repression. Nevertheless, the prophets of Hassan's imminent eclipse have been confounded by the advocacy on the part of all strata of Moroccan society of an ever more aggressive Saharan policy. Members of the OAU *ad hoc* committee who talked with leaders of the UNFP, USFP and PPS were struck by the identity of their views on the Sahara, despite marked ideological differences between them and with the king on other issues.[34] Even the extremist Union des Forces Révolutionnaires du Maroc excepted the Sahara while condemning the government's other policies, and Morocco's newest party, Rassemblement National des Indépendants (RNI), outdid the Istiqlal at its constituent congress in October 1978 by its members' insistence on 'recuperating' Tindouf and the Touat oases, and by the violence of their denunciations of Algeria.

It was the Polisario's surprise attack on Tantan in late January 1979 that marked a turning-point in the government's strategy, though not in its objectives. The assailants' near success alarmed Moroccan public opinion and shocked the king into reorienting his country's diplomacy, making more concessions to the domestic opposition and restructuring the military command. In response to the party leaders' demands for formation of a government of national union and of people's militias in the frontier regions, and for alleviation of the misery of the poor, the king convened a special session of the Chamber of Representatives on 10 March 1979. In his speech to that body, Hassan described the situation in southern Morocco as 'verging on the intolerable', and he announced the appointment of a new premier to head a reshuffled cabinet and of a national advisory defence council. That council, he said, would be composed of two representatives from each legal party and also from among veterans of the old ALN, whose task would be to propose 'all necessary measures' so as to check the Polisario's infiltration into Morocco. Once again the king's policy of associating all political groups with his policies succeeded in buying him time. He has used this respite effectively in the military domain, but ineffectively in dealing with the deplorable economic situation, and disastrously in international organisations, where his vacillations and aloof attitude have alienated all but Morocco's staunchest friends.

At home, Hassan's Saharan policy continues to bring him unprecedented popularity among the political elite, but the price they demand for prolonging support is rising fast. Ironically enough, the king's refusal to accept the principle of self-determination for the Sahraouis has been the means, or has supplied the leverage, to promote democracy — within limits — in Morocco itself. Since 1975 the takeover of the former Spanish Sahara has been used by Hassan to win support and by the legal opposition parties to wrest concessions from the king. It was the issue on which the palace conducted its campaign during the four-tiered elections that took place from November 1976 until June 1977,[35] and they gave the king a clear-cut majority in the form of so-called independents who took 141 of the 264 seats in the new chamber. In using the Sahara issue, the king not only appealed to his subjects' patriotic fervour but also capitalised on their long-standing resentment of Algeria's control of the Saoura, Touat and Tindouf, and their more recent indignation at the Algerians' support of the Polisario. As to the legal opposition parties, their members, too, backed Morocco's crusade to recover its 'national heritage',[36] and because their support was rewarded by long-sought concessions — such as the abolition of press censorship and a revision of the electoral registers, not to mention an elected parliament — they were willing to overlook 'irregularities' in the electoral process in return for a share in the government power.

Hassan's Achilles heel on the home front has been and still is his inability to check inflation, which has been running at the annual rate of 20 per cent, to fill the nation's coffers sufficiently to pay Morocco's creditors and to meet the official pay-roll, and to relieve the misery of the great mass of the population. Under these circumstances, just how long the leaders can keep their followers in line is open to doubt, for the king can neither afford to meet their demands nor to ignore them. Therein lies a greater danger to his throne than that represented by the Polisario's successes.

The Moroccan Armed Forces

The importance of Morocco's army in determining the outcome of the Sahara war transcends its purely military aspect, for it can — and has tried to — play the contradictory roles of bulwark and of nemesis to Hassan II. When he was an impulsive and inexperienced crown prince, Hassan had been entrusted by his father with the task of organising the Royal Armed Forces (FAR) from among veterans of the French and Spanish colonial armies and the ALN. Consequently, the training, military experience and loyalties of its members varied, notably as between Berber troops and their officers and between the latter and the king.[37] In short, the FAR was heterogeneous and loosely organised and from the outset had no precise national borders to defend in the south and east.[38] Because the ALN considered itself to be the only authentic national army, it acted as a catalyst in the Hispano-Moroccan dispute over Ifni and Tarfaya, but by 1960 it had yielded control of the deep south to the central authorities.

As of 1962 the FAR numbered 40,000 men, whose corps of 884 commissioned officers had been trained at St Cyr or Toledo or Meknes. Spread too thin over an area that was expanding in the south, and dispersed among the former French military posts along the Algerian 'frontier', the FAR suffered from poor logistical support, as became evident during the *guerre des sables* in 1963. Three years later, obligatory military service was introduced, but only some 5,000 conscripts a year were called up to swell the ranks of an army that took pride in being composed predominantly of professional soldiers.[39] It was apparently for professional or ethical reasons, unrelated to political objectives or personal gain, that high-ranking — mainly Berber — officers made two attempts to assassinate the king in 1971 and 1972.

By the end of the latter year, the officer corps had been seriously purged but the overall size of the FAR showed no corresponding reduction. Indeed, it was increased to about 80,000 men (of whom the army accounted for 55,000) when the king began serious preparations for the Green March. Still unsure of the FAR's loyalty and fearing to let it confront the superior Spanish forces, Hassan despatched military units to 'protect' the unarmed civilian marchers. Therefore, by the time the Madrid pact was signed on 14 November 1975 the Moroccan armed forces had been carefully positioned to relay the Spanish troops as they withdrew from their desert posts, although their presence in former Spanish territory was not publicly acknowledged until 28 November. The months between mid-November 1975 and late April 1976 witnessed some of the fiercest fighting of the war and the only combats in which Algerian troops were known to have participated. In the Saquiet El Hamra the Moroccans were able to take over successively all the posts held by the Polisario Front but not to cut the latter off from its supply bases in the Tindouf region.

Checkmated in the Moroccan zone, the Polisario redirected its main military attacks against Mauritania, with only occasional raids to sabotage the phosphate conveyor belt at Bu Craa. Rather than engage in a trial of strength with the Moroccan army, the Polisario leaders' preferred strategy was to try to undermine that army's loyalty to the throne and to make the war so disastrously expensive for the Rabat government as to provoke a popular uprising of the overtaxed and undernourished Moroccan masses. Although the Moroccan forces have sustained serious losses, these have not been on the scale publicised in the Polisario communiqués[40] and not to the point of undermining

Morocco's ability in 1977 and 1978 to arm and send some 2,800 troops to fight in Zaïre and nearly 9,000 to bolster Mauritania's defences. Contrary to the portrayal of Hassan as a firebrand by some journalists, it has been the king who has moderated the martial ardour of his officers and of the political parties who want to carry the war into Algeria.

As substitutes for such a dangerous course, Hassan offered two alternatives in 1979. One was a reactivated auxiliary armed force called Aosario (the Association of Native Saharans formerly under Spanish rule), which had been formed in 1976 by former members of the More-hob[41] for the purpose of conducting guerrilla operations inside Algeria. Aosario leaders described their organisation to the OAU *ad hoc* committee members as a 'people's militia' whose mission was 'to release fellow-Saharans held as refugees in the Tindouf concentration camps', and in April 1979 it claimed to have ambushed an Algerian convoy in that region.[42] Like the Polisario Front, of which it was a pallid replica, the Aosario offered the advantages of carrying the war into enemy territory – an act of aggression for which the Moroccan authorities could disclaim any responsibility.

Much more spectacular has been the well-publicised large-scale *Opération Ohoud*,[43] which was launched in February 1979 but did not get under way until late October.[44] Preparations for this combined air and land operation were as meticulous as those that preceded the Green March four years earlier. Its mission was to wipe out the hidden bases in the Tiris El Gharbia from which the Polisario drew its supplies and launched its raids on Moroccan strongholds. Both materially and psychologically, *Opération Ohoud* – which, as of this writing, is still in progress – represents a hazardous departure from Hassan's previous defence strategy, and it has been marked by the publication of Morocco's first 'victory bulletins' and displays of Sahraoui war prisoners. On the material side, it required a huge investment – in 1979 the war was estimated to be costing between $2 and $5 million a day – for a country seriously short of foreign exchange and credit. It is also a risky compromise between guerrilla operations, at which the Polisario are past masters, and conventional warfare, for which the Moroccan army has been organised in view of an eventual clash with the regular Algerian forces. Psychologically, the king has staked his personal prestige on the success of *Opération Ohoud* and his throne on the loyalty of Colonel Dlimi and of Colonel Mohamed Abrouq, the new commander of the armed forces in southern Morocco.

The Administrative Organisation of Morocco's New Provinces

On 23 November 1975, nine days after the Madrid pact was signed, Ahmed Bansouda, director of the king's cabinet, was named to represent Morocco in the tripartite administration installed under that agreement to govern the former Spanish Sahara in collaboration with the *yemaa*. Two days after his appointment, Bansouda reached El Aaiun, and by the end of November a direct telephone line had been opened between it and Rabat. By that time, too, broadcasting from the stations of Rabat and Tarfaya had superseded the former Spanish radio network. During the first week of December, the Moroccan flag was raised over the town, eight Moroccan ministers who were flown in for that ceremony inaugurated an air service between El Aaiun and Rabat, and President Khattri Ould Jamani and Vice-President Sheikh Ahmed Ould Bechir, accompanied by their followers in the *yemaa*, returned by plane to Rabat, where they swore allegiance to the king.[45]

The early months of 1976 introduced new names, administrative units and boundaries into Saquiet El Hamra. El Aaiun, except for the town, became Laayoune; Cape Bojador (a miniature desert with a light-house, a well and some 600 inhabitants) was renamed Boujdoura; and Smara was simply reorganised administratively. Governors were appointed to head the new provinces, and eighteen months later the southern portion of Tiznit was amputated to form the new province of Tata.

How many of the area's former residents preferred exile in Algeria to being 'Moroccanised' in their homes, and what proportion tacitly sympathised with the Polisario, were the subjects of speculation and differing opinions among the foreign journalists who visited the three provinces soon after the Moroccan takeover.[46] In 1976 estimates of the number who had already fled from the region ranged from 33 per cent to 50 per cent. More recently, the settled population of the three provinces has come to approximate what it was in the Spanish era — that is, between 55,000 and 60,000 — hence it appears that from one-half to one-third of those now living there must be immigrants from the north or returnees. If, as some reporters maintain, the Moroccan authorities have dealt harshly with those Sahraouis who are openly — or are suspected of being — pro-Polisario, they have also made great efforts in their so-called three-year urgency plan (1977-80) to attract as many nomads as possible to the towns and to induce them to settle there. Indeed, this programme may prove to be oversuccessful in attracting settlers beyond Rabat's capacity in personnel and funds to maintain, for the main settlements have become centres for duty-free imports and the free distribution of food, medical care and schooling.

In a grandiloquent speech on 17 November 1975 King Hassan stated that 'we did not conquer the Sahara because it has phosphate deposits . . . but to build schools, hospitals . . . and to guarantee peace, well being, and prosperity',[47] adding that the anticipated revenue from the Bu Craa phosphates would provide only two-thirds of what Morocco planned to spend annually in its Saharan provinces. By June 1976 Rabat had already sent there four doctors, 38 nurses and 47 teachers to instruct the 3,000 or so Sahraoui children then attending the local schools. But it was at Boujdoura, where a wholly new town was being built from the sand up, that the most spectacular changes were taking place. By the end of 1977 it had acquired not only its first stone houses but a desalination plant that was supplying a public fountain from which the nomads were drawing their first free-flowing water.[48] Smara was provided not only with the same facilities but also a national Islamic institute.[49]

The government's overall policy was defined at a meeting at Smara in December 1977 that was attended by all the governors and elected representatives from the new provinces, as well as their counterparts from Agadir, Tantan, Tiznit, Ouarzazate and the deep south — that is, the officials and representatives of an area covering one-fourth of all Morocco. The convening of this 'estates general' in itself betokened the government's intention of eliminating any demarcation between what had been southern Morocco and the newly acquired territories, as well as that of encouraging administrative decentralisation. It also foreshadowed the evolution of Smara as headquarters for the administration of the Moroccan Sahara and of El Aaiun as its commercial capital, thus duplicating the two northern poles of attraction at Rabat and Casablanca. Among the measures proposed at this conference as leading to those objectives was the development of communications such as roads, airfields, ports and broadcasting stations. The major long-term projects for the area are the creation of industries based on phosphates, fishing and tourism.

Rabat, like Nouakchott, early decided against a hasty integration of the new provinces into the country's national economy, and so as a temporary measure it perpetuated the free-trade zones that had been instituted by Spain, although this decision deprived its treasury, already badly depleted by war-caused expenditures and the sharp decline in revenues from mineral exports. In Morocco the cost of only the first instalment of its development plan amounted to 600 million DH, and even to meet its initial expenditures the government had to draw on national revenues and the regional development funds, as well as to increase taxes and also raise loans in the world and domestic markets. A further financial drain has been the payment of wages to the 4,000 or so Sahraoui labourers working in the new provinces at twice the rate paid in Morocco proper. Similarly, double pay for Moroccan soldiers and government employees serving in the Saharan provinces has helped to arouse, or to sustain, enthusiasm for the Greater Morocco policy.

It is indicative of the Moroccan leaders' concept of the government's political role in the new territories that a high priority was early assigned to the training of local cadres, as heralded by the appointment of Sahraouis as governors of two of the three provinces. From the outset the king was concerned that the Sahraouis should not be 'overwhelmed by an influx of administrators and technicians from the north',[50] but that they should have the hope of being trained themselves to qualify for such posts. This policy was in line with the resolutions adopted by the Conseil de la Jeunesse Sahraouie at Tangier as early as April 1976, a meeting which in itself was an unprecedented and imaginative example of the Rabat authorities' campaign to enlist the co-operation of the region's youth. Most of the hundred-odd delegates attending that meeting were former members of the PUNS or the FLU, who expressed their deep attachment to Morocco, their concern for the future of the Saharan provinces as an integral part of the fatherland and their desire to play a responsible role in its development. Although not all the delegates present endorsed the division of the former Spanish Sahara between Mauritania and Morocco, or favoured granting more autonomy to the new administrative units, or approved of giving more responsibilities to local Sahraouis, this conference did meet the Moroccan government's main objective in organising it — that is, to prove that not all the youth in the Western Sahara had espoused the cause of the Polisario.[51]

The process of integration was carried a long step further in the spring of 1977. On 19 April Khali Henna Ould Rachid became the first Sahraoui to occupy a ministerial post in the Moroccan cabinet, and on 3 June he was elected along with three other Sahraouis to the new Chamber of Representatives at Rabat. According to the Moroccan authorities, 90 per cent of the *pashas*, *caids* and *khalifas* in the Saharan provinces are Sahraouis, and all of the 213 lower officials — *moqaddam* and sheikhs — are local-born.[52] In the Tiris El Gharbia, which the Moroccan army wrested from the reluctant Mauritanian administrators and soldiers in August 1979 and which was renamed Oued Eddahab, there has been a rerun of the scenario played out in the Saquiet El

Hamra four and a half years earlier. In October 1979 Khali Henna Ould Rachid, again secretary of state for Saharan affairs, toured the area, duly noted the many weak spots in its socio-economic infrastructure, and began organising municipal elections in Dakhla.[53] As in the three more northerly Saharan provinces, the minister's tour was preceded by the sending to Dakhla of medical personnel and teachers, and it was followed by the shuttling between that town and Rabat of a steady stream of technicians, public-works engineers and political leaders, including notably 360 tribal chiefs and Notables who were flown to Rabat to swear allegiance to the throne.[54] Logically, the next step should be publication of a plan to align Oued Eddahab's development with that of the older provinces and to promote its inhabitants' 'marocanité'. But Rabat must also soon make difficult decisions as to its priorities, for there are simply not enough funds available to carry out existing programmes.

Morocco and the International Community

The history of King Hassan's relations with the international community has been one of almost unmitigated failure. This has been due not only to the aggressive diplomacy practised by the Polisario and Algeria but also to the king's own deprecatory attitude toward the Arab League, the OAU and the UN. Hassan has not tried to promote the overall purposes of those bodies but rather to involve them on his behalf, as organisations, in Morocco's perennial disputes with its neighbours. The support given the king initially by most of the members of the international organisations has gradually fallen away because they have been alienated by Hassan's aloof and sometimes contemptuous attitude, his inconsistencies in policy and the consequent lack of credibility he has increasingly inspired.

In the early 1960s domination of the Arab League by Nasser, Hassan's avowed adversary and the saboteur of the Casablanca bloc, closed off that organisation to the king. Subsequently he continued to believe that it could never serve his cause because of the divisions among its members in general and with regard to himself in particular. A member government's relations with Israel were the criterion by which the League passed judgement, and Hassan's record in this respect was mixed. On the debit side of the League's ledger was Hassan's 'fratricidal war' with fellow-Arabs and Muslims (the Polisario Front and Algeria), his ambivalence toward the PLO and, far more damning, his cordial relations with President Sadat, whom he had encouraged to visit Jerusalem. Off-setting these liabilities were the outstanding military performance by Moroccan troops during the 1973 war, Morocco's playing host twice to the Islamic Conference and finally Rabat's eventual rupture of diplomatic relations with Cairo subsequent to the conclusion of Egypt's peace treaty with Israel.

As to Morocco's relations with individual Arab countries, they ranged from hostile to cordial. The above-mentioned factors had a primordial influence on the Arabs' attitude, but ideology also played a determining role in the case of governments either markedly radical or strongly conservative. Arab hardliners such as Colonel Khadafi of Libya found Morocco's conservative, pro-Western, capitalistic monarchy intolerable, and short of recognising the RASD — for reasons unrelated to Morocco's claims to the former Spanish Sahara — did everything possible to bring about Hassan's defeat. Saudi Arabia, at the other end of the ideological gamut, discreetly financed both Hassan's army and his economic projects (except for the interval during which the king actively supported Sadat's peace initiative) in order to maintain Morocco as a bulwark against the spread of Algerian and Libyan radicalism.

Similarly, Hassan early became discouraged with the UN and the OAU. In 1961 he had vainly tried to prevent Mauritania's admission to the UN, and in 1974 that body's successive resolutions favouring a referendum to be held in the Spanish Sahara proved embarrassing to the king after he had decided to assert, unilaterally if need be, Morocco's 'historic rights' to that area. The next year, the sibylline judgement rendered by the World Court did not bring Hassan the legal satisfaction he had anticipated in proposing its intervention, and the support given by the UN fact-finding mission in the Western Sahara to the Polisario's claim to represent the Sahraoui people could not but displease the king. In view of these setbacks, Hassan's decision in early 1979 to bring his complaint against Algeria's armed aggression before the Security Council was surprising, and it is understandable only in the light of his deteriorating military and diplomatic situation. Soon, however, he judged his prospects there so poor that abruptly and without explanation he postponed lodging his complaint, and this once again left the issue up to the OAU, to which the UN and the Arab League had been trying unsuccessfully for some years to shift responsibility.

Hassan's record with the OAU was only slightly less discouraging than that with the two other international bodies. He had refused to attend its constituent congress in 1963 because of the presence there of Mauritania's president. After joining the OAU later that same year, he chose it over the Arab League as the organisation more likely to resolve to his satisfaction the issues that had led to the *guerre des sables*. Although the committee appointed by the OAU to study that case failed to reach a consensus, its policy of procrastination produced a *modus vivendi* between Morocco and Algeria that lasted for more than a decade. Unfortunately the same delaying tactics proved less effective when applied to the same protagonists beginning in 1975.

On one pretext and another, the OAU continued to avoid the Sahara issue until mid-1978, when the *coup d'état* in Mauritania compelled its heads of state to take some stand. This took the form of appointing an *ad hoc* committee to contact all the parties concerned in the dispute and to prepare a report for the next summit meeting at Monrovia, scheduled for July 1978, which would recommend ways of ending it. Hassan's last-minute refusal to attend that meeting enabled him to avoid the humiliation of witnessing the acceptance by the OAU of the committee's recommendations for a ceasefire and a referendum in the former Spanish Sahara. This defeat was compounded by the UN General Assembly's adoption on 2 November of a stronger resolution by a larger majority,[55] asking that Morocco end its occupation of the Western Sahara and, with the Polisario as representing the Sahraoui people, to help establish a just peace in conformity with the objectives laid down by the UN, the OAU and the non-aligned nations. When this recommendation was endorsed by the *ad hoc* committee meeting again at Monrovia a few days later, Morocco was not represented there and to all appearances was quarantined by the international community.

During the year in which the OAU committee was holding its hearings, Hassan, realising that the tide was running against him, made peace overtures to both Algeria and the Polisario, but the concessions he proposed did not include the basic one of any compromise in regard to Morocco's sovereignty over the disputed area. His one positive contribution toward a negotiated peace was his proposal to convene a conference of all the Saharan borderland nations from the Atlantic to the Red Sea, for the purpose of ironing out disputes and of planning joint economic development of the whole desert. Although this could hardly be considered a major contribution to the cause of peace, it did appeal to such black African states as Chad and Mali, which felt threatened by Libya's expansionism in the Sahara at their expense.[56]

'A plague on both your [Arab] houses' has been the attitude of the great majority of the sub-Saharan heads of state. Only President Senghor of Senegal has intervened openly and, as a rule, in Morocco's favour, not so much to support Rabat's claims to the Western Sahara as to protect the interests of the black tribesmen living on the banks of the Senegal River and to prevent the formation by the Polisario and Algeria of an aggressive Arabo-Berber nation along Senegal's northern frontier. The Third World's all-purpose yardstick in judging conflicts among its members has been their attitude toward national liberation movements, and for this Algeria has received high marks. That Morocco's takeover of Tiris El Gharbia, to which its historic claims are even more dubious than those to Saquiet El Hamra, has not been well received by Third-World nations is shown by the recent and rapid growth in the number of them that have recognised the RASD.

Generally speaking, Hassan's skill as a diplomat has been at its lowest ebb in international gatherings and at its peak in discreet bilateral negotiations. Only mediocre success has attended his formation or sponsorship among political exiles of nominally independent groups, such as the FLU, the Aosario and the Front Islamique et Démocratique de Mauritanie, which openly and with fanfare conduct operations against regimes opposing Morocco's objectives. In government-to-government relations, Hassan has almost consistently been on good terms with the Western nations from which he wants — and often receives — arms, funds and diplomatic support. He capitalises on their determination to maintain a moderate government as long as possible in northwest Africa's most strategic area — an objective that overrides their disapproval of the autocratic and imperialistic aspects of his regime.

Morocco's relationship with Spain under both Generalissimo Franco and King Juan Carlos is the outstanding example of Hassan's successful coupling of threats with patient courtship. Its rewards were Ifni, Tarfaya and the Madrid pact, and its penalty a bloody and expensive war that may yet, however, net him further material gains. Geographical proximity to the Canary Islands, the *presidios* and the coastal fishing grounds has given Morocco the whip hand, if not the control, over areas that Madrid considers vital to its national interests. To be sure, Algiers, too, has trump cards to play in preventing Spain from giving its full support to Rabat. On the positive side, Spain needs Algerian hydrocarbons, and, on the negative side, it desires the cessation of Polisario attacks on Spaniards fishing in 'Sahraoui waters' and of Polisario encouragement of the Canary Islands independence movement. These are potent enough forces, in conjunction with Spanish left-wing leaders, for Premier Adolfo Suarez and his Union of the Democratic Centre party to make some minor and largely *pro forma* concessions to the Polisario, but not strong enough to offset Madrid's perennial dependence on Rabat's goodwill. During King Juan Carlos's long-postponed state visit to Rabat in June 1979, a deal was reportedly made whereby Madrid pledged not to rescind the Madrid pact or to recognise the RASD, in return for Hassan's promise to hasten ratification of the Hispano-Moroccan fishing agreement, to soft-pedal Moroccan claims to the *presidios* and to subscribe to Spain's insistence on the 'Spanish character' of the Canary Islanders.

France has long been Hassan's most dependable source of foreign aid, and his frequent visits to Paris testify to this dependence on French goodwill. However, President Giscard d'Estaing's support began to falter in 1978 when France's increasingly chilly relations with Algiers began to harm seriously French business interests there. More recently, Paris has tended to look upon Morocco's takeover of Dakhla as indicating that Hassan's appetite for conquest is getting out of hand. Thus French concern about Morocco's growing aggressiveness has to some extent replaced its earlier fear of the spread of Algeria's revolutionary influence, especially as the latter country is passing through a period of transition following Boumediene's death.

Morocco's relations with the superpowers have undergone greater changes since 1975 than have those with other nations. In the case of the Soviet Union, the changes are unrelated to the Saharan war and derive directly from that country's growing need for agricultural fertilisers and consequently for Morocco's phosphate. An agreement signed in March 1978, which has been called the *marché du siècle*, marked the triumph in Soviet policy of economic considerations over its ideological affinities for Algeria and the Polisario, and gave an immediate stimulus to Moroccan morale, as well as an eventual boost to its economy.

Quite the contrary has been the evolution of American-Moroccan relations, which have always been friendly and based primarily on political and strategic considerations — an orientation that has been confirmed by the Saharan war and influenced by concurrent developments in Iran. Late in 1979 the official United States policy of neutrality in the Western Sahara conflict risked being reversed by the administration's proposal to sell to Rabat combat aircraft and electronic equipment on condition that Morocco would work towards negotiating an end to the war. This proposed policy change generated considerable opposition in the press and in Congress, where its most articulate spokesman was Representative Stephen Solarz.[57] This congressman argued against delivering offensive weapons to King Hassan on practical grounds as well as those of principle. In the first place, he contended, it would run counter to traditional American values by encouraging Morocco to cling to land and resources that properly belonged to the indigenous population of the former Spanish Sahara, as represented by the Polisario Front. Moreover, it would alienate Algeria, which has become a major trading partner of the United States, and a majority of the Third World nations, which have formally registered their support for the RASD. Solarz minimised the possibility that forcing the king to make appreciable concessions to the Polisario might cost him his throne, or might further damage the American image as a reliable ally, which has already been tarnished by its failure to give active support to the shah of Iran. He acknowledged the debt owed by the United States to King Hassan for his early support of Sadat's peace initiatives in regard to Israel, his despatch of troops to fight in Zaïre, and his hospitality to the shah of Iran, but maintained that it could be more constructively repaid by promoting Morocco's economic development than by supporting the king in his continuance of an 'unjust, costly, and unwinnable war'.

Time and the outcome of the war alone can test the validity of the foregoing arguments, for, as of the present writing, military operations are continuing in the Western Sahara.

Peace — or a War of Attrition?

Some sort of Sahraoui state is almost certain to emerge from the present conflict, but both its form and its substance are still obscure. Morocco, albeit beleaguered and impoverished, remains determined to reduce such a state to its simplest form and smallest dimensions. The Polisario, undeterred by its manpower losses and stimulated by international encouragement and continuing aid from Algeria and Libya, seems equally determined to attain fully-fledged statehood and thus to make Rabat pay the maximum price for peace in the Western Sahara.

On the eve of the 1980s speculation about an end to the four-year conflict in the Western Sahara and the chances for, and terms of, a negotiated peace there seem to be in order. All the many self-appointed mediators of the war, and almost all its participants, want to stop the destruction of that huge area's limited human and natural resources, but thus far the belligerents cannot agree on the timing or conditions for peace. Many of the basic elements in the situation are known, but others remain unknown or are perceived only as in a glass darkly. Nevertheless, any analysis of the background to the Sahara conflict should conclude with a weighing of the positive against the negative factors for peace, and sort out the known ones from those that are still obscure or unknowable.

Topping the list of positive factors is what might be called a negative asset — that is, the absence of active intervention in the Saharan war by the superpowers, and very little on the part of France and Spain, the two European nations that have the oldest historic ties and the greatest economic interests in the area. Although this fortuitous international void applies only to direct armed intervention and not to the supply of arms and funds to the combatants, it does set the Western Sahara apart from such other African trouble spots as Angola and Ethiopia and facilitates a settlement of the conflict by reducing it to local terms. This localisation of the issues is clearly implied in the successive resolutions passed by the UN and the OAU, almost all of which have recommended a ceasefire and the holding of a referendum to determine the will of the Sahraouis as to their future status. In practical terms, however, this seeming simplification of the situation raises thorny problems, such as who is a Sahraoui, how can Sahraoui votes be cast and counted, and under what auspices can the will so expressed be made known and enforced?

More important than such legalistic and practical questions is that of the likelihood of a peace that depends on the will to compromise on the part of all the warring parties. Mauritania has chosen to opt out of a war from which it emerged not only without any compensation for its serious losses, but with its precarious unity further undermined and its sovereignty jeopardised. Of the remaining participants in this war, Morocco has the most vital interests at stake, but whatever may be its outcome the Polisario Front will have won more than it has ever had before. If the war's outcome is favourable to Rabat, Morocco stands to acquire a quasi-monopoly of world phosphate exports, the means to develop a flourishing economy, and a primacy position in the Maghreb that would enable King Hassan to play a stronger role internally and internationally. On the other hand, there is the risk of a popular uprising or an army *coup d'état* that could cost the king his throne and possibly his life, in the event of a military defeat in the desert, or a concession to the Polisario that might incite hardline Moroccan nationalists into provoking a war with Algeria. In view of its human, economic and emotional dependence upon a victory, Morocco has the least inclination to compromise.

If, in the domestic context, the Saharan war is Hassan's greatest asset as well as his heaviest liability, it is basically irrelevant to Algeria's vital interests. The successors of Houari Boumediene do not share his emotional commitment to the defeat of Morocco, and, as they never tire of telling international audiences, their country has the least to gain materially from a Polisario victory. Psychologically, however, Algeria does have a vested interest in the outcome, for at stake are its prestige as one of Africa's leading revolutionary nations and its claim to hegemony in the Maghreb. Nevertheless, backing the Polisario is, on the whole, a gamble that Algeria can well afford to take inasmuch as it does not seriously divide its population, entails no loss of Algerian lives, and has the help of Libya and the USSR in footing the Polisario's bills and supplying it with arms. Indeed, Algeria stands to gain — if the Polisario wins — not only those advantages laid down in the treaty of Ifrane[58] but also a share in the Bu Craa mine and a port on the Atlantic for Gara Djebilet's iron ore exports.

On the debit side of the ledger, however, there are certain risks. These are that Algeria might inadvertently find itself at war with Morocco, or confronted by a more militantly nationalistic government at Rabat than that of Hassan, and of receiving unacceptable demands by a victorious Polisario for control of the Tindouf region. In fact there is no assurance that the RASD, once installed in the Western Sahara, might not team up with Tripoli to exert pressure on its former Algerian benefactors. At Algiers, therefore, as well as at Rabat, there is a predisposition to compromise along predictable lines that could, with certain adjustments, prove acceptable to both governments. Inasmuch as Morocco's fortunes have been generally declining during the past few years, Hassan has felt constrained to propose direct negotiations to Algeria. He almost succeeded in bringing Boumediene to the negotiating table, but the latter's fatal illness prevented their meeting at Brussels in the autumn of 1978, as had been prearranged.

If Hassan cannot afford to lose the war, Algiers can hardly afford to win it, so committed is its government to making the Polisario a partner in any agreement it reaches with Rabat. It would indeed be an anticlimax to the desert conflict were Algeria and Morocco to establish a working partnership for the purpose of holding in check the combined ambitions of the Polisario and Libya. The Polisario Front is the behemoth born of Spain's maladroit efforts to withdraw in good order from the Sahara, nurtured by Boumediene and Khadafi, and developed into a growing and still largely unknown force. Gone are the days when the Polisario could be discounted as a nuisance, as Algerian mercenaries or as an aggregation of disparate tribesmen held together by no bonds stronger than their refusal to accept any external authority. For the first time, in November 1977, Hassan admitted that the Polisario had become dangerous, and a year later he took the positive step of urging its members to 'return home', where, he implied, some ministerial posts would await them. Hassan has preferred a solution in which the Polisario would merge, or unite in some way, with Mauritania, or possibly become an autonomous unit in a Maghrebian federation, but under no foreseeable circumstances could he accept the establishment on Morocco's frontier of an RASD that, although nominally independent, would actually be subservient to Algeria and Libya.

If the precondition for peace in the Sahara is to be a fundamental agreement between Morocco and Algeria, the king wants it to be negotiated between himself and President Chadli, whereas the latter insists that the king deal directly and exclusively with the Polisario leaders. Those leaders, for their part, insist that the precondition for their even opening negotiations with Morocco is that Rabat recognise the RASD as a sovereign government. Moreover, the RASD has defined no boundaries for the state which it proposes to govern, operating apparently on the assumption that by their very nature nomads take little account of national frontiers, but more probably with the intention of pushing them into Mauritania and Mali as deeply as possible.

'Petit Sahraoui, à quel sauce veux-tu être mangé?' asked a journalist sympathetic to the Polisario cause in 1976. Although today the assumption of such a Polisario victimisation in any agreement reached between Morocco and Algeria is no longer valid, its leaders are taking precautions to see that they are not given short shrift. They are careful not to define too clearly the kind of nation they hope to create in the Sahara,[59] so as not to alienate potential foreign supporters, and seem to anticipate that that state's orientation, like its boundaries, will be determined by circumstance. To European left-wing leaders, who are the Polisario's most sympathetic foreign audience, its spokesmen voice suitably revolutionary Marxist sentiments, while to an American congressman they deny any commitment to the Soviet Union and indicate that they will look to the Western nations for guidance and technological skills. They quite properly assume that few of their interlocutors know much about their antecedents or have considered the disruptive effects that any Sahraoui state might have on the unity of Mauritania, Mali and possibly Senegal, on execution of the OMVS projects or, finally, on human life generally in the Sahara.

Of all the sub-Saharan states, Senegal and Mali have been the most deeply affected by the Western Sahara struggle and potentially could be by the possible establishment of a sovereign Polisario state. This is due not only to their governments' ethnic loyalties to the Senegal River black tribesmen, but also to their common interest in supporting a biracial Mauritania as a buffer state between their frontiers and an expansionist Arab Maghreb. Polisario troops operating from bases inside Mali against Mauritania have continued to recruit warriors from among the dissident Malian Touareg, and more of them could easily be attracted to a sovereign state under RASD governance. Even Nigeria, distant as it is geographically and politically from the Western Sahara, has been active as co-chairman with Mali of the *ad hoc* OAU committee in trying to settle the desert war, as part of its recent aim to establish its leadership of the borderland black Saharan states.

From regarding the RASD as a comic-opera state composed of picturesque but quarrelsome camel-breeding nomads, foreign opinion seems to have swung back so far in the other direction as now to view the 'Sahraoui phosphate republic' as peopled by courageous patriots, pioneers and embryonic statesmen. If the existence of a state is based on a discipline, cohesion and sense of nationhood that has been born of life in the desert under wartime conditions, the RASD can certainly qualify to be so designated. As to the economy on which it would presumably be based, it is hard to envisage any productive role for the present generation of Sahraouis, which is composed mainly of guerrilla fighters and survivors of refugee camps who are averse to farming and fishing and who possess none of the education required to qualify them for clerical or professional posts.

There is no doubt but that the Western Sahara has the mineral — though not the food — resources needed to support a population estimated by the Polisario leaders at a maximum of 150,000 persons, but the processing and exporting, if not the extracting, of those ores would require the prolonged presence of foreigners in the area. At the same time, the Sahraoui themselves could no longer live like nomads, for nomadism expired in the desert when the animal herds were decimated by the drought and the war.

Perforce the Sahraouis must remain or become sedentaries, either in encampments or in shanty towns adjacent to the existing settlements; in either case they will have lost, or will lose, their Bedouin character. Moreover, the RASD, like all other central governments, is the avowed enemy of nomadism, whose essential tribalism, regionalism and anarchism — the nomad's hallmarks — it has already singled out for extinction. No government, whatever its ideological stripe, can long afford to tolerate the existence in its midst of bands of loosely organised and dispersed families and fractions that refuse to accept schooling other than Koranic, or taxation, or any other hindrances to their freedom. Inasmuch as no means of survival other than pastoral nomadism has as yet been devised for humans attempting to live under stark desert conditions, the Sahraouis must perforce gravitate to the Sahara's northern or its southern periphery. Thus the heartland of whatever state can be built on those desert sands will be devoid of human life, and the few Western Saharans that still practice the traditional means of livelihood will be restricted to the date-palm oases and the foggy coastal pasturelands.

Notes

1. *Jeune Afrique*, 9 April 1976.
2. *El Chaab*, 16 April 1976.
3. *Jeune Afrique*, 30 Jan. 1976.
4. See *Jeune Afrique*, 19 Oct. 1974.
5. Ibid., 10 June 1977; *Europe-Outremer*, no. 574 (Nov. 1977). As of early 1978, the population of the Thirteenth Region was said to be 12,897. *Le Monde*, 31 March 1978.
6. See *Le Monde*, 17 Feb. 1978.
7. Of the town's active male population, 916 were unemployed, and there were 33 functionaries, 32 nurses, 26 skilled workers, 17 teachers and one farmer. A Dakhla sheikh was said to receive more salary than a Mauritanian deputy, and a Dakhla member of the *yemaa* was paid twice the salary of a Mauritanian cabinet minister. This pay scale seemed to substantiate the propaganda pledge made by the Polisario that in its 'phosphate republic', the Sahraouis would enjoy the highest per capita income in the Western Sahara. See Bechir Ben Yahmed, 'On Peut, On Doit, Eviter la Guerre', *Jeune Afrique*, 25 Nov. 1977.
8. 'La Mise en Valeur du Tiris El Gharbia', *Europe-Outremer*, no. 574 (Nov. 1977).
9. See articles by Moudjib Djibril in *Afrique Nouvelle*, 22, 29 Aug. 1978.
10. *Marchés Tropicaux*, 10 Nov. 1975.
11. *Le Monde*, 5 March, 10 April 1976; *El Chaab*, 22 March 1976.
12. Had the authorities chosen to develop Mauritania's available water and fish resources rather than finance building a steel plant, copper foundry and generating electrical current for hinterland settlements, agricultural production would have been at least maintained, and the imports of food and the rural exodus diminished.
13. Total losses amounted to half the cattle; 30 per cent of the sheep, goats and camels; and from 90 to 100 per cent of its cereal crops. By the end of 1977 food stocks had fallen so low as to require the importation of 72,000 tons of foodstuffs in addition to the donations in kind made by international organisations. According to the national census of 1977, the nomads then accounted for only 33 per cent of the total population of 1,400,000, as compared with 65 per cent in the mid-1960s.
14. See *Europe-Outremer*, no. 574 (Nov. 1977); *Jeune Afrique*, 25 Jan. 1978; *Afrique-Asie*, 20 Feb. 1978.
15. As of November 1975, the army numbered about 1,000 men, including a paratroop unit; the air force 200; the navy 100; and the gendarmerie some 700. It was the fierce fighting at La Guera and Bir Moghrein in December 1975 that gave Mauritania's armed forces their first combat action.
16. *West Africa*, 30 May 1977.
17. Abdelaziz Dahmani, writing in *Jeune Afrique*, 19 July and 2 Aug. 1978.
18. Col. Mohamed Khouna Ould Heydalla succeeded Col. Ben Salek as head of the general staff and Co. M'Barek was named ambassador to Bonn by the CMRN.

19. See pp. 281-2.

20. *Jeune Afrique*, 21 Jan. 1979.

21. See pp. 61-2.

22. These men were members of the group known as Ashab Errissalah, or 'signers of the letter' which had been sent in 1972 to Daddah urging him to promote liberal economic and democratic policies in place of socialism.

23. *Le Monde*, 4-5 Jan. 1979.

24. The blacks felt that Mauritania, as a biracial state, should resign from the Arab League, while the Moors claimed that for the same reason it was inequitable for the country to contribute public funds to an organisation such as the OMVS, whose only beneficiaries would be the black sedentaries of the Senegal River valley.

25. For a detailed discussion of the ethnic conflict, see *Jeune Afrique*, 31 Jan. 1979, and 'Analyse de la Situation Nationale', *Revue Française d'Etudes Politiques Africaines* (Feb. 1979).

26. Jiddou's fellow ministers who made up the so-called CMRN left wing, sometimes called Baathists or Muslim extremists, were Sidi Ahmed Bneijara and Mohammed Yehdid Ould Brezilel. Viyah's pro-Moroccan faction included Colonels Khouna Ould Heydalla and Mohamed Ould Ahmed Louly.

27. *The Economist*, 31 March 1979; *Le Monde*, 22 March 1979.

28. To show impartiality in foreign policy, Salek eliminated Col. Viyah from his government and replaced Major Jiddou by a black officer of equal rank, Thiam El Hadj, and Brezilel by Col. Mohamed Ould Ahmed Louly.

29. See p. 68.

30. The nominal founder of the Front was Alioune Diawo, an eccentric former member of the Mauritanian gendarmerie, possibly Senegal-born. The Front's name derived from the Walo, Fouta and Guidimaka regions of the Senegal River valley.

31. A similar attempt to dispose of Col. Jiddou by naming him ambassador to Tunis failed because he refused to leave the Mauritanian political scene and the Tunisians refused to accredit him.

32. *Le Monde*, 28 Nov. 1975 and 10 April 1976; *Marchés Tropicaux*, 13 Feb. 1976.

33. See *Marchés Tropicaux*, 11 Feb., 11 March and 2 Sept. 1977; *West Africa*, 20 Dec. 1976 and 3 Oct. 1977.

34. They expressed the conviction that the Sahara issue was simply a problem of decolonisation requiring reconciliation only because of the tension artificially generated by Algeria's ambition to dominate the region. *Jeune Afrique*, 7 Aug. 1979.

35. Elections for municipalities and communes were held on 12 November 1976; for the provinces and prefectures on 25 January 1977; for the agricultural, industrial and artisanal occupations on 21 February 1977; and for the legislature on 3 June 1977.

36. Not only did Ali Yata of the PPS and Maître Abderrahim Bouabid of the USFP participate in the king's diplomatic offensive to win international support in 1974-5, but they outdid Hassan in their proposals for developing the Western Sahara and in their denunciation of Algeria. Paul Pascon, a Moroccan sociologist associated with the PPS, even drew up a detailed programme for settling the Sahraoui nomads in the coastal region of Saquiet El Hamra. See 'La Marche Verte', pp. 22-4.

37. A. Caram, 'Note on the Role of the Berbers in the Early Days of Moroccan Independence' in E. Gellner and C. Micaud (eds), *Arabs and Berbers* (Duckworth, London, 1973), p. 272.

38. I.W. Zartman, *Morocco: Problems of New Power* (Atherton Press, New York, 1964), p. 92.

39. Moroccan soldiers have been employed by several presidents of sub-Saharan states to serve as African counterparts to the Swiss Guards of eighteenth-century Europe. Their martial reputation was further enhanced by their performance on the Golan Heights in Syria during the Arab-Israeli war in 1973.

40. In 1977 the Polisario claimed to have killed some 20,000 Moroccan soldiers, or about the same number as all the Moroccan troops stationed in the Sahara. Estimates by observers at that time of all Moroccan losses range between 1,200 and 1,500, not counting those due to desertions. By 1979 the size of Morocco's armed forces, including paramilitary units, was thought to approximate 120,000 men.

41. See pp. 137-8.

42. *Le Figaro*, 7 May 1979.

43. Ohoud was the name of a seventh-century battle in Arabia wherein the Prophet Mohammed was victorious. This nomenclature was another evidence of Hassan's flair for associating religious with military action.

44. The intervening months were spent in amassing 7,000 men selected from various units of the regular army, 1,500 vehicles and an experienced general staff headed by Col. Ahmed Dlimi, the king's closest military adviser. About half of the troops were said to be natives of the Tiris El Gharbia region.

45. *Marchés Tropicaux*, 12 Dec. 1975.

46. *Le Monde*, 3 March 1976; *Jeune Afrique*, 12 March 1976; A. Gaudio, *Le Dossier du Sahara Occidental* (Nouvelles Editions Latines, Paris, 1978), p. 304.

47. Hassan II, *Le Défi* (Albin Michel, Paris, 1976), p. 182.

48. *Christian Science Monitor*, 23 Dec. 1977.

49. Abdelaziz Dahmani, 'Au Sahara, la Frénésie de Construire', *Jeune Afrique*, 8 March 1978. See also P.A. Dessens, 'Le Problème du Sahara Occidental Trois Ans après le Départ des Espagnols', *Maghreb-Machrek*, no. 83 (Jan.-Feb.-March 1979).

50. *Marchés Tropicaux*, 11 March 1977.

51. *Jeune Afrique*, 14 May 1976; Gaudio, *Le Dossier*, pp. 390-5.

52. 'Morocco Settles No-man's Land', *Middle East Journal* (June 1979).

53. *Bulletin d'Afrique*, 3 Oct. 1979; *Marchés Tropicaux*, 17 Aug. 1979.

54. *Marchés Tropicaux*, 17 Aug. 1979.

55. The OAU resolution had been passed by a bare two-thirds majority, whereas in the UN General Assembly there were 83 votes in favour to 5 against and 43 abstentions.

56. Col. Khadafi's support for one faction of the Frolinat posed a threat to the N'Djamena government, and his sponsorship of a Mouvement Berbère in Tripoli alarmed the Bamako authorities, who feared it might revive Touareg dissidence.

57. He was chairman of the subcommittee on Africa of the House Foreign Affairs Committee when he made a study tour of the Western Sahara in August 1979. Later he expressed strongly his views on the issues involved in an article published in *Foreign Affairs* (Winter 1979-80).

58. See p. 236.

59. See pp. 250-1.

ANNEX: TRANSFRONTIER TRIBES

The Reguibat Confederation

'The people of the clouds', as the Reguibat call themselves, are of marabout Berber origin, although they have borrowed from the Arabs their language, religion, way of life and dress, and some of them even claim *chorfa* descent.

The Reguibat's common ancestor was Sidi Ahmed Reguibi, a fourteenth-century saint who reputedly delivered his fellow Berbers from Arab domination. Subsequent to his death, disputes between his sons over the division of his camels split the Reguibat into two confederations, the Sahel and the Lagouacem or Charg. After the French established control over southern Morocco, the Reguibat left the Oued Draa region. The Sahel confederation moved into the Spanish Sahara and the Mauritanian Adrar, digging wells for their herds on both sides of the frontier. Their preferred pasturelands lay in Spanish territory, which they left for Mauritania only during severe droughts.[1] The Lagouacem Reguibat's trek area lay to the west, extending as far as the Adrar des Iforas and Aïr, for their huge herds quickly exhausted the pastures that they shared with other tribes in some areas. The Reguibat confederations, far from being mutually hostile, used the same brand mark for their camels and, on occasion, even co-operated in their raiding operations.

In the fourteenth century the Reguibat had been peaceable marabouts and herders. Four centuries later, however, the growth in their herds and in their prosperity made them the target for attacks by warlike neighbours. To defend themselves and their animals, the Reguibat — first the Sahel and then the Lagouacem — transformed themselves successfully into warriors. In the process they became wholly nomadic, carrying out armed raids that netted them rich booty in animals and slaves. By the end of the nineteenth century, when the French forces entered the region from both the north and the south, the Reguibat were well on their way to establishing hegemony there, and by the eve of the First World War they had superseded the Blue Sultan, Ma El Ainin, and his son, El Hiba, as France's most formidable opponents in the Western Sahara.

Although the two confederations sometimes carried on joint military operations, they shared no overall leadership, nor was there any single chief in command of either confederation. Even the fraction chiefs exercised little authority, which was vested in a *djemaa* composed of the 'wealthiest, most intelligent and virtuous Notables'.[2] *Djemaa* membership was not related numerically to the size of the tribe or fraction, nor were its decisions binding on all members. Those tribesmen who consistently rejected the *djemaa*'s rulings did not try to impose their viewpoint but simply moved away to another encampment. Custom determined the division of spoils from armed raiding: one-third went to the warriors, one-third to those who carried firearms and one-third to the owners of the mounts used in the raid.

Camels were the Reguibat's pride and joy as well as the source of their basic food — milk — and of the wool they wove into tents and coverlets. Reguibat proverbs testify to the primordial role played in their lives by camels, which were said alone to assure happiness and to be objects worthy of dispute. It was the search for food for their camels that made the Reguibat the widest-ranging nomads in the Sahara, covering as much as 2,000 kilometres in a year. And it was the camels' perpetual need for pasture that brought the Reguibat into conflict with other tribes, both pastoral and agricultural, and also with the French, whose military power forced them into temporary submission or into seeking refuge in Spanish territory.

As a result of their unceasing mobility over so vast a region that they escaped control by a strong single government, the number of Reguibat and of their camels has never been accurately known. Estimates for the two confederations made in the 1960s placed the total number of tribesmen at about 30,000, including their servitors, and that of their camels at 70,000 to 100,000, in addition to about the same number of sheep and goats.[3] Since then, however, the losses and displacements occasioned by the drought of 1968-73 and the war in the Western Sahara have invalidated even the best-informed guesswork. Because they were at least in theory governed by France and Spain, who were often at loggerheads in the area, the adroit Reguibat escaped close supervision simply by crossing the political frontier that in any case they have never recognised. Both admirers and detractors of the Reguibat agree that they are courageous and hardy, highly practical and shrewd traders, suspicious of any outsiders, pious and credulous Muslims, and above all resistant to authority. Periodically they co-operated with the French and Spanish colonial administrations or made temporary alliances with Ma El Ainin, the Moroccan Liberation Army and the Boumediene government of Algeria, either to gain some material advantage or to safeguard their freedom of manoeuvre, but in no case has their loyalty been fully committed.

Between 1934, when the majority of Reguibat submitted to the French, and 1955, on the eve of Moroccan independence, the confederations remained relatively quiescent. They expanded their trek area into southern Morocco and Algeria, selling their camels in Goulimine and Tindouf, and also penetrating more deeply into Spanish territory, where they bought imported goods at Villa Cisneros and El Aaiun.[4] The Reguibat's ardour for pillage was not abated by prosperity alone but rather by the security measures taken by the French in Mauritania and by the Spaniards in Rio de Oro.

In 1932 new French military posts and *méhariste* platoons had been established in northern Mauritania at the same time as the region was placed under a single military commander, who was also in charge of Reguibat affairs. The key to controlling the Reguibat, however, proved to be an agreement reached on 5 August 1933 between the authorities in charge respectively of the Confins Algéro-Marocains and of northern Mauritania[5] to co-ordinate the administration and policing of the trifrontier region. Within a year the area's pastures and markets — and consequently their use by the Reguibat — were brought under French control. Also in 1934 the Spaniards occupied Smara and established a few permanent forts to keep guard over the waterholes of that region. This expansion of Spanish military power into the desert from the coastal area marked a sharp reversal of the policy that had prevailed during the early days of the Spanish Republic,[6] when it seemed that the high cost of maintaining the Saharan colonies might induce Madrid to cede them to France.[7] Within a few years, however, Spain had decided that its Saharan possessions provided an important fuelling stop for its planes serving South America and for the Canary Islanders' fishing and shipping operations, and Madrid proceeded to extend its control from the coast into the hinterland.

The French then gave up hope of joint police activities in the Reguibat region, and in December 1934 they created a free-trade zone encircling the Spanish territory with a view to luring the Reguibat away from the duty-free markets of Villa Cisneros and El Aaiun, then provisioned by sea with European merchandise. This proved successful, for the Reguibat in increasing numbers frequented Goulimine and Tindouf to sell their camels and buy imported goods at favourable prices. The construction of wells and of some 9,000 kilometres of new tracks in the Tindouf region expanded the Reguibat's pasture area and consequently their herds, and also revived the caravan trade between Atar,

Tindouf and Goulimine. Subsequently, Reguibat cameleers further benefited in French territory by being hired to provision the local French military posts. In 1936, however, the French authorities began tightening the screws by requiring Reguibat tribesmen to get authorisation to leave French for Spanish territory, and then refused to allow them to circulate in French-controlled areas unless they had made their formal submission to France and paid taxes to the French colonial government.

Throughout the Second World War, relations between France and Spain deteriorated further as a result of the flourishing contraband trade between Rio de Oro and Mauritania. They became frankly antagonistic in 1953 after Madrid had openly encouraged Arab nationalism in the Maghreb and refused to recognise the sultan that France had installed in Morocco after exiling Ben Youssef to Madagascar. Beginning in 1955, however, developments related to Morocco's impending independence changed the picture in the Western Sahara, and three years later the two colonial regimes co-operated there militarily for the first time.

In many respects 1956 proved to be a momentous year for the Western Sahara in general and for the Reguibat in particular. They were subjected to conflicting pressures from France, Spain, Algeria, Mauritania and Morocco, of which the last-mentioned was the most effective. Because it was a dry year in the Saquiet El Hamra, the Reguibat moved their herds into the pastures of Oued Draa, where they were propagandised intensively by the Istiqlal party. Its leader, Allal El Fassi, urged the Reguibat to rally to King Mohammed V and to join the Army for the Liberation of the Sahara, a recent offshoot of the Moroccan Army of Liberation. Reguibat from the Goulimine area formed the first contingents, and their example was followed by fellow-tribesmen from the Tindouf and Smara regions, but many Reguibat chiefs elsewhere were too cautious to commit themselves.[8]

Moroccan radio broadcasts beamed to Reguibat tribesmen throughout the Western Sahara stressed the inevitability of the imminent withdrawal of both colonial powers from that area, and such assertions naturally aggravated the unrest in the Tindouf region, already stirred up by FLN propaganda. Then, in July, the arrival at Rabat of the Mauritanian dissident politician, Horma Ould Babana, and the prospect of a semi-autonomous government council to be set up at Nouakchott in 1957 were new elements in an already complex situation that the Reguibat were able to use to their advantage. Caught between the conflicting fires of Moroccan and Mauritanian nationalism, they preserved their freedom by playing one off against the other. Furthermore, in the Reguibat's view the position of France had been seriously weakened by Morocco's accession to independence in April, the abortive Suez invasion in November and French inability to end the Algerian revolt after two years of war.

Spain recognised Morocco's independence a few days after France did so. It also ceded to Rabat the land lying between Oued Draa and the 27°40' parallel and withdrew all its garrisons from Saquiet El Hamra excepting those along the coast, thus confirming the encouragement Spain had been giving to Moroccan nationalists since 1945. By permitting the Army of Liberation to occupy much of Saquiet El Hamra and even giving it logistical support, the Spaniards enabled that army to use Smara as a base for attacking Atar in December-January 1956-7. This Moroccan offensive almost dislodged the French garrisons from Adrar, and it so alarmed the Paris government that troops were flown into northern Mauritania from Dakar. The attack also induced the Lagouacem Reguibat, including their venerable *caïd* Lahbib Ould Bellel, to join the Army of Liberation, which by July 1957 was in control of all the hinterland of Rio de Oro and Saquiet El Hamra, thus jeopardising France's hold on Mauritania.

The French retaliated by seizing the herds of those Reguibat who had joined the Moroccan forces, imprudently leaving their tents behind in the French zone. The loss of their animals slowed down the Reguibat's northward exodus and gave pause to the Spaniards, who, for the first time, allowed French reconnaissance planes to fly over their territory and gave French troops the right of hot pursuit on land. In June the arrival of a new Spanish commander-in-chief, General Zemalloa, coincided with the unrest caused by the Moroccan irregular forces at Ifni, and both developments laid the groundwork for the successful joint Franco-Spanish operations against the Army of Liberation early in 1958.[9] These operations destroyed the Army of Liberation's bases in Saquiet El Hamra and re-established the Spanish and French posts throughout the Western Sahara. The royal Moroccan armed forces took over the positions held by the Army of Liberation in the Draa region, and Spain tried to revive its friendship with Morocco by ceding Tarfaya to it in 1958.

If the defeat of the Moroccan irregulars ended Franco-Spanish military co-operation, it also terminated the support given the Army of Liberation by the Reguibat. As had been the case with their previous equally opportunistic alliances, the Reguibat deserted partners from whom they could no longer expect practical advantages, and they made their peace with France — that is, the power which had proven its military strength and which controlled the surest pastures in the Western Sahara. At Goulimine, the *caïd* Bellel discreetly sent his son to the French post at Ben Tili to ask France's pardon and permission to use Mauritanian pastures for his herds — in part, to be sure, because the Moroccans had offended the *caïd* by placing him under the orders of a youthful recent graduate of the Rabat *lycée*. Indeed, it was the Moroccans' condescending attitude toward them and their way of life that contributed to the Reguibat's defection from the Army of Liberation. Furthermore, the puritanical Muslim Reguibat were shocked by the Moroccans' drinking of wine and wearing of Western clothes, and were alienated by being treated not as comrades in arms but as miserable nomads.[10]

The Reguibat's volte-face began soon after the siege of Atar had been lifted, and their rallying to France reached its most spectacular manifestation at Bir Moghrein (formerly Fort Trinquet) in April 1958, when 300 Reguibat asked for pardon (*aman*). But now the Reguibat had to deal not only with the French authorities but also with Mokhtar Ould Daddah, who was soon to become the first president of the Islamic Mauritanian Republic. At that time, however, Daddah was an unknown quantity to the Reguibat, and he had to impress them with his authority as well as win them over by his tact. He kept the Reguibat emissaries waiting several weeks for an interview but when it took place he did not humiliate them by highlighting their surrender in a public ceremony,[11] and he permitted some of their chiefs to keep their arms. In private talks he tried to persuade them to sell their camels in Mauritanian markets rather than in Goulimine and generally to co-operate with Mauritania's merchants.

Like the French administration before him, Daddah failed to enlist the Reguibat's loyalty, and indeed his sole hold over them was their need to use freely northern Mauritanian pastures. Unlike the French, however, Daddah did not have the military force required to ensure respect for his country's frontier. If the Reguibat no longer supported Morocco, Daddah's main adversary, neither would they accept being ruled by the Moors, for the Reguibat's primary concern was as always to maintain their independence. Events during 1958-9 had awakened in them a new consciousness of their identity, and in listening to broadcasts received by their transistor radios they had become more aware of the outside world.[12] Politics as such did not interest the Reguibat, and they played no part in the political life of either independent Mauritania or Morocco. Yet among the younger Reguibat, intelligent and energetic men like Khatri Ould Youmani[13] and Hamdi Ould Bou Ali realised that their fellow-tribesmen must learn how to deal with their predatory neighbours if they were to defend their independence and the newly discovered mineral wealth of their area. Reportedly they sought French help in setting up an autonomous Reguibat confederation,[14] but they received no official support from France although French troops remained at Bir Moghrein until 1964 and at Tindouf until 1962. The Reguibat, therefore, had every interest in prolonging the disputes between Mauritania and Morocco and between Morocco and Algeria in the early 1960s, but the sanctuary that they continued to enjoy in Rio de Oro and Saquiet El Hamra depended on Spain's remaining in control of the only buffer state still existing in that area.

When Spain was reluctantly yielding to international pressure and preparing to decolonise its Saharan province in the late 1960s, it set up limited local-government institutions.[15] Because of their numerical strength and their reputation for wealth in animals, piety and prowess as warriors, the Reguibat easily dominated those institutions, and for the same reasons the Reguibat supplied the top leadership and the majority of militants for the Polisario Front, the most effective of the anti-Spanish resistance movements. Regardless of the exact number of Reguibat active in the Polisario forces, the aggressive tactics and the intransigent demands made by that Front bespeak its control by the Reguibat.[16] No matter which government eventually wins control of the Western Sahara, it will have to deal with the Reguibat as the strongest indigenous force in that area.

The Ma El Ainin

For three generations, beginning in the late nineteenth century, Sheikh Ma El Ainin (called the Blue Sultan) and his joint family — which now numbers several thousand, including their servitors — played a dramatic, colourful and, except in the religious domain, largely ineffectual role in the Western Sahara. The sheikh was born in Hodh to a distinguished family of Qadriya marabouts, and went to Mecca in his youth. For 25 years thereafter he wandered through the Western Sahara before building a fortified *zaouia* at Smara in 1895.[17] It was from Smara that he launched a crusade to drive the European infidels from Mauritania and, above all, from Morocco. As the French troops advanced north from Senegal early in the twentieth century, Ma El Ainin began to receive support from the Idaouaich of Tagant, the Lagouacem Reguibat, some

Tekna and Ouled Delim tribes, the Sultan Ould Aida of Adrar, and, above all, the Sultan Abd El Aziz of Morocco. Lacking a power base of his own, Ma El Ainin had to rely on the fitful following he enlisted as a religious leader, and in Mauritania his only positive achievement was to have organised Coppolani's assassination in 1905, thus delaying the French conquest.[18]

In Morocco the sheikh was more successful in bolstering Sultan Abd El Aziz's authority south of the Draa, thanks to the aid that Ma El Ainin received from such varied sources as the powerful Ait Atta confederation, the Spaniards at Cape Juby and Ifni, and Kaiser Wilhelm II of Germany.[19] Yet there, as elsewhere, Ma El Ainin's plans were set at naught by France's military and on occasion diplomatic strength. He withdrew to Tiznit, where he died in 1910, but not before he had inspired four of his sons to pursue his *jihad*. El Hiba, the strongest of them, marched on Marrakech after the French had established their protectorate over Morocco in 1912 and had himself proclaimed sultan there. After a few weeks, however, his followers melted away and, like his father, El Hiba was forced to return to the Sahara, where he died in 1918. Two of his brothers made equally determined and futile attempts in the desert to stem the tide of European conquest. One of them withdrew to Tarfaya after the French had pacified the Western Sahara in 1934, and the other fled to Tantan following the Spanish reoccupation of Smara in 1958, and even in the El Aaiun region they never fully accepted rule by Spain or Spanish patronage. Still another brother, however, accepted French rule and, as of the late 1950s, was living with his family alternately in St Louis and the Mauritanian Adrar.[20]

Thus ended the remarkable sequence of religious wars conducted by the Ma El Ainin family over half a century. Today the sheikh is remembered in the western desert less as a militant political leader than as the founder at Smara of the xenophobic, puritanical Goudfiya brotherhood, whose doctrines continue to be preached in the *zaouias* his followers founded in northern Mauritania and southern Morocco. Ma El Ainin and his sons had failed to establish a temporal state such as that founded by their Senoussi prototypes in Fezzan, but they remained intransigent leaders uncompromisingly opposed to Christianity and Western materialism. They were not a spent force even after their decisive defeats, and they maintained their coherence and, to some degree, their influence as a group, notably at the sultan's palace.

The Ma El Ainin were unique in that repeated failures to reach their goals by force, the achievement of sovereign status by Mauritania and Morocco independently of their efforts, and the honours and posts offered them by the Spaniards,[21] deflected their zeal not to trade or to the accumulation of wealth but to professional fields. As of 1973, members of the Ma El Ainin tribe who had received training mainly in Moroccan schools were serving as magistrates or doctors in such places as Tarfaya, Ifni, Tantan and Taroudant, and others worked for the Moroccan government as diplomats or administrators.[22] In upper official circles they kept alive the concept of the Islamic state which has no frontiers but which draws all Muslims together around the sultan as commander of the faithful.[23] Given their Moroccan orientation psychologically and geographically, it seems unlikely that the Ma El Ainin have been induced by the Polisario Front to join its ranks, except possibly during the Front's initial phase as an anti-Spanish resistance movement.

The Ouled Delim (Oulad Dlim)

Most of the members of this warrior tribe have long lived along the coast of the Spanish Sahara, mainly in Rio de Oro, where they numbered some 3,000 in 1949. Their defeat by the Reguibat in the early twentieth century was followed by the acceptance of French rule in 1934 on the part of those Ouled Delim tribesmen living in the Port Etienne region, who thereafter paid taxes to the colonial administration, albeit irregularly and reluctantly.[24]

In that area, the more peaceable Ouled Delim gradually turned from camel- to sheep-rearing. Some of the Ouled Delim living nearest to the sea became the only Saharan tribesmen other than the Imraguen to take up fishing on a commercial scale.[25] In Spanish territory, however, the warlike traditions of the Ouled Delim remained stronger,[26] and it is their tribes that provided most of the Saharan members of the Spanish police and *méhariste* units.[27] As in the case of the Reguibat who conquered them, the acceptance of such service to foreign rulers implied no commitment of Ouled Delim loyalties, so that members of that tribe have held leadership positions in the anti-Spanish movements and there were at least two known mutinies by Ouled Delim *méharistes* in the Spanish camel corps. Among the Polisario forces, the Ouled Delim are believed to constitute the tribal element second only in importance to that of the Reguibat.

The Tekna Confederation

Although the Tekna trace their ancestry back to the Almoravid period, the first written record of their name dates only from the sixteenth century. In the last few centuries their trek area has expanded, extending from Villa Cisneros to Tagounit and from Ifni to Iguidi. Their oases are concentrated in Oued Noun, which is the heartland of the Moroccan Tekna, and their close Berber relatives live in the Anti-Atlas. In the Spanish Sahara the Tekna were to be found throughout Rio de Oro and Saquiet El Hamra, as well as farther inland. As the pastures along the coastal areas are more abundant because of the prevailing humidity, the pattern of Tekna migrations in modern times has been in a generally north-south direction, as has also been that of their commercial activities.

The Tekna's mixed Arabo-Berber origin and bilingualism, geographical dispersion, occupational differentiation, and division into two *leffs* (Ait Jmal and Ait Bella), whose membership is unstable, make them difficult to define as a tribal confederation.[28] Yet blood ties bind the patriarchal families together, and the Tekna are reputed to be the only tribe of the Western Sahara whose prayers have always been said in the name of the sultan of Morocco.[29] Their tribal solidarity has been reinforced by the complementary nature of their resources, which are exceptionally varied. Although they were mainly sheep-herders in the Spanish Sahara, the Tekna of Oued Noun in 1960 owned 700,000 goats, 30,000 camels and more than 100,000 date palms, and they also grew wheat and barley besides extracting a few tons of salt.[30] Trading, however, has been the Tekna's common denominator, and one that they developed so ably to supplement their insufficient natural resources in Oued Draa that they became the leading caravaneers along the tracks between Mauritania and Morocco. The *Amagir* (sometimes called *Al-mugger*), or annual trade fairs, that they organised, were renowned throughout the Western Sahara, where they have survived to this day.

According to an estimate made in 1942, the number of Tekna tribesmen living in French and Spanish territory totalled some 44,500, loosely organised into twelve tribes.[31] Some of these tribes can be classified as nomadic and others as sedentary, but still others are nomadic or sedentary to varying degrees. Like the Reguibat they have become increasingly nomadic, but in the case of the Tekna primarily for economic reasons. Moreover, because they are primarily traders, the Tekna tribesmen remained on fairly good terms with both the French and Spanish administrations and with other confederations, notably the

Reguibat, who at one time may have been their vassals and whose herds they also permitted to pasture in the Tarfaya region in exchange for suitable gifts. It may well have been their long association with the Reguibat that induced some Tekna tribesmen to join the Army of Liberation of the Sahara briefly in 1957.

The Kounta Confederation

Through their membership in a branch of the far-flung Qadriya Brotherhood, the Kounta comprised both warrior and marabout tribes, which were bound together by common religious and trading interests. Initially, the prefix 'Kounta' attached to a family's tribal name denoted those who had studied at the founding *zaouia*, but gradually it came to be applied to widely dispersed and heterogeneous member tribesmen. The Kounta's religious prestige enhanced their commercial potential, and they successfully combined propagating their faith with expanding their trade over a vast area. Small colonies of Kounta tribesmen and itinerant Kounta traders were to be found along all the caravan routes from southern Morocco to Portuguese Guinea and from eastern Senegal and Soudan to Touat, as well as throughout the Mauritanian sahel.

The Kounta resembled the Tekna confederation more than any other nomads in the Western Sahara in that they united outstanding piety with prosperity. Also, both Kounta and Tekna tribesmen maintained generally peaceable relations with the French, who assured the security indispensable to their trade. Moreover, inasmuch as the Kounta's habitat lay wholly in French-controlled areas and they could not easily escape French control by escaping into Spanish territory, they had an even more compelling reason for remaining on good terms with the ruling power. After an initial adverse reaction to the French occupation of Trarza, Tagant and Adrar, the Kounta became more co-operative with the colonial administration. Indeed, before the First World War, the Kounta marabouts in southern Morocco even helped the French to recruit *goumiers* among their own followers, and as such the Kounta fought alongside French troops during the campaigns that preceded establishment of the protectorate.

At the same time, Franco-Kounta relations in Soudan had been equally friendly, and the Kounta co-operated with the French army against their traditional enemies, the Oulliminden Touareg. About 1913, however, this relationship began to deteriorate as a result of changes in the Kounta leadership. Hamoadi, chief of the Kounta in the Bourem region, died in 1912, and the erratic behaviour of his successor, El Maimoun, aroused French suspicions of his loyalty as well as that of the Kounta *goum*.[32] During the First World War, France alienated the Kounta by imposing taxes, requisitioning their animals and services, forcing Kounta tribesmen to farm what proved to be unarable land so as to increase the local food supply, ignoring El Maimoun's authority by setting up new administrative units that subdivided the tribes, and by restricting their trek area in such a way as to force the dispersal of their herds.

During the late 1920s and 1930s the situation gradually improved. Thanks in part to the lessons learned from experience and in part to the analysis made in the early post-war years by Paul Marty of France's mistakes in dealing with the Kounta, the French authorities in Soudan formulated a more enlightened Kounta policy. More confidence was placed in El Maimoun, whose authority over his tribesmen was thereby enhanced, the Kounta marabouts were treated with more consideration and respect, the tribes were regrouped in one administrative subdivision, and the Kounta *goum* was reconstituted and better armed. The calm that generally prevailed throughout the Kounta area during the Second World War confirmed the effectiveness of this new policy.

A census of the Soudanese Kounta and their animals taken in 1942-3 indicated such a fantastic growth in the number of tribesmen from an estimated 8,100 in 1937 to some 18,000, and of their cattle, sheep, goats and camels from about 63,000 to more than 144,000, that the accuracy of this and previous counts was cast into doubt.[33] It is certain, however, that both the Kounta and their herds were experiencing an unprecedented expansion and one that was being achieved at the expense of their traditional rivals, the Touareg. Serious incidents occurred because the ire of the Touareg was aroused by the Kounta's growing participation in the *azalai* (salt caravan), for the Touareg considered the transport of salt from Taoudenni to Timbuctu and its sale there to be their monopoly. Negotiations between them, conducted by the French authorities, led to an agreement in August 1942 which limited the number of Kounta camels permitted to participate in that trade to 6,000.

The post-war reforms had little direct immediate effect on the Kounta's evolution. They were indifferent to the new political opportunities, and their religious leaders actively opposed the opening of a school in 1947 to train nomad children with a view to their becoming cadres for the administration. It was not until the local administrator persuaded the chief Qadriya marabout to send his son to that school that it could begin to function normally. By 1947 its pupils numbered

44, of whom two were the sons of chiefs and 28 the sons of Notables. The Kounta, however, continued to insist that all they wanted was to trade in peace, and this they did with great skill and success. The Kounta were essentially transporters and distributors, and to only a limited degree were they producers, selling and exporting their own live-stock and animal products. For about three-fourths of the merchandise that they traded – consisting of salt, grain, dates and textiles – they acted as caravaneers and middlemen between the northern oases and sub-Saharan Africa, where their religious eminence gave them an additional advantage upon which they readily capitalised.

The Ouled Bou Sba

Like the Ouled Delim, the Ouled Bou Sba are of Maql Arab origin and have lived dispersed on both sides of the Franco-Spanish frontier, and they have undergone a similar economic and psychological evolution. Both tribes have nomadised in larger numbers in the Rio de Oro than in the Akjoujt region of Mauritania. The Reguibat, after defeating the Ouled Delim early in the twentieth century, then crushed the Ouled Bou Sba, who a few years later were also conquered by the French.[34]

In both cases their successive defeats deflected the two tribes from bellicose to more peaceful pursuits – but of differing economic character. Whereas the Ouled Delim in Mauritania became producers rooted in the rural economy, the Ouled Bou Sba, after trying to farm in the Tiris, became more dispersed and specialised in trade and developed a commercial network that extended from southern Morocco as far as Portuguese Guinea.[35]

Notes

1. *Afrique Française* (Nov. 1932).
2. Capt. Dupas, 'Notes sur la Confédération des Reguibat Lagouacem, 1937' (CHEAM, Mémoire No. 770, 20 Feb. 1937).
3. J. Paillard, 'Le Problème des Reguibat' (CHEAM, Mémoire No. 4202, Nov. 1967).
4. G. Salvy, 'Le Sahara du Nord-Ouest' in *L'Economie Pastorale Saharienne* (La Documentation Française, *Notes et Etudes Documentaires*, No. 1730, 21 April 1953); F.E. Trout, *Morocco's Saharan Frontiers* (Droz, Geneva, 1969), pp. 225 et seq.
5. Dupas, 'Notes sur la Confédération'.
6. *Heraldo*, Madrid, 27 March 1932.
7. J. Charbonneau, *Sur les Traces du Pacha de Tombouctou* (Paris, 1936), p. 13.

8. H. de Boisboissel, 'Situation au Sahara Occidental à la Veille de l'Indépendance Mauritanienne' (CHEAM, Mémoire No. 3787, Jan. 1963).

9. See pp. 108, 154.

10. Lieut. Cros, 'L'Evolution en Mauritanie et Plus Particulièrement chez les Reguibats, 1955 à 1960' (CHEAM, Mémoire No. 3510, 25 March 1961).

11. G. Dugué, *Vers les Etats-Unis d'Afrique* (Editions des Lettres Africaines, Dakar, 1960), pp. 57 et seq.

12. Cros, L'Evolution en Mauritanie'.

13. Khatri's career aptly illustrates what the anonymous author of 'La Marche Verte' euphemistically calls the flexibility of Reguibat policy. In 1958 Khatri, representing his Reguibat fraction, spoke out against Moroccan claims to Mauritania and the Spanish Sahara at a PPM congress; in 1959 he appealed to France for aid against the Army of Liberation for the Sahara and went to Dakar to get arms to fight the Moroccan irregulars. After supporting Daddah when Mauritania became independent, he joined the pro-Spanish forces and was elected president of the *yemaa* in 1967. In 1970 he was arrested in connection with the anti-Spanish riots at El Aaiun, but was restored to the good graces of the Spaniards. In the spring of 1975 he met secretly with El Ouali but apparently failed to make a deal with the Polisario, so that on 3 November 1975 — about ten days before the Madrid pact was signed — he came out in favour of King Hassan and of Moroccan claims to the Spanish Sahara.

14. Cros, 'L'Evolution en Mauritanie'; see also de Boisboissel, 'Situation au Sahara Occidental', and Paillard, 'Le Problème des Reguibat'.

15. See pp. 108-11.

16. In an interview with Spanish journalists in September 1974, two Reguibat members of the *yemaa* declared that there was never any question of the Sahraouis uniting with Morocco or Mauritania, and in the event that those countries tried to use force against them, the Sahraouis would join Spain in repelling the invaders. See *Marchés Tropicaux*, 4 Oct. 1974.

17. H. de la Bastide, 'Une Grande Famille du Sud-Marocain: Les Ma El-Ainin', *Maghreb-Machrek*, no. 56 (March-April 1973).

18. See p. 42.

19. Trout, *Morocco's Saharan Frontiers*, pp. 156 et seq.

20. *Le Monde*, 23-4 March 1958.

21. J. Mercer, *Spanish Sahara* (Allen and Unwin, London, 1976), pp. 248-9.

22. de la Bastide, 'Une Grande Famille'.

23. J. Recoules, 'Les Frontières de l'Etat Marocain', *L'Afrique et l'Asie*, no. 52 (1960).

24. A. Gaudio, *Le Sahara des Africains* (Julliard, Paris, 1960), p. 44.

25. O. de Puigaudeau, *Pieds Nus à Travers la Mauritanie* (Plon, Paris, 1936), p. 18.

26. P. Marty, *Les Tribus de la Haute Mauritanie* (Comité de l'Afrique Française, Paris, 1915), pp. 4-32.

27. Mercer, *Spanish Sahara*, p. 131.

28. F.E. Trout, 'The Return of Ifni to Morocco', *Genève-Afrique*, vol. IX, no. 1 (1970).

29. T. Desjardins, *Les Rebelles d'Aujourd'hui* (Presses de la Cité, Paris, 1977), p. 78.

30. R. Pelissier (ed.), *Les Territoires Espagnols d'Afrique* (La Documentation Française, *Notes et Etudes Documentaires*, No. 2951, 3 Jan. 1963).

31. G. Salvy, 'La Crise du Nomadisme dans le Sud Marocain' (CHEAM, Mémoire No. 1563, May 1949).

32. P. Marty, *Etudes sur l'Islam et les Tribus du Soudan* (3 vols., Leroux, Paris, 1918-19, 1920-1), vol. 1, pp. 152-4.

33. J. Genevière, 'Les Kountas et Leurs Activités Commerciales' (CHEAM, Mémoire No. 1240, 31 Dec. 1947).

34. Salvy, 'Le Sahara du Nord-ouest' and 'Le Sahara du Nord et Rédaction d'Ensemble' in *L'Economie Pastorale Saharienne*; J. Cauneille, 'Les Nomades Reguibat', *Travaux de l'Institut de Recherches Sahariennes*, vol. 6 (1950), pp. 85-100.

35. Pelissier, *Les Territoires Espagnols*.

BIBLIOGRAPHY

La Acción de España en Sahara (Instituto de Estudios Africanos, Madrid, 1977)

Adam, A. *La Maison et le Village dans Quelques Tribus de l'Anti-Atlas* (Larose, Paris, 1951)

——'Les Sahariens à Casablanca' in *Le Sahara* (7ème Colloque d'Histoire, organisé par la Faculté de Lettres d'Aix-en-Provence, 1967)

Allal El Fassi. *La Vérité sur les Frontières Marocaines* (Editions Peretti, Tangier, 1961)

'L'Aménagement Hydraulique de la Vallée du Draa et le Barrage El Mansour Eddahbi', *Industries et Travaux d'Outremer*, no. 224 (July 1972)

Andrianamanjara, R. 'Labour Mobilisation in Morocco', *Journal of Modern African History* (March 1973)

Anthoniez, R. 'Les Imraguen Pêcheurs Nomades de Mauritanie', *Bulletin de l'IFAN*, série B, part I (July-Oct. 1967); part II (Oct. 1968)

Area Handbook for Mauritania (The American University, Washington, DC, 1972)

Area Handbook for Morocco (The American University, Washington, DC, 1972)

Arnaud, J. *La Mauritanie: Aperçu Historique, Géographique, et Socio-économique* (Le Livre Africain, Paris, 1972)

Arnaud, R. 'Le Pacificateur de la Mauritanie: Xavier Coppolani', *Revue des Deux Mondes* (15 April 1939)

Ashford, D.E. 'Politics and Violence in Morocco', *Middle East Journal* (Winter 1959)

Assidon, E. *Sahara Occidental: Un Enjeu pour le Nord-ouest Africain* (Maspéro, Paris, 1978)

Aubinière, Commandant, Y. 'La Hiérarchie Sociale des Maures' (CHEAM, Mémoire No. 1496, 1949)

Azam, Capt. P. 'Les Cités Rurales du Ktaoua' (CHEAM, Mémoire No. 2038, 1946)

—— 'Sédentaires et Nomades dans le Sud Marocain: le Coude du Draa' (CHEAM, Mémoire No. 1009, 1946)

—— 'La Structure Politique et Sociale de l'Oued Draa' (CHEAM, Mémoire No. 2039, 1947)

Ba, M.A. 'Reguibat', *Bulletin d'Etudes Historiques et Scientifiques*

(July-Sept. 1933)

Badday, M.S. 'Rio de Oro: Madrid Se Dérobe', *Revue Française d'Etudes Politiques Africaines* (Oct. 1970)

Balta, P. 'La Crise du Sahara', *Le Monde*, 27-8 Nov. 1975

—— 'Lettre de Tindouf', *Le Monde*, 29-30 Jan. 1978

—— 'Le Maroc à l'Heure de l'Unité Nationale', *Le Monde*, 4-7 March 1975

—— 'Le Maroc entre Deux Feux', *Le Monde*, 18-19 April 1979

—— 'La Politique Africaine de l'Algérie', *Revue Française d'Etudes Politiques Africaines*, no. 132 (Dec. 1976)

—— 'Le Sahara Occidental Suscite les Convoitises de ses Voisins', *Le Monde Diplomatique* (Aug. 1975)

Barbier, M. 'L'Avenir du Sahara Espagnol', *Politique Etrangère*, no. 4 (1975)

Baro, A. 'L'Enseignement Technique et la Formation des Cadres', *Europe-France-Outremer*, no. 299 (Nov. 1970)

Barrada, H. 'Mais Quelle est Donc la Politique de la France?', *Jeune Afrique*, 4 October 1978

Bastide, H. de la. 'Une Grande Famille du Sud-Marocain: Les Ma El-Ainin', *Maghreb-Machrek*, no. 56 (March-April 1973)

Bayart, J.F. 'Le Conflit du Sahara Occidental', *Revue Française d'Etudes Politiques Africaines*, no. 158 (Feb. 1979)

Bechet, J.L. 'A Qui Sont les Iles?', *Jeune Afrique*, 10 May 1978

Bennoune, M. 'Mauritania. Formation of a Neo-Colonial Society', *Merip Reports*, no. 54 (Feb. 1977)

Ben Miske, A. *Front Polisario, l'Ame d'un Peuple* (Rupture, Paris, 1978)

Ben Yahmed, B. 'On Peut, On Doit, Eviter la Guerre', *Jeune Afrique*, 25 Nov. 1977

Berri, Y. 'Le Sahara à la Haye', *Jeune Afrique*, 5 Oct. 1974

Bertrand, A. 'Gravures Rupestres, Monuments Préhistoriques, Traditions Orales: L'Histoire Ancienne de la Haute Vallée du Draa' (CHEAM, Mémoire No. 4495, April 1976)

Besley, F. 'Aperçu sur les Croyances, Coutumes et Institutions des Maures' (CHEAM, Mémoire No. 1415, 1948)

—— 'Un Etat Sahraoui?', *Le Monde*, 6 Jan. 1976

Beyries, J. 'Evolution Sociale et Culturelle des Collectivités Nomades en Mauritanie' (Comité d'Etudes Historiques et Scientifiques d'AOF, *Bulletin*, tome XX, 1937)

—— 'La Mauritanie' in *L'Economie Pastorale Saharienne* (La Documentation Française, *Notes et Etudes Documentaires*, No. 1730, 21 April 1953)

Biarnès, P. 'Mauritanie: Au delà des Amitiés Traditionnelles', *Le Mois en Afrique* (April 1967)

—— 'Nouakchott se Préoccupe de l'Avenir du Sahara Espagnol et de l'Amélioration de ses Rélations avec Dakar', *Le Monde*, 4 Dec. 1969

Bisson, J. 'Les Nomades des Départements Sahariens en 1959', *Travaux de l'Institut de Recherches Sahariennes*, vol XXI (1962)

—— 'Nomadisation chez les Reguibat L'Gouacem' in *Nomades et Nomadisme au Sahara* (*Recherches sur la Zone Aride*, XXX) (UNESCO, Paris, 1963)

Boisboissel, H. de. 'De l'Adaptation des Maures au Cadre d'une Armée Moderne' (CHEAM, Mémoire No. 3500, April 1961)

—— 'Situation au Sahara Occidental à la Veille de l'Indépendance Mauritanienne' (CHEAM, Mémoire No. 3787, Jan. 1963)

Boiteux, L.A. 'La Question des "Confins" Sahariens Doit Etre Réglée d'Urgence', *Marchés Tropicaux*, 3 March 1958

Bombote, D. 'Nationalisation de la Miferma: Révolution Economique', *Afrique Nouvelle*, 15-21 Jan. 1975

Bonnefous, M. *La Palmeraie de Figuig: Etude Démographique et Economique du Sud Marocain* (Service des Statistiques, Rabat, 1952)

Bonte, P. 'Pasteurs et Nomades – L'Exemple de la Mauritanie' in *Sécheresses et Famines du Sahel* (Maspéro, Paris, 1975), vol. II

Bordarier, R. 'Mauritanie 1954', *Encyclopédie Mensuelle d'Outre-Mer*, doc. no. 31 (Oct. 1954)

Berricand, Lt. Col. 'La Nomadisation en Mauritanie', *Travaux de l'Institut de Recherches Sahariennes*, vol. V (1948)

Boyer, N. 'Le Problème des Frontières du Maroc' (CHEAM, Mémoire No. 4237, 1968)

Brassac, F. 'Réflexions sur le Développement par l'Irrigation dans le Sud-Marocain', *Maghreb*, no. 52 (July-Aug. 1972)

Bremard, F. *L'Organisation Régionale du Maroc* (Librairie Générale de Droit et de Jurisprudence, Paris, 1949)

Brenez, J. 'L'Observation Démographique des Populations des Milieux Nomades. L'Enquête de Mauritanie', *Population* (July-Aug. 1971)

Britsch, J. 'La Frontière Algéro-Marocaine au Sahara', *Revue Militaire Générale* (Dec. 1966)

Brosset, D. 'Les Némadi: Monographie d'une Tribu Artificielle des Confins Sud du Sahara Occidental', *Renseignements Coloniaux*, no. 9 (Sept. 1932)

Bull, M.R. 'Spain's African Enclaves', *Middle East International* (Oct. 1975)

Capot-Rey, R. 'Le Nomadisme Pastoral dans le Sahara Français', *Travaux de l'Institut de Recherches Sahariennes*, vol. I (1942)

—— *Le Sahara Français* (Presses Universitaires de France, Paris, 1953)

Caram, A. 'Note on the Role of the Berbers in the Early Days of Moroccan Independence' in E. Gellner and C. Micaud (eds.), *Arabs and Berbers* (Duckworth, London, 1973)

Caro Baroja, J. *Estudios Saharianos* (*Arch. del Instituto de Estudios Africanos*, VIII, no. 35)

Carrington, S. 'La Lutte pour l'Indépendance du Sahara Espagnol', *Le Monde Diplomatique* (Aug. 1974)

Catroux, G. 'Le Maroc et le Sahara', *Le Monde*, 7 March 1957

Caudron, J.P. 'Huit Jours avec le Front Polisario', *Croissance des Jeunes Nations* (Feb. 1976)

Cauneille, J. 'Les Nomades Reguibat', *Travaux de l'Institut de Recherches Sahariennes*, vol. VI (1950)

—— and Dubief, J. 'Les Reguibat Lagouacem', *Bulletin de l'IFAN*, série B, no. 17 (1955)

Cazaunau, J. 'Le Relèvement du Niveau de Vie dans les Régions Sahariennes et Présahariennes au Sud de l'Atlas', *Encyclopédie Mensuelle d'Outre-Mer* (Jan. 1957)

Célérier, J. 'Réhabilitation du Sahara', *Cahiers Nord-Africains*, special issue, *L'Avenir Humain du Sahara* (Sept.-Oct. 1954)

Chaffard, G. *Les Carnets Secrets de la Décolonisation* (Calmann Levy, Paris, 1965)

Chambard, P. 'La Politique Minière', *Europe-Outremer*, no. 549 (Oct. 1975)

—— 'Le Nouveau Drame de la Sécheresse', *Europe-Outremer*, no. 574 (Nov. 1977)

Chambon, A. 'Les Populations de Race Noire et d'Origine Servile dans la Subdivision d'Aioun-el-Atrous' (CHEAM, Mémoire No. 3503, undated [1961])

Chappelle, F. de la. 'Problèmes Actuels du Sahara. Rio de Oro et Territoire d'Ifni' (CHEAM, Mémoire No. 179, 1937)

—— 'Les Tekna du Sud-Marocain', *Afrique Française* (Nov. 1933)

—— 'Une Cité de l'Oued Draa sous le Protectorat à Nomades Nesrat', *Hespéris*, vol. IX (1929)

Charbonneau, J. *Le Sahara Français* (Cahiers Charles de Foucauld, Paris, 1955)

Chassey, F. de. *Mauritanie 1900-1975* (Editions Anthropos, Paris, 1978)

—— 'Tension Politique en Mauritanie', *Le Monde Diplomatique* (June 1973)

Cherel, J. 'Secteur Traditionnel et Développement Rural en Mauritanie',

Tiers Monde, vol. VIII, no. 31 (July-Sept. 1967)

Colin, J.P. 'Réflexions sur l'Avenir du Sahara Occidental', *Revue Française d'Etudes Politiques Africaines*, nos. 152-3 (Aug.-Sept. 1978)

Cooley, J.K. *Baal, Christ, and Mohammed* (John Murray, London, 1965)

Coram, A. 'Note on the Role of the Berbers in the Early Days of Moroccan Independence' in E. Gellner and C. Micaud (eds.), *Arabs and Berbers* (Duckworth, London, 1973)

Couleau, J. *La Paysannerie Marocaine* (Conseil National de Recherches Scientifiques, Paris, 1968)

Crimi, B. 'Le Dernier Quart d'Heure', *Jeune Afrique*, 28 Nov. 1975

Cros, Lieut. 'L'Evolution en Mauritanie et Plus Particulièrement chez les Reguibats, 1955 à 1960' (CHEAM, Mémoire No. 3510, 25 March 1961)

Cubillo, A. 'Après le Sommet Algéro-Marocain', *Africana* (June 1970)

Daoud, Z. 'La Bataille du Sahara', *Lamalif* (Aug.-Sept. 1970)

Delavignette, R. *Les Vrais Chefs de l'Empire* (Gallimard, Paris, 1934)

Désiré-Vuillemin, G.M. 'Coppolani en Mauritanie' *Revue des Colonies*, trimestres 3-4 (1955)

—— *Les Rapports de la Mauritanie et du Maroc* (pamphlet published by Service des Archives Nationales de la Mauritanie, St Louis-du-Sénégal, 1960)

Desjardins, T. *Les Rebelles d'Aujourd'hui* (Presses de la Cité, Paris, 1977)

Dessens, P.A. 'Le Litige du Sahara Occidental', *Maghreb-Machrek*, no. 71 (Jan.-March 1976)

—— 'Le Problème du Sahara Occidental Trois Ans après le Départ des Espagnols', *Maghreb-Machrek*, no. 83 (Jan.-Feb.-March 1979)

'Le Développement, Problème No. 1 de la Mauritanie', *Europe-France-Outremer*, no. 431 (Dec. 1965)

Dahmani, A. (articles in *Jeune Afrique*, 1974-9)

'Le Différend Frontalier entre le Maroc et l'Algérie', *Maghreb*, no. 2 (March-April 1964)

'Le Droit des Sahraouis à Disposer d'Eux-mêmes', *L'Afrique et l'Asie*, no. 116 (premier semestre 1978)

Doutrelant, P.M. 'Guerre d'Usure au Sahara Occidental', *Le Monde*, 6-8 (Aug. 1976)

Dubie, P. 'La Vie Matérielle des Maures', *Mémoires de l'IFAN*, no. 23 (1955)

Dubief, J. 'Les Reguibat Lagouacem. Chronologie et Nomadisme', *Bulletin de l'IFAN*, série B, tome 17, nos. 3-4 (Dakar, 1955)

Dugué, G. *Vers les Etats-Unis d'Afrique* (Editions des Lettres Africaines, Dakar, 1960)

Dunn, R.E. 'Berber Imperialism: the Ait Atta Expansion in Southeast Morocco' in E. Gellner and C. Micaud (eds.), *Arabs and Berbers* (Duckworth, London, 1973)

—— 'The Trade of Tafilalet: Commercial Change in Southeast Morocco on the Eve of the Protectorate' (African Studies Association paper, 1970 annual meeting)

Dupas, Capt. 'Notes sur la Confédération des Reguibat Lagouacem, 1937' (CHEAM, Mémoire No. 770, 20 Feb. 1937)

Duret, Capt. 'Au Contact des Grands Nomades' (CHEAM, Mémoire No. 2144, 10 Feb. 1953)

Duteil, M. (articles in *Jeune Afrique*, 7, 14, 21 Nov. 1975)

Eagleton, W., Jr. 'The Islamic Republic of Mauritania', *Middle East Journal* (Winter 1965)

'L'Economie Marocaine', *Europe-France-Outremer*, special issue (Sept. 1965)

L'Economie Pastorale Saharienne (La Documentation Française, *Notes et Etudes Documentaires*, No. 1730, 21 April 1953)

Enquête Démographique (Ministère de Finance, du Plan et de la Fonction Publique (Mauritanie), Paris, 1972)

'L'Espagne et l'Afrique', *Marchés Tropicaux*, special issue (17 Dec. 1966)

España en el Sahara (Servicio Informativo Español, Documentos Publicos, No. 9, Madrid, 1968)

Essono, S. 'La Mauvaise Carte', *Afrique-Asie*, 15 May 1978

Eydoux, H.P. *L'Homme et le Sahara* (Gallimard, Paris, 1943)

Faure, R. 'La Palmeraie de Tafilalet' (thèse du 3ème cycle, Faculté des Lettres et Sciences Humaines, Paris, 1968)

Faure, Y.A. 'De l'OERS à l'OMVS', *Revue Française d'Etudes Politiques Africaines*, no. 133 (Jan. 1977)

Fessard de Foucault, B. 'Le Parti du Peuple Mauritanien', *Revue Française d'Etudes Politiques Africaines* (Oct.-Nov. 1973)

—— 'Le Quatrième Congrès du Parti du Peuple Mauritanien', *Revue Française d'Etudes Politiques Africaines* (May 1976)

—— 'La Question du Sahara Espagnol', *Revue Française d'Etudes Politiques Africaines* (Nov.-Dec. 1975)

Fondacci, P. 'Maures et Serviteurs Noirs en Pays Nomades d'AOF' (CHEAM, Mémoire No. 811, 4 April 1946)

—— 'Les Némadis' (CHEAM, Mémoire No. 1009, 1946)

'La Fuite en Avant', *Afrique-Asie*, 20 February 1978

Funck-Brentano, C. 'Bibliographie du Sahara Occidental', *Hespéris*, vol. XI (1930)

Gaillard, M. 'Deux Oasis du Bani: Tata et Tissint' (CHEAM, Mémoire No. 1558, 1950)

'La Gauche Marocaine et l'Algérie', *Jeune Afrique*, 11 June 1976

Gaucher, G. 'Irrigation et Mise en Valeur du Tafilalet', *Travaux de l'Institut de Recherches Sahariennes*, vol. V (1948)

Gaudio, A. *Les Civilisations du Sahara* (Collection Marabout-Université, No. 141, Paris, 1967)

— 'Le Développement Economique du Sahara', *Marchés Tropicaux*, 2 July 1976

— *Le Dossier de la Mauritanie* (Nouvelles Editions Latines, Paris, 1978)

— *Le Dossier du Sahara Occidental* (Nouvelles Editions Latines, Paris, 1978)

— 'Ifni, la Suisse après le Sahara', *Jeune Afrique*, 27 July 1971

— 'Mauritanie 1977. Une Economie entre Guerre et Paix', *Marchés Tropicaux*, 22 April 1977

— *Le Sahara des Africains* (Julliard, Paris, 1960)

— 'Le Sahara entre la Guerre et la Paix', *Africa*, Dakar (Dec. 1978)

— *'Sahara Espagnol' – Fin d'un Mythe Colonial* (Editions Arrisala, Rabat, 1975)

— 'Les Sahraouis qui se Veulent Marocains', *Africa*, Dakar (Dec. 1978) Note. For an extensive annotated bibliography on the Western Sahara, see A. Gaudio, *Le Dossier du Sahara Occidental*, cited above.

Gellner, E. 'Patterns of Rural Rebellion in Morocco during the Early Years of Independence' in E. Gellner and C. Micaud (eds.), *Arabs and Berbers* (Duckworth, London, 1973)

— and Micaud, C. (eds.) *Arabs and Berbers* (Duckworth, London, 1973)

Genevière, J. 'Les Kountas et Leurs Activités Commerciales' (CHEAM, Mémoire No. 1240, 31 Dec. 1947)

Gerteiny, A.G. *Mauritania* (Praeger, New York, 1967)

Gouraud, H.J.E. *Mauritanie, Adrar, Souvenirs d'un Africain* (Plon, Paris, 1945)

Greene, M.H. 'Impact of the Sahelian Drought in Mauritania', *African Environment* (April 1975)

Gretton, J. *Western Sahara: The Fight for Self-determination* (The Anti-Slavery Society, London, 1976)

— 'Algeria Losing Interest in Polisario?', *The Times*, 30 May 1978

— 'War Above, Iron Below', *International Herald Tribune*, Paris, 7-8 July 1979

Hammoudi, A. 'L'Evolution de l'Habitat dans la Vallée du Draa', *Revue de Géographie du Maroc*, no. 18 (1970)

Hart, D.M. 'The Tribe in Morocco: Two Case Studies' in E. Gellner and C. Micaud (eds.), *Arabs and Berbers* (Duckworth, London, 1973)

Hassan II. *Le Défi* (Albin Michel, Paris, 1976)

Henriet, Lieut. *L'Extrème Sud dans l'Economie Marocaine* (Editions Internationales, Tangier, 1939)

—— 'Un Problème de l'Extrème-sud Marocain' (CHEAM, Mémoire No. 6, Oct.-Nov. 1937)

Hernandes, F. and Cordero Torres, J.M. *El Sahara Español* (Instituto de Estudios Políticos, Madrid, 1962)

Hodges, T. 'Western Sahara, the Escalating Confrontation', *Africa Report* (March-April 1978)

Howe, M. 'Oil and Politics Mix in the Sahara Desert', *Mainichi Daily News*, Osaka, 15 March 1957

Hultman, T. 'The Struggle for Western Sahara', *Issues* (Spring 1977)

Jacques-Meunié, D. *Greniers-Citadelles au Maroc* (2 vols., Arts et Métiers, Paris, 1951)

—— 'La Vallée du Draa au Milieu du XXe Siècle' in *Maghreb et Sahara* (Société de Géographie, Paris, 1973)

Junqua, D. 'La Mauritanie Prise au Piège', *Le Monde*, 15-17 Feb. 1978

—— 'Les Mauritaniens, Conquérants Malgré Eux', *Le Monde*, 10 April 1976

—— 'La Politique Maghrebine de la France', *Croissance des Jeunes Nations* (Sept. 1976)

Kalfleche, J.M. 'Sahara: Hassan Offre des Portes de Sortie à l'Algérie', *Le Figaro*, 21 Aug. 1979

Kazadi, F.S.B. 'Carter's Saharan Foray', *Africa Report* (March-April 1978)

Kone, A. 'Perspectives d'Avenir d'une Communauté Mauritanienne' (CHEAM, Mémoire No. 3932, 1964)

Lafeuille, R. 'La Crise Economique chez les Nomades de Mauritanie de 1940 à 1944' (CHEAM, Mémoire No. 756, 5 September 1945)

Laroui, A. *L'Algérie et le Sahara Marocain* (Serar, Casablanca, 1976)

Lattre, J.M. de. 'Le Minerai de Fer de Gara-Djebilet', *France-Outremer* (Aug. 1957)

—— 'Pour une Communauté Eurafricaine du Fer: le Gara-Djebilet' (Comptes Rendus des Séances de l'Académie des Sciences Coloniales, No. 5, July 1957)

Lavrancic, K. 'Damming the Senegal — At Last', *West Africa*, 18 June 1979

Lazrak, R. *Le Contentieux Territorial entre le Maroc et l'Espagne* (Dar el Kitab, Casablanca, 1975)

Le Borgne, C. 'Les Nomades Chameliers de Mauritanie, Evolution du Nomadisme et de la Richesse Chamelière' (CHEAM, Mémoire No. 2241, 8 Oct. 1953)

Le Boulleux, Lieut. 'L'Esclavage dans l'Ouest Saharien' (CHEAM, Mémoire No. 3824, 1963)

Lemoyne, M.R. 'Pénétration des Maures en Afrique Noire' and 'La Transformation Modèrne de l'Economie des Nomades du Sahara Occidental' (CHEAM, Mémoire No. 1009, 1946)

Le Naelou, Y. 'Problèmes Politiques à Kenadsa en 1960-62' (CHEAM, Mémoire No. 4137, Jan. 1965)

Lenoble, M. 'L'Enseignement Français en Pays Maure' (CHEAM, Mémoire No. 2454, 1954)

—— 'Premières Ecoles du Campement en Mauritanie' (CHEAM, Mémoire No. 2350, 1954)

Leriche, A. 'Les Haratin', *Bulletin de Liaison Saharienne*, no. 6 (Oct. 1951)

—— 'Notes sur les Classes Sociales et sur Quelques Tribus de Mauritanie', *Bulletin de l'IFAN*, série B, XVII (Jan.-April 1955)

Lesourd, M. 'Le Nomadisme en Voie de Sédentarisation — Sahara Atlantique — Les Reguibat' (CHEAM, Mémoire No. 3868, Dec. 1963)

Lienz, C. 'Vallée du Dadès', *Encyclopédie Mensuelle d'Outre-Mer* (July 1955)

Limagne, J. 'La Politique Etrangère de la République Islamique de Mauritanie', *Revue Française d'Etudes Politiques Africaines* (March 1972)

Luze, de. 'La Société Maure de 1942 à 1946' (CHEAM, Mémoire No. 2246, 9 Oct. 1953)

—— 'La Subdivision de Tamchakett en 1945' (CHEAM, Mémoire No. 2169, 1953)

Maalouf, A. 'Pleins Feux sur le Gaz', *Jeune Afrique*, 3 May 1978

Maazouzi, M. *L'Algérie et les Etapes de l'Amputation du Territoire Marocain* (Dar el Kitab, Casablanca, 1976)

Maghreb et Sahara, *Acta Géographica* (special issue, Société de Géographie, Paris, 1973)

Maillot, D. 'La Politique Marocaine de Non-dépendance', *Revue Juridique et Politique d'Outre-Mer* (Jan.-March 1963)

Marais, O. 'The Political Evolution of the Berbers in Independent Morocco' in E. Gellner and C. Micaud (eds.), *Arabs and Berbers* (Duckworth, London, 1973)

'La Marche Verte' (anonymous typescript, 15 Dec. 1975)

'Le Maroc dans la Voie de la Démocratie', *Europe-France-Outremer*, special issue (June 1963)

'Le Maroc: un Nouveau Départ', *Europe-France-Outremer*, special issue (April-May 1972)

Martel, M. 'Mémoire sur le Coutumier des Confédérations Constituant les Tribus Controlés par le Territoire du Tafilalet' (CHEAM, Mémoire No. 97, 28 Jan. 1937)

Martin, H. 'Les Ouled Bou Sba' (CHEAM, Mémoire No. 300-326, 1937)

—— 'Les Tribus Nomades de l'Ouest et du Nord Mauritanie, du Sahara Espagnol, et du Sud Marocain' (CHEAM, Mémoire No. 300-328, 1939)

Martinet, G. 'Ma El Ainin et le Sakiet El Hamra', *Lamalif* (Aug.-Sept. 1970)

—— 'Les Tribus de la Sakiet el Hamra', *Lamalif* (Oct. 1970)

Marty, P. *Etudes sur l'Islam et les Tribus du Soudan* (3 vols., Leroux, Paris, 1918-19, 1920-1)

—— *Les Tribus de la Haute Mauritanie* (Comité de l'Afrique Française, Paris, 1915)

'La Mauritanie à l'Heure du Fer et du Cuivre', *Europe-France-Outremer*, no. 363 (Feb. 1960)

'La Mauritanie à un Moment Décisif de son Histoire', *Europe-Outremer*, no. 519 (April 1973)

'Mauritanie — Dix Ans d'Indépendance', *Europe-France-Outremer*, no. 490 (Nov. 1970)

'Mauritanie — Les Grands Projets de Développement Sont en Cours', *Europe-France-Outremer*, nos. 459-60 (April-May 1968)

'Mauritanie — Les Premières Exportations de Minerai de Fer', *Europe-France-Outremer*, no. 402 (July 1963)

'La Mauritanie Mobilisée', *Europe-Outremer*, no. 574 (Nov. 1977)

'Mauritanie 1954', *Encyclopédie Mensuelle d'Outremer*, doc. no. 31 (Oct. 1954)

'Mauritanie '60', *Industries et Travaux d'Outre-mer*, no. 75 (Feb. 1960)

'Mauritanie — 15 Ans d'Indépendance (28 November 1975)', *Europe-Outremer*, no. 549 (Oct. 1975)

Mercer, J. *Spanish Sahara* (Allen and Unwin, London, 1976)

Mergui, R. 'Le Maroc, Israel, et les Juifs', *Jeune Afrique*, 3 May 1978

—— 'La Grande Riposte', *Jeune Afrique*, 21 Nov. 1979

Méric, E. 'Le Conflit Algéro-Marocain', *Le Monde Diplomatique* (Nov. 1963)

—— 'Le Conflit Algéro-Marocain', *Revue Française des Sciences Poli-*

tiques (Aug. 1965)

—— 'La Mauritanie n'est pas Mal Partie', *L'Afrique et l'Asie*, no. 64 (1963)

Miège, J.L. 'Les Origines de la Colonie Espagnole du Rio de Oro' in *Le Sahara: Rapports et Contacts Humains* (7ème Colloque d'Histoire, Faculté de Lettres d'Aix-en-Provence, 1967)

Molina-Campuzano, M. *Contribución al Estudio del Censo de Población del Sahara Español* (Instituto de Estudios Africanos, Madrid, 1954)

Monteil, V. 'Notes pour Servir à un Essai de Monographie des Tekna du Sud-ouest Marocain et du Sahara Nord-occidental' (CHEAM, Mémoire No. 1232, Sept. 1945)

—— 'Le Peuplement des Qsour du Bani' (CHEAM, Mémoire No. 1307, 1948)

Moore, C.H. 'One-partyism in Mauritania', *Journal of Modern African Studies* (Oct. 1965)

—— 'Political Parties in Independent North Africa' in L.C. Brown (ed.), *State and Society in Independent North Africa* (Middle East Institute, 1966)

Morgan, S. 'Crisis Time in Mauritania', *West Africa*, 30 May 1977

Morin, D.'Mauritanie An IV', *Marchés Tropicaux*, 12 Dec. 1975

'Morocco Settles No-man's Land', *Middle East Journal* (June 1979)

Moureau, Capt. 'Les Sociétés des Oasis. Une Race de Bani: Les Harratins. Parallèle entre son Evolution et Celle des Autres Races des Oasis' (CHEAM, Mémoire No. 2431, Jan. 1955)

Munier, P. *Le Palmier-Dattier* (Maisonneuve et Larose, Paris, 1973)

Naegele, A. 'Le Ksar d'Atar et sa Palmeraie en Mauritanie', *La Nature* (July 1957)

Niclausse, Capt. 'Une Tribu du Sud Marocain: Les Aït Atta du Sahara' (CHEAM, Mémoire No. 2681, 1956)

Noin, D. *La Population Rurale du Maroc* (2 vols., Presses Universitaires de France, Paris, 1970)

Nomades et Nomadisme au Sahara (UNESCO, Paris, 1963)

Oliva, P. 'Notes sur Ifni', *Revue de Géographie du Maroc* (Rabat), no. 19 (1971)

Ormières, J.L. 'Les Conséquences Politiques de la Famine' in *Sécheresses et Famines du Sahel* (Maspéro, Paris, 1975), vol. I

'Ould Daddah's Dilemma', *West Africa*, 9 February 1976

Paillard, J. 'Destin des Reguibat' (CHEAM, Mémoire No. 3085, 1959)

—— 'Le Problème des Reguibat' (CHEAM, Mémoire No. 4202, Nov. 1967)

Paul, J. 'Games Imperialists Play', *Merip*, no. 45 (March 1976)

—— 'With the Polisario Front of Sahara', *Merip*, no. 53 (Dec. 1976)

Pautard, A. 'Frontière Algéro-Marocaine: Le Conflit Reste Ouvert', *Revue Française d'Etudes Politiques Africaines* (April 1967)

Pelissier, R. 'Sahara Espagnol: La Ronde des Chacals', *Revue Française d'Etudes Politiques Africaines* (July 1970)

—— 'Sahara Espagnol: L'Escalade', *Revue Française d'Etudes Politiques Africaines* (Sept. 1974)

—— 'Spain Changes Course in Africa', *Africa Report* (Dec. 1963)

—— 'Spain's African Sandboxes', *Africa Report* (Feb. 1966)

—— (ed.), *Les Territoires Espagnols d'Afrique* (La Documentation Française, *Notes et Etudes Documentaires*, No. 2951, 3 Jan. 1963)

—— 'Territoires Espagnols d'Afrique', *Le Monde*, 24-5 Oct. 1967

Pitte, J.R. 'La Sécheresse en Mauritanie', *Annales de Géographie*, vol. 466 (Nov.-Dec. 1975)

'La Politique des Grands Barrages', *Europe-France-Outremer*, nos. 507-8 (April-May 1972)

Poncelin de Raucourt. 'Contribution à l'Etude de la Coutume des Aït Atta du Draa' (CHEAM, Mémoire No. 1209, 1947)

'Les Populations de Race Noire d'Aioun el Atrouss' (anonymous typescript, CHEAM, Mémoire No. 3503, 1961)

Pouchin, D. 'Le Désert Insurgé', *Le Monde*, 24-7 May 1977

'Préoccupations et Inquiétudes de la Communauté Noire de Mauritanie', *Revue Française d'Etudes Politiques Africaines*, no. 158 (Feb. 1979)

'Les Présides au Maroc et Ifni', *Revue Française des Sciences Politiques* (April 1968)

Price, D.L. 'Morocco and the Sahara', *Middle East International* (Aug. 1978)

—— *Morocco and the Sahara: Conflict and Development* (Institute for the Study of Conflict, Report No. 88, London, 1977)

—— *The Western Sahara* (*The Washington Papers*, vol. VII) (Sage Publications, Georgetown University, 1979)

'Le Problème des Phosphates au Coeur de la Souveraineté du Sahara Espagnol', *Marchés Tropicaux*, 13 June 1970

'Programme d'Action Nationale', *Le Peuple Sahraoui en Lutte*, Algiers (May 1975)

Puigaudeau, O. du. *La Grande-Foire des Dattes* (Plon, Paris, 1934)

—— *Pieds Nus à Travers la Mauritanie* (Plon, Paris, 1936)

—— *Le Sel du Desert* (Plon, Paris, 1940)

Recoules, J. 'Les Frontières de l'Etat Marocain', *L'Afrique et l'Asie*, no. 52 (1960)

—— 'Notes sur la Frontière Méridionale du Maroc', *L'Afrique et l'Asie*, no. 64 (1963)

'Rélations Hispano-Marocains', *Maghreb*, no. 33 (May-June 1969)

La République Islamique de Mauritanie (La Documentation Française, *Notes et Etudes Documentaires*, No. 2687, 29 July 1960)

République Islamique de Mauritanie. *Enquête Démographique 1965: Résultats Définitifs* (2 vols., République Française, Secretariat d'Etat aux Affaires Etrangères, Service de Coopération, Paris, 1972)

'La Rétrocession d'Ifni et les Relations Hispano-Marocaines', *Maghreb*, no. 33 (May-June 1969)

Reyner, A.S. 'Morocco's International Boundaries: A Factual Background', *Journal of Modern African Studies*, vol. I, no. 3 (1963)

Rezette, R. *Le Sahara Occidental et les Frontières Marocaines* (Nouvelles Editions Latines, Paris, 1975)

Robin, J. 'Moors and Canary Islanders on the Coast of the Western Sahara', *Geographical Journal*, vol. I (1955)

Roché, P. 'L'Irrigation et le Statut Juridique des Eaux au Maroc', *Revue Juridique et Politique* (Jan.-March, April-June, Oct.-Dec. 1965)

'Le Royaume de Maroc: Développement dans la Stabilité', *Europe-France-Outremer*, special issue (July 1968)

Safer, K. 'Au Sommet de Tlemcen: Le Problème des Frontières est Dépassé', *Africasia*, no. 17 (8-21 June 1967)

'Le Sahara Espagnol', *Maghreb*, no. 22 (July-Aug. 1967)

'Sahara Espagnol: L'Impatience du Maroc', *Revue Française d'Etudes Politiques Africaines* (Aug. 1974)

'Le Sahara ne Veut pas une Guerre', *Marchés Tropicaux*, 13 June 1975

'Le Sahara Nord-Ouest' in *L'Economie Pastorale Saharienne* (La Documentation Française, *Notes et Etudes Documentaires*, No. 1730, 21 April 1953)

'Sahara Occidental: Qu'est-ce que le Front Polisario?', *Jeune Afrique*, 26 December 1975

'Sahara Occidental: Se Conformer au Droit', *Révolution Africaine*, no. 810 (6 Nov. 1975)

Sahara Occidental: Un Peuple et Ses Droits (Harmattan, Paris, 1978)

Sahara: On Peut, on Doit Eviter la Guerre, *Jeune Afrique*, special issue, 25 Nov. 1977

'Sahara: Les Raisons d'une Offensive', *Lamalif*, no. 40 (June-July 1970)

Saint-Bon, Capt. de. 'Les Populations des Confins du Maroc Saharien' (CHEAM, Mémoire No. 27 bis, 11 May 1938)

Salvy, G. 'La Crise du Nomadisme dans le Sud Marocain' (CHEAM, Mémoire No. 1563, May 1949)

— 'Les Kounta du Sud-Marocain', *Travaux de l'Institut de Recherches Sahariennes*, vol. VIII (1951)

— 'Le Sahara du Nord-ouest' and 'Le Sahara du Nord et Rédaction d'Ensemble' in *L'Economie Pastorale Saharienne* (La Documentation Française, *Notes et Etudes Documentaires*, No. 1730, 21 April 1953)

Sane, J.K. 'Sahara Occidental: Un Conflit qui s'Envenime', *Afrique Nouvelle*, 17 Feb. 1976

Schaar, S. 'Hassan's Morocco', *Africa Report* (July 1965)

Schissel, H. 'La Mauritanie, la Guerre et les Ruines', *Le Monde Diplomatique* (Aug. 1978)

Schoen, Capt. 'Les Confréries Musulmanes dans le Sud-Marocain' (CHEAM, Mémoire No. 89, 30 Jan. 1937)

Serjac, J. 'Mauritanie et Maroc', *L'Afrique et l'Asie*, no. 45 (1959)

Sigisbert, G. 'La Révolution Agraire', *Europe-Outremer*, no. 542 (March 1975)

— 'Le Fer, l'Exploitation Actuelle', *Europe-Outremer*, no. 574 (Nov. 1977)

Solarz, S. 'Arms for Morocco', *Foreign Affairs* (Winter 1979-80)

Spillmann, G. 'Les Aït Atta du Sahara et la Pacification du Haut Dra', in *Collection Juridique*, vol. XXIX (Institut des Hautes Etudes Marocaines, Rabat, 1936)

— 'A Propos de la Frontière Algéro-Marocaine', *L'Afrique et l'Asie*, no. 75 (1966)

— 'La Situation au Sahara Occidental: Le Polisario', *Comptes Rendus Trimestriels des Séances de l'Académie des Sciences d'Outremer*, 17 February 1978

Stewart, C.C. 'Much Ado About Nothing', *West Africa*, 3, 10 November 1975

— 'Political Authority and Social Stratification in Mauritania' in E. Gellner and C. Micaud (eds.), *Arabs and Berbers* (Duckworth, London, 1973)

— and Stewart, E.K. *Islam and Social Order in Mauritania* (Clarendon Press, Oxford, 1973)

'La Structure Politique et Sociale de l'Oued Draa' (anonymous typescript, CHEAM, Mémoire No. 2039, 1947)

Swift, J. 'Une Economie Nomade Sahelienne Face à la Catastrophe. Les Touareg de l'Adrar des Iforas (Mali)' in *Sécheresses et Famines du Sahel* (Maspéro, Paris, 1975), vol. II

Taton, R. 'Mauritanie: Les Combats du Sahara ont Cimenté l'Unité de la Nation', *Europe-Outremer*, no. 552 (Jan. 1976)

— 'Le Pouvoir, l'Administration, et l'Opposition', *Europe-Outremer*, no. 519 (April 1973)

—— 'Un Problème Très Complexe' (and six other articles) in 'La Mauritanie Mobilisée', *Europe-Outremer*, no. 574 (Nov. 1977)

—— 'Le Sahara Occidental Vu du Coté Mauritanien', *Europe-Outremer*, no. 549 (Oct. 1975)

Les Territoires Espagnols d'Afrique (La Documentation Française, *Notes et Etudes Documentaires*, No. 2951, 3 Jan. 1961)

Thomas, M.R. 'Notes sur les Imraguen de Mauritanie' (CHEAM, Mémoire No. 757, undated [1944])

—— *Sahara et Communauté* (Presses Universitaires de France, Paris, 1960)

Tiano, A. *La Politique Economique et Financière du Maroc Indépendant* (Presses Universitaires de France, Paris, 1963)

Toupet, C. 'Orientation Bibliographique sur la Mauritanie', *Bulletin de l'IFAN*, série B (Jan.-April 1959; supplement in vol. XXIV (July-Oct. 1962)

—— 'Le Problème des Transports en Mauritanie', *Bulletin de l'IFAN*, série B (Jan.-April 1963)

—— 'Reguibat L'Gouacem' in *Nomades et Nomadisme au Sahara* (UNESCO, Paris, 1963)

—— and Pitte, J.R. *La Mauritanie* (Presses Universitaires de France, Paris, 1977)

Toutain, C. 'Sur une Evolution Economique de la Vallée du Draa' (CHEAM, Mémoire No. 4428, 1972)

Trancart, A. 'Base et Structure de la Société Maure' (CHEAM, Mémoire No. 1024, 1947)

Treyer, C. *Sahara 1956-1962* (Société Les Belles Lettres, Paris, 1966)

Trout, F.E. *Morocco's Saharan Frontiers* (Droz, Geneva, 1969)

—— 'The Return of Ifni to Morocco', *Genève-Afrique*, vol. IX, no. 1 (1970)

Vallée, C. 'L'Affaire du Sahara Occidental devant la Cour Internationale de Justice', *Maghreb-Machrek*, no. 71 (Jan.-March 1976)

Vieuchange, M. *Smara, Carnets de Route* (Plon, Paris, 1932)

Voisin, C. 'L'Islam Maure' (CHEAM, Mémoire No. 1009, 1945)

Weiner, J.B. 'The Green March in Historical Perspective', *Middle East Journal* (Winter 1979)

Weiss, D. and Taton, R. 'Les Hommes d'Affaires Mauritaniens', *Europe-Outremer*, no. 549 (Oct. 1975)

Westebbe, R. *The Economy of Mauritania* (Pall Mall, London, 1972) .

—— *Mauritania: Guidelines for a Four-year Development Program* (World Bank, Washington, DC, 1968)

Wolfers, M. 'Letter from Mauritania', *West Africa*, 13 Jan. 1975

Woronoff, J. 'Différends Frontaliers en Afrique', *Revue Française d'Etudes Politiques Africaines* (Aug. 1972)

Yata, A. *La Mauritanie, Province Authentiquement Marocaine* (Imprimerie Al Maarif, Casablanca, 1960)

'La Yemaa ò Asambléa Géneral del Sahara', *Africa* (Instituto de Estudios Africanos, Madrid, 1967)

Zartman, I.W. *Morocco:Problems of New Power* (Atherton Press, New York, 1964)

—— 'The Sahara: Bridge or Barrier?', *International Conciliation*, no. 541 (Jan. 1963)

INDEX

CHINA
FORMOSA
WEST R
Canton
Hong Kong
Hanoi
Haiphong
HAINAN
N. VIETNAM
LAOS
MEKONG R
Hué
S. VIETNAM
Dalat
Nhatrang
Saigon
CAMBODIA
South China Sea
Bontoc
Baguio
LUZON
PHILIPPINE ISLANDS
Manila
MINDANAO
Zamboanga
JOLO
N. BORNEO
SARAWAK
KALIMANTAN (BORNEO)
SULAWESI (CELEBES)
Banda Sea
INDONESIA
Jakarta
Java Sea
Flores Sea
JAVA
BALI
Ocean